D1600888

Fluid Iron

mgun
907

FLUID IRON

State Formation in Southeast Asia

Tony Day

University of Hawai'i Press
Honolulu

University of Ottawa
LIBRARIES

b24375445

© 2002 University of Hawai'i Press
All rights reserved
Printed in the United States of America

02 03 04 05 06 07   6 5 4 3 2 1

Library of Congress Cataloging-in-Publication Data
Day, Tony.
Fluid iron : state formation in Southeast Asia / Tony Day.
p.   cm.
Includes bibliographical references and index.
ISBN 0–8248–2507–1 (hardcover : alk. paper)—ISBN 0–8248–2617–5
(pbk. : alk. paper)
1. Asia, Southeastern—Politics and government.   2. State, The.
I. Title.
JQ750.A58   D393   2003
959.05'3—dc21   2002004636

University of Hawai'i Press books are printed on acid-free
paper and meet the guidelines for permanence and durability
of the Council on Library Resources.

Designed by University of Hawai'i Production Department
Printed by The Maple-Vail Book Manufacturing Group

JQ
750
.A58
D393
2002

To
Joan and Robert, my source and strength;
Rob, Chris, Ben, and Sam, my life and light;
Sarah, my world and home

Contents

Preface

This book began as an introductory undergraduate history course on the state in Southeast Asia that I co-taught with Craig Reynolds at the University of Sydney in the late 1980s. We offered the course for several years and then moved on to other things. In the back of our minds, though, was the thought that we had the makings of a short book that could be both accessible to nonspecialists and provocative in a historiographical sense for scholars of Southeast Asia. We felt there was a real need for an easy yet intellectually satisfying book on a major topic for a part of the world that even Australians, just next door, knew relatively little about. So between field trips to Southeast Asia and relocations to other universities we mapped out a structure and in 1996–1997 received a grant from the Australian Research Council to pursue the project. Through e-mail, occasional meetings in Sydney, and joint panel appearances we worked away on families, cosmologies, bureaucracy, and hegemony, publishing an article or two, but feeling that we still had a long way to go. In 1998 I moved to Chapel Hill, North Carolina, with my wife and two youngest children. The tyranny of distance and the further separation of paths and priorities brought my stimulating and happy collaboration with Craig on the state in Southeast Asia to an end.

The book that I eventually wrote has stayed close to the major themes and stylistic aims that Craig and I explored years ago. Neither Craig nor I was interested in producing a hefty tome about the "state" in a comprehensive manner. My own few areas of expertise, as well as my many blind spots and weaknesses, are all too readily apparent. But the intention was and is a modest one: to explore some interesting ideas and theories, to critique the field in a generous, deft, but incisive way, and to stimulate reflection on an important but relatively neglected topic in Southeast Asian studies for reasons that I set forth in the book. The style is clear and accessible. Quotations from primary and secondary sources are ample and sometimes long, with a view to introducing nonspecialists to what has been written in and on Southeast Asia in the hope that they will want to read more. Quoted passages will also serve, I hope, as the basis for solid agreement with or reasoned dissent from the arguments that are presented. The book is meant to be debated as well as to inform.

Without the years of collaboration with Craig, the book would never have been written. As we often told one another after a meeting on the run, the discussions we held about ideas and plans for the book were the best conversations about Southeast Asian history that either of us could remember. Craig will see how much I have deviated from some of our shared thoughts, but he will also find much that is his and our own. I have tried my best to emulate his clarity and succinctness of expression, but one or two sentences may have managed to revert to my more naturally convoluted and clausal style.

I thank the Australian Research Council for my share of our joint grant. It enabled me, combined with a semester of regular study leave from the University of Sydney, to spend a year of fairly uninterrupted reading, thinking, and preliminary writing. It also brought me to conferences in Bangkok, Melbourne, and Honolulu, where Craig and I tried out some of our ideas. The grant gave us, too, the extraordinary services of Chris Buckley, former student, Sinologist, and brilliant thinker, who as our research assistant collected materials, but more importantly, wrote searchingly thoughtful bibliographic essays of his own that opened my eyes to new writers and approaches. I also want to thank the University of Sydney's Department of Indonesian and Malayan Studies, now no longer in existence, and especially Peter Worsley, for giving me time off and support. Peter and my other colleagues at Sydney comprised one of the few and most distinguished bastions of dedicated research and teaching on the literatures and histories of Indonesia anywhere in the world. There are now even fewer of these centers left.

I am grateful to the late O. W. Wolters, the teacher and scholar who introduced me to Southeast Asian history and whose ideas and enthusiasm for the subject are so evident in the pages of this book. To Henk Maier go many and warmest thanks for his incisive and positive annotations on early drafts; his enthusiasm for the little I had to show him helped me immeasurably. To Michael Peletz I owe crucial guidance, late in the day when I thought I was almost done, in how to present my theoretical and methodological framework; I was much in need of his generosity, clarity, and anthropological expertise so that I could summon forth, out of the depths of what now seems a pretty garbled earlier attempt, a formulation of what my book is all about. Sarah Weiss read everything from start to finish, saved me from infelicities and errors, gave me love and encouragement, and patiently waited for the end to come. Audiences at Monash University; the Australian National University; the Universities of Washington, Wisconsin, and Chicago; Cornell and Harvard Universities; and conferences in Honolulu and Bangkok heard talks based on material for the book and were both critical and encouraging. I thank the editors of the *Journal of Asian Studies* and *Modern Asian Studies* for permission to use material, reworked and recontextualized, that appeared in two earlier articles (Day 1996b; Day and Reynolds 2000). Lois Bateson graciously gave me her permission to use Ida Bagus Madé Togog's painting, "The Making of a Mythic Sorcerer," on the front cover of the book. Tony and Claire Milner haven't had much to do with the book directly, but their friendship has sustained me over the years. I have often thought of them, of Braidwood, and of our times together.

To Jim and Florence Peacock I owe many thanks for their warm welcome to us in Chapel Hill. The University of North Carolina's Center for International Studies gave me financial support in 1999 and an opportunity to lead a weekly seminar on Southeast Asia at which a draft of my chapter on violence was thoughtfully discussed. At the invitation of Peter Coclanis and the UNC Department of History I taught survey courses on Southeast Asian history in 2000–2002, which has helped me keep my regional perspective on the state. Michael Hunt, also of the history department, kindly read and commented on two draft chapters, inviting me to discuss bureaucracy at his weekly graduate seminar on world history. To all these friendly Chapel Hillians I give my thanks for their help and support.

Pam Kelley, acquiring editor for the University of Hawai'i Press, encouraged Craig and myself to submit a book proposal half a lifetime ago, then waited patiently as global dislocations and palace coups took their toll. Pam's periodic inquiries as to how things were going and enthusiastic support when something, anything at all, appeared have been crucial. I cannot thank her enough. To Susan Biggs Corrado, copy editor for the Press, I owe my thanks for her meticulous and skillful work. As for the two anonymous readers from the Press, I hold them directly responsible for whatever improvements may have been made to the final draft. Their constructive criticism added months to the project. I hope they're satisfied with the final product! If not, and this goes for everyone else involved, then only I am to be blamed for the poor result.

1
Studying the State in Southeast Asia
Definitions, Problems, Approaches

A casual reader of the daily paper has trouble avoiding questions about the nature and role of the Southeast Asian state. "What a Mess!" exclaims the headline from Thomas L. Friedman's op-ed article on contemporary Indonesia in *The New York Times* (Friedman 2000). "Indonesia," Friedman writes, "the world's fourth most populated country, is the prime example of a new kind of state: the 'messy state' " in which "you never quite know" who is in charge and where "levers get pulled but they come off in your hand." Meanwhile, as post-authoritarian Indonesia flounders, across the Straits of Melaka in Singapore the prosperous subjects of a much smaller, neater, and transparent authoritarian regime sip cappuccinos outside shopping malls along Orchard Road as they worry about the effects of economic downturn in the United States on Singapore's all-important microchip industry (Morris 2001) or ponder getaways to "the mysterious Angkor Wat . . . this enchanting part of Cambodia, complete with its centuries-old temples" in exchange for the purchase of a mobile phone (Explore 2001). Once the center of one of Southeast Asia's most powerful states, Angkor Wat is an enduring monument to the appeal and longevity of despotic state power in Southeast Asia. But its latest popularity also reminds us that global forces of communication and economic change have been shaping the identities and challenging the sovereignty of the "comprador states" of Southeast Asia for centuries (Abu-Lughod 1989, 310). Messy Indonesia, orderly Singapore, monumental Angkor: these three apparently contrasting geographic and temporal locations of the state in Southeast Asia draw our attention to the larger history and significance of state formation in a region of the world where states have been rising and falling, communities forming and fracturing, economies booming and busting, and where the very identity of "Southeast Asia" as a coherent cultural region and analytic concept has been coming in and out of focus for a very long time.

The state in every part of the world is a very old and enduring product of human cultural practice. It is both revered and reviled, far removed from everyday life for some, oppressively omnipresent within it for others. It is also one of the most difficult forms of social practice to understand (Held 1985, 1). In Southeast Asia, the state has a far longer history than the nation, but its role in Southeast Asian history has been both elusive (Schulte Nordholt 1996, 1–11) and obscured by a scholarly preoccupation with nationhood and modernization (McVey 1995b, 2–3). In American academia, state theory, which received fresh attention in the 1960s and 1970s, has been challenged by students of Michel Foucault as well as scholars of globalization who argue that political spaces are no longer under the territorial control of nation-states. Antistatism is rampant in popular American political discourse (Steinmetz 1999, 9–11). Today, however, globalization and its economic consequences, the spread of new information technologies, and the movements of populations across borders and around the globe are drawing fresh attention to states everywhere, including those of Southeast Asia. The fact that national revolutions and decolonization have been slow to foster the development of democracy in Southeast Asia adds new urgency to questions about state formation there as both a product and agent of social, cultural, and economic change, or stasis (cf. Scokpol 1979).

Definitions of the "State"

This book is about state formation in Southeast Asia. It is not about the state as a finished product or structure that has existed in "traditional," "colonial," or "modern" forms, but about the state as a kind of human practice. Notwithstanding my emphasis on the process of state making, I need to begin my discussion with some well-known definitions of the state—definitions that inform a large body of scholarship on the topic both inside Southeast Asian studies and beyond it. Consider the following formulation offered by a social scientist whose work has been influential in some of the debates about the nature and role of the modern state in Southeast Asia:

> It is an organization, composed of numerous agencies led and coordinated by the state's leadership (executive authority) that has the ability or authority to make and implement binding rules for all the people as well as the parameters of rule making for other social organizations in a given territory, using force if necessary to have its way. (Migdal 1988, 19)

As Joel Migdal remarks, the terminology for this definition comes from the sociologist Max Weber (1864–1920), whose writings emphasize the role of legitimate authority, rational bureaucracy, control over territory, and violence in the formation of the modern state (Gerth and Mills 1974). Weber is also famous for his studies of patrimonialism in non-Western, premodern societies and of charismatic authority, a form of leadership that can be found in every historical era and one that Weber contrasted with rational, bureaucratic rule. In Weber's words,

> In contrast to any kind of bureaucratic organization of offices, the charismatic structure knows nothing of a form or of an ordered procedure of appointment or dismissal. It knows no regulated "career," "advancement," "salary," or regulated and expert training of the holder of charisma or of his aids. It knows no agency of control or appeal, no local bailiwicks or exclusive functional jurisdictions; nor does it embrace permanent institutions like our bureaucratic "departments," which are independent of persons and of purely personal charisma.
>
> Charisma knows only inner determination and inner restraint. The holder of charisma seizes the task that is adequate for him and demands obedience and a following by virtue of his mission. His success determines whether he finds them. His charismatic claim breaks down if his mission is not recognized by those to whom he feels he has been sent. (Gerth and Mills 1974, 246)

Although Migdal pays no attention to charismatic authority in his study of Third World states, the fluid, formless characteristics of charisma as described by Weber have been a focus of interest for those who study states and political power in Southeast Asia. Patrimonialism and bureaucracy are the other Weberian topics that have received wide coverage in the scholarly literature on the region.

Karl Marx (1818–1883) is another nineteenth-century German theorist whose ideas about the state deserve to be mentioned here. In general, Marx thought that the state served the interests of a particular, dominant class in its struggle with rival classes in society. In his early works, however, particularly his *Critique of Hegel's Philosophy of Right* (1843), Marx argues that the state is "relatively autonomous" from class struggle (Held 1985, 26). Bureaucracy exercises a further kind of autonomy of its own inside the state, Marx contends, since it "takes itself to be the ultimate purpose of the state" (Tucker 1978, 24). This view of the relative autonomy of the state, and of bureaucracy within the state, receives even more emphasis in Marx's famous essay, *The Eighteenth Brumaire of Louis Bonaparte* (1852), where he analyzes the French state under Louis Napoleon Bonaparte:

> This executive power with its enormous bureaucratic and military organisation, with its artificial state machinery embracing wide strata, with a host of officials numbering half a million, besides an army of another half million, this appalling parasitic growth, which enmeshes the body of French society like a net and chokes all its pores, sprang up in the days of the absolute monarchy, with the decay of the feudal system, which it helped to hasten. . . . The parliamentary republic, finally, in its struggle against the revolution, found itself compelled to strengthen . . . the resources and centralisation of government power. All the revolutions perfected this machine instead of smashing it. The parties that contended in turn for domination regarded the possession of this huge state edifice as the principal spoils of the victor. (Tucker 1978, 606–607)

This vision of the autonomous, despotic power of the modern state echoes another characterization of the state in Marx's writings: that of the Asiatic Mode of Production (AMP) (P. Anderson 1974, 462–549). Here Marx draws on a long line of earlier European political theorists who from the time of the Renaissance had located the origins and operations of "despotism" first in Turkey, then in Persia and India, and finally in China (P. Anderson 1974, 462). In Perry Anderson's words, Marx's definition of the AMP consists of the following elements:

the absence of private property in land, the presence of large-scale irrigation systems in agriculture, the existence of autarchic village communities combining crafts with tillage and communal ownership of the soil, the stagnation of passively rentier or bureaucratic cities, and the domination of a despotic state machinery cornering the bulk of the surplus and functioning not merely as the central apparatus of repression of the ruling class, but as its principal instrument of economic exploitation. Between the self-reproducing villages "below" and the hypertrophied state "above", dwelt no intermediate forces. . . . The political history of the Orient was . . . essentially cyclical: it contained no dynamic or cumulative development. The result was the secular inertia and immutability of Asia, once it had attained its own peculiar level of civilization. (P. Anderson 1974, 483)

Marx's thinking about the role of the state in class struggle has been influential in Southeast Asian studies, particularly among writers and scholars from the region itself, but the concepts of the AMP and of the autonomous, despotic state are also widely found in works that do not otherwise espouse a Marxist orientation.

Understandings of the Southeast Asian state have been most influenced by Weber, followed by Marx, but there is a third theorist whose thinking both echoes and challenges these writers and who has become important in shaping approaches to questions of power in Southeast Asia: Michel Foucault (1926–1984). Whereas Weber stresses the structures and legitimacy of the state and Marx its sometimes autonomous, sometimes class-based role in social struggle, Foucault shifts the discussion away from the question of the state as such to one of relations of power:

I don't want to say that the State isn't important; what I want to say is that relations of power, and hence the analysis that must be made of them, necessarily extend beyond the limits of the State. In two senses: first of all because the State, for all the omnipotence of its apparatuses, is far from being able to occupy the whole field of actual power relations, and further because the State can only operate on the basis of other, already existing power relations. The State is superstructural in relation to a whole series of power networks that invest the body, sexuality, the family, kinship, knowledge, technology, and so forth. (Foucault 1980, 122)

As Anthony Giddens points out, Foucault's analysis of "the emergence of novel types of administrative power" is reminiscent of Weber's studies of bureaucracy (Giddens 1984, 151). Throughout his work, Weber displays an interest in social conflict and the nature of domination that is similar to Foucault's concern with the struggles, processes, mechanisms, and multiple social locations by and in which power is formed (Bendix 1960, 268–270, 289–449). Weber, Marx, and Foucault are all concerned with historicizing the state, or the relations of power that, as Giddens puts it in his discussion of the similarities between Weber and Foucault, are "symptomatic" of the state (Giddens 1984, 151), but only Weber frames his research in world-historical terms involving the examination of Asian case studies as well as premodern historical examples. Weber emphasizes the importance of religious and other cultural factors affecting state formation in premodern and non-Western situations, but he largely ignores cultural factors in his examination of the process of "rationalization," which he treats as the primary cause and end of modernization. This dichotomy between traditional/non-Western/cultural and modern/Western/rational kinds of state formation—and the "Orientalist political teleology" that this binary and historicist way of thinking implies (Steinmetz 1999, 16; Chakrabarty 2000; K. Taylor 1998)—is perhaps the most important and pervasive legacy of Weberian thinking in the scholarship on Southeast Asia.

Locating the State in Southeast Asia

There is no comprehensive survey of writing on the state in Southeast Asia, although two review articles by anthropologists—one on the scholarship dealing with premodern "indigenous states of Southeast Asia" (Bentley 1986) and the other on studies of the state and culture in contemporary Southeast Asia (Steedley 1999)—are illuminating and wide-ranging. What I want to do here is give an overview of the main lines of inquiry into the state in Southeast Asia. I will try to show how this body of work reflects ideas derived from the work of Weber, Marx, and Foucault, but I do not intend to propose a comprehensive theory or typology of the Southeast Asian state (cf. Reynolds 1990) or make an exhaustive examination of scholarship about it. The point of the exercise is to provide the reader with a critical introduction to some of the major examples of existing approaches to the subject as well as a context for understanding my own methodological preferences and aims, which I will set forth in the final section of the chapter. I will organize my discussion around the Weberian dichotomy between "traditional"/non-Western and "modern"/ Western categories, since this binary way of thinking about states accounts for virtually everything written about the state in Southeast Asia. Weber's dichotomy also provokes a question I began thinking about some time ago and which I will consider throughout this study, namely, whether the distinction between tradition and modernity can or should be maintained once we compare the evidence about the nature of state formation from different eras and regions for Southeast Asia as a whole (Day 1986; Corrigan and Sayer 1985, 193; Latour 1993).

The best-known and most influential examinations of the Southeast Asian state (or statelike political formations) that exhibit Weber's interest in the role of culture in shaping political behavior in traditional contexts can be found in the works of Clifford Geertz, O. W. Wolters, and Benedict Anderson. In his essay "Centers, Kings, and Charisma: Reflections on the Symbolics of Power," first published in 1977 (1993, 121–146), and his book *Negara: The Theatre State in Nineteenth-Century Bali* (1980), Geertz draws on European philological and historical reconstructions of the Southeast Asian state (e.g., Heine-Geldern 1956; Coedès 1968; Pigeaud 1960–1963; Worsley 1972), as well as Weber's concept of charisma, to develop a model of the "Indic state" in Southeast Asia. This state form is loosely organized around a king whose person and ritual behavior constitute an "exemplary center" and model of hierarchical order in social worlds characterized by intense status rivalry and the dispersal of political authority. In Geertz's view, culture and power were distinctly different political forces in nineteenth-century Balinese society (C. Geertz 1980, 19). Geertz's definition of the "theatre state" derives from Weber's idea of charisma (via the work of Edward Shils): it is a form of charismatic authority located in "the point or points in a society where its leading ideas come together with its leading institutions" (C. Geertz 1993, 122–123). Thus the "ceremonial life" of the Balinese state becomes a Weberian "charismatic claim":

The ceremonial life of the classical negara was as much a form of rhetoric as it was of devotion, a florid, boasting assertion of spiritual power. . . . The state cult was not a cult of the state. It was an argument, made over and over again in the insistent vocabulary of ritual, that worldly status has a cosmic base, that hierarchy is the governing principle of the universe, and that the arrangements of human life are but approximations, more close or less, to those of the divine. (C. Geertz 1980, 102)

Geertz argues, therefore, that the ritual "theatre" of the exemplary center in Southeast Asia is "the heart of things" for an understanding of the Indic state, one that represents a non-Western alternative to the (Weberian) view of the modern state as "a monopolist of violence within a territory" or (as a Marxist might argue) an "executive committee of the ruling class" (C. Geertz 1980, 122). Notwithstanding the "multiple, fragile, overlapping, and personal, . . . complex and changeful"—as well as violent—nature of political alliances at the local level in the Indic state formation in Bali, Geertz concludes that the Balinese "theatre state" and its charismatic king had as much political reality and practical efficacy as modes of state domination found elsewhere that are based on the exercise of rationality and violence (C. Geertz 1980, 134).

In his *History, Culture, and Region in Southeast Asian Perspectives*, which was first published in 1982, then revised and expanded in 1999, Wolters examines a similar if much wider range of evidence from "traditional" Southeast Asia to reach very different conclusions about the nature of the state. Wolters argues that the term "state" is an inappropriate rubric for political relations in early Southeast Asia, except possibly in Vietnam by the fourteenth century (Wolters 1988). Even in Vietnam, " '[g]overnment' was not a matter of elaborate institutions but of a relaxed unbureaucratic style of public life, where importance was attached to man-management and ceremony and where personal qualities of leadership and example played a major role" (Wolters 1994, 6). Migdal's definition of the modern state is indeed unsuitable in accounting for the political practices Wolters describes. The template for the early Southeast Asian process of stateless historical development is Hinduization, a mode of acculturation carried out by self-Hinduizing "men of prowess" who appropriated and "localized" Indian ideas about divine power and kingship to create *maṇḍala* (sacred, centered spaces). Early Southeast Asia was dotted with these "unique centers," which "represented a particular and often unstable political situation in a vaguely definable geographical area without fixed boundaries and where smaller centers tended to look in all directions for security" (Wolters 1999, 27–28). Wolters' use of Weberian concepts and allusions to Geertzean conceits to disprove rather than affirm the existence of a political entity that could be called a state is well illustrated by the following characterization of the "man of prowess" at work inside his *maṇḍala:*

> In the situation I have just sketched, the ruler was not an autocrat; he was a mediator, accessible and able to keep the peace and mobilize many disparate groups. He needed to attract loyal subordinates to his entourage and to satisfy their self-esteem. One way of doing this was by organizing exciting court occasions at which the entourage was made to feel that it belonged to his company of faithful servants. This system is sometimes described as "patrimonial bureaucracy." The personal type of government, indicated by Weber's term, made a virtue of improvisation, and an illustration is provided by the Angkorean rulers' creation of special posts with ceremonial functions and prospects of future favors in order to attract particular sections of the elite to their side. (Wolters 1999, 29)

"Charismatic" is a better Weberian term to describe what Wolters means by a man of prowess. As a set of analytic terms, "man of prowess," "*maṇḍala*," and "localization" provide Wolters with an effective way of connecting parts of Southeast Asia that remained largely untouched by Hinduization (northern Vietnam, the Philippines) to those that were (the Malay world, Java, Cambodia, Burma, and Siam). Wolters does not deny that state-forming concepts arrived in Southeast Asia from India and China, but he is concerned with demonstrating the continuousness of the region's early historical development and defining its unique identity as a cultural region. Men of prowess were crucial agents in the formation of a cultural entity that can be called "early Southeast Asia," but it was really the process of localization itself, a suprahuman form of cultural "agency" emanating from the region and acting through men of prowess and the educated elites who served them, that subdued and transformed foreign concepts and prevented states from forming. Foreign ideas became "fragments," Wolters says, that "[submitted] to the influence of local cultural statements" (Wolters 1999, 65). This (seemingly natural) historical process through which various combinations of foreign and local cultural statements came together to form "the cultural mosaic we call 'Southeast Asia' " is one of the most important attributes of Southeast Asia as a regional concept according to Wolters (1999, 65).

Wolters is particularly interested in reading cultural texts— temples, inscriptions, poems, historical narratives—for evidence of what he thinks happened during localization. Thus the "visible signifiers" of Angkor Wat, built during the first half of the twelfth century, came to stand for "a Khmer formulation . . . into which Indian conventions of Viṣṇu and the golden age have retreated so completely that they have become, in a literal way, decorative" (Wolters 1999, 63). Similarly, in his analyses of Vietnamese court poetry from the fourteenth century, Wolters argues that Chinese poetic conventions and references to China's golden age under sage-rulers were used to celebrate the uniqueness and antiquity of Vietnam's own cultural space, rather than assert foreign political norms or lay claim to disputed territory. These same poetic enactments, in another reading of the same texts, might well be called contributions to the formation of a state (Wolters 1999, 71–78; 1988, 3–53; see chapter 5).

Both Wolters and Geertz eliminate questions of "power" from their examinations of the Southeast Asian "state." In an essay he first published in 1972 (1990, 17–77), Anderson addresses the nature of Javanese power directly, but in a way that still does not bring the state directly into view. Like Geertz, Anderson argues that Javanese political ideas are fundamentally different from those in the West. The approach he takes to apprehend them is based on Weber's idea that social action needs to be explained in terms of the "subjective meanings" attached to them by the agents who carry them out (B. Anderson 1990, 19). Anderson's adoption of the term "Power" to denote his ideal-type Javanese keyword for understanding Javanese political thought and action is also Weberian. Like Geertz in *Negara*, Anderson presents his essay as a constructive critique of Weber's concept of charisma. Anderson argues that charisma needs to be historicized and specified in a cultural sense:

> If . . . we accept that "charisma" involves belief in Power, it should
> be clear that in both the historical and analytic sense, "charisma"
> precedes rational-legal domination. Study of the Javanese polit-
> ical tradition demonstrates that in Old Java, all rule was charis-
> matic insofar as it was based on belief in Power. Bureaucracy
> there was, but it drew its legitimacy and authority from the radiant
> center, which was seen to suffuse the whole structure with its
> energy. In such a society, "charisma" was not a temporary phe-
> nomenon of crisis, but the permanent, routine, organizing prin-
> ciple of the state. (B. Anderson 1990, 76)

Notwithstanding his commitment to history, Anderson's embrace of a cultural ideal-type for explaining Javanese political thinking and behavior results in the imposition of a kind of timelessness
on Java that we also find in Geertz's treatment of Bali or Wolters'
examination of early Southeast Asia. Political ideas and actions during the Sukarno period in Indonesia (1950–1965) are explained by
examples taken from "Old Java," a designation that itself spans several centuries of Javanese politics and cultural change. The Javanese
idea of Power has the same kind of suprahuman agency in the creation of unstable, centered political formations as does the "exemplary center" in Geertz's Indic Southeast Asia or Wolters' localizing
"prowess" in early Southeast Asia. In all three cases the focus of
analysis is the political center of a social formation that is not, or is
only weakly or irrelevantly, a state. The one element of significant
historicization in Anderson's discussion, one that foreshadows the
Marxist and anticultural turn that his work took after his 1972 essay,
is found in the suggestion that concepts of Power from Old Java in
modern Indonesia are but temporary "residues" of a previous cultural mode that exercise a "continuing cultural hold" of a negative
kind on the minds of Sukarno and his successors (B. Anderson 1990,
73, 77). Anderson thus posits a disjunction between Old and New
Java that in effect raises implicit questions about the cultural authenticity of "the Javanese idea of Power." The thought that "Javanese
Power" is an atavism echoes Marx's characterization of the use of
classical Roman culture by the French state under Louis Napoleon
and lays a methodological basis for treating modern Southeast Asian
culture as "invented," inauthentic, and a tool of state domination. In

the 1972 essay, however, the Javanese idea of Power is a modular cultural concept that Anderson deploys over several centuries of Javanese history as a way of giving a unique cultural shape to the conduct of politics in Java irrespective of time or particular locale. As in the writings of Geertz and Wolters, the state in Anderson's essay is virtually invisible as either an object of or keyword in the analysis of power.

I want now to take a brief look at some of the studies of "traditional" Southeast Asia that draw on or draw away from the ideas of Geertz, Wolters, and Benedict Anderson in order to bring the elusive Southeast Asian state more clearly into view. Michael Aung-Thwin, for example, tries to close the separation, insisted on by Geertz, between the ideology of the "exemplary center" and practical economic activity in his study of Pagan, the most powerful state formation in Burma before the fourteenth century (Aung-Thwin 1985). The kings of Pagan were exemplary centers and men of prowess in their realms, but their chief importance in Pagan history was as redistributors of merit, since it was the accumulation of merit and its redistribution in the form of donations to the building and upkeep of temples that explains, in Aung-Thwin's view, the cyclical nature of the rise and fall of the state in Pagan. Power in early Burma, unlike the case in Anderson's Old Java, was meant to disperse, to be converted into prosperity and security for all those who chose to serve either the king or the Buddhist *saṅgha* (community of monks) in pursuit of merit for themselves and their families (Aung-Thwin 1985, 78, 86–91).

Anthony Milner's early nineteenth-century Malay "ceremonial ruler" (1982) is closer to Geertz's model than Aung-Thwin's Pagan *cakkavattī* (world conqueror). Like Wolters and Anderson, Milner uses literary texts to tease out the "categories of experience" that help us understand Malay political behavior (Milner 1982, 112). What he discovers through reading them is not a state, but a *kerajaan*, or the "the condition of having a raja" (Milner 1982, 114). Milner provides a demonstration, based on early nineteenth-century case studies taken from another part of Southeast Asia, that, as Geertz had argued for Bali, ceremonial, symbolic kingship was effective in a practical sense. Like Aung-Thwin, Milner concludes that having a raja also conditioned the nature of economic activity in the Malay world. In *kerajaan* terms, having wealth, which could be acquired legitimately by any means, including piracy, only became politically significant when it was converted into an entourage of followers, a conversion that gave the wealthy man *(orang kaya)* the power to challenge the authority of the king. Rather than risk direct confrontation with the ruler, *orang kaya* who found themselves caught up in the life of a *kerajaan* had another option: accumulating *nama*, or reputation, rather than wealth. The quest for immortal *nama* through loyal service to the raja had a force that activated the entire *kerajaan* system, with the same kind of appeal and function as ascetic "prowess" in Wolters' early Southeast Asian *maṇḍala* (Milner 1982, 104). *Nama* and prowess resemble the accumulation of merit in Pagan in that all three contributed to the creation of hierarchical, statelike formations.

Both Aung-Thwin and Milner develop synchronic, ideal-type cultural models of state formation that do not involve examination of the effects of transcultural contact or difference over time. Of the approaches to the Southeast Asian state considered thus far, only Wolters considers the question of transcultural interaction at all seriously, but "localization" emphasizes the smooth assimilation of foreign concepts into preexisting cultural patterns in Southeast Asia, rather than possible disruptions, conflict, or change. Although Aung-Thwin mentions spirit worship and ethnic diversity in Pagan, his analysis of Burmese kingship, unlike E. R. Leach's study of political systems in upland Burma (1965), does not develop a sense of how forms of transcultural contestation, emulation, or resistance might have affected the development or workings of state formations. Milner suggests that one of the texts he examines was written as a manual on *kerajaan* doctrines intended for Bataks living under the authority of the Malay raja of Deli in late nineteenth-century East Sumatra, but there is no further reflection on how interethnic relations in Sumatra or the contacts and confrontations between Malays and Europeans that had been going on since the early sixteenth century might have contributed to the formation of the *kerajaan* as ideology or practice (Milner 1982, 87).

Barbara Andaya's book on the struggle for control of the pepper trade in Southeast Sumatra in the seventeenth and eighteenth centuries (1993), on the other hand, addresses the effects of Dutch-Malay relations on political activity directly. Andaya shows that the rivalry between Malay rajas and representatives of the Dutch East India Company (VOC) was carried out in terms of conflicting cultural perceptions and values. On the Malay side, actions were governed by assumptions about authority, trust, and social cohesion based on kinship; oral memories of the heroism of former kings; and Javanese-style state ritual practices and attitudes toward kingship handed down from the seventeenth century and described in written Javanese-language texts. In Dutch eyes, Javanese-Sumatran modes of political authority were merely displays of "base pomp" that failed to conceal the weakness of the raja's "actual" authority, especially in the unruly, multiethnic upriver regions where pepper was grown. Although the Dutch exploited such practices as exchanging gifts in order to win Malay commercial allies, they refused to be turned into trusted kin. Their own practices were governed by cultural attitudes toward contracts and orderly, bureaucratic states. The victor in this clash of cultures was neither side, but rather the market forces of international trade that brought them into contact and conflict in the first place. Andaya does not suggest that either the Malays or the Dutch modified their views about the state in fundamental ways, even though the glory and power of both the rajas and the VOC had faded by the beginning of the nineteenth century.

Unlike Aung-Thwin, Andaya does not factor religion into her account of kingship, although the period she examines was one in which appeals to Islam in the face of European incursions were widespread. She is also not interested in the problem that occupies the thinking of Geertz, Wolters, and Anderson, namely, the lack of fit between Western state theory and Southeast Asian political practices. Sumatran assumptions about the role of kinship in political affairs are not so much an analytic problem as a given in her historical account. This account is full of diachronic complexity and forward movement, but the market rather than culture explains, in the end, the way things turn out.

Culture is given a much more powerful and nuanced role to play in another study of Sumatra, Jane Drakard's book on seventeenth-century Minangkabau, the "kingdom of words" (1999). Drakard's case study is even more paradigmatic of the apparent contradiction between "real" and "titular" political authority than the examples studied by Geertz, Wolters, Anderson, and Milner. Located in the interior of Sumatra, where its state rituals had a very limited audience, with only legendary claims to former glory in the fourteenth century and without any apparent institutional or organized military ability to impose its will, the royal court of Minangkabau was nonetheless extraordinarily influential for hundreds of years. It exerted its authority through words—inscribed in royal letters and on royal seals—that circulated through the peripheral regions of the Minangkabau "state," attracting loyalty and creating unity. "It was the words and names inscribed and broadcast in royal letters and credentials from the interior," Drakard writes, "which had the power to unite"(Drakard 1999, 133).

Drakard uses Foucault to argue that, for the Minangkabau in the seventeenth century, words, seals, and regalia were substantive "resemblances" and effective agents rather than mere symbolic "representations" of royal power (Drakard 1999, 139; Foucault 1973). In this cultural world, there was an unbroken, "intimate relationship between signifier and signified" that explains why seals and letters brought about obedience to the king even though he was distant, unseen, and powerless to enforce his authority except through the agency of the mysterious *besi kawi*, or "force of iron," that brought disease to rice crops and humans if they disobeyed the king's authority (Drakard 1999, 153, 264). Drakard shows that the language of royal letters drew on the imagery of universal overlordship taken from the traditions of the earliest Tantric Buddhist rulers of Minangkabau as well as metaphors of all-pervasive heavenly fragrances and waters found in the Qur'an. "We might say," she says, "that the letters bring together and concentrate the elements of the kingdom for use on occasions when the idea of kingdom needed to be condensed for the purposes of dissemination" (Drakard 1999, 234). Far from being atavistic residues from "Old" Minangkabau, concepts about royal authority drawn from Buddhism and Islam were repeatedly activated in the seventeenth and eighteenth centuries by means of the circulation of "seal letters" *(surat cap)* that stimulated an ongoing process of state formation in the Minangkabau-controlled regions of Sumatra and the Malay Peninsula. Like Andaya, Drakard takes up the question of Javanese cultural and political influence in Sumatra and locates its effective beginnings in the fourteenth century.

Drakard localizes cultural concepts in seventeenth-century Minangkabau by showing how royal words were interpreted and used by the conflicting groups of human agents who enacted the historical events she examines. She analyzes Dutch cultural assumptions in even greater depth than Andaya. Seventeenth-century Dutchmen lived and thought on the other side of Foucault's epistemological watershed: they understood words not as resemblances but as "representations" of a preexisting reality. For them, the *surat cap* were pompous claims to "bare titles," lies, and forgeries. But VOC agents also had a sense, derived from their own political experience in the Netherlands with the royal House of Orange, which exerted its royal influence in subtle rather than direct ways on the political decisions of the stadtholders, that it was important "for form's sake" *(kwansuis)* to establish diplomatic relations with the bombastic and hypocritical Minangkabau rulers (Drakard 1999, 70, 76). Drakard shows that, paradoxically, the Dutch enhanced rather than weakened the authority of the Minangkabau kings and their circulating letters through their negotiations with them about commercial matters. Apart from the unseen king and his agents, the Dutch also had to deal with various claimants to the Minangkabau throne who stirred up anti-Dutch unrest through appeals to Islam and the circulation of royal letters—"forgeries," according to the Dutch—through wide areas of Sumatra, Java, and the Malay peninsula. In her analysis of the careers of Rajas Sakti, Kecil, and Ibrahim, Drakard offers a very precisely historicized critique of the notion of charisma, since she shows that in all three cases the rebel leaders used the language of the *surat cap* to "[fashion] a language of resistance" that affected people who never saw the three rajas in person, but only read or heard their letters (Drakard 1999, 183, 246). Like the Dutch, the three rebel rajas used royal letters and seals in ways that increased the substantive and effective reality of words. Raja Kecil was even referred to by the Dutch metaphorically as "in himself a *cap*," so hegemonic did the influence of royal letters become (Drakard 1999, 200). Drakard shows how Minangkabau kings, their various verbal signs (constructed out of Javanese, Tantric Buddhist, and Islamic as well as Minangkabau cultural concepts), VOC agents, and Minangkabau rebels interacted to form (what I would venture to call) the seventeenth-century Minangkabau state through a process of transcultural contestation and adaptation.

Drakard remarks that Minangkabau power was "too diffuse" to be easily co-opted by the Dutch. The VOC was much more successful in infiltrating, and, indeed, in being infiltrated by, the more visible and geographically centered Javanese state. The VOC had established the base of its Southeast Asian operations in Batavia in 1619, and over the course of the seventeenth and eighteenth centuries it was drawn into closer and closer political and cultural interaction with a succession of Javanese states located in Central Java. Merle Ricklefs charts the course of this interaction in his studies of Kartasura, Surakarta, and Yogyakarta during the seventeenth and eighteenth centuries (1974, 1993, 1998). Although he insists that cultural identities remained "unbridgeable" over the two centuries surveyed in his books, Ricklefs demonstrates that a process of cultural interaction between the VOC and Javanese made them co-creators of a culturally hybrid Indic-Islamic-Javanese-Dutch kind of state formation (Ricklefs 1993, 226).

Ricklefs argues that Islamic Sufi concepts of the king as a "Perfect Man" united in a mystical union with both God and his subjects, combined with ritual royal practices as old as Majapahit, offered a temporary solution to political disorder and Dutch encroachments in the early eighteenth century (cf. Milner 1983). This solution dissolved in the face of Kartasura's destruction by Chinese marauders in 1742 (Ricklefs 1998). The sacking of Kartasura cast doubt on the effectiveness of Sufism as a political strategy for safeguarding the Javanese state, so much so that from that time onward, the elite of Central Java turned away from both Islam and the cultural heritage of Majapahit and became directly dependent on the Dutch for their survival. This hybrid Dutch-Javanese state was challenged twice: once at the end of the eighteenth century, when Javanese ideas about the need for dynastic change at the beginning of a new Javanese century led to the founding of Yogyakarta, a state that reduplicated rather than departed from the existing state form (Ricklefs 1974); and once in 1825–1830, when Dipanegara unsuccessfully rebelled under the banner of Islam and in the name of the Just Ruler *(ratu adil)*, a poltical concept derived from messianic Buddhism.

It is clear from Ricklefs' studies that Indic, Islamic, and Javanese cultural concepts and practices were used both to combat and collaborate with the VOC in the formation of a state in ways that involved constant tinkering with the mix of cultural elements in search of one that would "work." This is a dimension of state formation that Wolters would have called the "localization" of Indic and Islamic ideas in Central Java in the seventeenth and eighteenth centuries. Another dimension of transcultural interaction, the process by which Dutch concepts and practices were localized to serve Javanese political aims in the court world of Central Java, does not emerge clearly from Ricklefs' work, although the overall process by which a kind of hybrid Dutch-Javanese state came into existence by the end of the eighteenth century is very clear. Jean Taylor's study of the social world of Batavia in the seventeenth to early nineteenth centuries demonstrates that Dutch culture was indeed localized and combined with "Asian" elements at the center of Dutch power in Southeast Asia during the same period studied by Ricklefs (J. Taylor 1983).

Viewed from outside the courts of Central Java, from Batavia or from the north coast of the island, the eighteenth-century Dutch-Javanese state appears to have a less monolithic form than the one Ricklefs depicts. Luc Nagtegaal has called this state form a "network" consisting of "a personalized structure . . . in constant flux" (Nagtegaal 1996, 52). A state of flux is also what we can expect to find when we turn our attention to the Tagalog region of Luzon in the Philippines in the sixteenth century, according to Vicente Rafael (1988). Rafael presents a picture of stateless society in which local men of prowess, called *datu,* exerted authority over shifting networks of followers who were indebted to them in various ways and to various degrees of bondage. Into this situation intruded the Spanish at the end of the sixteenth century. During the next three centuries, the Spanish "converted" natives to Christianity and their political forms of shifting alliances into a fixed hierarchy leading from the village via the colonial bureaucracy all the way to the Spanish king and his God. Positioned on the boundary between the village and the colonial state, the *datu,* now known as *principales,* exacted tribute for the Spanish from their followers in exchange for access to the Spanish God and the promise of eternal life in His heaven. Although he is not interested in the question of state formation as such, Rafael clearly demonstrates how Spanish colonization and conversion to Christianity created a state where none had apparently existed before.

I say "apparently" because in the process of developing his main theme—Wolters' idea of localization in early colonial Luzon—Rafael suggests that tendencies toward state formation preexisted the Spanish and helped shape the way political relationships developed under Spanish rule. Rafael refers to the work of W. H. Scott (W. Scott 1982; see also 1994), who studied early Spanish accounts of Filipino societies in order to reconstruct the nature of preconquest social and political orders. Scott is clear about the hierarchical nature of pre-Spanish Tagalog society and produces linguistic evidence to suggest that Malay practices based on Indic and Muslim concepts of kingly status and power had been brought to preconquest Manila from Melaka and Brunei (W. Scott 1994, 191–198). Rafael is more interested, however, in the nature of transcultural change that occurred once the Spanish had landed. He calls this process of change "translation," the Tagalog localization of Christian concepts and practices in the face of Spanish attempts to convert and dominate them. Overall, he concludes at the end of his study, "[t]ranslation, in whatever mode, leads to the emergence of hierarchy, however conceived" (Rafael 1988, 211).

But in the Tagalog case, translation also gave rise to expressions of resistance along the way. In an analysis of an early seventeenth-century Tagalog primer of Spanish, for example, Rafael shows how the treatment of Spanish words had the effect of "inoculating" the Tagalog reader "against the larger shock of conquest" (Rafael 1988, 65). In other contexts as well—during confession, for example—Tagalog "converts" employed various strategies to avoid being victimized by the evil spirits that animated incomprehensible Spanish words. What is also telling for an understanding of state formation in Rafael's analysis of how the language and techniques of conversion were turned against the Spanish priest is the important role of fear and the search for protection—values that Alfred McCoy, in an essay on "animist religion and Philippine peasant ideology" (1982), argues are centrally important in political cultures throughout Southeast Asia. The desire for invulnerability made the promise of dying a "beautiful death" and entering the Christian heaven a powerful incentive for submission to the authority of Spanish priests and Tagalog *principales,* as did the "fear of being overcome by *hiya,*" or shame, in relations of indebtedness (Rafael 1988, 127). Rafael demonstrates the cultural and affective basis for the formation of a hierarchical, colonial state even as he illustrates the manifold ways in which, in a colonial situation, the state's authority could be deflected and avoided.

Keith Taylor's studies of early Vietnam (1983, 1986a) offer another perspective on the role of transcultural translation in state formation. Starting in the third century B.C.E., Chinese armies, officials, and merchants came to northern Vietnam in search of exotic forest products and out of imperial concern with the security of the southern frontier. Vietnamese political culture took shape during the centuries of Chinese occupation (until the ninth century C.E.) as a product of the interaction between: 1) Chinese ideas about "civilization," the imperial state, and the patriarchal family; 2) Austronesian concepts of manly prowess, bilateral family structures, and the power of deceased heroes and local spirits; and 3) Indic Buddhism. As Wolters also argues, Taylor shows that the overall effect of attempts to convert Vietnamese to Chinese civilized norms was to "strengthen local sensibilities" (K. Taylor 1983, 208; 1986b). Chinese characters were being used to "translate" Vietnamese words as early as the eighth century c.e. (K. Taylor 1983, 206; 1986b). Rather than suppress indigenous spirit cults and the exaltation of military prowess exercised by the paramount political leader—as Christianity did in the Tagalog region during the sixteenth and seventeenth centuries according to Rafael—Vietnamese Buddhism coming from India as well as northern China was "elastic," providing the basis for a "dynastic religion" under the independent Lý rulers (1009–1225) that allowed the ruler to "[arouse] the slumbering spirits and [galvanize] them into a supernatural shield to protect the nascent kingdom" (K. Taylor 1983, 174; 1986a, 149). The dominant cultural forces at work in the formation of the Vietnamese state up to the thirteenth century came from the Indic Cham kingdom to the south and from China and Buddhism, as well as from the deep Austronesian cultural past of the coastal Vietnamese. Vietnam's Austronesian heritage and the ongoing tension between Chinese state models and Vietnam's Southeast Asian cultural environment are also evident in Wolters' studies of fourteenth-century Vietnam (1988), Alexander Woodside's book on the Vietnamese state in the early nineteenth century (1971), and Li Tana's examination of the formation of a distinctive political culture in southern Vietnam during the seventeenth and eighteenth centuries, when both the Nguyễn state and the Tây Sơn rebellion had more in common with Indic Cham and Khmer culture, Buddhism, and the beliefs of upland groups like the Jarai than with the Confucianist states of the Lê/ Trịnh north (1998).

Reynaldo Ileto's writings on Tagalog popular political culture in the nineteenth century also reveal the persistence of an indigenous type of state in the Philippines that, according to Rafael, had already been suppressed and transformed by Spanish colonialism in the sixteenth century. Looking at popular uprisings and religious texts in the nineteenth and twentieth centuries, Ileto argues that Christian concepts and Spanish structures of authority did not supplant Tagalog ones but were themselves retranslated into a coherent system of beliefs and practices that resembled those of Indic Southeast Asia (Ileto 1979, 1982, 1998). The Christlike heroes of the two most popular Tagalog oral poems of the nineteenth century that inspired popular anticolonial insurgencies well into the next century, as well as popular representations of the nationalist hero Rizal, exhibit characteristics of an Indic man of prowess who uses both physical force and spirituality to gather an entourage and form a hierarchical "state" that is situated on or near a mountain, which is both a symbol and source of supernatural power. Ileto demonstrates that such Tagalog translations of Spanish ideas and practices underlay and outlived the nationalist revolution of the late nineteenth century (Ileto 1979). Unlike peasant politics in Hue-Tam Ho Tai's study of millenarianism in nineteenth- and twentieth-century Vietnam (1983), the forms that peasant protest take in Ileto's book never evolve from primitive/religious to rational/secular types of social movement along a linear Weberian trajectory.

Ileto's work on the nineteenth century connects popular social movements with earlier state forms in Southeast Asia and is an exception to the approach taken in most studies of the Southeast Asian state in the colonial and postcolonial periods. In the works I have been considering, the concept of the (modern) state is kept at bay as scholars attempt to understand and describe political processes in a region that they assume has certain shared cultural characteristics of its own that give a similar form to "states," or whatever other term seems more appropriate, from one end of Southeast Asia to the other. In all of these works, cultural concepts are central, as is human agency, to the building of states. In many of the works I have surveyed, there is also an alertness to the processes of transcultural interaction in the formation of states (or statelike forms) that is an important dimension of the role of culture as such in state formation in Southeast Asia.

But I now turn my attention to the ways in which "modern" colonial and postcolonial states have been represented and to shifts in the ways in which both culture and human agency are treated in such studies.

The tendency to downplay questions of human agency and the role of culture in the creation of the Southeast Asian state is present in works that examine state formations in the precolonial past from the perspective of their failure to develop in the direction of fully modern Western states. Anthony Reid and Victor Lieberman are the best-known proponents of the view that premodern Southeast Asian history and the precolonial state can be studied using Weberian notions of religious rationalization, bureaucratic centralization, and a natural tendency for impersonal forces to push state development in the direction of modernity and capitalism in a Weberian sense (Lieberman 1984, 1993, 1999; Reid 1993).

A theme common to both Reid's and Lieberman's work on the sixteenth and seventeenth centuries is a general "trend towards centralized, if personal, government" in the region and the deterministic conclusion that "a period of absolutism was probably required . . . if bureaucratic and legal institutions were to emerge strong enough to enable the states to continue to compete with ever stronger rivals" (Reid 1993, 260–261; Lieberman 1993, 1999). In the following passage, we can observe how this Weberian prognosis is combined with a characterization of the Southeast Asian king that is based on the "Oriental despot" stereotype taken from Marx's AMP:

> The powerful rulers of the age of commerce appeared absolute in theory and in practice. They proclaimed supernatural status in their titles and rituals; they claimed the right to dispose of the land and wealth of their subjects; and numerous accounts testify to the arbitrary killing and dispossession of vassals who got in their way. Such absolutism found theoretical justification in long-standing Southeast Asian adaptions of Indian ideas of the supernatural king, and there were always foreigners (Brahmans, peripatetic ulama, European adventurers) ready to help ambitious kings give substance to such ideas. But it must be remembered that absolutism had to deal with an underlay not of feudalism, still less of constitutionalism, but of autonomous lineages, tribes, and entrepreneurs not yet incorporated into state structures. (Reid 1993, 251)

What is the role of culture in explaining "absolutism" in this passage? Indic concepts have become ideologies to be manipulated by "ambitious" rulers in a rational way so as to impede the forces of an emerging bourgeois, capitalist new order. The relationship between the indigenous "underlay" of Reid's Southeast Asian Indic state and the state itself has the feel of the dichotomous world of

Marx's AMP, where "between the self-reproducing villages 'below' and the hypertrophied state 'above', dwelt no intermediate forces" (P. Anderson 1974, 483).

It is also worth taking a moment to reflect on the term "absolutism" here. On comparative historical grounds, the use of the term "absolutism" to characterize Southeast Asian states under kings like Sultan Agung of Mataram, Sultan Iskandar Muda of Aceh, Narai of Ayutthaya, or Tha-lun of Toungoo is not very convincing. Not only were these "absolutist" rulers exceptional rather than typical in the period, but the states in which they lived did not closely resemble the absolutist states in seventeenth- and eighteenth-century Europe, either in theory or practice. The features that made European states "absolutist"—that is, the concept of "sovereignty" as a "co-ordinated system of administrative rule"; the theories about how kings and fathers mirrored one another and reinforced each other's claims to absolute authority; the bounded, territorial form of the state; diplomatic training; intelligence gathering; international congresses; the "balance of power" concept; mastery of the seas; the legal concept of private ownership; the administrative and fiscal reforms brought about through the constant waging of war; the appearance of "incarceration" as a mode of social control; and the new mode of anonymous and disciplined armies—do not have parallels or echoes in Southeast Asia that are strong enough to be meaningful (Giddens 1985, 83–121; Stone 1979, 110; Hunt 1993). In his Marxist interpretation of European absolutism, moreover, Perry Anderson insists that the crucial, defining feature of the absolutist state is one that is never explored by either Lieberman or Reid in the Southeast Asian case: the nonlinear, overlapping "concatenation" of modes of production during the European age of absolutism, which through their very simultaneity and interaction produced the emergence of European capitalism (P. Anderson 1974, 420). As Anderson observes,

> [C]oncrete *social formations* . . . typically embody a number of co-existent and conflicting modes of production, of varying date. In effect, the advent of the capitalist mode of production in Europe can only be understood by breaking with any purely linear notion of historical time as a whole. For rather than presenting the form of a cumulative chronology, in which one phase succeeds and supersedes the next, to produce the successor that will surpass it

in turn, the course towards capitalism reveals a *remanence* of the
legacy of one mode of production within an epoch *dominated* by
another, and a *reactivation* of its spell in the passage to a third.
(P. Anderson 1974, 421, emphasis in original)

Thus in the Europe of the Renaissance and absolutism, there
was not only global expansion outward through geographic space,
but also a rediscovery backward through time of classical learning
and Roman law. The rediscovery of the classical past served not only
to stimulate the development of science and political theory, but also
to increase rights of private property even as the absolutism of the
state continued to grow (P. Anderson 1974, 428–429). "For the apparent paradox of Absolutism in Western Europe," Anderson writes,
"was that it fundamentally represented an apparatus for the protection of aristocratic property and privileges, yet at the same time the
means whereby this protection was promoted could *simultaneously*
ensure the basic interests of the nascent mercantile and manufacturing classes" (P. Anderson 1974, 40, emphasis in original). Bureaucratization under absolutism, which was stimulated by the emergence
of capitalism, was also paradoxical, since it institutionalized the sale
of offices that was a throwback to the old order, "a kind of moneterized
caricature of investiture in a fief" (P. Anderson 1974, 33). In Southeast Asia during the same period, law reinforced status and hierarchy rather than individual property rights and contract, one of the
many differences that renders the Western "absolutist" or "bureaucratic" model for defining the Southeast Asian state problematic
before such terms have been localized and translated into ideas that
can better explain Southeast Asian concepts and practices and their
historical development (Hooker 1978, 17–119). I will return to these
large historiographical issues in due course.

It has been easiest simply to treat colonialism and capitalism in
nineteenth- and twentieth-century Southeast Asia as processes so
powerful and alien to "traditional" societies that culture and forms
of cultural interaction and localization seem irrelevant or suspect as
analytic categories. J. S. Furnivall, a colonial administrator and scholar,
coined the phrase "plural society" to describe the social effect of the
development of capitalist economies in European colonies in a way
that stresses the leviathan-like nature of the colonial state and the
insignificance of cultural interaction between social groups in colo-

nial societies (Furnivall 1991; Day and Reynolds 2000, 21–22). I quote from Furnivall's influential characterization of colonial society, replete with its echoes from Marx's AMP, at length:

> All tropical dependencies, and indeed all tropical countries, so far as they have been brought within the modern world, have in common certain distinctive characters in their social structure. In Dutch colonial literature they are often said to present a dual economy, comprising two distinct economic systems, capitalist and pre-capitalist, with a western superstructure of business and administration rising above the native world in which the people, so far as they are left alone, lead their own life in their own way according to a traditional scale of values in which economic values rank so low as to be negligible. . . . But the western superstructure is only one aspect of a distinctive character, common to all tropical dependencies, that cannot fail to impress even the most casual observer: the many-coloured pattern of the population. In Burma, as in Java, probably the first thing that strikes the visitor is the medley of peoples—European, Chinese, Indian, and native. It is in the strictest sense a medley, for they mix but do not combine. Each group holds by its own religion, its own culture and language, its own ideas and ways. As individuals they meet, but only in the market-place, in buying and selling. There is a plural society, with different sections of the community living side by side, but separately, within the same political unit. (Furnivall 1956, 303–304)

Furnivall's notion of the pluralizing, nonhybridizing effects of colonialism and capitalism under the aegis of an all-powerful state, used in combination with other theoretical ideas that are for the most part Foucauldian and Marxist, underlies the approach of a very large number of studies of power and society in modern Southeast Asia. Phrases like "discrepant histories" (Rafael 1995c), "dissociated identities" (Kipp 1996), and "fragmented vision" (Kahn and Wah 1992) in the titles of books about states and societies in colonial and postcolonial Philippines, Indonesia, and Malaysia, respectively, have a Furnivallian ring, and much stress is laid in them on the "technologies" and Oriental despotism of state rule and on the resulting fragmentation and dislocation of society and culture. To the extent that culture is examined in these and similar studies, it is largely as the product (Steedley 1999, 441–442) or "invention" (Hobsbawm and Ranger 1983) of the state, rather than as a force that also shapes the powerful inventiveness of authoritarian state formations and their cultural interventions. The conditions of colonialism over-determine the ritual means by which "Java" is reinvented by the Surakarta courts in the nineteenth century, according to John Pemberton, for example, and "invented" Javanese culture, in a reified and inauthentic form inherited from the colonial period, becomes a despotic technology of state rule during the New Order (1966–1998) (Pemberton 1994). Pemberton's interest in a single, determinant, state-manipulated form of Javanese culture precludes an examination of how weddings in nineteenth-century Surakarta, and later, could be ritual sites of multiple, contested meanings that tell us something about the struggle over, not just the imposition of, state power (Day 1996a). The role of colonial discourse in shaping Javanese culture is also the subject of Laurie Sears' study of Javanese shadow-puppet theatre, although here the puppeteers themselves are highlighted as agents who react to colonial and postcolonial imperatives in ways that empower them to respond creatively to the colonial inventedness of Javanese culture (Sears 1996a). The state is highly Oriental and dominant again in a series of essays Sears edited on female roles and identity in Indonesia, however, as it is in Ann Stoler's writings on bourgeois society in colonial Southeast Asia more generally (Sears 1996b; Stoler 1995b, 1996, 1997).

As treated in these studies, which are tinged with Foucauldian ideas yet preoccupied, as Marx would have it, with the "superstructural State" in a way that frustrates the application of Foucault's insistence on the microdynamic nature of power, as well as in studies that take a robust "political economy" approach to colonialism and its legacies, the "state," "capitalism," and "colonial discourse" are monolithic forms of domination and the primary agents in the making of history (Ortner 1984, 141–144; Stoler 1995a; Jomo 1986; Gomez and Jomo 1997). The roles of human agency and culture in the process by which the state itself is formed are left unexplored even in political economy studies that examine the "indeterminacy, fluidity, and dynamic character" of the state in its interaction with capital (Searle 1999, 10; Robison 1986; Hewison 1989; MacIntyre 1990; McVey 1992a; Winters 1996). Studies of the modern Southeast Asian state that focus primarily on institutions and politics in the tradition of Weber, on the other hand, allow us glimpses of human actions and unfolding events in which cultural factors are acknowledged as important, if not analyzed in depth (Girling 1981; R. Taylor 1987; Pasuk and Baker 1995; Crouch 1996). It follows from both the modified Foucauldian and political economy conceptualizations of the state in Southeast Asia and Furnivall's idea of "plural society" that any interaction between society and state that does occur will take the form of "resistance," "rebellion," or "nationalism," rather than a more ambivalent kind of transcultural localization and hybridization in which human agents involved in relations of power and the formation of states engage in complex acts of domination, submission, and resistance in ways that are shaped by culture. As Sherry Ortner observes, James Scott's studies of peasant resistance to colonial and postcolonial rule in Southeast Asia and elsewhere entail "a refusal of thickness," an inattention to "the ambiguity of resistance and the subjective ambivalence of the acts for those who engage in them" that results in a "virtually mechanical" account of how peasants and states interact. Scott's account dissolves both culture and human agency (which cannot "[exist] apart from cultural construction") as explanatory factors (Ortner 1995, 186; J. Scott 1976, 1985, 1990). Nationalism, the major theme of Benedict Anderson's writing, undergoes a similar cultural thinning that has as a corollary an emphasis on the role of an oppressively and opaquely monolithic state, the nation's nemesis (B. Anderson 1990, 1991, 1998). Although Anderson has continued to examine Javanese culture in specific textual and biographical contexts, he no longer sees its role as one of shaping the nature of Power, but as a site of "civil war" against itself as it resists defeat at the hands of revolutionary Indonesian nationalism, which has few specific cultural characteristics of its own. "Culture" in Anderson's thinking on Southeast Asian nationalism comes to be associated with "old" social formations and with the suppression of nationalist imaginings and social revolution. As my own choice of words implies, "nationalism," the "state," and other abstractions become the primary agents in the making of history in Anderson's writings on modern Southeast Asian politics, rather than human beings involved in particular transcultural, state-forming or state-resisting situations.

Two studies that have been much influenced by the anticultural turn in Anderson's thinking make the debunking of cultural modes of analysis a central theme. In his 1999 book on bossism in the Philippines, John Sidel takes issue with McCoy's use of Migdal's "strong society, weak state" thesis (Migdal 1988). McCoy argues that the weakness of the Filipino state is culturally "synergistic" with the activities of the country's powerful yet "fissiparous" rent-seeking kinship networks (McCoy 1994, 1–32). Sidel turns McCoy's thesis on its head, arguing instead that it was state formation in the Philippines, most crucially the introduction of American-style electoral politics at the local level under American colonial rule, that created possibilities for family "dynasties" and bossism to form:

> State formation in the Philippines after the precolonial era permitted the survival of private, personal control over the instruments of coercion and taxation. Successive phases of state formation supplanted the charismatic basis of local strongman authority with new bases of local power—derivative and discretionary enforcement of the law and accumulation of land and capital—and, in the American period, extended private control to include the provincial and national agencies of an emerging state apparatus. (Sidel 1999a, 18)

After examining several local variations of bossism in the Philippines, Sidel concludes his study by looking at other examples of bossism in Southeast Asia, in which a similar "conjuncture in state formation and capitalist development" can be observed. This conjuncture is the moment when "the trappings of formal electoral democracy are superimposed upon a state apparatus at an early stage of capital accumulation" (Sidel 1999a, 146). In Thailand, for example, Sidel finds no evidence to support the idea that "the strength of 'traditonal élites' and clientalistic demands in society constitutes the crucial precondition for the emergence and entrenchment of local bossism" (Sidel 1999a, 151). Bosses in the Philippines, as elsewhere in Southeast Asia, derive their power from coercion and wealth; cultural claims to legitimacy are a "myth." As Sidel puts the matter (in a way that actually brings the "state" into view):

> Through the idiom of the family, the mayor, governor, or congressman defines his relationship to his constituency as inherent,

permanent, and primordial. By consanguinity, affinity, ritual co-parenthood, and ritual feasting, he purports to incorporate the community into his extended family, obscuring the impersonal and contractual aspects of various relationships of dependence. . . . With his family name engraved on numerous local monuments and stenciled on the signs of various establishments, the local boss strives to achieve and sustain his status as both symbol and root of his bailiwick's very essence. (Sidel 1995, 160)

Sidel quashes the thought that there may be an active, cultural connection between old-style *datu* "prowess" and modern bossism. Manifestations of charisma, as well as belief in magical amulets and supernatural intervention, can still be found in the Philippines, Sidel says, but they are associated with tribal chiefs, priestesses, and social outlaws—individuals who tend to oppose the state (Sidel 1995, 152–156). Such individuals are in any case easily co-opted by predatory bosses (Sidel 1995, 156). Culture from both the "old" and the "new" Philippines, in Sidel's view, when not appropriated by the state in the form of legitimizing myths, expresses popular nationalism and disempowered (rather than culturally empowering) resistance to the state (Hedman and Sidel 2000, 140–165).

Geoffrey Robinson's book on political violence in Bali debunks culture in much the same way that Sidel does, although he gives Balinese culture as reinvented under Dutch colonial rule an important role to play in the unfolding events leading to the massacres of 1965–1966 (Robinson 1995). Robinson argues that Geertz ignored the actual political and social turmoil of Bali when he conducted field research there in the late 1950s. Robinson also contends that Geertz's model of the Balinese theatre state is based on a Dutch colonial construction of Balinese culture as harmonious and apolitical (Robinson 1995, 6–9). Like Sidel, Robinson traces the lineages of the modern state, which he defines as "a set of potentially powerful political structures and institutions whose precise historical significance varies depending on their relationship with societal forces" (Robinson 1995, 10). Using this flexible and culture-free definition, Robinson shows how the massacres of 1965–1966 were an outcome not of primordial rivalries and traditional values, but of the history of successive state formations in Bali and their social and economic effects on the island's population.

Robinson lays particular stress on the legacy of both Dutch and Japanese colonial rule. Under the Dutch, traditional Balinese elites were "resuscitated" and their power enhanced (Robinson 1995, 308), a policy continued by the Japanese. Both colonial regimes used these elites to exploit Balinese labor, creating class tensions. The Dutch politicized the issue of caste privilege and Balinese culture, while the Japanese taught Balinese new forms of anti-Western, nationalist organization. After 1945, the weakness of the central state allowed both old and new kinds of political conflict to take place on Bali, intensified by the participation of the military and the police. The potential for intra-Bali violence was also increased by the fact that states encompassing the whole of Bali were historically weak, so that "smaller state-like structures" gained in influence (Robinson 1995, 311–312). From the colonial period onward,

> [t]he precise pattern of political conflict in Bali depended on the local configuration of socioeconomic and cultural forces, and the way these forces interacted with impulses from the outside. Despite Bali's reputation for social and political harmony, a wide range of potential sources of conflict existed there throughout the twentieth century, including rivalries between noble houses, caste disputes, class conflict, ideological differences over cultural and political matters, and anger arising from real or perceived economic injustices. (Robinson 1995, 312)

In conclusion, Robinson claims that the sources of political violence in Bali and elsewhere are the result of "certain structural features of the broader political environment" rather than "the character, temper, or cultural makeup of a given political community" (Robinson 1995, 313). Paradoxically, he shows in detail throughout his book how a "somewhat exaggerated respect for Balinese religion and custom" on the part of all the agents concerned played an important role in relations of power and conflict and hence in what Balinese understood the "state" to be (Robinson 1995, 144).

My aim in this section has been to indicate some of the main themes and approaches in studies of the state in Southeast Asia from early to contemporary times. My survey confirms that as we move forward through time, the "state" becomes a more solid and acceptable, if still opaque, term, even as culture becomes an increasingly suspect analytic concept for understanding the nature of Southeast Asian political processes, or disappears entirely from view. As far as the "fate of culture" is concerned, to borrow a phrase from Ortner (1999), the shift can be explained in part by a difference in the nature of historical sources: the historian of early Southeast Asia before the coming of Europeans has to rely on materials that are products of Southeast Asian cultures—literary texts, inscriptions, and temple remains. Before the nineteenth century, when investigations into every aspect of Southeast Asian life led to the writing of voluminous reports by Europeans, European sources are still a sketchy basis for studying the Southeast Asian past, especially since most of Southeast Asia was not under any form of direct European rule. In studies of the nineteenth century onward, however, Western sources and Western (predominantly Weberian and Marxist) analytic categories that are themselves expressions of European rather than Southeast Asian cultures reign supreme as Southeast Asia is swept up into the mainstream of Western history via colonialism and the imperialisms of the cold war and globalization. The apparent dominance of Western institutions, like "the modern bureaucratic state," and Western epistemologies, like "nationalism," in Southeast Asia from the late nineteenth century onward seems to require a reading of the sources, even indigenous ones, that is ipso facto "occidented" toward a teleological understanding of the "progress" of Southeast Asian history, away from "culture" and toward social forms and practices that conform to the same universal, rational categories that Weber employed to describe Western capitalism and the Western bureaucratic state. Few analysts have stopped to consider the fact that Weber's own critical terms are culture-bound.

The "occidentalizing" effect of colonialism in Southeast Asia on the categories used to understand Southeast Asian history is even apparent in the argument John Smail put forward in 1961 for an "autonomous history of modern Southeast Asia" (Smail 1993). Smail writes that historians should focus on "domestic" Southeast Asian history and on the creative adaptation of European ideas and institutions, but from a neutral viewpoint and in terms of "a single thought-world of universal history." As I have indicated in my survey of writings on the Southeast Asian state, Western categories, especially Weberian ones, are also dominant in the way cultural features of early Southeast Asian state formations are discussed. Not only is the likelihood of a neutral moral viewpoint highly suspect, but the possibility of an autonomous Southeast Asian history that is not already greatly determined by cultural forces coming from outside as well as from within the region is hard to imagine.

If avoidance of the term "state" in the work on early Southeast Asia allows for an examination of state-forming practices in ways that keep the definition of the state and its teleology open to revision, in the case of most of the work on the "modern state" in Southeast Asia from the nineteenth century onward, an assumption is made that we already know what the "modern state" is, even though "it" is in fact never analyzed as such. The paradoxical conclusion that can be drawn, therefore, is that the cultural specificity of the Southeast Asian state is clearer in its early forms when its definition as a "state" is fuzzy, and fuzzier when the state's modern structures and functions seem absolutely clear.

How can we resolve this paradox and put culture "back in" to the study of the colonial and postcolonial Southeast Asian state? Would it help, for instance, if we expand Wolters' notion of localization and think of Southeast Asian history from early times to the present as an overlapping series of localizing, transcultural processes, differentially distributed over the whole region and occurring over many centuries at different rates in different places? For one thing, "colonialism" could then be located in this series in all its heterogeneity, rather than being treated in a reductive way as an unbridgeable watershed that divides the "traditional" Southeast Asian past from the "modern" present. As Sears observes in her critical reevaluation of Smail's essay, the issue at stake in the study of "modern" Southeast Asian history is not the formation of a single, universal moral viewpoint about its "autonomy," but the "partial, situated" nature of the knowledges that can be posited about it (Sears 1993, 19). Sears is suspicious of Dipesh Chakrabarty's call, similar to Smail's, for "provincializing Europe," since it may result in a compulsion "to rewrite yet again the history of Indian-European relations from an Indian perspective with a damning moral viewpoint" (Chakrabarty 2000). Instead she asks for an approach to colonialism in Southeast Asia that

> concentrate[s] on the ways in which new knowledges were brought into being as the result of the interaction between colo-

nizers and colonized and the ways in which these knowledges were continually transformed as they moved between various circles of Europeans and . . . Southeast Asians as well as between elite and peasant groups. (Sears 1993, 13)

Sears suggests a process in colonial Southeast Asia that is different in quality but not in kind from interactions between cultures in earlier periods of time. Although she dislikes the term "hybridity," her sense of the transformative "interaction between colonizers and colonized . . . as well as between elite and peasant groups" disputes the reality and heuristic usefulness of representing colonial societies as "plural" in Furnivall's sense (Sears 1993, 9). Her understanding of colonial society is closer to what Mary Louise Pratt means by "contact zone," as "the space in which peoples geographically and historically separated come into contact with each other and establish ongoing relations, usually involving conditions of coercion, radical inequality, and intractable conflict" (Pratt 1992, 6), or what Homi Bhabha means by hybridity, the "inter" or "in-between space" in colonial cultures where the translation, negotiation, appropriation, imitation, resistance, and Smail's "creative adaptation" take place (Bhabha 1994, 38, 112–113). I would go even further and argue that the process of transcultural "hybridization" that Sears describes can be used as a synonym for what Wolters means by "localization" in premodern as well as colonial and postcolonial contexts (see Wolters 1999, 55–56, n. 58). As Robert Young puts it in his discussion of the etymology of the word "culture," "colonization rests at the heart of culture," which always "participates in a conflictual economy acting out the tension between sameness and difference, comparison and differentiation, unity and diversity, coherence and dispersion, containment and subversion" (Young 1995, 31, 53). To understand hybridization and localization in this way, as properties of culture itself (and I have been using all three terms, along with "transcultural," in a virtually interchangeable way in this chapter), pushes the meaning that Wolters intended for his term "localization" in a direction that expands its meaning and invites questions about the heterogeneous and contested nature of the localization process, questions that draw attention to the role of power in cultural relations and to the role of culture in the formation of states. To return "colonialism" in an anti-historicizing, nonteleological way to the diversity and flow of South-

east Asian history, therefore, allows us to locate the state in a continuous series of overlapping, cultural localizations in which "tradition" and "modernity" or the varieties of conflicting forces involved
in transcultural practices are not mutually exclusive. It is now time
to offer a definition of the Southeast Asian "state" of my own that
embraces the historiographical issues I have raised and that inaugu-
rates the argument in the remainder of the book.

An Approach to State Formation in Southeast Asia

Here is my own working definition of the state, one that appropri-
ates and adapts ideas and words taken from definitions found in the
writings of Weber, Marx, Foucault, Geertz, Wolters, Benedict Anderson, and a number of other writers on the subject:

> The state is a complex agent that acts through culturally con-
> structed repertoires of potent, rational, authoritative, magical,
> symbolic, and illusory practices, institutions, and concepts. The
> state is distinct from yet interactive with societal forces, in ways
> that vary according to time and place. The state regulates power
> and morality and organizes space, time, and identity in the face
> of resistance to its authority to do so.

The definition is designed to facilitate comparisons. Overall, the
terminology I use makes the definition applicable to "traditional,"
"colonial," as well as "modern" state formations, thereby suspend-
ing judgment about the need for categorical distinctions between
states in different times and places. The first sentence of the definition makes reference to "practice theory" and its rejection of mechanical or structural models for explaining culture, history, or politics
(Ortner 1984, 144–157; Dirks, Eley, and Ortner 1994, 11–17). Of primary importance in practice-theory approaches is the agency of
human beings, of their intentions and desires, in forming states.
The same emphasis applies to the study of culture, which Raymond
Williams defines succinctly as the "whole social process" (Williams
1977, 108). The cultural processes of state formation are never complete. The state never becomes a fully, finally constructed "thing,"
nor does its power act independently from or simply upon human
actors (Ortner 1996, 6–12; Giddens 1984, 9; Inden 1990, 23; Steinmetz
1999, 9). It is made and remade by human beings who form a "com-

plex agent." This agency is constrained, shaped, and guided by cultural concepts and practices such as "daily routines, initiations, courses of study or apprenticeship, meetings, assemblies, courts, parades, processions," as well as bureaucracies, rituals, armies, and so on (Inden 1990, 26; Ortner 1996, 12; Hobart 1990a, 95). It is in this sense, as a complex human agent, that states can be said to "act." This is not to say that the state-as-complex-agent acts as one mind and body. Its internal complexity consists of multiple networks, conflicts, ambivalences, and resistances as well as dominations (Ortner 1995, 175; Giddens 1984, 16; Peletz 1996, 348–355). The state consists, like cultures or societies, of power networks and struggles. Like peasants, states have their own internal politics that must not be "sanitized" so as to make them seem monolithic or naturally "legitimate" (Ortner 1995, 176–180). Nor should states be detached from the cultural forces that resist and so shape the ways in which they are constructed (Ortner 1995, 186; Corrigan and Sayer 1985; Sayer 1994; Steinmetz 1999, 1–49). As cultural forms in the process of their making, states can best be thought of less as total "structures" or holistic "theatres" than as assemblages of "repertoires," provisional—if often long-enduring—modes of collective human action and thinking constrained by "rules of the game" (Ortner 1996, 12–16) that "emerge from struggle" and affect the way in which states act and change over time (Tilly 1993). These repertoires accumulate power or potency, which gives them the authority to act in coercive ways that are at once rational, symbolic, and magical (S. Errington 1989, 292; Sayer 1994, 375; Inden 1990, 241; Taussig 1992, 111–140; Bourdieu 1991; Taussig 1997; Wiener 1995, 183–221). The state is also, as Philip Abrams has argued, "in every sense of the term a triumph of concealment . . . [that hides] the real history and relations of subjection behind an ahistorical mask of legitimating illusion" (Abrams 1988, quoted in Joseph and Nugent 1994, 19). The power of the very "idea" of the state is such that "'it' slips very easily off the tongue" (Sayer 1994, 372), making us think that "it" is more coherent and eternal than it is (Mitchell 1999, 76). Most theorists, including Foucault, assume that the boundaries that separate the "state" from "society" are thus clear and unproblematic. But this assumption begs the question, implied by the ideational nature and illusoriness of the state, of how to describe the process by which the state's "limits" or boundaries are constructed and maintained. "At what point," Timothy Mitchell asks, "does power enter channels fine enough and its exercise become am-

biguous enough that one recognizes the edge of [the state] apparatus? Where is the exterior that enables one to identify it as an apparatus" (Mitchell 1999, 76)? Finally, the definition lists the most
important things states as complex agents do. States consist of networks of power that connect them to society, which states attempt to
regulate through various coercive means that include the imposition
of what Émile Durkheim called "moral discipline" (Corrigan and
Sayer 1985, 4–6). State formations also organize space—a better term
than Weber's "territory" for analyzing state practices in different
times and places (de Certeau 1988, 117)—as well as time and social
identity in distinctive ways that reveal both the strength and the limitations of the state as an assemblage of repertoires made up of practices, institutions, and concepts that struggle for dominance against
social forces that resist the state's authority (Giddens 1984, 35, 152;
Williams 1977, 108–114).

In the next four chapters I make use of the definition I have
given above to examine state formations in Southeast Asia. The
phrase in the title of this book, "fluid iron," which I take from a
Dayak magic spell and to which I will return in chapter 3 (Tsing 1993,
77), is meant to suggest the malleable nature of the state-forming
process, in which coercive concepts and resistant practices are both
involved. In chapter 2 I take up questions of kinship and gender in
order to examine complex agency in the Southeast Asian state and as
a good place to look for the boundary that separates state and society.
In chapter 3 I examine textual examples of the ways in which Southeast Asian states are constituted as cosmologies, or what Foucault
calls "truth regimes." My interest here is in cutting the category of
"cosmological state" loose from its Weberian mooring in "traditional" Southeast Asia. My use of works of literature and art in this
and other chapters in my book builds on the practice of many other
historians of Southeast Asia, but it is also a response to Williams' call
for the study of "works of art" in the cultural analysis of the "active
and formative" ways in which hegemonic power is exercised (Williams
1977, 113–114). The texts I discuss in chapter 3 allow us to examine
the processes and conflicts by which potent and authoritative state
concepts that regulate power and morality as well as organize space,
time, and identity take shape and are represented, purified, and hy-
bridized at all levels of society in cosmological forms that can be
found in any period of Southeast Asian history. Chapter 4 is con-

cerned with dehistoricizing—that is, detaching from a Western historical teleology—that most typically "modern" of state institutions, bureaucracy, in a way that sheds light on its character as a very old repertoire of Southeast Asian practices, one that can be described as both rational and ritualistic. In chapter 5 the cultural form of the Southeast Asian state becomes more evident as I examine the relationship between two apparently contrasting expressions of state coercion in a variety of examples. I show how the interaction between these two coercive forms reveals the magical nature of the Southeast Asian state.

My argument will proceed in a comparative manner that will cross temporal, disciplinary, as well as cultural boundaries in Southeast Asia and Southeast Asian studies, but the insights I seek to develop will always be "partial" and "situated" with respect to cases I have spent time studying, that interest me, or that I have access to through the languages I read. Any impression that my treatment of the scholarly literature aspires to be all-inclusive in both a regional or interdisciplinary sense is accurate only to the extent that it reflects my interest in developing a comparative, interdisciplinary approach to the question of the state. My intention, however, remains one of merely suggesting, in as convincing a manner as possible, ways of thinking across and beyond the reigning dichotomies that separate "traditional" from "modern" Southeast Asia, the study of culture from the study of history and politics, one part of Southeast Asia from another. I will have something more to say about Southeast Asia as a regional concept at the end of my book, but for the purposes of the next four chapters, "Southeast Asia" serves as a heuristic frame for my analytic readings and reinterpretations of primary and secondary sources about the state. Finally, throughout my discussion, I hope to develop a better understanding of state formations in Southeast Asia as significant "projects" that have been undertaken by Southeast Asians themselves. "The importance of subjects (whether individual actors or social entities)," Ortner reminds us,

> lies not so much in who they are and how they are put together as in the projects that they construct and enact. For it is in the formulation and enactment of those projects that they both become and transform who they are, and that they sustain or transform their social and cultural universe. (Ortner 1995, 187)

2
Ties That (Un)Bind

Newspapers and academic journals have featured reports for many years about family politics in the Philippines, the economic power and corruption of ex-President Suharto and his children, and the business holdings of the Thai royal family. And yet kinship, the "family," and the ways in which gender inflects relations of power in Southeast Asia are new subjects of serious study in the historiography of the region (see, e.g., J. Taylor 1983; McCoy 1994; Andaya 1993, 1994, 2000b; Wolters 1999). One of the most important reasons for the neglect of kinship, the family, and gender as a major topic of historical research, to extend the argument made by Craig Reynolds in his essays about the writing of modern Thai history, is that historians of Southeast Asia generally have tended to focus less on gender and power relations in the region and more on definitions of the nature of Southeast Asian "power" and state "structures" that leave actual relations of power out of the picture (Reynolds 1994, 1995, n.d.). Typically, neither culturally defined concepts of "power" nor states are marked for gender or theorized in terms of the real networks of power that constitute them.

In this chapter I want to examine how kinship, families, and gender are involved in and affected by state formation in Southeast Asia. Notwithstanding the "looseness" of the entourages based on bilateral kinship practices that are found in the fabric of Southeast Asian states new and old, a factor that has been used variously to label early states as "fluid" and contemporary ones as autocratically "patrimonial," I argue that extended family-like networks and the ideologies that give these networks coherence and longevity constitute a characteristically Southeast Asian mode through which relations of power have assumed statelike form, in whatever shape or size, throughout the region's history. This line of argument goes against the grain of approaches to the relationship between "family" and "state" that understand them to be "the two competing institutions in the development of a society" (Forster and Ranum 1976, viii; McCoy 1994). A closer look at examples of the ways in which kinship networks and families become states and in which states lose their statelike identities to become the contending factions that they have always been, linked through kinship and kinlike bonds, provides a better understanding of how the boundaries between states and societies in Southeast Asia have been formed and transgressed.

I will argue that families and kinship groups are complex agents that help to explain similarities between Southeast Asian states over time that have not been carefully examined. Extended Southeast Asian families are also an important site of state control, as well as a template for generating ideologies of control. Relations of power are inflected according to gender but also generation. Fathers, mothers, and children, not simply as sociological agents but also as "imaginative constructs" (Hunt 1993, 196), have played important roles in the creation or destruction of states in Southeast Asia. The tendency of different state formations to "feminize," "masculinize," and "infantilize" those who participate in the life of the state is another important aspect of the "familyism" of Southeast Asian states. My mode of argumentation, here and in the chapters that follow, will be to break down linear, teleological understandings of Southeast Asian history and to take issue with static explanatory categories. Relations of power that constitute states in Southeast Asia are practices made out of "fluid iron," as coercive as they are changing and subject to evasion or resistance.

Familial States and Their Ancestors

To call Southeast Asian states "familial states" (to borrow a term from Julia Adams, whose work on the Dutch state in the seventeenth century will be discussed in chapter 4) should not call to mind the patriarchal dynastic families of Europe. The agents at work in Southeast Asian state formations are kinship networks, "a working coalition drawn from a larger group related by blood, marriage, and ritual" (McCoy 1994, 10). Yet scholars of colonial and postcolonial

Southeast Asia speak of the "patrimonial" or "patron-client" character of modern states in Indonesia, Thailand, Malaysia, or the Philippines as if they are talking about a European historical phenomenon that has become universal (Winters 1996; Crouch 1996; Anderson and Kahin 1982; Pasuk and Baker 1995). As the term "patrimonial" indicates, the typology of states developed by Max Weber, rather than research extending back into early Southeast Asian history, is being invoked in these studies to give a label to the prominent role of families and kinlike entourages in Southeast Asian states. The interest in the label is primarily classificatory and moral rather than analytical: such states are "bad" and "premodern" because they are "patrimonial" and so violate the teleological imperative of world history written from a Western point of view (Chakrabarty 2000; Steinmetz 1999, 16). The historical reasons for, and the cultural form and mode of operation of, such states—and the possibly ambiguous meanings of their "familial" characteristics—are never explained, except as an expression of some ill-defined "feudal" legacy from the past.

One approach to uncovering the historical origins of patrimonialism in contemporary Southeast Asia is to look back to, but no farther than, the colonial period, where there is abundant evidence of a process by which families became entrenched in bureaucratic positions of power or seized on state office as a method of gaining access to wealth and status. In Java, Bali, Sumatra, Johore, and the Philippines during the nineteenth and twentieth centuries, to take several examples, colonial policies and the effects of capitalism turned a motley group of sometimes old, sometimes arriviste regional families into intermarrying and "legitimate" elites who maintained their family members in office over several generations and depended on the state for their power and longevity (Sutherland 1979; Fasseur 1992a; Robinson 1995; Dobbin 1983; Trocki 1979; McCoy 1994; B. Anderson 1998, 192–226; Sidel 1997). In these cases, the primary cause of familyism in the state seems to be Western colonialism. In Thailand, on the other hand, a pattern of family control over the bureaucratic institutions of the state developed in the seventeenth and eighteenth centuries, notwithstanding the fact that Ayutthaya was not a strong, centralized state (Wyatt 1994, 90–130; Wolters 1999, 142–143). Kinship networks continued to both strengthen and weaken the state in the nineteenth and twentieth centuries (Englehart 2001, 76; Hewison 1989, 206–214). This example of networking familyism has an indigenous origin, therefore, although the role of trade as the source of the wealth, cohesion, and power of families like the Bunnag, rather than control over agrarian manpower by "men of prowess," suggests similarities with examples from colonized Southeast Asia. As I will discuss in more detail in chapter 4, the Dutch East India Company and its successor colonial state were themselves "familial" states in which familyism and capitalism developed hand in hand, creating a synergy with the "network state" of Central Java (Adams 1994a, 1994b, 1996; Nagtegaal 1996; J. Taylor 1983; Fasseur 1992a). In the nineteenth century, the similarity between the Siamese state and the familial states of colonized Southeast Asia grew clearer. Westernizing reforms under King Chulalongkorn (r.1868–1910) put the king's brothers and half-brothers in charge of state ministries. In 1910 nine out of twelve cabinet posts were occupied by members of the royal family, and in the same year all of the senior posts in the army were held by members of the royal family or by high-ranking nobles with family connections to the throne. The new, Western-style educational institutions were also monopolized by the royal clan and the nobility related to them. The modern bureaucracy itself served as a recruiting ground for turning the nobility of the provinces into *"kharatchakan,* the servants of the (royal) state" (Pasuk and Baker 1995, 235–239). These patterns persist in the pervasive patron-clientage of the contemporary period. "In a 1977 survey," report Pasuk and Baker (1995, 239), "95 percent of a sample of bureaucrats reckoned that advancement in the bureaucracy depended on patron-client relations."

But the question arises: if familyism developed in Southeast Asia as a result of colonialism, or economic conditions similar to those under colonial rule, what preexisting political and cultural factors made such a Southeast Asian response possible, even inevitable? What is the prehistory of the familial colonial or postcolonial state in Southeast Asia? How do we get from the fluid, autonomous, flexible, power- and prowess-filled worlds evoked in the writings of Benedict Anderson and O. W. Wolters to the "patrimonial" family-dominated scenes of the colonial and postcolonial eras? Perhaps colonialism and capitalism should be seen as reinforcing and fulfilling, rather than only transforming, state-forming impulses and responses that have a long history in the region.

Wolters, drawing on the work of Thomas Kirsch on the role of bilateral kinship in the organization of society in Angkor, has made the influential argument that in early Southeast Asia the "cultural emphasis [was] on 'person' and 'achievment' rather than on 'group' and 'hereditary' status" (Kirsch 1976; Wolters 1994, 6). Wolters' studies of early Vietnam illustrate this emphasis, and he implies that the gradual adoption of Chinese dynastic state forms there from the tenth century onward must be viewed as a progressive failure of the Southeast Asian localization process (Wolters 1988, xxxiii–xxxiv). The question that needs to be asked, then, is whether the political "dynasties" that arose in the colonial and postcolonial times in Southeast Asia (e.g., Sidel 1999a) depart from or confirm a cultural pattern that has deeper roots in Southeast Asian history. The point was made some time ago that bilateral kinship networks can in fact serve to strengthen social and political structures in contemporary Southeast Asia, so it is time to investigate the situation in earlier times (Hüsken and Kemp 1991).

A "dynastic" impulse at work in the process of state formation can indeed be detected in Southeast Asia from very early times. The same status competition between kinship networks and the same problem of controlling kin who become ancestors that explain the important role of personal "prowess" also underlie the adoption of practices and institutions of centralizing Indic, Sinic, or Islamic kingship to form states. The synergy between bilateral kinship, hierarchy, and state formation yields evidence of a predisposition to react to colonialism in a "familial" mode.

Paul Mus' essay of 1933, in which he examined the process by which Hindu religious practices "underwent fixation, localization" in the village ancestor cults of early Champa, is an early precursor to Wolters' writing on localization (Mus 1975). But what do we imagine took place when Southeast Asian village ancestors were turned into Hindu gods, or when Sanskrit came to Cambodia or Java? In Sheldon Pollock's view, the role of Sanskrit in Southeast Asia was not, to quote Wolters on localization, to bring "ancient and persisting indigenous beliefs into sharper focus," but to cause "the very creation" of (new) forms of Southeast Asian culture "and to be itself changed in the process" (Pollock 1998a, 33). In other words, localization is transformative, not simply absorptive and adaptive. Pollock encourages us, therefore, to reread the following passage from Wolters' discussion of the *devarāja* cult's founding in ninth-century Cambodia, in which he lays stress on the ease with which local cultural practices absorbed Hindu concepts and procedures:

> Pedro Chirino, a Spanish missionary of the early seventeenth century who was familiar with Tagalog society in the Philippines, tells us that those who had distinguished themselves would attribute their valour to divine forces and take care to select burial sites that would become centres for their worship as Ancestors. This is the conceptual framework in which I am inclined to interpret the meaning of the much discussed *devarāja* cult. . . . The cult, established by tantric procedures of initiation and only after a long series of triumphant campaigns in many parts of the country, assimilated the king's spiritual identity to Śiva as "the king of the gods," a definition of Śiva that matched the overlord status that the king had already achieved. . . . [Jayavarman] realized that his achievements had guaranteed his status as an Ancestor among all those Khmers who were connected with his kinship group, which was bound to be an extended one because it was organized in accordance with the principle of cognatic kinship. (Wolters 1999, 19–20)

As well as noting that early Tagalog and Khmer societies were bilateral, Wolters also indicates in this passage that they were hierarchical and concerned with status distinctions. Writing on the relationship between rank and gender in Polynesia, Sherry Ortner argues that here, as well as in hierarchical societies like those of Southeast Asia, the "sex/gender" system interacts with the "prestige" system in distinctive ways (Ortner 1996, 59–115). Since the criteria for prestige, such as *"mana"* for Polynesia or "potency" for Southeast Asia, are "encompassing" and furnish the basis for the construction of social hierarchy, it follows that an important task of analysis is the identification of "hidden *possibilities*" for "prestige-oriented action" for both men and women in bilateral, hierarchical societies (Ortner 1996, 62, emphasis in original). The arrival of Hindu religious and political ideas in early Cambodia, made available only to those with access to the learned Brahmans who could read, interpret, and give instruction about Sanskrit texts, would have furnished one such "hidden" opportunity for "men of prowess" to increase their status by adopting what Pollock calls the "cosmopolitanism" of Sanskrit culture. This culture transformed them from local chiefs into "world conquerors," or *cakravartin*. Once he had absorbed Sanskrit cosmopolitanism, it would certainly have felt natural for the powerful and hierarchical Jayavarman to think of himself as a *devarāja*, but this self-identification also served crucially to demarcate the boundary between old Khmer society and a new Khmer-Indic "state," a difference that would henceforth have to be maintained through state-forming and boundary-demarcating practices, institutions, and concepts. The Sanskrit term *"cakravartin"* marks the crucial difference between a local society and a cosmopolitan state in early Cambodia. As Wolters puts the matter, without intending to lay stress on the factor that is crucial for identifying the emergence of the state:

> There would have been men of prowess in various Southeast Asian societies long before any question of Śiva-like metaphors arose, and nothing that accompanied "Hinduization" would have represented a major discontinuity at the dawn of early Southeast Asian history *except a differentiation between those who imagined that they belonged to the "Hindu world" and those who lived in forests and others who were unaware of that world.* (Wolters 1999, 113, emphasis added)

State formation in Angkor as elsewhere in early Southeast Asia allowed kinship networks both to expand and achieve a certain coherence, which was commemorated in genealogical inscriptions. The tendency toward lineage formation and statelike solidarity was also encouraged through the institution of *varṇa*, which were not caste groupings as in India, but court functions, usually ceremonial in character, carried out by the members of a family who had been given quasi-hereditary right to perform them (Sedov 1978, 118–120; Mabbett 1977, 435). Like members of the royal family, as well as families generally who sought to participate in the life of the state, *varṇa* lineages derived their income from and developed a sense of family solidarity by means of cult temples and the populated lands connected to these. Particularly from the reign of Sūryavarman I (r.1002–1050) onward, the epigraphical record is rich in genealogies of, and recorded land grants to, families of state officials and loyalists (Vickery 1985). The Trapaeng Don On inscription from the early twelfth century, for example, allows us to glimpse the process through which "person," "family," and "king" became bonded to one another in a "state" (Coedès 1951, 180–

192; cf. Kenneth Hall's purely economic reading of this inscription, K. Hall 1985, 162–163). In the Khmer portion of the inscription, the author, who entered the service of Udayādityavarman II (r.1050–1066) at the age of eighteen as guardian of the sacred buffaloes, describes the birth and progress of his family fortunes:

(1–2)   Success! Happiness! Homage to Śiva! This inscription was written in 1051 śaka.

(2–8)   Arriving at the age of eighteen years, I served in the caste [*varṇa*] of the sacred bulls, in 989 śaka [1067 c.e.] under the reign of S. M. Śrī Udayādityavarman; then under S. M. Sadāśivapada [Harśavarman III], S. M. Parama-kaivalyapada [Jayavarman VI], S. M. Paramaniṣkala-pada [Dharanīndravarman I] and S. M. Śrī Sūryavar-madeva. I showed my devotion to them, following my destiny, and conquered the enemies of Their Majesties.

(8–12) These kings showed me their favor in all kinds of ways. With the possessions which they deigned to grant me and with the produce of the labors of my people I constructed sanctuaries, I bought slaves, purchased lands, redeemed properties [sold because of earlier debts], put up boundary markers, made barrier dikes, built walls, dug canals and tanks for water.

(12–14) I established foundations in the years mentioned, offered slaves, lands for each half of the month, wet-rice fields for the upkeep of the cult, wet-rice fields for the officiants, the head priest, for the care of the temple slaves, which my family from the country of Svay Pañcaka has an obligation to continue to assure.

(14–17) I have offered these slaves and lands in order to assure provisions for the sanctuaries, I piled up dikes and constructed bridges across which roads could pass. I offer the fruit of my merit to the king as if this were a royal foundation; I desire nothing but the fruit of my devotion to my master.

(17–38) [Same details about the amounts of rice and numbers of slaves found in the Sanskrit text; the male and female slaves are listed by name, with their children, who are unnamed.]

(38–43) All these rice fields, lands, these means of subsistence,

> these slaves of the gods will belong to the member of my
> family who will be a pandita and will take charge of the
> sanctuary, be priest to these gods and give orders to
> these slaves of the gods and others. May he neither sell
> nor disperse the slaves and land of the gods. As for my
> family, may those who would sell or encourage the dis-
> persal of these slaves and lands of the gods be reported
> to the Court as guilty of having harmed a spiritual
> master. (Coedès 1951, 190–192; my translation of the
> French version)

Inscriptions like Trapaeng Don On, or the more famous Sdok Kak
Thom (Mabbett 1977), tell us something more than that Angkorean
kings depended on male prowess and bilateral kinship networks to
create and maintain the state. The inscription records the author's
commemoration and reactivation of his own past acts, which constitute his personhood and agency in relation to a succession of kings,
to their enemies, to his male and female slaves, to his priests, to other
subjects of the king who traveled the roads he built, to his family,
to the gods, and to his descendants for whom he hopes to become a
powerful and beneficent ancestor. The inscription represents a person
who was both autonomously active and also energetically subservient
to a state that he helped to build. In the process of transforming himself and the countryside, this loyal subject closed the social and cultural distance between himself and the kings he served; to use Fenella
Cannell's words describing a beauty contest in contemporary Bicol,
he engaged in the "pleasures of empowerment . . . and also [moved]
towards a transformation in which what is distant, powerful, and oppressive is brought closer and made more equal" (Cannell 1999, 254).

If we look for a modern parallel in the Philippines to this model
state-builder from Angkor, a good choice would be Doña Sisang's
henchman Grasing de Guzman, one of five violent brothers who allied
themselves with her Central Luzon landowning family. In Brian
Fegan's words,

> After his criminal notoriety of the 1950s faded, Grasing's career
> and reputation matured into those of a political king maker, busi-
> nessman, and philanthropist. His influence in regional politics
> and with national government officials made him an effective

go-between and peacemaker in provincial rivalries. . . . On behalf of Doña Sisang and her heirs, he manipulated tenants on the estates in such a way that the land reforms of presidents Magsaysay in 1954 and Macapagal in 1963 had little effect on estate income. . . . As Cabanatuan City expanded, the seven-hundred-hectare estate on its outskirts became valuable urban land. Grasing manipulated its tenants into surrendering their cultivation rights, allowing the Buencamino-de Leon estate to convert rice land into the Kapitan Pepe Memorial Park cemetery and urban subdivision, both of which he managed. Growing rich from this managerial and political base, Grasing invested in land in Nueva Ecija and Bulacan provinces, in piggeries, a tractor pool, a short-time motel, and urban real estate. He became a patron of fiestas, sporting competitions, and athletic teams, and a "friend of the poor" on whose largesse and interventions a constant stream of supplicants waited. (Fegan 1994, 83)

Unfortunately for Grasing, his lack of connections to the centralizing Marcos regime led to his downfall and arrest when martial law was declared in 1972. But other members of the de Guzman family thrived once Marcos fell from power. Like the author of the Trapaeng Don On inscription, Grasing and his brothers were "men of prowess" in the very old Southeast Asian meaning of that term. They were also similar to the state-building Khmer and his relatives in that their combined efforts constituted what Fegan calls

a political family . . . a political unit whose power—whether to get its will done or block its opponents—is, first, transferable from one member to another over time, and, second, extends beyond its blood members to allow it a leading role in the politics of its particular area. . . . At the heart of [the de Guzmans'] continuous political prominence lies an esprit de corps and sense of corporate honor that binds the family and impels it to throw itself into public affairs as a unit rather than withdraw to the concerns of member households. (Fegan 1994, 101)

The author of the Trapaeng Don On inscription expresses a similar esprit de corps extending over several generations, one that in his time and place was put at the service of a centralizing state. Like early

Javanese states that promoted temple building and wet-rice agriculture for similar reasons, individuals and kinship networks that made up complex state-forming agents in Angkorean society sought personal status and wealth. They also developed a certain lineage consciousness, which coalesced around and precipitated wet-rice agricultural activity and the building and maintenance of family or royal ancestor cult temples (Dove 1985; Christie 1986). The emphasis on family discipline and the hierarchy of authority necessary for wet-rice regimes is also found in records about state formation in twelfth- and thirteenth-century Vietnam (Wolters 1988, 12–13; K. Taylor 1995, 60–61). The author of the Trapaeng Don On inscription exhorts members of his family collectively to commit themselves to fostering the development of family resources, what the Sdok Kak Thom inscription calls *kulopāya* (Sedov 1978, 119), through service to the state, a message that has a thematically close if temporally distant echo in a contemporary Thai film genre called *nang chiwit* (film of life), which represents "the importance of keeping family assets together no matter what the cost" (Hamilton 1992, 270). *Nang chiwit* films make an Angkor-like case for individual initiative that serves the interests of both family cohesiveness and a desirable familyism that can buttress the collective loyalty of individuals to the state.

There is no tension expressed in the Trapaeng Don On inscription between individual action and familyism, between "exalted rhetoric" and the "tenuousness" of the whole state enterprise (Reid 1993, 202; cf. Drakard 1999). Rather, forces that historians of premodern Southeast Asia tend to read as opposites were interactive constituents of the Angkorean state formation. Viewed in such terms, the Pagan-like scenario for the decline of Angkor described by Hagesteijn (Hagesteijn 1987; cf. Aung-Thwin 1979; 1985, 183–198), involving increasing royal donations of land to royal functionaries who, with the growing influence of Buddhism, contributed to their own personal salvation cults rather than to state temples, can be reread as a history of the dynamism of kinship networks striving to achieve the welfare of the state in ways that also maximized their own interests.

As in nineteenth- and twentieth-century Bali or eleventh-century Lý Vietnam, kings in Angkor were not simply "mediators" between kinship networks: they were shamanic mediums who governed relations between the realms of the living and the dead, whose potential for bringing harm to the living was increased once their powers had been augmented and universalized through their incorporation into royal Hindu cults (Wiener 1995, 56, 74, 129; Hobart 1990b; K. Taylor 1986a). We might therefore entertain the possibility that encounters between early Southeast Asian kings and ancestral spirits involved ambiguities of high risk as well as high, potential gain. If this were so, then such encounters would be similar to those observed by anthropologist Cannell in healing seances among the poor of Bicol in the Philippines during the 1980s. She writes:

> Looking at Bicolano healers, we see people who still represent themselves as constructed in some ways through cycles of "indebtedness" to superordinate powers of various kinds. . . . These are not elites, however, but people who themselves say they "have nothing" and who feel themselves to be in a painfully subordinate position, without thereby seeing themselves as having no rights, or no claim to dignity.
>
> In Bicolano healing, we can see a complex and multiplicitous response to this situation; healers in fact do not think of their relationship with their *saro* ["spirit-companions"] in any single way (as, for instance, a kind of patron-clientage); they think of it in at least three ways at once. From one viewpoint, it *is* patronage, a benevolent gift. From a second, it is its inverse, a relation of inevitable exploitation. From the third point of view, it is a relationship of intimates in which *tawo* ["people we don't see"] and human "become used to each other." All these possibilities are held within the healer's sights. The general superiority of the power of the spirits is a given, but the outcome of any particular encounter is not. And the notion of intimacy with the spirits is perhaps the most intriguing moment in the dynamic, holding out as it does at least the ghost of a chance that the sacrifice which healers make straddled between two worlds will succeed both in calling "help" into the world, and in eliciting a recognition of equal value —if not equal power—of those who request it. (Cannell 1999, 105)

This passage from Cannell encourages us to think that "men of prowess" in early Southeast Asia were themselves, like the ordinary people who were their servants, in a subordinate and dangerous position vis-à-vis the spirits and Hindu gods they sought to placate and enlist. She suggests a way of defining kingship in early Southeast Asia as a dynamic set of unequal power relations in which kings sought benevolence from and intimacy with the gods, so that centralizing, power-concentrating measures could be developed in order to reduce the dangers and uncertainties that occur when humans and spirits seek to dominate or help one another.

In Angkor, cults to deceased members of the royal family—dangerous, as in Burma, because of their spirit status as well as the rivalrousness of the living bilateral kin who deified them (Aung-Thwin 1983)—transformed relatives into powerful Hindu gods through acts of public ritual and temple building that created the social conditions for a greater centralization of power. What the French art historian Philippe Stern called the "rhythm" of temple construction in the reigns of the most powerful Angkorean kings always followed a set pattern: first, irrigation works were built; next, shrines for the Indic deities identified with the king's deceased parents and important ancestral relatives were constructed; last, the king established a temple-mountain symbolizing the cosmographic form of the "state" and dedicated to the worship of the king himself, once he had become an ancestor (Chandler 1996a, 37–38). In Angkor the architectural and ceremonial representations of states as centered, sacred *maṇḍala* were made possible by and continued to foster the worship of the king's deceased family (Wolters 1999; Higham 1989). "Doing these good deeds," concludes the dedicatory inscription of the temple of Ta Prohm (1186), built to house the image of the mother of Jayavarman VII (r.1181–c.1218) along with 260 other family-associated deities, "the king with extreme devotion to his mother, made this prayer: that because of the virtue of the good deeds I have accomplished, my mother, once delivered from the ocean of transmigration, may enjoy the state of Buddha" (Coedès 1963, 96). The king's devotion to his mother was such that 3,140 villages and 79,365 people, "of whom 18 were great priests, 2,740 officiates, 2,202 assistants, and 615 dancers," were assigned to the temple, making it a familial state "nested" within the Angkorean state where ritual and economic activities dedicated to the family cult also served to reproduce the formation of the state as a whole (Mabbett and Chandler 1995, 207; Tambiah 1976, 114). Ta Prohm was also the headquarters of a "hospital system" consisting of 102 "halls of diseaselessness" to which the king donated medicine (Mabbett and Chandler 1995, 206–207).

This last example allows us to draw several conclusions about the process of state formation in early Cambodia. The building of Ta Prohm reiterated, by means of a visible, monumental, and ritually active statement, the message that Jayavarman's mother and her extensive kin, whose paternal ancestors included the kings who had ruled Cambodia during most of the eleventh century and whose maternal forbears were related to the kings of pre-Angkorean Cambodia (Coedès 1968, 169), were not just a "kinship network," but active participants in the formation of a state. The Sanskrit word for devotion, *bhakti,* implies that all who joined the king in serving the temple—in which the queen mother was deified as Prajñāpāramitā, the "mystic mother of the Buddhas" (Coedès 1968, 174)—"participated" *(bhakti)* in the life of the Buddha through devoted service to the state (Inden 1990, 235). As in other Southeast Asian societies, early and contemporary, Jayavarman's deified mother, enclosed within a female space that was encompassed by Jayavarman's extensive and expanding male domain, had a compassionate, protective, and advisory role to play in the life of the state (Andaya 2000a, 236–238; cf. the role of mothers in Pramoedya 1982). The localization of Hindu and Buddhist cultural practices that resulted in the state form found in early Cambodia served to expand the possibilities for women to achieve high status, which was of more concern than their reproductive role as wives and mothers (Ortner 1996, 59–115), even as it increased the stratification of Khmer society, enhanced the authority of males, and idealized and so controlled a woman's role in Indic terms (Ortner 1996, 43–58; Andaya 2000a). At the same time, in order to understand this passage from the Ta Prohm inscription as part of a discourse about gendered relations of power as well as a statement about male prowess, we need to notice how it hints at a powerful affective bond between mothers and sons and wonder how this bond might have functioned in practical politics as well as political ideology. It is not just the politics of early modern Europe that is elucidated when we take "actors' expressed feelings about ancestors and descendants, political privilege, and family line" into account (Adams 1999, 108). Thomas Kirsch discussed long ago how such passages demonstrate the strategic political function of Angkorean bilateral genealogies (Kirsch 1976). We can also bring out the intensity of emotion that is expressed in the inscription, wonder about the queen's role in politics (as a living person or as an ancestral spirit), and think about how a man's understanding of "prowess" would have been shaped by his love for a mother who was powerful in her own right.

The words of the inscription can be compared to passages from the nineteenth-century Tagalog *Pasyon* (Passion) story that I will discuss later in the chapter, as well as to the following passage from the Siamese folk epic *Khun Chang Khun Phaeng*, which dates from the sixteenth century (Pasuk and Baker 1995, xvii). In the lines below, one of the sons of Khun Phaeng takes leave of his mother, who is eventually killed by order of the king because of the sexual and political rivalries that continue to swirl around her and endanger the state:

> Phlai Ngam is full of compassion for his mother.
> Looking at her he perceives tears running over her face
> And kneels down before her in a loving gesture.
> Once I am grown up I will come and look after you.
> Destiny now decrees that we must part.
> I must take leave of you because of this villainous man [i.e.,
>   Khun Chang, his stepfather and enemy of his father
>   Khun Phaeng]
> And shall go in search of my father. Let me be lucky to find him.
> I shall not forget your kindness, mother, I shall come back.
> Dear mother of mine, I know you love me.
> There is no else like you, not in ten or a hundred thousand.
> Whether eating or sleeping you will care for me.
> When I leave you and your house, it is only my body that parts.
>   (Wenk 1995, 41–42)

I will say more about the symbolic role of the "mother" and of maternal love in state ideologies later in the chapter. But it is important to note in passing here that the Angkorean woman deified in Ta Prohm joins a long list of Southeast Asian women, one that includes the widow of the last Lý ruler; Majapahit's Rajapatni; the anticolonial hero Dipanagara's great-grandmother; Indonesia's Ibu Tien Suharto; Doña Sisang from Central Luzon in the Philippines; King Mongkut's "formidable" consort, Chaochommanda Wad (1841–1939); Thailand's Queen Sarikit; and Imelda Marcos (Wolters 1999, 230; Prapañca 1995, 69–76; Carey and Houben 1987, 31; Pemberton 1994, 152–161; Rendra 1979; Fegan 1994; Hong 1998, 339; Bowie 1997, 141; Rafael 2000, 122–

161). All of these high-status women are remembered for their effective, in some cases brutal, power in state affairs.

It is also worth thinking more about what such passages of commemoration signify as "memorials" to a powerful female ancestor. Mark Hobart has written that in contemporary Bali,

> [r]emembering and forgetting . . . are vital preconditions of action. It is not just that when human neglect is recalled (*kaelingan*) by the ancestors they take steps; or when humans remember what is required of them all is likely to be reasonably well. Memory and consciousness (or, for that matter, forgetting) are not passive faculties, they shape the pattern of agency. Humans are not the helpless victims of bloody-minded ghosts; rather they take part in the process of recreating the dead, who are patients slowly being transformed back into agents, through remembering them. (Hobart 1990b, 329)

Once they were recited and their images ceremonially revisited, inscriptions, literary texts, and temple sculptures activated the same kind of power in early Southeast Asia to quicken the agency of departed kin, making them co-participants in the formation of networks of power that constituted "states." In the form of idealized images constructed out of words, rituals, and stone, ancestors in early Southeast Asia became—like movies about the "deified" national heroine, overseas Filipino worker Flor Contemplacion, executed on March 17, 1995, for her alleged role in a double murder in Singapore—sites for the development of "a language of commonality" and of identification with the state (Rafael 1997, 288; Hedman and Sidel 2000, 160–161).

Elsewhere in early Southeast Asia, kings sought to reanimate their female as well as male ancestors in order to make them active participants and allies in the political process. In Burma, for example, the rulers of Pagan (c.849–1287) developed Mon cults of familial and territorial guardian spirits into a state cult of the Thirty-Seven Nats (Aung-Thwin 1983). In the eleventh century, King Aniruddha "made the Shwezigon Pagoda the official abode of the Thirty-Seven Nats, in effect allowing this Buddhist temple to become also the ancestral stele of all Burmese royalty" (Aung-Thwin 1985, 54). This cult of dangerous spirits, all of whom had died unjust and violent deaths at the hands of the state, helped form the state and its domination over space and time. The pantheon served to unite opposing factions within the extended royal family, Aung-Thwin writes, while each of the *nats* (ancestral spirits) became identified with a regional guardian spirit and as such

> "received" a fief from the reigning king. Any human living in the territory belonging to a particular nat propitiated that nat no matter where he or she moved to. While the king ruled the temporal world, his deposed ancestors watched over the supernatural as guardians in a realm the former could never hope to control while alive. (Aung-Thwin 1985, 55)

The king and queen of the *nat* pantheon, Min Mahagiri and his sister, became household guardian spirits who were worshiped by ordinary families as spirit agents of the state. At the same time, Burmese kings expressed their relatedness to ordinary humans by referring, as Kyanzitthà did, to their role in society as being like that of "a father who wipes away the nasal mucus from the noses of his children" (Aung-Thwin 1983, 59). On a more practical level, the state extended its control over manpower as well as time through various kinds of bondage involving the tattooing of bondsmen and the keeping of "meticulous" written records that specified the connections between hereditary function and ethnicity (Aung-Thwin 1985, 90). This institutionalization of personal ties brought the "state" clearly into view. The active agents at work in forming the state of Pagan were the networks of kin consisting of the living as well as the departed, men as well as women, many of whom were at enmity with one another. To the extent that "the state" functioned as an agent in early Burmese history, it did so as a complex of agents vying with one another for dominion over the universe.

Large, central temples in Angkor at which ancestors were commemorated and reanimated, as well as smaller, local ones, which often had institutional links to those at the center, had an integrative role in a political and economic sense. Temple networks in early Cambodia thus give us the impression of having formed a mappable "structure" of economic and political relations (K. Hall 1985). But it would be wrong to attribute too much modern, Western, administrative structural form or economic rationality to the fluid, unpredictable role of temples as outposts on the frontiers that separated masters from slaves, the living from the dead, the civilized from the barbaric. Wild frontier regions that separate the living from the living or from the dead in Southeast Asia have always posed a threat to state formations and their "official" version of reality, and the persistently defiant "otherness" of the humans and spirits that inhabit them has helped states form boundaries around their ideological and geographic spaces (Steedley 1993; Kamala 1997; Li 1998; Jónsson 1996; Chandler 1996b, 76–99). On the other hand, it is undeniable that Southeast Asian temple networks, whether in Angkor, fifteenth-century Java, or twentieth-century Bali, constituted an "amalgamating," "rallying," "mobilizing" tendency, even if this tendency implies nothing at all about the permanence of the state thus formed (K. Hall 1985, 136–168; Noorduyn 1982; Noorduyn and Teeuw 1999; Day and Derks 1999, 329–332; Boon 1977, 100–102; Schulte Nordholt 1991; cf. Wolters 1999, 108). This tendency represents a desire for consolidated domination and "participation" *(bhakti)* that is also implicit in the drive to seek greater prestige through the accumulation of kin, ancestral spirits, and godlike, Indic attributes. As Jeremy Beckett has remarked, commenting on theories of patron-clientage in the Philippines that fail to explain the existence of the "political family" as a significant political force,

> [C]onceptually, as well as practically, a plethora of dyadic [patron-client] ties cries out for some kind of aggregation. . . . While a family may be divided or fragmented momentarily, the norms and sentiments that define it transcend particularities, and so secrete the power to generate a reaggregation. (Beckett 1994, 289)

In Angkor and early Java, as well as in Lý Vietnam, where the king's role was "to establish a personal relationship of trust and loyalty with the different local spirits, thus bringing them into the 'center,' incorporating them into the Việt identity being developed at the court" (K. Taylor 1986, 149), temples were places where economic activity was integral to the attempt to enlist the loyalty of ancestors as well local guardian spirits, gentry, and peasants. In Pagan Burma, those who spent money for religious purposes acquired merit for themselves and their families and thus enhanced chances of all their relations for salvation. It was the king's duty as *dhammarāja* (king of righteousness) to promote merit-making in this way, and as king he also had to demonstrate that he was a "king of merit," or *kammarāja*, by donating more wealth to religious buildings and endowments than anyone else. The networks of merit-making individuals who participated in creating the Pagan state also contained families who possessed inheritable control over lands and labor donated to monks, who were often relatives of the donors, so that individual religious practices were enmeshed in kin loyalties (Aung-Thwin 1985, 56–62, 144, 147–148). In southern Thailand, lineages developed in families that claimed hereditary status in connection with the foundation and upkeep of monasteries that were sanctioned by Ayutthaya (Gesick 1995, 44, 47). In eighteenth-century Perak, while the ruler succeeded in delimiting the hereditary claims of the powerful nobility, he could not deny the royal birth of members of his own family, who formed a contentious network of relatives "marking time, waiting for the death of the ruler so that they could be promoted to a position closer to the sultanate" (Andaya 1979, 32). In all these cases, "time" in the form of concepts of timeless spiritual guardianship, eternal salvation, or hereditary (im)permanence was defined, and in varying degrees controlled, by the state.

Thus far we have been surveying examples of practices, institutions, and concepts that highlight the importance of kinship networks and status competition for understanding the formation of Southeast Asian states. But the sources for and the perspective on this question are elitist. We also need to ask how far the dynastic ambitions and ancestor-consciousness of elites penetrated into the countryside and the minds of peasants and villagers.

Anthropological writing on Southeast Asia raises doubts about just how appealing and coercive the ideology of ancestor worship and state-promoted familyism would have been. Some anthropologists, for example, have stressed the shallowness of peasant genealogical memories (S. Errington 1989, 204), while others have noted the "de-emphasis of intragenerational seniority and genealogical precision" (Hefner 1985, 79). Others have suggested that a strong contrast and opposition exists between those aspects of village life associated with women—nurturance, spirit cults, and matrilineal kinship—and those connected to men—potency, political authority linked to the central state, and patrilineal lineage (Keyes 1977, 132; Andaya 2000a). In modern Theravada Buddhist societies in particular, writes Keyes,

[n]owhere ... do we find social action constrained by kinship patterns to the degree that it is in either India or China. Although
one may have certain responsibilities to one's kinsmen because
of an ascriptive status determined by past Karma, one also has
the responsibility to oneself in determining what actions one will
undertake since these actions will have consequences for oneself.
... Even in those areas where kinship structure has been relatively strongly emphasized, religious beliefs have still tended to
preclude any significant development of ancestor worship, such
worship being almost invariably associated with unilineal kinship. (Keyes 1977, 165–166)

It would be difficult either to prove or disprove the presence of
ancestor-consciousness in early Southeast Asian peasant communities given the elite origins and bias of the sources. But one can imagine
that peasants have always and everywhere been living in relations of
power involving social and economic competition, even in relatively
egalitarian peasant societies (Hefner 1985, 101). This is the Foucauldian "view of subjects as materially constituted by power relations
and always part of them" (Ong 1990, 259; Ong and Peletz 1995, 188).
Such relations, it could be argued, would have been susceptible to
manipulation by states, which promoted ancestor-consciousness as a
form of centralizing social control while at the same time holding out
"positions of power" to peasants and their families who were not
all that different from elites in hierarchical societies in which the
"endemic search for individual patrons who would demand a smaller
share of their wealth" also provided opportunities for enhanced status
(Lieberman 1984, 166).

In Central and East Java before the eleventh century, for example,
the local nobility, known as *rakai* and *rakryan*, a kinship term for "older
brother," were given tax exemptions for villages and lands under
their authority if these were set aside for the building of ancestor
temples and their subsequent upkeep. *Sīma* (freehold, from Sanskrit
sīman, boundary) grants appear to have been used strategically by
the king or other grantees to deprive rivals of sources of income and
manpower (A. Jones 1984, 79–80). From the beginning of the eleventh
century, when there was "a proliferation of upwardly-mobile wealthy
families of lesser status" in East Java vying for status distinctions,

these *sīma* became a form of family investment (Christie 1986, 73). The inscriptions that record *sīma* grants by the king to nobles or wealthy families suggest how villagers were stimulated to participate in this surge of *sīma* investment: peasant families in relatively egalitarian villages were offered privileges and marks of status by the king in exchange for their allegiance (de Casparis 1981). In the early tenth-century inscription of Kubukubu, the text records the distribution of clothing and money to villagers as an expression of the king's largesse *(anugraha),* then concludes with a blood-chilling curse that threatens all who might violate the terms of the sacred charter:

> All those people who are evildoers, who interfere with the sacred stone which was consecrated by everyone, the representative of the Hyang Kudur [i.e., the sacred village "foundation" stone] and the servants of the

> Rakryan, the patih [i.e., the king's representative] and the representatives of all the villagers, will be as the egg which has been crushed and shattered and cannot return to its (previous) form, its head having been cut off, and also their property will be confiscated together with their whole family *[grha sĕdaya],* their children, their wives, their fathers and mothers, and their relatives *[wwang sanaknya]* and their families *[kadangnya],* their whole family *[hatūtan grhanya]* included.

> None of them will meet with mercy, they are the left-overs on the cauldron of Yama, and they will go to hell, the abode of Yama, and going to the

> Forest may they be seized by a snake, may they be seized in the mouth of a tiger and may they fall; going to the fields may they be seized by a

> Seamonster; swallowed by a crocodile, pulled in by the gods who live in the water; going on the sea may they sink and go down, be eaten by a porpoise, a whale,

And seized by a *lampay* [i.e., a kind of sea] snake. This will be the fate of those who would despise and interfere with the *sīma*. Śrī Dharmmodaya Rakryan Watukura Haji Balitung from his kraton. (A. Jones 1984, 174–175)

These threats of hellfire and brimstone against present and future generations of those who might violate the sanctity of the *sīma* at Kubukubu suggest that the writing of the charter and the holding of the ritual to sanctify it inscribed a "state" upon the Javanese landscape, one that "encouraged" village people, through practices that were no less coercive for being ritualistic, to think of their families as an extended network of living and departed kin. The Kubukubu inscription enjoins ordinary villagers to think of themselves and their families as belonging to the king's hierarchical, kin-based political order and to participate in the king's own consciousness of time and ancestral power, by means of which he imagined that he could control the world of the village, the powerful supernatural forces associated with the ancestors, and time itself. Engaging repeatedly in ritual activity and acquiring enhanced status enabled villagers to participate *(bhakti)* in the state.

By the eleventh and twelfth centuries, the holders of *sīma* grants in East Java were being enticed to participate in the life of the state by more material means, for they were allowed, in the words of the inscription of Kambang Śri, to

use a *kutlimo* umbrella, to use a white Chinese (?) tiered umbrella, to use whatever is used by those of the interior of the *nāgara*, to build a yellow pavilion, to eat royal foods such as castrated goat, *badawang* turtle, wild *pulih* boar, wild *matinggantungan* boar, *taluwah*, castrated dog, broken *awawara*; they are allowed to use a carved couch in their *balé* . . . they are allowed to wear *ringring bananten, patarana banaten,* to wear patterned cloth: gold colored, broken patterned . . . *ajön*, grasshopper-patterned, floral, water lily patterned, halved . . . seed patterned, yellow colored, *awali* cloth, *dulang pangṇḍarahan, dodot* . . . with green water lilies, tumeric *sadangan, nawagraha, pasilih galuh.* (quoted in Christie 1983, 22)

Ordinary village families received fewer but similar marks of status from the king. By the time Prapañca described royal progresses through the countryside of East Java in the middle of the fourteenth century, four-fifths of some inscriptions were filled with lists of the king's officials (Christie 1983, 23). By this time, too, regional chiefs had been replaced by members of the royal family (Kulke 1991, 19). Thus from the beginning of the tenth century until the middle of the fourteenth we can observe a process of state formation that had spatially and temporally expansive, hierarchical, and centering tendencies, a process through which villagers were being drawn into the cultural world of elite kinship networks and status competition through ritual means. The objective for human agents involved in this process was not the creation of a permanent, centralized, urbanized state as such, but rather participation in opportunities for greater and greater prestige, practices that produced the "effect" of a "centrist" state (Mitchell 1999; cf. Wolters 1999, 135–142; S. Errington 1989, 64–95, 232–272; Christie 1991). If we compare the situation I have just described to that of village Java during the nineteenth century under the Dutch and again in the late twentieth century under the New Order, it is striking how similar the three cases appear. As in East Java of old, the authority of nineteenth- and twentieth-century village heads and their families, who sometimes held power over several generations, grew stronger, and village society became more stratified as those in a position to do so embraced "familyism" and took part in rituals of solidarity with the centralizing state (Elson 1994, 154–178; Hüsken 1989; Murai 1994). The dynamic at work here has less to do with colonialism—and nothing to do with urbanization (Boomgaard 1989)—than it does with seizing opportunities for enhanced status that could also be used to consolidate and extend kinship networks and power.

Vietnamese history after the emergence of the first indigenous line of rulers, the Lý (1009–1225), provides another good illustration of the dynamic interaction of families, ancestor spirits, and kings in creating a complex, state-forming agent. The early Lý rulers were remembered in a text written at the beginning of the fourteenth century as kings who summoned forth male and female spirits, especially those living in regions near the capital Thăng-long. These spirits were enlisted in defense of the country and to strengthen the power of the ruling family (K. Taylor 1986a; Wolters 1988, xvi–xxxv; Lý 1999). As part of this process, the royal clan sought to reform and discipline Buddhism, which it used "to control magical practices in the villages that could be detrimental to the interests of the State" (Wolters 1988, xxv; K. Taylor 1986a). In Keith Taylor's words, "'Lý dynasty religion' comprised popular religions in the process of being folded into a national cult of royal authority," a process that can be observed in the tenth-century Javanese Kubukubu inscription cited earlier (K. Taylor 1986a, 149).

Lý Phật Mã, for instance, with whom six spirits were associated, was reportedly told in 1043 to display his "majesty, glory, and military power" by attacking the Chams, lest "different clans and nobles" at home fail to send tribute or show respect in the manner of the Chams. During the 1044 war the wife of the slain Cham king, Mị Ê, was carried away to Vietnam, where she committed suicide by throwing herself into a river. Local people built a shrine to placate her sorrowing spirit. Later, Lý Phật Mã established a royal cult to her and so commemorated the transformation of an enemy into a female guardian spirit (K. Taylor 1986a, 156–169; Lý 1999, 24–26). The cult to Mị Ê also expressed Lý Phật Mã's dedication to family values, underlined by Taylor in the following anecdote:

> King Lý Phật Mã was often impatient with officials who cloaked their arguments in references to the Chinese classics and histories. When a group of rebellious brothers disputed his succession in 1028, an advisor, who had gone to China on a diplomatic mission in 1011, cited the precedents of T'ang T'ai Tsung and Duke Tan of Chou as good rulers who killed rebellious brothers. Phật Mã replied: "Of course, I know all about T'ang T'ai Tsung and Duke Tan of Chou. But I want to hide the wicked crimes of my brothers and allow them to withdraw and yield of their own volition for, of all things, my own flesh and blood is most precious!" (K. Taylor 1986a, 150)

Relatives of the Lý queens controlled the court bureaucracy through the high (military) post of *thái úy*, while Buddhist monasteries sought links with and patronage from the Lý family because it was clearly, already in 1009, the "largest, without equal." The Lý rulers also used patronage of Buddhism and control over monastic wealth to transform local spirit and ancestral cults into "a national cult of

royal authority," which sought to convince "powerful regional clans
... that the Lý kings were men of virtue, competent to deal with the
supernatural powers of the land, able to obtain supernatural blessing
for the prosperity of the realm" (Wolters 1976, 219; K. Taylor 1986a,
149, 150, 156, 162–163, 170). Commenting on the Lý family's incom-
plete adoption of Confucian dynastic principles for regularizing the
succession (principles that were eventually instituted by the usurping
Trần family, who infiltrated the Lý clan through marriage), Wolters
describes the proto-institutionalization of familyism under the Lý in
a way that highlights the formation of a "boundary" between the
state and society:

> The family had to set itself as far apart as possible from other
> families in order to prevent it from being absorbed into a coalition
> of families, linked together by marriages and other modes of alli-
> ance. Otherwise, leadership would sooner or later be exercised
> by the person in every generation who could mobilize most sup-
> port from these allied families, all of whom could regard them-
> selves as being of comparable status. (Wolters 1976, 213)

The Lý case suggests the existence of a complex, gendered Southeast Asian state agent in which men, women, and spirits struggled
with one another for preeminence. Under the Trần (1226–1400), new
rules for regulating royal marriages and transitions from one ruler to
the next; the use of kinsmen as officials; the further development of
Confucian-style bureaucratic practices (made possible by greater
"dynastic" stability); the move to introduce Confucian principles
into the village; and the formation of a royal school of Buddhism—
all such measures continued a trend toward state formation in which
family solidarity was becoming more important as both a source of
state power and as a site of state domination (Wolters 1988, 10, 118–
122; 1999, 143–151). The Confucian scholarly attack on the Mahayana
Buddhist doctrine of *upāyukauśalya* (individualistic salvation) during
the reign of the Trần king and *dhyāna* Buddhist adept Minh-tôn
(r.1320–1357), because it stimulated monks to accumulate wealth and
"husbands and wives" to leave their families and villages, is another
indication of growing family power and solidarity (Wolters 1979,
446; 1988, 17–18).

The Family as Site of Control and Resistance

Michel Foucault has argued that in Europe the "family" was first transformed from a "model" of what he calls "governmentality" into an "instrument" for controlling populations in the middle of the eighteenth century (Burchell et al. 1991, 100). There is no shortage of examples demonstrating that colonial and postcolonial states in Southeast Asia have also intervened in family life to define and control its racial composition, ritual practices, gender roles, and reproductive output (e.g., Stoler 1995b, 1996, 1997; Boomgaard 1989; Pemberton 1994; Brenner 1998; Ong and Peletz 1995; Chua 1997a, 1997b; Sears 1996b; Sen and Stivens 1998; Van Esterik 2000). Although some of these studies reinforce the idea of an all-powerful, authoritarian Southeast Asian state, others invite attention to the contested, ambivalent "manifold forms of domination" that interested Foucault (Held 1985, 306; Peletz 1995; Ong 1995; B. Anderson 1996; Sen 1998; Stivens 1998).

It is also the case that an instrumental view of families and populations appeared very early in Southeast Asia, if not in Europe as well (Blum 1978). It grew clearer in late fourteenth-century Vietnam, for example, when court officials, in response to disorder in the countryside, urged the introduction of schools for teaching family values to villagers (Wolters 1988, 36). In fifteenth-century Vietnam, an expanded bureaucracy and village headmen armed with greater authority "attempted to implant among the peasantry respect for patrilineal and primogeniturial norms" as part of a drive to register families and tie villages to the state, rather than allow them to fall into the hands of competing aristocratic clans (Whitmore 1997, 668). In the late eighteenth and early nineteenth centuries, both the rebel Tây-son and the victorious Nguyễn states sought to register populations and keep them in their villages (Whitmore 1997, 685). "If soldiers defected from [Emperor] Gia-long's armies," writes Alexander Woodside, "their parents, brothers, and 'lineage relatives' were immediately found and canvassed for replacements. And if the canvass was a failure, responsibility was then spread outward to the village, which in turn had to supply the men" (Woodside 1971, 39).

The concern to "fix" peasant families to the soil is also found in mid-fourteenth-century Java. In a passage from the court poem

Deśawarṇana, a courtier who is in charge of agricultural matters (and also an uncle by marriage to the king), followed by the king's father, followed by the king himself, all address the assembled gentry and chiefs about regulating the countryside and ensuring its increased productivity (Prapañca 1995, 89). The king's uncle states that "the main thing is the ricefields" and the settled populations attached to them; "the inhabitants should not push off to other areas when they open up new land." The king's father "approve[s] the size of districts to be made; But let the number of hearths within their borders be counted at the end of each month." To which, in a concluding image drawn from Sanskrit manuals of good governance, the king adds:

> For the palace and its own area are like a lion and a deep wood:
> If the fields are ruined, then the city too will be short of
> sustenance.
> If there are no subjects, then clearly there will be other islands that
> come to take us by surprise.
>
> Therefore let them [i.e., the villagers] be cared for so that both [the
> court and the countryside that supports it with food and
> manpower] will be stable. (Prapañca 1995, 90)

In nineteenth-century colonial Java, Dutch officials were as concerned as their Trần or Majapahit counterparts about irregularities and disorder in the countryside (Elson 1994, 155). The Dutch colonial cultivation system was designed to make agricultural lands produce profit as well as sustenance, and to do so required "permanent, tightly defined communit[ies] of people, which could easily and efficiently be subjected to control from above." This idea would have been as comprehensible to reforming Trần or Lê officials as it would have been to Vietnamese Communist party officials in charge of collectivization, who also, like their bureaucratic ancestors or King Hayam Wuruk of Majapahit, saw strict control of the countryside as the best means of mobilizing manpower against the constant threat of external enemies (Kerkvliet 1995, 401; Elson 1994, 156). Depending on the district, control in colonial rural Java could have involved the regulation of such matters as sexual behavior and the movements of unmarried men and women (Boomgaard 1989, 139–164). These intrusions of the colonial state into family practices in the countryside, together with Hayam Wuruk's concern that his village chiefs follow certain orderly procedures for preparing feasts intended to woo village support for the state (Prapañca 1995, 89), should be kept in mind when we read Anna Tsing's account of the introduction of "orderly" meals, the idea of the conjugal family with a male head, and "orderly" farming and settlement practices to the realm of the Meratus Dayak of Kalimantan by New Order Indonesian officials in the 1980s (Tsing 1993). Without multiplying examples further, it is clear that the family has been a site of control from early times in Southeast Asia and that such evidence contradicts the claim that the instrumentalizing of the family is a purely modern phenomenon. But how can we get a better idea of the process by which such control may have been resisted as well as enacted?

Victor Lieberman has written a landmark history of "the decline of royal authority" in Restored Toungoo Burma at the end of the seventeenth century, in which he bases his analysis on Western normative categories used to talk about orderly states (Lieberman 1984, 139–198). It is possible to read Lieberman's detailed account in a different way. In this new reading, the chief causes of "decline" express another kind of history in which Southeast Asian families can be seen as fractious, ambivalent participants in the formation of state cohesion and control.

At the beginning of the seventeenth century the strong founder of the Restored Toungoo line of kings, Nyaungyan Mìn (r.1597–1606), together with his two sons and successors, subdued invaders and reorganized the older, decentralized state in which regional overlords were relatives of the king, ruling over their territories as lesser but regal potentates. The Restored Toungoo rulers appointed nonrelatives to regional posts, forced princes of the blood to live at court, and settled endogamous "service platoons" *(ahmú-dàn)* close to Ava. Successions, as elsewhere in Southeast Asia, were chronically unstable, however, and rivalry between princes stimulated nonroyal lineages of prominent officials to increase their power. The history of the extended family of chief minister Twìn-thìn-hmù-gyì—"a virtual dynasty of chief ministers who attempted to direct the government for the better part of three generations"—at the very end of the seventeenth century bears witness to the fact that the study of state formation during the Restored Toungoo period can focus less on the questions of kingship and the decline of kingly authority and more

on the contestation of power among the families who were participating in the life of the state (Lieberman 1984, 150).

The upswing in commercial activity throughout Southeast Asia
in the early seventeenth century, moreover, while facilitating the centralization of power in the hands of strong kings, seems to have done
more to undermine the "absolutism" of Restored Toungoo states by
giving powerful nonroyal families at court access to wealth in the
form of disposable cash. Commercial wealth as cash rather than in
kind enabled nonroyal power brokers to induce men, women, and
children who belonged to the ruler's *ahmú-dàn* to leave the king's
service and move into their own entourages as debt-slaves.

Indeed, the most fascinating aspect of this process lies in the
history of what Lieberman calls "the mobility of clients at all levels"
of society, which "underlay the fluidity of political authority" in Restored Toungoo Burma. We can get some idea of what this history
entails through Lieberman's discussion of the rise of debt-slavery
and of the vain attempts of late seventeenth-century kings to control
the movement of people out of the royal *ahmú-dàn*, as recorded in
royal edicts (Lieberman 1984, 152–181; Than Tun 1985).

The service platoons, which were the principal source of corvée
labor for the king's building projects and of fighting men for the
royal army, were theoretically endogamous and their specific service
functions hereditary. From the reign of the first Restored Toungoo
king, Nyaungyan Mìn, however, we learn that "mixing" of platoons
through intermarriage and the flight of men from one platoon to another occurred. Nyaungyan Mìn is said to have remarked, in words
that seem to foreshadow the sentiments of colonial officials worried
about the disorderly effects of *métissage* (racially mixed marriages) in
the Netherlands Indies and French Indochina (Stoler 1997):

> My royal subjects are not well differentiated, but mixed together.
> Only if I organize them into separate platoons so that we can
> clearly distinguish them, will my royal sons, grandsons, and great-
> grandsons in succession be able to know [what people they con-
> trol]. (quoted in Lieberman 1984, 103)

The pace of intermarriage between and flight from *ahmú-dàn*
increased as royal authority "declined" in Burma over the course of
the seventeenth century. Thus what we read between the lines of the

royal edicts of Burma from the period is the same outburst of upward mobility, stimulated by commercial wealth and unstoppable by the "absolutism" of the state, that can be observed in the history of ministerial families or indeed in the widespread movement of peasants into debt-slavery.

How the contest between royal control and popular mobility was played out can be gathered from what the edicts suggest about strategies and counterstrategies of marriage and disposal of children. In general terms, people in "ignoble platoons" tried to buy or marry their way into higher-status platoons and less burdensome forms of service. Thus an edict of June 11, 1664, tells us that men from the *ahmú-dàn* in charge of feeding and training the king's elephants were selling their children to moneylenders and also attempting to move them into higher *ahmú-dàn* to which their wives belonged. From an edict of June 14, 1666, we learn that members of the royal family were attempting to expand the size of their entourages by encouraging their slaves to intermarry; the edict declared that two-thirds of the children born to a free woman who took a slave for her husband would be "free." An edict of August 13, 1671, shows that members of the jailers', gatekeepers', and prison warders' platoons were attempting to move their children outward and upward; they were also selling their children into debt-slavery. Moneylenders who took part in such transactions were to forfeit their earnings. Two years later, an edict prohibited the selling of children in general to settle debts. An order of December 12, 1675, attempted to shore up *ahmú-dàn* loyalties in the form of the king's pledge to protect the rights of the children of deceased platoon men to inherit their fathers' property. A long edict of April 10, 1679, records that platoon members were using initiation into the Buddhist monkhood, marriage, voluntary debt-slavery, and flight to the households of the nobility to move themselves and their children out of undesirable *ahmú-dàn*. In another order of the same year, the king accused platoon members of seeking work in new districts because they wanted "an easy life." A third edict of 1679 went so far as to attempt to control the sexual and musical amusements of young men by ordering them to stop "playing on the flute dirty ditties on the city streets." Another edict that year reveals that people were selling themselves into debt-slavery for "trivial" amounts. A long edict of April 27, 1691, which lists more than two hundred *ahmú-dàn* and orders that all children born of "mixed marriages" be assigned to the lower platoon, suggests the pervasiveness of the impulse toward upward social mobility among those in royal service at the end of the seventeenth century (Than Tun 1985, 23–24, 27, 29, 30–31, 44–45, 55–59; Lieberman 1984, 167, 168–169, 171, 174).

A reasonable argument can be made, therefore, that the history of seventeenth-century Burma could concern itself less with the institution of kingship and with the "decline" of an "absolutist" state and more with the agency of dependents in the processes of entourage formation, debt-slavery, and the search for enhanced status. The seventeenth-century Burmese inscriptions suggest a history of state-forming agency that resembles that of the sixteenth-century Tagalogs described by Vicente Rafael:

> Sixteenth-century Tagalog class structure . . . was characterized by forms of indebtedness and servitude that were transferable and negotiable, allowing for random submission to authority. We might infer that rendering tribute and performing labor were less signs that memorialized one's submission to the master than ways of bargaining with him, of plugging into a circuit of indebtedness in which one could hope to accumulate the means to shift social registers. By moving from a lower to a higher rank, one could expect to reduce the amount of labor one had to render, thereby reserving part of oneself from the demands of authority. (Rafael 1988, 145)

It is here, in the fluid shifts from submission to authority to avoidance of both, that the history of state formation in premodern Burma and the "stateless" Philippines, in which families were extended or broken apart and then reconfigured as "entourages," unfolded.

Bondage to Debt and Family

There is agreement between historians of premodern Southeast Asia that the control of manpower, the gathering of dependents, and the formation of entourages were the work of those who sought power to form states (Reid 1988, 120; Wolters 1999, 164). Although the acquisition of what Benedict Anderson calls "Power" or Wolters terms "prowess" played an important role in the formation and leadership of entourages, which also grew as a result of the capture of men and women during war (Bowie 1996), "the most characteristic source" of dependents in Southeast Asia was debt-slavery (Reid 1988, 121). As the Burmese example discussed above indicates, the practice of debt-slavery entailed mobility for the "slave" and more than one possibility for securing "guarantees [of] one's social existence, protection and well-being" (Cannell 1999, 236). In other words, relations of power in premodern Southeast Asian states, in which "everyone was in some kind of bondage relationship" (Reid 1983, 168), were certainly fluid, but those who lived within them could never be "free." Irrespective of local meanings of words for "freedom" in relation to forms of bondage, no one, not even a king, was free of the "concrete *relations* operating between the members of the social order," which were always defined in terms of some degree of debt-slavery, "benevolent or oppressive" (Thanet 1998, 164; Cannell 1999, 237; Reid 1998; 1999, 136–137; Aung-Thwin 1985, 75–76). The opposite of bondage was "solitude" in the sense described by an undated Cambodian *cpāp* (poem describing good conduct; see Jacob 1996, 28–31):

> True solitude is being an orphan, lonely, desolate;
> It is possessing learning, but not teaching others,
> It is not having children to love you. (Chandler 1996b, 51)

However much based upon economic and status considerations, debt-slavery was typically conceived of and experienced in terms of familial relations between parent and child. It is worth recalling the words of the Ta Prohm inscription quoted earlier as we read the following comment by an anthropologist writing on families in modern Java as he summarizes the nature of the parent-child relationship:

> A parent is one who forgives his children all and passes on blessings, material and immaterial, to them throughout his lifetime and indeed beyond. In return . . . a person is obligated to feel a constant sense of indebtedness and unworthiness. (Jay 1969, 179)

In Confucianized and Hinduized premodern Southeast Asia, there was a widespread tendency to represent male paternalism in similar familial, rather than "absolutist," terms—terms that asserted emotional bonding between parents and children. The Trapaeng Don On inscription discussed earlier lists the adult male and female slaves of the sanctuary by name, implying a personalized relationship between master and slave. In fourteenth-century Vietnam, the adoption and institutionalization of Confucian norms produced a nostalgia among certain of the ruler's officials for an "older," more Southeast Asian kind of family-style entourage relationship between official and ruler, in which emotional loyalty to a charismatic, "father"-like leader (Vietnamese *vua*), rather than formalistic Confucian filial piety to a paternalistic emperor, would hold sway (Wolters 1982b, 118). In the nineteenth century, this kind of leadership was still expected of kings, fathers, and elder brothers, who were "supposed to rule primarily by example, by cultivating and projecting the inner quality of virtue *(duc),* not by promulgating an outer system of laws and institutions *(phap)"* (Marr 1981, 58; Woodside 1976, 265). Hồ Chí Minh is a good example of a Vietnamese leader who fulfilled popular expectations of good leadership similar to those demanded of a *vua* (Malarney 1997, 913; Tai 1992, 257). Indeed, in contemporary Vietnam there is a tension similar to the one that arose in fourteenth-century Vietnam between "two notions of virtue," the one defined in terms of adherence to Communist party (i.e., state) ideology and discipline, the other to "the conscientious fulfillment of one's social relations" on the local level (i.e., the level of concrete power relations).

Another example of how familial alternatives to formalized, hierarchical structures of authority were imagined is provided by the 1292 inscription of King Ramkhamhaeng. Here the Sukhothai king is represented not as the kind of divine Angkorean ruler known to his entourage and potential subjects from areas formerly under Angkorean control (Wyatt 1984, 54), but as a *pho khun,* "lord father" (Kirsch 1984, 254), exemplary as a son to his own father and as a fatherly leader of his people. In the well-known words of the inscription:

> In my father's lifetime I served my father and I served my mother. When I caught any game or fish I brought them to my father. ... When my father died, my elder brother was still alive, and I served him steadfastly as I had served my father. When my elder brother died, I got the whole kingdom for myself. ... In the time of King Rama Gamhen this land of Sukhodai is thriving. ... He has hung a bell in the opening of the gate over there: if any commoner in the land has a grievance which sickens his belly or gripes his heart, and which he wants to make known to his ruler

and lord, it is easy; he goes and strikes the bell which the King has hung there; King Rama Gamhen, the ruler of the kingdom, hears the call; he goes and questions the man, examines the case, and decides it justly for him. (Prasert and Griswold 1992, 265–267)

King Ramkhamhaeng's benevolent paternalism has been interpreted as presenting a Tai alternative to Angkorean-style kingship, or as offering a "civilized" and benevolently Buddhist style of rule as opposed to a more "primitive" and autocratic form of leadership practiced by Tai chiefs still living by pre-Buddhist Tai cultural values (Kirsch 1984, 262–263; O'Connor 1991). Looked at in terms of the present discussion, the idiom of Sukhothai kingship expresses not so much a uniquely, "essentially" Tai or Buddhist concept of "the state" as a strategic cultural statement about the position of the king in relations of power between competing families and ethnic groups (O'Connor 1991). It is an early formulation of what John Girling, using a Weberian vocabulary, calls the "continuing dialectic between bureaucratized, formal hierarchy and personalized, informal clientship" in modern Thai political culture (Girling 1981, 37).

An example of the skillful manipulation of the "informal" dimension of this dialectic by the modern Thai state is provided by Katherine Bowie's study of the Village Scout movement in Thailand during the 1970s (Bowie 1997). Founded in 1971 as a counterinsurgency force against communism, about five million people, or one-fifth the population of Thailand, joined the movement. During a five-day initiation ritual attended by Bowie in 1977, when the movement was at its peak,

[t]he instructors repeatedly reinforced the family metaphor, beginning with the first day when age reduction transformed villagers into children. Scout initiates were portrayed as younger members of the extended royal family. On the fourth day, as the climax approached, the initiates became subjects of a mythical village kingdom, a microcosm of the nation. The ritual ended with the initiates formally restored to adulthood but as children in the national family and subjects of the nation. Villagers associated the family ideology with self-sacrificing parents and caring siblings, with the moral-bonds of mutual support and love that bind families into a cohesive whole. (Bowie 1997, 236)

The ritual reinvention of familyism in service of the Thai nation-state highlights the failure of citizenship to replace debt-bondage or familyism in Southeast Asia as the mode in which individuals participate in the life of the state (Day et al. 1996). This failure is bound up with the fact that the "autonomous city" did not begin to develop in Southeast Asia until the 1970s (Reid 1993, 130; Pasuk and Baker 1998, 153–186, 216–243). During the centuries in which capitalism and colonialism interacted in Southeast Asia, even though Westerners in the region imposed a definition of "debt" on social relations that was purely monetary and strictly contractual, and despite the fact that they established institutions based on concepts of individualism, the long-term economic interests of the West were best served by the preservation of older forms of subservience to authority in the region (Andaya 1993, 83–91; Siegel 1997, 243–244; B. Anderson 1998, 192–226).

For Southeast Asians themselves, even in the colonial period, however, the ideas and emotions that bound members of entourages together should not be reduced to the economic motives that may have encouraged debt-slavery, or confused with the violence that enforced it (McKenna 1998, 61). Writing on the nineteenth-century state of Perak on the Malay Peninsula, Patrick Sullivan comments that the relationship of debtor to creditor "was never calculated in terms of a cash return"; indeed, "no amount of work or produce rendered to the creditor lessened the debt" (Sullivan 1982, 50). Debtors in Perak were properly known as *kawan*, or "companions." From other late nineteenth-century European comments on particular cases of debt-slave emancipation in premodern Sulu in the southern Philippines, we learn of the "affective loyalty" that bondsmen often felt for their masters:

> Told Juan he was now a free man, which he seemed to regard from the "heritage of woe" point of view, and seemed very melancholy. Mahomet addressed a few words to him when handing him over and burst into tears. Juan wept and Mohamet's wives howled, altogether it was very affecting. (quoted in Warren 1981, 218)

But what exactly was the process by which family ties were turned into bonds of generalized servitude, making them serviceable, in other words, to both entourage and state formation (Rafael 1988, 167; Sullivan 1982, 72)?

One of the best examples of the way in which obligation at the family or village level in Southeast Asia was transformed into a state-forming ideology of generalized indebtedness comes from the Philippines. Sixteenth-century Spanish accounts of the communities encountered by the Spanish in Luzon present village society as stratified, consisting of a hereditary, lineage-conscious nobility called *maginoo*, freemen, and *alipin*, or debt-slaves (W. Scott 1982). The authority of the village chief, or *datu*, according to the Spanish sources, derived in part from his claim to *maginoo* lineage, but more important was his personal ability to build powerful entourages of freemen and *alipin*. Rafael follows Wolters in stressing the achieved and provisional character of the early *datu*'s authority, although he acknowledges the observation William Scott takes from the Spanish sources that deference to the *datu* extended "to his family and descendants . . . to all *maginoo*, in short—and slander against any of them is severely punished" (W. Scott 1982, 103, quoted in Rafael 1988, 140).

There seems to have been an interplay in the sixteenth and seventeenth centuries between the desire on the part of Tagalog elites to "increase hierarchy" and the "potential for movement between social ranks" (Cannell 1999, 68, 237). The hierarchical, state-forming leanings of Tagalog elites can be glimpsed in the writings of the missionary Pedro Chirino, for example, whose comments on ancestor worship were compared to the concept of the *devarāja* cult in Angkor by Wolters earlier in this chapter. For Rafael, however, the crucial aspect of the *datu*'s power is that it did not derive from a source outside the village, but from "a circuit of indebtedness." Along this circuit services and deference were rendered, or denied, by those of lower social rank to those who were expected to provide leadership, protection, and "pity" (Rafael 1988,145).

> [I]ndebtedness was in constant circulation, ever displaceable: the burden of payment could always be shifted to someone else in the hierarchy, while payment itself could be deferred. The link between person and status was therefore far from stable. Notably missing from descriptions of Tagalog society are elaborate mythologies purporting to relate social divisions to a natural or cosmological order. Nor did meticulously compiled genealogies establish the historical basis for the privilege of one group or family over others. (Rafael 1988, 146)

This fluid situation was partly transformed by the linked processes of Spanish colonization and Christian conversion. The *datus* became village headmen, with rights of hereditary succession, titles, and economic privileges such as exemption from paying tribute to the state (Phelan 1959, 122). As in seventeenth-century East Sumatra or nineteenth-century rural Java, a European idea of nonreciprocal "debt," involving forced labor and obligatory repayment, exploited and gained dominance over older, more flexible practices of debt-slavery (Cannell 1999, 238; Andaya 1993, 83–91; Elson 1994, 198–199). But it was crucial to the Tagalog situation, Rafael argues, that rather than "synthesize" the two systems of obligation and dominance, the Tagalog *principales* kept them apart yet both in play and working for their own interests in tandem. New sources of status and wealth taken from the Spanish could be used to feed relations of "reciprocal indebtedness" between the *principales* and their village entourages (Rafael 1988, 166). The appeal of Christianity to villagers was that "while most low-ranking Filipinos were constantly caught up in cycles of demanding and anxiety-provoking debt and obligation both to other men and to the *anitos* [spirits and ancestors]" (Cannell 1999, 195), a Christian death and entry into heaven promised, in the words of a seventeenth-century Tagalog poem, "[n]o fear, no shock, no sleep, no sleeplessness, no anxiety in searching, speech will be fit and appropriate" (Rafael 1988, 173). The appeal, in other words, was similar to that of serving in less burdensome, higher-status platoons for the *ahmú-dàn* of Restored Toungoo Burma, a situation that must have also increased opportunities for making Buddhist merit. The Tagalog Christian heaven in the seventeenth century was also similar to the Malay *kerajaan*, "the state of having a king," where serving the raja according to the rules of *bahasa* ("fit and appropriate" speech and deferential behavior that expressed social hierarchy and maintained the form of the state) was juxtaposed with the condition of living outside the state, as described in one nineteenth-century text, in which people are "stiff with fear, there is a din of cries and frightening shouting, a sound of wailing and weeping" (quoted in Milner 1982, 94).

The "key to the actualization of Spanish power in everyday life" in the colonial Philippines was the Spanish priest (Rafael 1988, 151). The priest was a member of the colonial state bureaucracy, indispensable because of his fluency in the local language, but his power transcended what he derived from his place in the secular state structure:

> He was a representative not merely of the royal will but of the divine will as well. . . . Because he could move between the registers of divine and royal will, he could claim the ability to decipher native signs in terms of God's laws and natives' wishes in terms of the king's. (Rafael 1988, 152)

The Tagalog *principales,* who mediated between the Spanish and Tagalog worlds and who carried out much of the work of conversion, also increased their status and power by allying themselves with God, particularly by teaching converts about how to die a good Christian death (Rafael 1988, 193). Submission to the Tagalog *principales,* and ultimately to the Spanish king, involved giving tribute that was "exchanged" for "God's mercy and grace" in this life and the next, obtained through conversion to Christianity that offered the possibility of dying a "good death."

There is a close resemblance between this Tagalog transaction and the exchange of tribute and submission for divine grace and protection elsewhere in Southeast Asia. In the following fourteenth-century description of tribute being offered to King Hayam Wuruk of Majapahit during his royal progress of 1359, villagers present animals and cloth to the king and queen, who have "descended" to the countryside with their entourage like divine beings, in exchange for a "wiping away of impurities," or *moktang kleśa:*

> Out of devotion they brought gifts, competing with each other;
> Pigs, sheep, buffaloes, oxen, chickens and dogs in plenty,
> As well as cloth which they carried in one after another in piles;
> Those who saw it were amazed, as if they could not believe their
>   eyes. (Prapañca 1995, 44)

Rosalind Morris describes a similar exchange in her study of mediumship and modernity in contemporary northern Thailand (R. C. Morris 2000). Her account brings out the way "participation" *(bhakti)* in relations of power can be enacted in terms of an idiom of familial obligation so as to generalize these ties either to reinforce the state's authority, as in the case of the Spanish Philippines or Majapahit, or to challenge it, as in the case of contemporary Chiang Mai. Such challenges create new possibilities for forming alternative state forms:

> Many of the clients who visit [the medium] Naang Khao ... have placed themselves under the protection of one of her spirits and pledged themselves to a relationship of exclusive dependency on him. Those who believe themselves to be under the spirit's protection are called *luuk sit* or, more commonly, *luuk liang*. The latter means, literally, the children whom one feeds. Here, language reveals the fact that feeding can constitute powerful bonds of familial relations which can mimic and even substitute for blood ties. But such individuals ... have themselves paid a standardized fee for the privilege of the spirit's regal patronage, and they have agreed not to seek the services of another *cao* [lord] nor to allow any other *cao* to *suu khwan* (a rite of blessing normally performed by elders and people in authority). It is not difficult here to find the remembrances of previous eras and the kinds of debt patronage that defined the political economy of the old *müang*. When clients enter the circle of a spirit's power, they replicate the forms of citizenship [*sic*] that existed under the *cao*s of old Lannathai, when common people submitted themselves (or were forced to submit) to the personal rule of an individual and were promised protection in return for exclusive devotion. (R. C. Morris 2000, 85–86)

Through their translation of Christian scripture into Tagalog, Spanish priests also made use of indigenous notions of indebtedness, fear of the ghosts of dead ancestors, and love between parent and child in order to elicit "conversions" in which Tagalogs "availed themselves of the sacraments as a way of entering into a debt transaction with the Spaniards and their God." The "prototypical" love/debt relationship for the Tagalogs was that between mother and child, but in the seventeenth century this relationship was subordinated to that between father and son in relations of power introduced by the Spanish (Rafael 1988, 110–135, 151–155).

The generalizing power of the Christianizing version of indebtedness was that, like the royalization of local ancestor cults in early Java, Angkor, Lý Vietnam, or modern Chiang Mai, it placed the relationship between parent and child, master and servant, spirit and supplicant into an expanded and more controlling temporal and political framework. In the words of a late sixteenth-century text on the Ten Commandments in Tagalog:

> [W]e are all really slaves [*alipin*] of the Lord God and it is as if we were temporarily housed here on earth, and someday, if we are good and respectful to Him, He will house us all in heaven and treat us like His children and grant us His blessings here in His land. (quoted in Rafael 1988, 167)

As is also implied in the curse of the Kubukubu inscription from tenth-century East Java discussed earlier, the individual is here defined as being in an eternal state of indebtedness and "therefore in constant need of protection" (Rafael 1988, 168). The protection being offered, via the priests and officials of the Spanish state, replaces the primacy of the circulation of indebtedness inside the family and village with the promise of eternal life in the care of God the Father. Safety is contingent upon submission to the authority of God that is "premised on the fear of death" and on the deferment of the richest form of reward, to be granted in the afterlife (Rafael 1988, 202, 167–209). We also see this premise at work in the Kubukubu inscription, which threatens the entire extended family of those who violate the regulations of the state with a terrible death and a worse afterlife, tortured by Yama in hell. In nineteenth-century Siam, Rama III (r. 1824–1851) gave a sermon to criminals in which he "reminded them of the prospect of Karmic punishment for their crimes in the form of rebirth as destitutes without relatives or patrons to depend on, the worst state of human existence there was" (Hong 1984, 28). In fourteenth-century Vietnam the Confucianist scholar Lé Quát (?–1370), who deplored the lack of obedience to Confucian norms in the villages, noted the power of reward deferment in the Buddhism of his day for reinforcing the authority of the king:

> From the ruler and princes at the top of society down to ordinary people, everyone performs Buddhist acts. . . . When today they hand something over to a temple or pagoda, they are as happy as if they have received in return the guarantee that tomorrow they get their reward. Therefore from within the capital

to the provinces and prefectures outside the capital and to the villages and humblest places, the people follow Buddhism without being ordered to do so, and they believe in it without understanding it. (quoted in Wolters 1988, 12)

Obedience to authority sanctioned by Buddhism held out the promise of a death leading to a better form of dependency. Similarly, for those who responded to the call of the *ulama* (religious scholars) to die in the holy war against the Dutch in nineteenth-century Aceh, eternal life in paradise was to be a state transcending that either imaginable or possibly fulfilled by family and earthly wealth (Siegel 1979, 229–265). A comparable kind of transcendent comfort and dependency was offered to the Tagalog convert in this seventeenth-century hymn:

If your father and mother
in hell you see
still undiminished joy you'll have
you won't behave like an orphan.

For God is their Father
Their companion and friend
He alone is kept in mind
everyone else is forgotten. (Rafael 1988, 177)

In forgetting all other social obligations, the Tagalog Christian convert was enlisted for service in a new and expanded state-forming hierarchy centered on the Spanish king and the Christian God, a hierarchy enforced by the *principales,* the *datus* of old. In fourteenth-century Vietnam and nineteenth-century Aceh, the concept of the afterlife also served to reinforce rather than diminish the earthly power of the hierarchical state.

Gendered States and Transvestite Alternatives

The priests and *principales* who carried out the Christianization of Tagalog society used an idiom of family dependency, as well as the promise of heaven as an "all-encompassing unity of men and women, young and old, rich and poor," in an attempt to construct a rigid, "absolutist" hierarchy of authority centered on God the Father (Rafael 1988, 176). Barbara Andaya argues that in this and similar ways Christianity, like other "world religions" in Southeast Asia, strengthened patriarchy in the region (Andaya 1994, 2000a). Certainly, as the following quote by the early seventeenth-century Islamic Sumatran poet Hamzah Fansuri suggests, "world religions" offered the Southeast Asian individual an illusion of autonomy and childlike security under the care of an all-powerful male deity, one whose power transcended that of earthly rulers, while at the same time reinforcing the authority of masters over servants and parents over children at all levels of society through the use of religious idioms rich in references to kinship ties and enslavement (Reid 1993, 171; Rafael 1988, 168):

> In fact, the divine Sovereign
> Is always playing with His servants
> Since His names confirm themselves
> His countenance is everywhere
>
> He is the greatest of kings
> Called the only mighty one
> Plotting and resourceful
> He constantly conceals Himself inside a servant
>
> His devices are various
> He is both mother and father
> On account of His skillfulness
> The mass of mankind do not give heed to Him (quoted in Drewes
>   and Brakel 1986, 97)

A comparable and more contemporary example of a masculinist state discourse is analyzed by the anthropologist Clive Kessler in his essay on spirit seances in the northern Malay state of Kelantan in the early 1970s (Kessler 1977). In these curing sessions, the shaman, or *bomoh*, and his interlocutor, the *mindok*,

> liken the assemblage of [the patient's] four humoral elements to
> a realm, asking: "in what district, and in what village" *(dalam negri
> mana, kampong apa)* does the disorder lie? The matter, they declare,
> resembles that between slave and ruler, subject and sultan *(pasal*

hamba dengan raja, rakyat dengan sultan). The land, they observe, is fouled *(kotor)* with strife *(susah gadoh dalam negri).* They compare the patient to a battlefield *(medan perang)* or arena of conflict *(bom, gelenggang),* and liken their own intervention to a royal audience or council *(medan majlis)* where rivals are reconciled or restrained by a superior will. Thus the evening's business, they say, is like that of a strong ruler—to promulgate law and orderly custom *(malam ni nak jatoh hukum, meletak adat),* restoring authority, and curtailing strife. Since the patient's inner imbalance and illness . . . stem from a lack of inner strength, they must fortify [her] spiritual essence *(membuat semangat).* This task, in the political idiom of the *main peteri* [curing ritual], is characterized as and treated coterminously with the *perangkatan daulat,* the custom at Malay royal installations and state ceremonies of "raising" the spiritual strength that ensures a ruler's legitimate sovereignty and the integrity of his realm. (Kessler 1977, 320)

Colonialism, nationalism, and "modernity" subjected Southeast Asians to a conquering, middle-class European kind of masculinity that also engaged with the gender of Southeast Asian identities in significant ways (Gouda 1993; Locher-Scholten 1994; Stoler 1995b, 95–136; cf. Enloe 1990, 42–64). In the Netherlands Indies at the beginning of the twentieth century, European males were warned by one colonial author to resist the seemingly sensible inclination to imitate "the natives" in wearing "light, airy, and casual *(luchtige)* clothes": "This is contrary to Western civilization and its rules" (quoted in Mrázek 1997a, 127). Meticulously gendered, Western, and "civilized" dress codes were also decreed by the Thai nation-state in 1941 as one of the measures instituted after the fall of the absolute monarchy in 1932 to ensure what Phibun Songkhram, the Thai prime minister in 1938–1944 and 1948–1957, called "[t]he exhibition of high culture by the people" as "one sure way of maintaining the sovereignty of the nation" (quoted in Van Esterik 2000, 38). In the words of Scot Barmé:

The dress regulations formulated by the [Thai] state were extraordinary in their detail. Men, for example, were expected to wear hats, shoes and socks, jackets and long trousers. Female fashion . . . consisted of hats, skirts, blouses covering the shoulders, gloves, and high-heeled shoes. (Barmé 1993, 157)

The dress codes that are enunciated in both these cases helped enforce the coercive moral vision of a model Southeast Asian colonial state formation, one that was also adopted by the Thai nation-state in the early twentieth century, in which "imperial masculinity" and "imperial femininity," to borrow Rafael's terms, dressed at all times in "civilized" fashion for their "modern" roles in the public sphere, presided over a bourgeois domestic scene in which the wife attended to her children's education, supported her husband's career, and ruled over her "uncivilized" servants (Rafael 2000, 52–75; Fishel 1999; Stoler 1996).

The postcolonial nation-state of ex-President Suharto, "Father of Development," was equally paternalistic and infantilizing. These characteristics form part of an Indonesian state-forming response to a complex series of historical interactions between the family, the nation, and the state in which, according to James Siegel, a breakdown of the symbolic identification of the people with the "mother"-as-nation occurred (Siegel 1998, 11–29; Bodden 1996; Keeler 2002). As explained by Ariel Heryanto, in the ideology of "development" in New Order Indonesia,

> [t]he presence of a Father of Development *(Bapak Pembangunan)* [explains] *Pembangunan* [development] as a unit of social activity with "familial" characteristics. Such a Father is head of the family in the *Pembangunan* household not because he desires to occupy this position, but because of the will of destiny. As a Father, he is not a person chosen through an election, who is lent a mandate of authority for a limited time by his electors, and who must take responsibility for his actions as holder of this borrowed mandate. In the Indonesian family . . . there is a prohibition against children "sinning" . . . against their Father, no matter how culpable the Father in the eyes of his children. A Father is a father to his children not only during his lifetime, but even after his death. (Heryanto 1988, 21)

The masculinization of the postcolonial Southeast Asian state can also be traced to the reaction of males to the colonial experience and the process of modernization during the colonial and postcolonial eras (cf. Nandy 1983). For example, there is a large didactic literature written by Javanese men in nineteenth-century Central

Java—who were forced into impotent submission to Dutch colonial authority—that celebrates the submissive wife (Florida 1996). The attitudes found in these texts, which parallel those fostered by the Dutch Indies state, foreshadow those that came to inform "familial" state policies on family life and sexual behavior in Indonesia during the New Order (Suryakusuma 1996). The "reincarnation of the *satria*," or noble warrior, in the writings of male Javanese nationalists lives on in the Javanese militarism of the Indonesian National Army, one that was reinforced during the Japanese occupation of Java during World War II (T. Shiraishi 1981; Tsuchiya 1987; B. Anderson 1972). Colonialism had a similar stimulating effect on the development of masculinist ideology within the army and the nation-state in the Philippines (Rafael 1995a; McCoy 1994, 1999). In Vietnam the nation-alist male intellectual assault on familyism and its "tacit conspiracy" with "a corrupt bureaucracy" during the 1920s and 1930s liberated "filial piety" to serve as "the wellspring of patriotism" during the revolution and as a source of loyalty to Uncle Ho (Jamieson 1995, 154 and passim; Marr 1981, 333–334; Tai 1992, 224–257). In Thailand the glorification of the aggressive, resourceful male parallels the mis-representation of nineteenth-century royal consorts as subservient, companionable middle-class wives in contemporary popular histo-ries written for middle-class readers; both stereotypes perpetuate "feudal" *(sakdina)* gender relations in the contemporary Thai nation-state (Reynolds 1994, 1996, n.d.; Hong 1998). In Singapore Lee Kwan Yew's ideology of the "rugged society" promoted "private femi-ninity" and motherhood for women, "public masculinity" and polit-ical conformism for men (Heng and Devan 1995). Lee's doctrines and policies sought both to reverse the colonial stereotype of the "feminine" Asian and to discipline the population for success in the world of global capitalism (Ong 1999, 69, 152, 202). Meanwhile, throughout diasporic Chinese communities in Southeast Asia and around the world, according to Aihwa Ong, "earlier images of the Chinese railroad worker, laundryman, houseboy, and garment worker have been replaced by the masculine executive, a *homo economicus* model inspired in part by the so-called neo-Confucian challenge from across the Pacific." For these men, it has not been a Confucian idiom of filial piety that has served to conceptualize their world, but one of fraternal loyalty, as vividly represented in kung fu movies (Ong 1999, 130, 162). Southeast Asian diasporic Chinese families have turned "away from Confucian social ethics toward a family-centered notion of Confuciansim," due to the conditions created by Western capitalism in Southeast Asia (Ong 1999, 115). Light-years away in Cambodia, the genocide carried out by the Pol Pot regime (1975–1979) was enacted by Khmer Rouge soldiers, many of them children, who had been subjected to the antifamily doctrines and practices of the new regime. But these teenagers were also motivated by older Khmer male cultural imperatives, ones that had been undoubtedly warped by the colonial experience, such as the desire for "honor" and the need to display "bravery" (Hinton 1998a).

Yet I would argue that there is no simple, teleological connection between seventeenth- and twentieth-century expressions of patriarchy in Southeast Asia. As Andaya, Thomas McKenna, and Michael Peletz all demonstrate, Islam provided opportunities for women as well as men to participate in new forms of social hierarchy and prestigeful status display (Andaya 2000a; McKenna 1998, 48–55; Peletz 1996, 53–100). Men have not always come out unambiguously on top under the sway of "world religions" or colonialism (Ong and Peletz 1995; J. Taylor 1983). What is clear is that Islam, Buddhism, Christianity, and colonialism generally have strengthened rather than weakened the role of hierarchy in the formation of Southeast Asian states, but this statement says little about the ambiguities and complexities of the overall process as far as gender is concerned.

For example, in rural Vietnam in the 1990s, manifestations of a new pluralism can be seen in the formation of "criminal gangs, mutual credit associations . . . women's spirit medium groups," local male ritual associations, Elderly Women's Buddhist Associations, and in the reviving role of lineage identification "as ancestral halls have been refurbished, funeral funds for lineage members . . . established, and death anniversary ceremonies . . . grown more grand" (Malarney 1997, 916–917; 1996). Such developments amount to challenges to the dominance of the centralizing, (post-)Confucianizing, masculinist Vietnamese state, a process celebrated in Dương Thu Hương's 1994 novel *Paradise of the Blind*, in which "strong" women endure and eventually triumph over the corrupt, masculine order of postrevolutionary Vietnam. Aihwa Ong's essay on the state, female labor, family planning, and Islamic revivalism in contemporary Malaysia charts a similarly complex interaction between "weak" males and "strong" females, who derive part of their new independence from the "bodily containment" imposed by Islamic orthodoxy (Ong 1995). In another study, Ong notices a greater strategic flexibility in Southeast Asian states themselves. Using the analytic concepts of Foucault but formulating a definition of the "global-age" Southeast Asian state that sounds remarkably like Wolters' "relaxed" and "flexible" early Southeast Asian "polity," she writes that

> the typical ASEAN state makes different kinds of biopolitical investments in different subject populations, privileging one gender over the other, and in certain kinds of skills, talents, and ethnicities; it thus subjects different sectors of the population to different regimes of valuation and control. . . . Thus, globalization has induced a situation of graduated sovereignty, whereby even as the state maintains control over its territory, it is also willing in some cases to let corporate entities set the terms for constituting and regulating some domains. (Ong 1999, 217)

In the Philippines, the gendering of authority as male in sixteenth- and seventeenth-century Tagalog society was not the only template for the gender of authority in subsequent centuries. "Absolutist" and Christianized representations of childlike indebtedness to God the Father temporarily displaced another relationship that was just as enduring in Tagalog society, one that was also central in the portion of the Christian liturgy that became the focus of Tagalog religious devotion: that between mother and son, powerfully evoked in the story of Christ's bond with his mother Mary during the Passion. As Reynaldo Ileto shows, it was the emotion contained in the mother-child bond, the same emotion that motivates the character Phlai Ngam to seek justice in the Siamese poem *Khun Chang Khun Phaeng*, that turned into revolutionary fervor once Tagalogs perceived an analogy between themselves and Christ, who left his own mother in order to redeem mankind (Ileto 1979, 19). Ileto also shows, however, that Christlike authority figures in Tagalog anticolonial movements formed authoritarian, hierarchical "states" that resembled Indic Southeast Asian state formations (Ileto 1982).

For the Bicol region of the contemporary Philippines, however, Cannell doubts that even heaven has the power to distract Bicolanos from their "focus on ideals of exchange which maintain the continuities between 'help' and 'debt' " in the everyday here and now

(Cannell 1999, 196). The *Ama*, the wooden image of the "dead Christ" venerated and supplicated by Bicolanos, is "like the most powerful and exemplary of shamans" who like some ungendered "man of prowess" mediates between the dead and the living, successfully and "unscathed" (Cannell 1999, 198–199). The aspect that defines the *Ama*'s power is not his gender, but the fact that he cojoins "the qualities of the inanimate (wood) and the animate (a growing child) so that the differences between them become null" (Cannell 1999, 198). The *Ama* embodies and is an agent of "transformation," and as such enters into the politics of being poor in Bicol, where people are concerned with "*transformation* from states of greater hierarchy, distance and symmetry between persons to states of greater balance, intimacy and harmony" (Cannell 1999, 228, emphasis in original). While greater equality may be what the poor of Bicol seek from their spirits, the desire of individuals who participate in rituals that summon the aid of spirits in northern Thailand is for a "revalorization" of submission to "more intimate forms of debt," under the authority of mediums who "appear to be princes endowed with curative knowledges," as an escape from "the tyrannical indifference of rational bureaucracy" (R. C. Morris 2000, 53).

To focus too intently on the rise of the "masculine" Southeast Asian state, therefore, obscures the continuous, ambiguous play of gendered forces in the contest for power and the constant regeneration of hierarchy in Southeast Asia. One of the most interesting and oldest expressions of this contest is symbolic "cross-dressing." Androgyny, transvestitism, and incestuous twinship are very old expressions of state forms and practices in Southeast Asia where there was a dynamic "conceptual order in which the ability to incorporate seemingly opposed elements was read as a sign of potency" (Johnson 1997, 27; B. Anderson 1990, 28–29; Boon 1990, 94–114). Localizing the outside world in Southeast Asia has also been conceived of and enacted in ways that involve the incorporation of foreign ideas and practices through a kind of cultural "cross-dressing." In the earliest recorded representation of cultural contact between the outside world and Southeast Asia, the story of the state of Funan's founding near the mouth of the Mekong River in the first century C.E., the Brahman Kaundinya throws his javelin to mark the location of his new capital. He then clothes and marries the daughter of the local king, a "mystical union" of gendered as well as cultural opposites that was still being commemorated in court rituals in Angkor in the thirteenth century (Coedès 1968, 37–38; Keyes 1977, 66–67). Elementary school textbooks in the contemporary Philippines represent the "Filipino" as "naked and in need of being dressed in foreign gear" received from successive contacts with Chinese, Hindus, Spaniards, and Americans (quoted in Hedman and Sidel 2000, 142). Transvestite practices in contemporary Southeast Asia—whether as a temporary strategy adopted by migrant male workers from rural northeast Thailand to defend their masculinity and very lives from the devouring "widow ghosts" of official modernity (Mills 1995); as represented in fiction as the "happy, modern, sexy, Indonesian married woman as transsexual" who encompasses the contradictory identities of official bourgeois mother, feudal Javanese aristocrat, and modern, cosmopolitan person (B. Anderson 1996); or as transvestite beauty queens in the southern Philippines who attempt to resolve the conflicting claims of rival knowledges, Islamic and American, rival nations, Moro and Filipino, and opposing genders, male and female (Johnson 1997)—are popular attempts to conceptualize and wrest control of state-led processes of "modernization." Modernity is represented in national media throughout the region as an irresistibly desirable but well-regulated "woman" (Mills 1995, 259; Stivens 1998; Rafael 2000, 122–161).

The anthropologist James Peacock noticed something similar about the role of transvestite singers in performances of *ludruk* theatre that he attended in the East Javanese city of Surabaya in 1962–1963. The only performer who "regularly and directly exhort[ed] the audience" to be modern and loyal to the nation-state was the *ludruk* transvestite. His/her progressive words were seemingly belied by his/her old-fashioned, aristocratic female appearance. And yet s/he urged the audience to action: "Get up! Open your eyes!" But do not forget, Peacock writes,

> how the transvestite sings [his/her modernizing lyrics]: to the tune of a slow, droning, repetitive chant, accompanied by soft instruments, while smiling a fixed smile, and moving in decelerated, flowing fashion against a dreamy mural of a quiet palace courtyard. . . . A young Javanese said that when he heard the music accompanying these verses, he remembered a lullaby his mother used to sing to him when he was sick, and the term

"unify" in the nationalist verses made him think of being one
with his mother! (Peacock 1968, 209)

Here the symbolic layer that clothed the transvestite performer to
protect him/her and the audience from the dangers of a threatening
modernity was drawn from Javanese high-status culture. Combined
with his/her message of "development," the style of the transvestite's performance attempted to transform state power and its
program of modernizing nationalism into something protective and
maternal.

A similar kind of "strategic cross-dressing" in contemporary
Indonesia is practiced by powerful and mobile Meratus Dayak men
in their regular encounters with higher-status, lowland Banjar males
in the Indonesian province of Kalimantan (Tsing 1993). Anna Tsing
tells the following story of shaman Awat Kilay's visit to a Banjar
town:

> Hiking out of the foothills, we stopped at a Banjar village to have
> tea at a food stall. The Banjar men at the stall lit into Awat Kilay
> with aggressive joking, calling him a savage bandit who, presum-
> ably because of his Dayak nature, had a lifetime habit of plunder-
> ing and murdering Banjar travellers. Awat Kilay immediately be-
> came humble and shy. He seemed to shrivel up before my eyes,
> transforming himself from a powerful leader into a slight old
> man. He joined in the joke quietly, stressing that he was old and
> sexually impotent.

When he returned home, however, Awat Kilay was more confident
of his authority than ever. The "trick of transforming humiliation
into bravery," Tsing comments, "is crucial to the Meratus formulation of selfhood and identity. . . . In relation to sexuality, Meratus
men play into Banjar feminizations, yet turn them into local masculinity" (Tsing 1993, 199). Feminized modes of representing and
mediating the appropriation of Western modernity sharpen gender
stereotypes and differences (Cannell 1999, 225). But they also reenact
"typically Southeast Asian ways of dealing with relations of power"
in which the body becomes a temporary "lodging place for potency,
wrapped around" in "symbols of protective status" (S. Errington
1990, 46; Cannell 1999, 223). The person to whom the body belongs is

thereby "transformed" by proximity "to the power it imitates" (Cannell 1999, 223). In northern Thailand, a similar transformation seems to occur when the "polarities of asceticism and fertility" overlap:

> Some female mediums actually identify with [masculine power] outside of possession, meditating and observing the five Buddhist precepts in an effort to mitigate or even negate their menstruation and to seal up the orifices of a body they perceive to be dangerously porous. However . . . that identification is less with ideal masculinity . . . than with the asceticism or emasculation of the monk. In this respect, mediumship seems to inherit a tradition deeply inscribed in local myth and legend [in which] . . . the Buddhism of northern Thailand's golden age attributed enormous and similar potency to the bodies of both women and Buddhas. (R. C. Morris 2000, 122)

Summary

The examples of "transvestite" practices in Thailand, the Philippines, and Indonesia briefly considered above indicate that forces of change originating from outside Southeast Asia, social relations of power, and the ongoing formation of the state interact in complex ways that need to be understood in gendered terms. Like the "familial" state, the role of gender and concepts about gender in the formation of states has a very old, continuous, and yet varied history in Southeast Asia. In this chapter I have not only intended to demonstrate that longevity, but also to suggest some of the discursive ways in which gender and kinship act upon political processes in the region. The argument and evidence have cut two ways at the same time, putting kinship "back in" to the history of state formation in early Southeast Asia, where it has been downplayed, and "taking it out" as a monolithic, essentialized, "patrimonial" presence in the history of the modern state, to be replaced by a much more fluid and complex set of gendered and kinship interactions that are crucial for understanding the way the Southeast Asian state has been taking form for centuries.

In the case of early Southeast Asian history, thinking about the agency of kinship networks helps us see that there is a very old, very powerful tendency toward elaborate state formations in the region.

This tendency must then be taken into account when we examine the roles of colonialism, capitalism, and globalization in fostering certain kinds of "dynastic" and "patrimonial" states in modern Southeast Asia. Western causes alone are not responsible for "re-feudalizing" and "centralizing" indigenous Southeast Asian social and political practices. The evidence suggests that tendencies to form states in which hierarchy and kinship were elaborated and consolidated were already well in place, and these tendencies shaped indigenous responses to colonial and global forces. In arguing for the significance of kinship networks and gendered concepts and practices in modern history, I have been interested in suggesting the diversity and non-teleological nature of the ways kinship and gender frame actions that both reinforce and challenge the authority of the state.

Tracing the history of kinship networks and gendered powers in Southeast Asia allows us to glimpse one important dimension of the way in which states in the region have been formed. But how do we account for the massive, cosmological, monumental appearance of state formations like Angkor, the Thai nation-state, or Suharto's New Order? What cultural imperatives and desires do such state forms express or repress? To answer these questions we need to turn our attention to the interactions between knowledge and power to produce cosmological state forms and other signs of truth and "civilization."

3
Cosmologies, Truth Regimes, and Invulnerability

Questions about the role of knowledge in "the clash of domina-tions," to borrow a Foucauldian phrase from Hubert Dreyfus and Paul Rabinow (1983, 114; Dirks, Eley, and Ortner 1994, 5), have been raised before, particularly about colonial India (Breckenridge and van der Veer 1993; Cohn 1996). In Southeast Asian studies such ques-tions have typically not been asked by more than a handful of scholars (e.g., Manas and Turton 1991; B. Anderson 1992). The historical lit-erature, where it deals with questions of power, has been overwhelm-ingly concerned with narratives of political conflict within or be-tween states; or with indigenous concepts of power, such as those of the Javanese (B. Anderson 1990); or with alternative models to the "theater state" (C. Geertz 1980; 1993; Schulte Nordholt 1996; Robinson 1995). Michel Foucault's thinking has been taken up with the greatest enthusiasm and skill in anthropological studies of Southeast Asia that examine gender in the context of power relations, or attempt to understand the origins of colonial domination, or construct "geneal-ogies" leading back from present discourses into the Southeast Asian past (Ong and Peletz 1995; Pemberton 1994; Wiener 1995; Stoler 1995a, 1995b; Peletz 1996). In the case of studies that examine the colonial past, the central preoccupation is with the onset of colonialism as an origin for a particular discourse of power and with indigenous South-east Asian responses to that discourse. Especially in the strongly argued writing of John Pemberton and Ann Stoler there is a tendency to depart from Foucault's interest in history and the "infinitesimal mechanisms" of power in pursuit of an exposé of a unitary, mono-lithic, and static form of colonial and postcolonial state domination that had its beginnings in the late eighteenth century.

In the discussion that follows I want to examine some of the ways knowledge and the process of its transculturation shape agency in the formation of Southeast Asian states in a wide range of historical periods and social contexts, from early to contemporary times, in peasant movements as well as elite circles. The argument will seek to widen the focus on the colonial and postcolonial state and on Western knowledge systems in studies of knowledge and power in Southeast Asia and will cut across the dichotomy that such studies draw between "dominance" and "resistance" (J. Scott 1990). I will also continue to develop a case for claiming that "Southeast Asia" and its history in the fullest, deepest historical sense are an important heuristic framework for comparative analysis in our global age even as the region as a unit of historical inquiry is being critically reexamined and reconfigured (C. Reynolds 1995; Lieberman 1999; Lewis and Wigen 1997, 170–176). This does not mean that I am reviving old arguments for thinking of Southeast Asia as a unified and "autonomous" cultural whole (cf. Smail 1993). The repetition of certain features of Southeast Asian state formation across time and space does not imply the existence of static cultural identities or essences peculiar to Southeast Asia as a unified geographic, cultural, and historical region. Rather, the argument that certain features persist or recur from one era to another, from one location to another, in Southeast Asia seeks to deepen and expand our understanding of the possible parameters—past, present, and future—of what we mean by "Southeast Asian history" and to question the distinction between "tradition" and "modernity," a distinction that is itself a product of colonialism (Maier 1997b; Chakrabarty 2000). In the pages that follow, ideas and interpretive strategies taken from Foucault and Bruno Latour will be used to break down, rather than invent new forms of, totalizing, teleological, or essentialized "local" interpretation. I will also exploit the critical positions of a number of thinkers to examine possible ways of bridging the dichotomy between "tradition" and "modernity," the "global" and the "local," by focusing on the "networks of practices and instruments, of documents and translations" that have never ceased to connect the Southeast Asian present to the past, and Southeast Asia to the rest of the world (Latour 1993, 121).

In the first part of the chapter I take up the question of the "cosmological" form of the Southeast Asian state, a topic that has been well examined in studies of "traditional" Southeast Asian state formations (e.g., Heine-Geldern 1956; C. Geertz 1980; S. Errington 1989; Tambiah 1976; Lombard 1990). Simply put, the Southeast Asian state is said to be cosmological when its form and practices produce a magical correspondence between "the universe and the world of men" so that the state acquires power with which to dominate space, time, and social relations (Heine-Geldern 1956, 1). Arguably, though, all states make claims to universality, and all states are, by definition, "magical operations" filled with what Marx called "a cosmopolitan, universal energy which overflows every restriction and bond so as to establish itself instead as the sole bond" (Bourdieu 1999, 71; Marx quoted in Richards 1993, 152). I will argue that there is little difference between "traditional" and "modern" state formations in Southeast Asia as far as their cosmological aspect is concerned. The second part of the chapter concerns the struggle to gain encyclopedic, "total" mastery over knowledge in a colonial situation. As I pointed out at the beginning of the chapter, the relationship between state formation and the control of knowledge has been studied as a Western phenomenon in colonial India and Indonesia as well as in the "imperial" West more generally (Richards 1993), but the extent to which Southeast Asian states and social groups engaged in a similar kind of totalizing activity in colonial situations has not been examined. I focus, therefore, on a particular text from early nineteenth-century Java and its representation of the state as a dispersed, hybrid, entropic archive of cultural knowledge (cf. Richards 1993), a cosmic state in the process of dissolution and reconfiguration. This section ends with a discussion of the process by which the hybrid universe of Javanese language and culture was conquered and purified by the Dutch colonial state, only to reemerge as a source of hybrid opposition to state dominance during the New Order (1966–1998). I conclude the chapter with a general reflection on knowledge formation in Southeast Asia. I argue that whether monumentalized as a temple, worn as an amulet, or printed as a "modern" text, knowledge in the region is conceived of as a magical talisman that offers time-annulling protection against danger and misfortune. In this way, the acquisition and activation of knowledge at all levels of society, rather than counteracting the state, contribute instead to its continuous reformation/re-formation.

Cosmological Regimes and Civilizations

Indian-style kingdoms were formed by assembling many local groups . . . under the authority of a single Indian or Indianized-native chief. Often this organization was accompanied by the establishment, on a natural or artificial mountain, of the cult of an Indian divinity intimately associated with the royal person and symbolizing the unity of the kingdom. This custom, associated with the original foundation of a kingdom or royal dynasty, is witnessed in all the Indian kingdoms of the Indochinese Peninsula. It reconciled the native cult of spirits on the heights with the Indian concept of royalty, and gave the population, assembled under one sovereign, a sort of national god, intimately associated with the monarchy. We have here a typical example of how India, in spreading her civilization to the Indochinese Peninsula, knew how to make foreign beliefs and cults her own. (Coedès 1968, 26–27)

I begin my discussion with a quotation from one of the founding fathers of the academic discipline of "Southeast Asian history," Georges Coedès, who was himself a product of, and tireless contributor to, French colonial knowledge about Southeast Asia. Although Coedès defines "Indianization" in a way that leaves the nature of the process unclear, the passage unambiguously links "Indianization" to both the *mission civilisatrice* of French colonialism (here identified implicitly with the high "civilization" of India) and the spread of the nation-state as the universal form of modern social organization. In the historiography that Coedès did so much to shape, Indianization marks the onset of "history" in Southeast Asia. Whatever else may be disputable about the nature of Indianization, or what O. W. Wolters calls Hinduization, it entailed unquestionably one of the most significant transcultural interactions between knowledge and power in the history of the region. It was first and foremost a process that formed a certain discourse about power, a discourse that transformed "men of prowess" into "world conquerors"; kinship networks into bureaucratic hierarchies; and space, time, and identity into dimensions of the state that were both organized and "aestheticized" in a particular way (Pollock 1996, 216).

In his major reinterpretation of "Indianization," Wolters reformulated this process of state-forming acculturation so that it ceased to have the implication of a colonizing *mission civilisatrice* conferred on it by French colonial scholarship (Wolters 1982a, 9–15). Southeast Asia was already "civilized" in its own way so that the Indic was "localized" in Southeast Asian terms, not the other way around. Wolters cast his understanding of the process in terms of the "Hindu devotionalism" of the Southeast Asian "man of prowess," involving the male leader's education by "elitist teacher-inspired sects." This education led to the leader's self-identification with the god Śiva, "the sovereign deity who created the universe";

> [t]hus, the overlord's close relationship with Śiva meant that he participated in Śiva's divine authority. . . . He participated in sovereign attributes of cosmological proportions. . . . The chief's prowess was now coterminous with the divine authority pervading the universe. (Wolters 1982a, 11)

The cosmological symbolism, topographical form, and hierarchical properties of the "Indic" state alluded to by Wolters have been the subject of numerous studies, but only Wolters and Sheldon Pollock have paid attention to the transcultural nature of the practices involved in the "Indianization" process (Pollock 1996; 2000). Whereas Wolters treats Sanskrit (as well as Chinese) culture in Southeast Asia as a metaphorical veneer that never conceals or alters the local cultural forms it adheres to, Pollock argues that Sanskrit culture, particularly literature, introduced a new, powerfully transformative and prestigious political aesthetic into the region. The "Sanskrit cosmopolitanism" that spread throughout South and Southeast Asia in the first millennium of the common era "performed the imperial function of spanning space and time, and thus enabled one to say things with lasting and pervasive power" (Pollock 1996, 240–241). In Angkor, one of the most powerful states of early Southeast Asia whose name is Khmer for *nāgara*, the Sanskrit word for "state," Sanskrit inscriptions were "thoroughly infused with the idiom, intelligence, and political imagination of the Sanskrit subcontinent" (Pollock 1996, 220). Unlike Java, where already by the eighth century C.E. a "local genius can be glimpsed through the Sanskrit inscriptions," foreshadowing the vernacularization of Sanskrit literature by the beginning of the ninth century, Sanskrit in Angkor remained *"exclusively* the cosmopolitan language of elite self-presentation" until the end of the Angkorean period (Pollock 1996, 226–227, emphasis in original). Yet nothing in this transcultural process of Sanskrit "imperialism," according to Pollock, coerced the Khmer elite to adopt

Sanskrit language and culture in this way. As Pollock explains, the Sanskrit cosmopolis was a strange kind of non-Western, non-Latinate, seemingly noncoercive kind of cultural empire:

> The space of Sanskrit culture and the power that culture articulated were never demarcated in any concrete fashion; the populations that inhabited it were never enumerated; nowhere was a standardization of legal practices sought, beyond a vague conception of moral order *(dharma)* to which power was universally expected to profess its commitment. Nor was any attempt ever made to transform the world into a metropolitan center; in fact, no recognizable core-periphery conception ever prevailed in the Sanskrit cosmopolis. Every center was infinitely reproducible across cosmopolitan space, such that the golden Mount Meru and the river Ganga could be and were transported everywhere.... This entire culture-power complex was invented on the fly, so to speak, which makes the very idea of "Indianization" or "Sanskritization" a crude sort of teleology, erroneously supposing as cause what was only produced as effect. (Pollock 2000, 604)

With Pollock's thoughts in mind, I want to begin my discussion of the cosmological form of Southeast Asian states by reflecting on Eleanor Mannikka's analysis of the "journey into the philosophical concepts and numerical sets" of the temple of Angkor Wat (Morón 1977, 218; Mannikka 1996), the largest and most famous of the temple monuments of Angkor. This state dominated most of what is now Thailand, Cambodia, and southern Vietnam from the ninth century until the end of the thirteenth century.

The visitor to this twelfth-century temple crosses distances in entering and leaving the central temple along the west-east axis of 1,728 cubits—lengths equivalent to the duration of the Golden Age, or *kṛta yuga,* in Indian cosmology. Along this journey through the Golden Age s/he can look at wall carvings that allegorically represent, through scenes taken from the epic *Mahābhārata,* the career and glory of the king who commissioned the building of the temple, Sūryavarman II (r.1131–1150). First, the king is represented as Yama, the Indic god who sits in judgment over men and women in the afterlife. Scenes of the thirty-two hells give way to representations of the churning of the Sea of Milk over which the king presides in the form of Viṣṇu. The churning, which produces the elixir of immortality, requires the cooperation of opposing factions, thus signaling the need for unity of all who live under Sūryavarman's rule. Moreover, the temple is constructed in such a way that the bas relief depicting the churning is illuminated by the rising sun every morning, and the sun alternately favors the gods or the king, depending on the time of year. In winter the king is illuminated while the gods are in darkness; in summer Sūryavarman is in deep shadow (Morón 1977, 225). The central tower represents the central peak of Mt. Meru, the home of Viṣṇu (Mabbett 1983). To climb to the chamber where the image of the god was housed, the devotee had to traverse a space consisting of thirty-three units, a length that "represents the universe as a whole, embodied in Viṣṇu," and at "the same time . . . a universe in which divinity is not defined or confined by three dimensions" (Morón 1977, 243). "During the long walk to the upper elevation," moreover, "visitors . . . cross through a sequence of four *yuga* periods," thus traversing the entirety of cosmic time according to the Indic schema. The *yuga* symbolism is reiterated by the positioning of the four subsidiary Meru peaks around the central tower, a positioning that is also coordinated with the cycles of the solar calendar:

> In complementary terms, the total vertical length of all four corner towers . . . symbolizes a complete *mahayuga* period of 4,320,000 years. As a consequence, the four towers arranged around the central tower can symbolize both the real cycles of stars and planets around the north pole as well as the four *yuga* cycles. . . . As the north celestial pole, Mt. Meru remains immobile while time forever flows around it in an eternal movement. (Morón 1977, 249)

In light of Mannikka's studies, Wolters' contention that "the signifiers visible at Angkor Wat are drawn from Indian literature, but they signify a Khmer formulation associated with the Khmers' expectations of being Sūryavarman's contemporaries" (Wolters 1982a, 62, passim) understates the transformative power and significance of the Khmer elite's use of Indian concepts to conquer and then regulate cosmic time and space, as well as large areas of mainland Southeast Asia. Sūryavarman II's reign began when he killed his own great-uncle for the throne and witnessed the military expansion of the state into what is now present-day southern Vietnam and Thailand (Coedès 1968, 159–162; Chandler 1996a, 49–52). The building of Angkor Wat commenced at the beginning of his reign and was completed after Sūryavarman's death. The knowledge inscribed in the form and beauty of the temple was thus physically localized in a violent struggle for power extending over many years. As a devotee of Viṣṇu, Sūryavarman observed the requirements of *rajadharma,* the Indic norms of kingly behavior, which he fulfilled by becoming a copybook "world conqueror," or *cakravartin* (Tambiah 1976, 9–31). And the early Cambodian state formation is not the only place in Southeast Asia where we find this kind of state-sponsored construct of knowledge and power that asserted universal dominion over time and space. A thirteenth-century royal temple in East Java, Candi Jago, has Tantric Buddhist carvings of equally elaborate and arcane structure that reflect a Javanese king's concern with achieving universal domination in the age of another world conqueror, Kublai Khan (O'Brien 1988, 1990). In the imperial state of thirteenth-century Vietnam, meditational Buddhism and the incorporation of both legendary Chinese sages and ageless tutelary spirits into a pantheon of state-forming agents also served to conquer time and make it "a matter of no consequence" (Wolters 1999, 148).

Returning to Pollock's understanding of Sanskrit cosmopolitanism in Southeast Asia, we are confronted, therefore, with a number of paradoxes. First of all, if the acquisition of Sanskrit knowledge by the elite of Angkor enabled it to become "civilized," it did so in ways that also empowered the elite to seek domination over time, space, and all political rivals, domestic and foreign. If the Sanskrit cosmopolis, as a kind of cultural imperium, was beautiful, noncoercive, dispersed, and infinitely reproducible, its state form in Angkor was indeed beautiful, but nonetheless violent, centralizing, and a source of status competition expressed not only in the repetitive building of rival temple complexes by successive kings, but also through constant military struggle with Chams, Vietnamese, and Tais. The Sanscritic "beauty" of Angkorean temples elevated this violence and competitiveness to a level of cosmic and "cosmopolitan" significance.

Second, unlike the case in Java, Sanskrit cosmopolitanism in Cambodia remained the cultural domain and source of power for the elite alone. Although Angkor Wat is the first Khmer temple in which we find images of the living king and historical dates from his reign, it does not contain representations of everyday life, as does the Buddhist temple Bayon of Jayavarman VII (r.1181–1218) (Freeman and Jacques 1999, 78–101). The reliefs of the Bayon notwithstanding, Sanskrit cosmopolitanism did not stimulate a process of vernacularization in Cambodia that brought about a more localized and socially accessible and pervasive sense of shared cultural identity, the hybrid product of a transcultural process (Pollock 1996, 1998a). Thus for all its claims to universal domination over time, space, and peoples, Angkor Wat remains the expression of a state form in early Cambodia that is predominantly self-referential for the elite and foreign to the country at large, one that never became localized in Wolters' meaning of the term. In this respect, early Khmer state culture resembles the Westernized urban culture of postindependence Cambodia that was overthrown and smashed by the culturally alienated Khmer Rouge peasant armies for whom "the rice field is the university," "the hoe the pen" (quoted in Ponchaud 1989, 157).

Finally, and this is to return both to Pollock's insight about Sanskrit cosmopolitanism as a kind of cultural "effect" rather than a teleological cause of historical change and to Clifford Geertz's understanding of the Balinese Indic state as (powerfully) enchanting theatre, the cosmological state of Angkor, for all its massively numerological temples and extensive irrigation tanks and canals, rested not on technological functionality, but on a spatially and ritually elaborated cultural pun, one powerful enough to bring a "state" into massive, monumental, but nonetheless illusory, visibility (Mabbett and Chandler 1995, 148–155). Pollock writes that Sanskrit literature was a "poetry of polity" that provided not just a language that was "dignified" and "eternal" enough to express a king's fame, but also "conceptual affinities" between poetic and grammatical practices that were "mercilessly disciplined" and the "moral, social, and political order" (Pollock 1996, 209, 232, 240). The temporal and spatial coerciveness of Angkorean temples was thus immanent in and made possible by the Sanskrit poetry used to praise their founders. Yet the state temples and temple networks, the rituals and imperial wars that gave form to the Angkorean state were expressions of a "state effect" that was not only "mercilessly disciplined," but also as ambiguous as a pun in Sanskrit poetry. As Ian Mabbett has written,

> The ritual, architecture and statuary of god-kingship [in Angkor]
> . . . are a sort of language, where the words are however not arbi-
> trary symbols but potent forces that will produce for the manip-
> ulator the results he desires if the grammar is right. . . . [A]mbig-
> uous verses [in Sanskrit poems about Angkorean kings] are more
> than poetic fancies. They are part of the same language of am-
> bivalence that is constituted by ritual, architecture and statuary.
> . . . Nobody ever spells out in so many words the claim that a
> particular human being is divine . . . ; the exercise is designed not
> to inflate the status of an individual [*sic*] so much as to fit the
> world of men to the shape of the world of the gods according to
> sacred ritual, and thus make possible the transmission of favours
> and salvation from one world to the other. (Mabbett 1969, 217, 219)

Pollock and Mabbett help us see how the Angkorean cosmological state formation could be beautiful, coercive, and illusory all at the same time.

My second example of a cosmological state comes from nine-teenth-century Siam. Although the history of the modernization of Siam after the accession of Rama I in 1782 is conventionally told in terms of the modernizing agency of the Chakri monarchs and their extended family of scholar-officials, it is possible to conceptualize that agency in the history of modernity and nationalism in Thailand in terms of a struggle over knowledge and power. In this history Chakri kings employed rival epistemologies to forge the modern Thai nation-state.

One of these epistemologies was expounded in the *Traiphum,* or Three Worlds, cosmography (C. Reynolds 1976, 209; Reynolds and Reynolds 1982). Versions of this cosmography date from the four-teenth century, and the text was repeatedly redrafted and cross-checked against Pali sources between 1783 and 1802 by the order of Rama I "in order to promote both faith and knowledge" of the hyper-orthodox Buddhist variety insisted upon by the first Chakri monarch (Wyatt 1982, 20–27). Paintings of the Three Worlds cosmography covered the walls of monasteries in many parts of nineteenth-century Thailand, instructing "the illiterate, through the medium of their senses," as one European visitor to Bangkok put it. These paintings made graphic a powerful concept of universal social order and cosmic space. Wyatt points out that one of the "innovations" of the Rama I recension of the text was to reorganize the order in which the different levels of existence were presented (from lowest to highest in older versions), beginning this time with the "middle" level of mankind (Wyatt 1982, 24–25).

As can be seen in the case of Angkor Wat, Southeast Asian cosmologies typically contain narratives that explain the origins and power of hierarchy. A late sixteenth-century Visayan cosmology as recorded by the Spanish, to take an example from a part of Southeast Asia that lies on the periphery of the Sanskrit cosmopolis, conceives of the origins of social hierarchy in spatial and architectural terms that recall the centric form of Indic temples and states. The children of the primordial couple flee their father's anger:

> They scattered where best they could, many going into their father's house; and others stayed in the main sala, and others hid in the walls of the house itself, and others went into the kitchen and hid among the pots and stove. So, these Visayans say, from those who went into the inner rooms of the house come the lords and chiefs they have among them now, who give them orders and whom they respect and obey and who among them are like our titled lords in Spain; they call them datos in their language. From those who remained in the main sala of the house come the knights and hidalgos among them, inasmuch as these are free and do not pay anything at all; these they call timaguas in their language. From those who got behind the walls of the house, they say, come those considered slaves, whom they call oripes in their language. Those who went into the kitchen and hid in the stove and among the pots they say are negroes, claiming that all the negroes in the hills of the Philippine Islands of the West come from them. And from the others who went out of the house, they say, come all the other tribes there are in their world, saying that these were many and that they went to many and diverse places. (quoted in W. Scott 1982, 112)

The following passage from the *Traiphum* makes clear in similar terms that the seemingly "enlightened" and "humanisitic" Siamese revision of the early nineteenth century in fact gives emphasis to the central role of the king and the state in maintaining a hierarchical, Buddhist moral order:

> When mankind arose in the world, and began to gather in groups, those groups raised up a person of truth, justice, ability, force, and power to preside over them in order that they might be governed so as to live in peace and prosperity, safe from all dangers. When mankind had further progressed and states *(ban muang)* had been formed, a Bodhisattva appeared in the world of men, a man of merit, bravery, and ability surpassing all other people, so the assembled people invited him to become their leader, and he was named the King. (Wyatt 1982, 25)

The *Traiphum* of Rama I expresses familiar Southeast Asian aspirations of world conquest, casting its cosmological net over other Buddhist subjects such as the Mon and Lao, whose versions of the text, obtained during military campaigns, were used in compiling the dominant Chakri recension (C. Reynolds 1976, 210).

Beginning in the 1830s, Western knowledge about astronomy and geography began to compete with the Three Worlds cosmography. The result was not a victory of one kind of knowledge over the other, but their mutual accommodation so as to strengthen the modernizing elite and give impetus to the formation of a powerful nation-state. An early stage of this epistemological collaboration can be observed in the way in which Chaophraya Thiphakorawong's 1867 *Kitjanukit* (a book explaining various things) rationalizes Buddhism even as it attacks traditional Buddhist cosmography. The book gives instruction on Western geography and astronomy, yet it also confirms that while "the Buddha knew the truth of the earth, . . . the Buddha was also aware that what he knew was in conflict with people's belief," which, if challenged, would only lead to their neglecting "the path to salvation." Thus Thiphakorawong promoted "geography of the new kind with the approval of true Buddhism" (Thongchai 1994, 40–41). "Geography" and "true Buddhism" as epistemologies were both used to inform state-forming agency by reinforcing the accommodating policies that the elite had chosen as they confronted Western pressures in the middle of the nineteenth century.

A similar epistemological partnership was forged between Thai astrology and Western astronomy through the scientific activities of the reigning monarch himself, King Mongkut (r.1851–1868). On August 18, 1868, the sixty-four-year-old Mongkut traveled into malarial rainforests near Wako on the Kra Isthmus with a party of European officials to observe the solar eclipse he had predicted would take place that day, since, like Sūryavarman II, "he was obsessed by the calculation in every precise detail to prove his knowledge and the king's credibility" (Thongchai 1994, 45). When he returned to Bangkok (dying not long after from malaria contracted in Wako), Mongkut punished the court astrologers for their ignorance. Yet while visiting the peninsula he himself had made offerings to the traditional deities who had cleared away the clouds so that he could make his scientific observations of the August 18 eclipse. The lesson of the Wako story is surely that the "Father of Thai Science," who was also called the "Father of Thai Astrology," became the embodiment of a powerful epistemological convergence of rival knowledges and hence a "modern" *cakravartin.* For in the words of one of his biographers, quoted by Thongchai Winichakul:

> [Mongkut] understood astrology well, both in Siamese and European scripts. He could calculate the movements of the sun and all the planets in great detail, predicting solar and lunar eclipses so precisely that no one could match him. He also knew *yiokrapfi* [geography] very well, measuring the sun and stars accurately. . . . He was unremittingly faithful to the Three Gems of Buddhism. (quoted in Thongchai 1994, 57)

Such a nineteenth-century *cakravartin* would not be altogether out of place as a human devotee or deified as an ancestral statue of the god-king in the central chamber of Angkor Wat. In fact, the elite of fifteenth-century Ayutthaya imitated Khmer courtly and bureaucratic practices, developed a special court vocabulary based on Khmer and Sanskrit, and, rather than adopt the folksy, fatherlike style of Sukhothai rulership, elevated their kings "far above the level of [their] subjects, insulated by layers of officials from direct contact with them, and wrapped [them] in a cloak of mystery and sanctity compounded out of brahmanical religion from the cults of Śiva and Viṣṇu" (Wyatt 1984, 71–72). The Ayutthayan ruler Prasat Thong (r.1629–1656) built a model of the Hindu heavens outside his palace in 1638 and carried out a ritual there in order to "rectify time" at the end of the Buddhist millennium (Andaya 1999, 194). The Angkorean-Ayutthayan legacy of "a king closely identified with a Hindu divinity" continued into the nineteenth century, when Siam held control over the ruins of Angkor from the 1790s until the retrocession of Siem Reap to French Cambodia in 1907 (Keyes 1991b, 263, 265). King Mongkut himself laid claim to Angkor Wat's power in an act of imperialistic and hybridizing miniaturization. Penny Van Esterik comments:

> Recognizing the importance of the famous Cambodian temple Angkor Wat as an antecedent to modern Siam, King Mongkut had a model of the Khmer temple complex constructed in the Grand Palace in Bangkok some time in the 1860s. This model dates from the time when Thailand exercised sovereignty over Cambodia (1863). The temple model resembles the engraving of the principal façade of Angkor Wat from *Voyage d'exploration en Indo-chine* by Francis Garnier, 1873. The model was "Thai-ized" by the substitution of Thai architectural features for Cambodian ones. (Van Esterik 2000, 110)

In 1931 it was the turn of the French to reproduce a model of Angkor Wat at the Exposition Coloniale Internationale de Paris (Norindr 1996, 21). The exterior of the temple was reproduced according to exact measurements and with the use of molds of the original carvings, while another "exact representation" of French Indonchina as a "great modern state" was organized on three levels in the interior of the building, in a hierarchy of importance beginning from the ground up with a display of economic resources and products (quoted in Norindr 1996, 25). Peopled with native Khmers brought from Cambodia and ritualized with Buddhist rituals and courtly dances, the Parisian Angkor Wat was a hybrid, cosmological representation of the French Indochinese state that was compared by exposition officials to Persepolis, the Parthenon, and a cathedral from the Middle Ages. Once again, Sūryavarman's Angkor Wat represented a claim to universal domination over time and space (Norindr 1996, 26–28). The cosmological afterlife of Angkor Wat that was reincarnated in Chakri kings also surfaced in Laos during the 1990s, where members of the Thai royalty were worshiped in cults and honored as patrons of development and Buddhism (G. Evans 1998, 108–113).

By the 1880s Western "geography" and the concept of the "map" had become powerful conceptual tools for transforming the old Siamese *phraratcha-anachak* (royal kingdom), with its Angkorean cosmological outlook and practices, into a modern *prathet* (literally "common space," nation) in a way that allowed the older concept and its epistemological basis to retain a powerful afterlife within the boundaries of a new, dominant nation-state order and worldview (Gesick 1995, 12). Administrative reform and expansion into the north were carried out under the double aegis of "tributary over-lordship" (old) and "national sovereignty" (new), in the name of a kind of universalizing nationalism, that of "Us" Thai versus "Them" others (Thongchai 1994, 95–107). What the universal monarchy lost in dominion over infinite time and space the emergent nation-state gained in sovereignty and administrative control over a bounded national territory, which the court saw itself as protecting from European imperialism.

> The actions taken together constituted a code which signified two kinds of relationship simultaneously. On the one hand, it signified the premodern overlord/tributary relationship. On the other, it represented the new polity and political geography. (Thongchai 1994, 106–107)

The map of the new bounded nation-state served as a symbol for a royal foundation supporting the police and paramilitary forces, as well as the blueprint for a retrospective Thai national history that was already mapped upon territory in the distant past deemed "national" only by hindsight (Thongchai 1994, 137, 140–163; Keyes 1991b). In the late nineteenth century, the Siamese elite also began to imitate and consume European culture in order to obtain what Thongchai calls "the new cosmic power" of (Western) "civilization" *(siwilai)* (Thongchai 2000, 539; Cary 2000, 138–141). Through such activities as royal tours of Europe and Southeast Asia (Chulalongkorn 1993) or the planning of a national museum that would imitate European "world fairs" and museums where colonial products and peoples were put on display, the Siamese elite continued to build a cosmological state in which

Bangkok was likened to London, making Siam a parallel, though a smaller one, to the British Empire. In this sense, the rulers in Bangkok were likened to the British court, a center of the global *siwilai*. This was not a naïve pretension or ambitious delusion. On the one hand, the courts of Southeast Asia claimed a genealogy from the source of cosmic power, typically making the monarch a reincarnation of gods and the court itself a microcosm of the cosmic center. The legacy of this tradition, apparently, was alive and well in Bangkok at that time. On the other hand, the British Empire, a colonizer who conquered other nations, was not entirely dissimilar to the premodern polity of overlordship and empire that Siam was. For the Siamese elite, the traditional empire and modern colonialism were in certain ways compatible. (Thongchai 2000, 543–544)

Thus the role of such universalizing Western knowledges as "geography" and "nationalism" in the formation of the nineteenth-century Siamese state is not very different from that of the Sanskrit cosmopolitanism of early Cambodia or Java. Each kind of knowledge offered to provide those who received instruction in it access to the civilization of a Golden Age under the benevolent domination of a world conqueror or his modern, national, or colonial avatar. In Thailand today, schoolchildren are still taught the art of controlling time and space in a localization, eight centuries later, of the cosmological principles of Angkor Wat, which have become what Pierre Bourdieu would call a coercive, state-forming "embodied cognitive structure" in Thai society (Van Esterik 2000, 36–41; Bourdieu 1999, 70). *Kalatesa,* the Thai word for etiquette, is a Pali-Sanskrit compound from the words for time *(kala)* and space *(tesa).* Practicing correct *kalatesa* means showing respect to hierarchical authority through correct speech and manners; healing the body of disease by restoring the correct balance of body elements based on a knowledge of the place and time of the patient's birth and the onset of the disease; ensuring a good rice crop by harmonizing local and court ritual practices; using astrology to know and submit to the future; assenting to Prime Minister Phibun's dictum that "the exhibition of high culture by the people is one sure way of maintaining the sovereignty of the nation"; or accepting one's "proper" gender role (Van Esterik 2000, 38, 41). In Thailand, as throughout Southeast Asia today, "the little scenarios of etiquette" reenact cosmological repertoires of state authority that have a very long history (Ortner 1984, 154).

Moving on to my third example, in the scholarly literature on the Indonesian nation-state under Suharto (r.1966–1998), strong arguments have been made about the relationship between knowledge and state formation that challenge any assertion that "traditional" and "modern" concepts of cosmological knowledge in Southeast Asia are quite similar (McVey 1995a). In the earlier writings of Benedict Anderson (1990, 17–77) there is a tendency to stress the persistence of traditional attitudes toward knowledge and power, especially among the Javanese, which shaped and inhibited the transition of Indonesian societies to modernity. In later work, however, most notably in *Imagined Communities,* Anderson stresses the rupture not only between the traditional past and the modern present, but also between the utopian promise of authentic popular nationalism and the official nationalism of the contemporary nation-states of Southeast Asia.

In the following passage, Anderson reifies the nation-state and the knowledge formation it embodies in a way that poses problems for the kind of analysis that I have been pursuing.

> Successful revolutionaries also inherited the wiring of the old state: sometimes functionaries and informers, but always files, dossiers, archives, laws, financial records, censuses, maps, treaties, correspondence, memoranda, and so on. Like the complex electrical system in any large mansion when the owner has fled, the state awaits the new owner's hand at the switch to be very much its old brilliant self again. (B. Anderson 1991, 160)

Although Anderson is antipathetic to the state generally, the implicit contrast here is between the decayed institution of the nation-state that houses tyrannical "lords of the manor" and a state formation that is the living expression of the people and their culture. For example, Anderson makes an invidious comparison between Jayavarman VII's Bayon temple in early Khmer society and Suharto's theme park, Taman Mini, in contemporary Indonesia (B. Anderson 1990, 181–182). Anderson characterizes the discourses of "official nationalism," again by way of explicit contrast with those of an earlier and more authentic social formation, as "inventions" and "lies" (B. Anderson 1991, 161n).

Anderson's argument makes it difficult, in other words, to entertain serious questions about knowledge and the state in Suharto's New Order Indonesia that allow for real connections between the present and the past. This line of argument suggests that state-produced knowledge can only be regarded as inauthentic, masking the truth of a cunning struggle for total domination. (Suharto was famous for his cunning, but this is an attribute shared by all successful "men of prowess.") State-sponsored efforts at building ethnic identity or national unity are typically seen as transparently manipulative, because they demand that older symbols of power and royalty be included as signs of "tradition" (Bowen 1995, 1061; Steedley 1999, 441). Yet the phenomenal development of new technology in New Order Indonesia since the mid-1970s under the leadership of Suharto and his then minister for research and technology and later successor, Baharuddin Jusuf Habibie, demands some recognition of authenticity in its inspiration and historical formation if it is to be understood. Will we be able to apply the same kind of analysis of state knowledge to this case as we have to the other examples of universalizing knowledges that I have called cosmologies?

Arguments by Anderson and Pemberton assume a rupture between authentic and concrete "old cosmologies" and inauthentic, "monumentalized" yet "intangible" ideologies in contemporary Java (see Pemberton 1994, especially 148–196 and 269–310). In doing so, these arguments ignore the very old and still-unfolding history of cosmologies and monuments in Southeast Asia. For example, the following characterization of Taman Mini, which was completed in 1975, notes the time-transcending and conflict-resolving function of the theme park without identifying and then reflecting on the similarity of these functions to those of Angkor Wat and other early Southeast Asian temples:

> With the founding of "Beautiful Indonesia," Bapak (Father) [Suharto] and Ibu (Mother) [Tien Suharto] assumed the roles of model parents of an extended national family, privileged benefactors of an extensive inheritance. Displacing economic concerns with a patently "cultural" gift, this novel inheritance offered Indonesians a bequest they apparently could not afford to refuse. Built into the logic of such a bequest was a transference of culture that erased the difference between past, present, and future, and thus flattened time—and, with it, histories, including the extraordinary

violence of the New Order's own origins—into a continuously presented present. For "Beautiful Indonesia" was founded upon a peculiar sense of temporality. The obsession with connecting the past and future in the form of a present finds prolific expression at Mini through numerous so-called monuments *(monumen):* miniature replicas of ancient monuments *(candhi),* memorial monuments *(tugu),* and commemorative inscriptions *(prasasti).* (Pemberton 1994, 155)

The meaning of Taman Mini's time-immobilizing and universalizing message, one of many repetitions of similar statements found throughout the course of Southeast Asian history, cannot be said to be exactly the same as that of Angkor Wat, even though both structures exhibit an interest in symbolic numerology (see Pemberton 1994, 156), assert the transformation of a culturally diverse and conflict-filled empire into one where "difference" has been "tamed," "reified," and made "decorative" (S. Errington 1998, 222), and are modeled on contemporary "monuments" to universal domination over time and space: the Indic cosmic Mount Meru on the one hand, Disneyland on the other. Shelly Errington has even labeled Taman Mini a "cosmic theme park" in an ancient Southeast Asian sense because of the ways genealogies, state processions, and cosmographic, "centered space" have been used in the park, in addition to such nation-state-forming devices as the map, the census, and the museum (S. Errington 1998, 188–227). Sūryavarman II and Suharto are hardly identical kinds of Southeast Asian leaders, and yet both were powerfully motivated to build tombs for themselves during their own lifetimes in order to become "future anterior royal ancestors," to use Pemberton's felicitous phrase for describing President and Mrs. Suharto as destined for ancestral status on Mount Awakening near Surakarta in Central Java (Pemberton 1994, 166). I am also reminded here of Wolters' characterization of the cult founded on Mount Mahendra by Jayavarman II in 802:

> But his cult, I believe, was also something else. He realized that his achievements had guaranteed his status as an Ancestor among all those Khmers who were connected with his kinship group, which was bound to be an extended one because it was organized in accordance with the principle of cognatic kinship. He

therefore made arrangements, as the Sdok Kak Thom inscription
of 1052 describes, for the perpetuation of the cult to enable future
kings to invoke additional supernatural protection from their deified Ancestor. (Wolters 1982a, 7)

Nor are the historical conditions of the foundation of Suharto's or
Sūryavarman's monuments totally dissimilar. Political consolidation,
economic growth, territorial expansion, and the incorporation of different religions into one centralized but multifaceted state ideology
are part of the background to the origins and form of both monuments (see Chandler 1996a, 49–54; Bourchier 1984; Hefner 1993; T. Shiraishi 1996).

"Beautiful Indonesia" as an expression of New Order concepts
of "culture," and Habibie's technology as the exemplar of New Order
notions of "development" can therefore be seen as complementary
components of the same cosmology. Takashi Shiraishi provides an
excellent introduction to the rise of Habibie and to the economic
background of the timing of technological development in Indonesia
since the 1970s (T. Shiraishi 1996). Shiraishi's analysis, however, is
dependent upon Anderson's rewiring metaphor of the New Order
nation-state, so that Habibie's career and contributions to technological development are read merely as further articulations of the
growing authoritarianism of Suharto's rule rather than as embedded
in a struggle for power that has epistemological as well as political
and economic dimensions (see Bourchier 1984; Hefner 1993).

Suharto's drive toward rapid industrialization and technological autonomy seems less inauthentically sui generis when examined
in the context of the twelfth-century Angkorean and nineteenth- and
twentieth-century Siamese cases discussed above. The state in each
case seizes and technologizes knowledge to achieve not just control
over social relations, but a kind of universal domination over time
and space. In the Suharto-Habibie case we can observe how such an
objective involved the struggle between old and new epistemologies,
between mysticism and technology, within a statist discourse that
we may usefully call cosmological, rather than simply "corporatist"
—a term that is frequently used to describe the contemporary Indonesian state, but one that has a shorter historical reach and narrower
cultural range (Hefner 1993, 22; Bourchier 1997).

A good place to begin examining this conflict is Suharto's own ideas as expressed in his *Otobiografi* (Autobiography), published in 1989. I will look at three chapters, set in the mid-1980s, in which epistemological struggle is apparent. One of the discourses developed in the autobiography is that of the traditional, hierarchy-maintaining cosmic ruler who must set an example for his people. In chapter 84, titled "There Are Those Who Have the Wrong Idea," Suharto begins by paying exemplary respect to three state officials who have become "ancestors": Ali Murtopo, Adam Malik, and Sudjono Humardani. But the chapter is mainly concerned with refuting the view that these three well-educated and highly intelligent officials, now deceased, were superior to the president:

> Before Ali Murtopo died, there were people who liked to assert that Ali Murtopo was the one who decided things. Why? Maybe because he was a clever speaker, dared to say what he thought. . . . About Sudjono Humardani one could hear people say that he knew more than I did about mysticism. Even though Djono himself always paid obeisance [Javanese *sungkem*, literally "kiss the knees"] to me. He considered me to be older and more knowledgeable about *ilmu kebatinan* [science of mysticism].
>
> It's true, for me *kebatinan* is not the mysticism people currently think it is. As I said earlier, *kebatinan* is a science for bringing oneself close to God. . . .
>
> Djono liked to come to me bringing a book full of writings. He had a belief. And he liked to make proposals. I accepted these proposals in order to make him happy. I didn't just swallow these ideas.
>
> I analyzed them. I weighed them up—were they rational or not? If they were rational, if they entered the rational mind [Indonesian *masuk akal*], then I accepted them. (Suharto 1989, 440–442)

Suharto emerges in this passage as a "rational" mediator between mystical and scientific epistemologies.

The next chapter is titled "The Meaning of the Indonesian Air Show," the subject of which was held in 1986. Suharto discusses the importance of Indonesia's aeronautics industry, initiated and led by Habibie, and argues that it is a key to Indonesia's economic independence. But the cosmological significance of the industry as an expression of "development" seems to outweigh its practical usefulness.

As Ariel Heryanto points out, the Indonesian word for "development" *(pembangunan)* was coined in the 1930s in the midst of polemical debates over the nature of "modern" Indonesian culture (Heryanto 1988). During the New Order, the word was used to indicate the new, willed, man-made, technological "exploitation of natural and human resources." Like Angkor Wat, "development" was about building something that had never existed before "by mobilizing forces from OUTSIDE the object concerned" (Heryanto 1988, 16). We should also recall the representation of the churning of the Sea of Milk on the walls of Angkor Wat as an expression of collective social labor as well as an effacement of time as we read the following passage:

> The development of an aeronautics industry, of a naval industry and of other modern industries which use sophisticated technology is not just for show and is not undertaken without an awareness of the sacrifices which we are shouldering [*pengorbanan yang kita pikul*]. We carry out this development precisely because we are aware [*sadar*] of the great difficulty and pain which we have to expect in the future, if the Indonesian nation is to continue to compete with other nations in knowledge and technology [*ilmu pengetahuan dan teknologi*]. (Suharto 1989, 453)

The phrase *"pengorabanan yang kita pikul"* implicitly refers to traditional Javanese maxims about sacrifice and leadership, while the word *"sadar"* is an Indonesian-Javanese concept that carries overtones of an Islamic, exemplary ruler. Time has been expanded to become an infinitude of collective labor as well as collective salvation. Technological development is being thought about here in a temporal and social framework that has very old, Southeast Asian cosmological dimensions.

The next chapter is called "My Request: One Must Always Remember." To "remember"—Javanese *eling*—is an important concept in the neotraditional Javanese epistemology that Suharto sought to dominate in the face of competition from members of his own entourage, like Sudjono Humardani, or from critical mystics with powerful elite backers, like Sawito (Bourchier 1984). One should remember God, the ancestors and their teachings, one's place in the hierarchical order of things; to "forget" these things is to invite disease, death, and social disorder. In chapter 86 of Suharto's autobiography, the person who is asked to *eling* is Dr. B. J. Habibie, the son of a Bugis father and Javanese mother, whose fiftieth birthday coincided with the holding of the Indonesian air show. Suharto recalls how he personally recruited Habibie, luring him back to Indonesia from a high-paying aeronautics job in Germany. Would Dr. Habibie accept the president's offer?

> "I'm ready, Sir," he answered.
>
> Habibie's Eastern spirit was still youthful [note: The "youthfulness" of the East as opposed to the decrepitude of the West is a trope from pre-war Indonesian nationalist discourse]. He always asked my advice about how to approach life. He also asked for my photo and I gave him one that he picked himself, a photo of me when I was relaxing in traditional Javanese clothes.
>
> I gave it to him with the following teaching in Javanese: *Wong sing tansah eling, percaya mituhu marang kang murbeng dumadi, iku dadi oboring urip kang becik, sajatining becik.*
>
> (That is, we must always "remember," believe in God, have faith. Never should scientific knowledge [*berilmu*] lead to an abandonment of faith.)
>
> He put the portrait in his office. Then he made a copy of it and it was later printed in his book [i.e., the one published in his honor on his birthday].
>
> He considers me as his own parent. It is completely clear that he doesn't want to do wrong. He always asks for my guidance. The philosophy which I give to him is noted down by him. I know that this philosophy of struggle will be a source of no insignificance for him during his career and later during his retirement. (Suharto 1989, 456–457)

This passage, no less than the others from Suharto's autobiography quoted above, documents the struggle for dominance between human agents and their competing epistemologies in New Order Indonesia, a struggle that led to a synthesis of "scientific knowledge" and "faith" to form a dominant state cosmology. The Southeast Asian genealogy of this synthesis is ancient, but its local Javanese provenance can be traced at least as far back in time as the opening of the first Western school for the sons of "native chiefs" in colonial Java in

1879. At that time it was argued that the Western "religion of knowledge" *(agama kawruh)* combined with the Javanese "religion of judgment" *(agama budi)*, rather than Islam, offered the true basis for "being Javanese" (Drewes 1966, 326 and passim). In his study of the first Javanese nationalist organization, the Budi Utomo, Akira Nagazumi cites a 1904 newspaper article describing a debate between several Javanese judges about the meanings of three Javanese/Indonesian words for "knowledge": *pengetahuan, ilmu,* and *budi.* The following passage echoes Suharto's thinking as well as his politics in the choice of *budi* as the master term, "the attribute that [gives] balance and unity to mere fragmentary knowledge" (Nagazumi 1972, 36):

> Budi can be likened to a king enforcing order in his country: He discusses and seeks to understand, contemplates and works toward creating a prosperous and refined life for his subjects; the soul in the human body is therefore like a lamp inside a house, serving to illuminate the structure. A man with budi abhors trouble and seeks not to become involved in anything that would make him feel sorry. . . . The man with budi behaves with ilmu. Ilmu is to know what should be done, whereas budi is to know what, by whom, how, where and why something should be carried out, lest the acts should become useless. . . . The state of a kingdom depends on budi. A kingdom that lacks budi will be flawed, and thus it will be ineffective. . . . The common man need be concerned with merely his own work, but the king is responsible for the work of all mankind. (quoted in Nagazumi 1972, 36–37)

Budi, it should be noted, is a Sanskrit word *(buddhi)* that arrived in Java centuries ago when the island was part of the "Sanskrit cosmopolis" (Zoetmulder 1982, 266).

Understood in terms of their genealogical connections to early Javanese nationalism, and beyond that to the Sufi mystical doctrines that shaped state formation in the first half of the eighteenth century and continued to inform Javanese cultural debates in the nineteenth and twentieth centuries before entering the statist discourse of the New Order, the cosmological assertions of Suharto and the New Order Indonesian state appear no more or less religious than they are "modern" and technological (Ricklefs 1998; Tsuchiya 1987; 1990; Reeve 1985). The notion that the beliefs of the New Order leadership were secular and "concerned with this world and not that beyond" obscures the similarities between the three examples of Southeast Asian state formation in a cosmological mode that we have just considered (McVey 1995a, 26). This mode also appears elsewhere in contemporary Southeast Asia, no more strikingly than in the guise of the bodhisattva-like Mahathir Mohamad's neo-Sufi "Vision 2020" of the perfectibility of Malay men in the Golden Age of global information technology (Milner 1983; Mahathir 1998).

The Formation of Regimes of Truth

> Each society has its régime of truth, its "general politics" of truth: that is, the types of discourse which it accepts and makes function as true; the mechanisms and instances which enable one to distinguish true and false statements, the means by which each is sanctioned; the techniques and procedures accorded value in the acquisition of truth; the status of those who are charged with saying what counts as true. (Foucault 1980,131)

In the preceding section I examined the universalizing knowledges of several Southeast Asian state formations. In each case Brahmans, kings, or Western-educated experts and advisors were the authorized possessors of truth that was synonymous with the political order of things as well as with the "natural" order of the world. The sun and seasonal changes helped determine the cosmological design of Angkor Wat and in turn illuminated its meaning. The Chakri monarchs mastered astronomy and geography and used them to naturalize the workings of the heavens above and the boundaries around the Thai nation-state below. Suharto's Javanism was fashioned to be the natural basis and goal of technological development in New Order Indonesia. In each case, potentially opposing truths, and the human combatants in knowledge wars between the foreign and the indigenous, have been made to seem harmonious corollaries of an even greater truth to which the state lays claim. But how were such struggles actually situated within the "networks" (Latour 1993) and "mobile systems of relationships" of power (Gordon 1980, 236; Foucault 1980, 114) that did the work of constructing and maintaining monumental, cosmological state forms? I want to develop an

approach to answering this question by tracing the network of connections that link the Sanskrit cosmopolis to colonial India to colonial Java to the colonial regime of the Netherlands Indies to New
Order Indonesia and the Western academy.

We might begin by following one of the threads that connects
knowledge to power in colonial Java back to what David Ludden has
called the formation of "Orientalist empiricism" in India (Ludden
1993). In a moment we will meet up with several important agents
on behalf of this kind of knowledge in Java. But first I want to sum-
marize Ludden's account of how it was formed.

Ludden argues, against Edward Said but very much in the spirit
of Foucault, that it is necessary to imagine a shifting, historically contextualized relationship between knowledge and power in order to
understand the stages through which the search for Western empirical knowledge about India developed. In the late eighteenth century
officials whose thinking was influenced by the Enlightenment sought
a universal kind of knowledge about India that was not strictly utili-
tarian and bound to the needs of colonial rule (Ludden 1993, 252).
During the transition to European rule over India in 1722–1820, however, the requirements of centralized government altered the nature
and uses of the knowledge that was collected. Not just indigenous
rulers, but also the "Indian intelligentsia" had to be placed under
colonial control:

> To subordinate these men, Europeans had to appropriate knowl-
> edge that was locked away in the minds of Indian commercial,
> judicial, military, and revenue specialists. By appropriating knowl-
> edge toward this end, Europeans discovered India for them-
> selves, in their own terms, by converting knowledge from native
> sources into English language forms that were systematic, scien-
> tific, and accessible to means of truth-testing that were becoming
> the pride of European culture. . . . In addition, military operations
> and political centralization required that data which had never
> been produced by Indian rulers be generated and controlled by
> government; such data constituted new facts for the creation of
> orientalism as a body of knowledge. (Ludden 1993, 253)

The kinds of knowledge gathered not only became more spe-
cialized, ultilitarian, and "British," they were also labeled as " 'empirical,' . . . which made colonial knowledge into a set of factualized

statements about reality" (Ludden 1993, 258). This was once again a kind of "universalization" of knowledge by the colonial state:

> Indology, revenue surveys, and commission reports came to share the same epistemological terrain and positivist knowledge about all societies, culture, and political economies. Separate streams of knowledge about India could thus intersect and enrich one another, and facts from investigations in India could be integrated with facts from around the world in political economy and world history. (Ludden 1993, 258)

Empirical knowledge about India became first authoritative, then indistinguishable from definitions of "actual law-abiding behavior and thus of religious norms that guided traditional life." What was already "known" became not only normative, it was actually "discovered" and "seen." "Factualized representations of India became official wisdom," and so what Said calls Orientalism was born (Ludden 1993, 259). Ludden concludes his analysis by arguing that Orientalism served to transmit British empiricism to Indian nationalist thinking.

Ludden does not, however, explain if or how empiricism was contested in its march from British Enlightened science to Indian nationalistic ideology. As I observed earlier about the work of Pemberton and Stoler on colonial Indonesia, studies based on Foucault's writings about knowledge and power tend to trace simple genealogies of domination rather than chart complex struggles for power in the manner advocated by Foucault (1980, 83–85). The regimes of knowledge and truth encompassed by "colonization," like "Hinduization" and all the major premodern "-izations" labeled as such by historians of Southeast Asia, far from representing the natural and inevitable historical transformations as so often described in both indigenous and Western historiographies, were contested and fragmentary rather than monolithic and unitary. In thinking about "Islamization" in Southeast Asia, for example, we can deconstruct the accounts of seamless transition as recounted in state myths of conversion found in Indonesian and Malay societies (R. Jones 1979) or as presented in eighteenth- and nineteenth-century Central Javanese court histories (Ricklefs 1972). This can be done by making use of accounts that bring out the ongoing clash of discourses occasioned by Islamization, from the sixteenth century (Drewes 1978) to the late eighteenth (Ricklefs 1972 and 1998; Soebardi 1975; Drewes 1966; Day 1983a) to the twentieth (Hefner 1987 and 1993).

Colonization throughout Southeast Asia, as in India, was a struggle not just over land and wealth, but over the construction and uses of knowledge. Colonial institutes of learning and their massive output of research and observation on all aspects, past and present, of colonial Southeast Asia attest to the Western attempt to dominate the production of knowledge (Day and Reynolds 2000, 20–24; Peletz 1993, 70–78). But to examine the Western dimension of this process alone would be to foreclose the possibility of understanding the nature and the role of "subjugated knowledges" in the formation of a dominant, statist regime of truth. I want now to pick up the thread of knowledge formation in colonial India and follow it to Central Java in the nineteenth century. My interest is to develop an understanding of the struggle over knowledge in Southeast Asian colonial situations that is as complex, ambiguous, nuanced, and tenuous as a "genealogy" in Foucault's sense or a "network" in Latour's.

In Java the human sciences inspired by the Enlightenment and the colonial need for local knowledge converged at the end of the eighteenth century. A decision by the Dutch Society of the Sciences to establish a branch in the colonies led in 1778 to the founding of the Batavian Academy of the Arts and Sciences (Bataviaasch Genootschap van Kunsten en Wetenschappen). According to its charter, the academy, which was the first of its kind in Asia,

> [would] attempt to stimulate all arts and sciences and . . . eagerly receive anything which deals with the natural history, antiquities, customs and mores of the peoples. However, its principle goal [was] to make such matters the subject of its investigations which [would] be beneficial to the agriculture, trade, and particular welfare of these settlements. (The and van der Veur 1973, 3)

Contributions to the first eighteen volumes of the *Transactions* of the Academy, which cover the period up to 1843, reflect the scientific goals of the institution and the rather loose relationship between the gathering of knowledge and the goals of colonialism during these years. Thus we find "short descriptions" of islands in the Indonesian archipelago as well as of Japan, China, and India, but also articles on children's diseases in Batavia and on a variety of topics concerning natural history and agriculture, as well as an essay on the bird of paradise. But there are also articles on Javanese language, "antiquities," and indigenous histories; sea charts (proposing improvements to Dutch maps using English and French ones as models); and racial themes. All of these subjects would feature more prominently later in the nineteenth and twentieth centuries once empirical knowledge had become "Orientalized" and more closely aligned with the objectives of the colonial state (The and van der Veur 1973, 98–109).

But it was the British, armed with "Orientalist empiricism," who provided the Dutch with the greatest single impetus to the scientific collection of empirical data about Java on the model of the energetic investigations of Thomas Stamford Raffles, John Crawfurd, and Colin Mackenzie during the British occupation of the island between 1811 and 1816. The cultural and intellectual shock waves of the example set by these British gentlemen and antiquarian-orientalists —who gathered manuscripts, laid siege to and overran native palaces, and reorganized the chaotic state of European colonial administration in Java—were felt until the end of the colonial period by Dutch "Indologists" and administrators.

To scholars of Southeast Asia, Colin Mackenzie, later surveyorgeneral for India, is the least well known of the three, but it was he who planned the siege of the Yogyakarta *kraton*, which fell to the British in June 1812. Mackenzie also traveled around East and Central Java collecting Javanese manuscripts earlier in that same year, compiling materials that were used by both Raffles and Crawfurd in their publications and that now comprise a major collection of late eighteenth- and early nineteenth-century Javanese manuscripts housed in the India Office Library in London (Weatherbee 1978; on Mackenzie's career in India, see Dirks 1993; 1994; Cohn 1996, 76–105). A closer look at Mackenzie's "Enlightened" objectives and a sketch of the modus operandi of European seekers after Enlightenment—a process that was underway in Central Java from the time of the founding of the Batavian Academy of the Arts and Sciences and that apparently produced a response from Javanese intellectuals—provides one of the earliest opportunities to examine the struggle over knowledge as the colonial state was formed in Southeast Asia.

Mackenzie's "A General View of the Results of Investigations into Geography, History, Antiquities, and Literature in the Island of Java," written after he had returned to India in 1813, is based on "encyclopedic," universalizing assumptions like those of published studies by Raffles and Crawfurd. The essay is divided topically into five sections that, taken together, constitute a totalizing concept of knowledge: charts, both geographical and hydrographical; military; territorial; history and antiquities; and manuscripts (Blagden 1916, xxiii–xxxii). Most of the information in all of the categories except history and antiquities was already available to Mackenzie in the archives of the VOC. With regard to history and antiquities, Mackenzie begins by noting how little had been accomplished by the Dutch despite the founding of "a Society of Sciences," which had been revived by the British in the hope that it could still "contribute essentially to the general culture of science, and of commercial economy, and of useful knowledge in these" (Blagden 1916, xxvi). Mackenzie remarks that his prior experiences in India have helped him to "remove difficulties arising from prejudices of education and religion" during his investigations, but he was hampered by a major problem. Because he was without "the powerful aid of the penetrating acute genius of the Brahmans," he had trouble making translations into English, especially from Javanese. The Dutch colonists themselves were either ignorant or "from a repugnance to travelling and fatigue, arising from indolence, and from habits widely dissimilar to ours" unavailable to assist him (Blagden 1916, xxvii).

Mackenzie thus placed the local Dutch and Eurasians he encountered in Java in the same Orientalist category as "indolent natives"! However, as Donald Weatherbee shows, this characterization is misleading, for the new scholar-overlords from Great Britain in fact made extensive use of resident "enclyclopedists" of Javanese culture, including Dutch, American, Eurasian, as well as Javanese and Chinese informants. We know from his correspondence during 1812–1813, for example, that Mackenzie drew on the knowledge and linguistic skills of the American naturalist Thomas Horsfield, who had been living in Surakarta since 1801 and had traveled down the Solo River and through East Java in 1805–1807 investigating "climate, soil, mountains, rivers and productions of Java" as well as medicinal plants (Horsfield 1814; de Haan 1935, 582–584). Mackenzie also made use of the services of the Eurasian translators J. G. Vincent and J. W. Winter (father of the better-known C. F. Winter), who had close contacts with a large number of Javanese aristocrats in Semarang, Surakarta, and East Java, all of whom provided Mackenzie with manuscripts and assisted him with translations (Blagden 1916, 218–224). Other Eurasian informants, translators, and owners of manuscripts from this period include F. von Winckelman, who lived and worked in Semarang, and J. D. J. d'Arnaud van Boeckholtz, who later assisted Raffles with his translation of the "Brata Yudha" and whose father, F. van Boeckholtz, made drawings of Hindu-Buddhist antiquities while he was stationed in Salatiga in the early 1780s (de Haan 1935, 503–504, 665–666). Mackenzie also states in a note to "A General View" that "an ingenious native of Java has since this accompanied Colonel MACKENZIE to India, and has already made some progress in translating from the Javanese," but we learn nothing more about this person (Blagden 1916, xxvii).

We can form an impression of how Mackenzie went about collecting information on Java by leafing through Mackenzie's "Narrative of a Journey to Examine the Remains of an Ancient City and Temples at Brambana [Prambanan] in Java," a trip he made in January 1812 and described in his travel journal (see Blagden 1916, 98), then published in 1814. On January 19, Mackenzie arrived at the ruins at "about 9 A.M. by very deep bad roads."

> After some refreshment, about half past eleven A.M. Mr. Knops and myself, with the Draftsman, and some villagers provided by the Chinaman (by the Sooracarta Gentlemen's orders) proceeded in more form to perambulate the ruins; chairs were provided, covered with canopies of leaves and each carried by 4 men on poles of bamboo, but my impatience did not always permit me to avail myself of this convenient coverture from the sun's scorching rays, amidst the tantalizing ruins that surrounded us. (Mackenzie 1814, 7)

Later in the day Mackenzie noted:

> We enquired and sought in vain for inscriptions and characters; an aged Mantree who was our Ciceroni, intimated there were some in the ruins of the upper part, and I clambered in quest of them upon the ruinous roof; but what was pointed out consisted merely of single characters or figures which seemed cut on the stones. (Mackenzie 1814, 14)

At day's end the explorer wrote:

> Returned at six A.M. [*sic*] much fatigued, though highly gratified with our inspection of these antiquities—the evening was fair and pleasant.—We were lodged in the Chinaman's house where we were accommodated with the open hall on pillars in front, with chairs and tables, where we sat, wrote and eat. . . .
>
> The evening was passed after dinner in writing our notes, and in Mr. Knops' takingdown [*sic*] the traditionary [*sic*] account of Buka Embok Lora-Jongran, as translated verbally by one of the younger Chinese, from a village-Mantree who promised to bring a MSS containing its history in the morning. (Mackenzie 1814, 16–17)

Mackenzie, Raffles, and Crawfurd were the most visible, but by no means the only, participants in such founding moments of "Javanology"—the systematic, encyclopedic, empirical study of Javanese language, literature, history, and culture in the Netherlands and the Netherlands Indies. The aim of this study was to uncover the "truth" about Java (Tsuchiya 1990). In the extracts from Mackenzie's journal quoted above one is struck by a paradoxical mixture of innocent, boyish curiosity and imperialistic arrogance, as if Mackenzie and his party had some natural right to "perambulate the ruins" and demand explanations about them. Nicholas Dirks captures in pertinent fashion the same mixture of detached Enlightenment inquisitiveness about "universal and objective truths" and the "brutality of conquest" implicit in the colonial appropriation of local knowledge in his characterization of Mackenzie's paradoxical encounter with antiquities in India, where he was surveyor-general from 1815 until his death in 1821:

> Let us recall the picture where Mackenzie is marching in with his native assistants to draw the ruined Hindu temple. The temple has been rent by the riotous energy of the natural world; it is about to be lost forever to the undergrowth. Mackenzie is clearly enamoured by the Hindu past, seeking to recover it through his collections . . . [t]hus the paradox of Mackenzie's presence. On the one hand, the massive documentation of Mackenzie's empirical project is carried out with as little mediation as possible; Mackenzie eschews writing catalogues and annotations in favor of

continuing to collect. But on the other hand, Mackenzie's very absence is what constantly legitimizes his presence; it is the fact that India's histories and traditions would soon disappear if allowed to follow their natural course that reminds us that without Mackenzie's active efforts the process of recovery and transcription —representation itself—could not take place. (Dirks 1994, 229)

It would be a mistake, however, to follow Dirks or Ludden (1993) too closely in assigning primary agency to European scholar-imperialists in the construction of colonial regimes of truth. As C. A. Bayly argues, the "colonial information order" in India

was erected on the foundations of its Indian precursors. For instance, indigenous police descriptions and sociological understanding of the classes of beings were incorporated into the British canon by means of the testimony of native informants. Of course, this information was reclassified and built into hierarchies which reflected the world view of the Britons of the early nineteenth century. Nevertheless, Indian sociologies, forms of religious thought and beliefs about criminality were active, not passive elements within these constructs, and Indians almost immediately began to critique them from the inside. (Bayly 1996, 179 and passim)

As I have noted in my comments about Mackenzie's "informants," and as his account of the visit to Prambanan also testifies, British research on "the actual state of knowledge" about Java was already intertwined with and based on "facts" and ideas that were being generated and written down by the Javanese themselves in response to the colonial requests for "information" that were being made upon them. Next to the many texts that were being produced, copied, and created to order for colonial investigators at the beginning of the nineteenth century, one work stands out, not only because of its encyclopedic scope and size, but also because of the way in which it contested the authority of the colonial state (Behrend 1997).

A Shastric Encyclopedia

In 1814, the *Serat Centhini*, a massive poetic compilation of knowledges of all sorts about Java, was written in the residence of the crown prince of Surakarta, Central Java. As Tim Behrend's research demonstrates, this text had older antecedents (Behrend 1987 and 1997). But it seems probable that, given everything else we know about the visibility of and Javanese participation in the Enlightenment investigations of all aspects of Javanese life and culture at the beginning of the nineteenth century, and given the features that distinguish the 1814 text from its predecessors, the much-expanded 1814 version of the *Serat Centhini* was a response to the Enlightenment and to the formation of the colonial state in Java.

According to Behrend, the seventeenth- and eighteenth-century recensions of what became the *Serat Centhini* of 1814 are concerned with the travels during an unspecified time by various characters through villages in a geographically vague if identifiably Javanese countryside. During these wanderings "lists of animals and foods" as well as "theological points" are enumerated or discussed. In his study of one of the source texts for the 1814 *Centhini*, Behrend makes clear that the "encyclopedism" of the later text is already present in the earlier story's wide-ranging attention to questions of religious practice and knowledge. But in the 1814 text, the number of characters and information was vastly expanded to cover every imaginable facet of Javanese experience and knowledge, both secular and religious. The text also acquires a historical setting—Java after the sacking of the Islamic coastal state of Giri in 1625 by the forces of Mataram—and a place—the detailed geography of the length and breadth of the same island. "History" was not a novel concept in Central Java at the beginning of the nineteenth century. But it is noteworthy that the 1814 *Centhini* is apparently the first Javanese encyclopedic poem about the quest for religious enlightenment to be historicized. The text's "historicity" is one of the features that suggests a resemblance to European writing and modes of thinking about the Orient from the same period, making it in one sense an expression of the transculturation of one universalistic mode of knowledge to another.

The kinds of knowledge now inquired about and recounted include, in Behrend's listing, "*primbon* (numerology and divination), *pakem* (wayang stories), *suluk* (Islamic mysticism), *piwulang* (etiquette and morals), *kawuruh kalang* (building lore), *jampi-jampian* (herbology and medicine), *musawaratan para wali* [stories about the Islamic saints and their deliberations], *babad* (history), *jangka* (predictions), *sastra wadi* (mystical meanings of the alphabet), *dasa nama* [lists of synonyms for use in literary compositions], *pikih* (Islamic law), *anbia* (tales of the [Islamic] prophets), *katuranggan* (equestrian lore) and many others," including *kawruh* (knowledge) about birds, krisses, sex, women, ascetics, legendary pre-Islamic and Islamic heroes, dates, calendars, non-Islamic "Buda" religion, Islamic prayers and rituals, childbirth, marriage, weddings, butchering, exorcism, wealth, thievery, music, dancing, magic, mountains, springs, grave sites, and death (Behrend 1997; Pigeaud 1933). The 1814 *Centhini* includes within itself a multitude of what might be called "manuals" of knowledge, presented during incidental conversations in the course of a long and meandering narrative. This presentation of knowledge in manual-like segments as well as the seemingly unstructured way in which these manuals are strung together mark one of the obvious differences between the text and a European encyclopedia. Benedict Anderson's characterization of the manual passages in the *Centhini* as "unalphabetized, poetic Yellow Pages"—an understanding that reflects a Western Enlightenment notion of how knowledge should be organized dating back to the late eighteenth century when such "scientific," totalizing, and obsessively tidy constructions of human knowledge as Jean Le Rond D'Alembert's 1751 diagram of the "Detailed System of Human Knowledge" were composed (D'Alembert 1995 [1751], 144–145)—pinpoints one of the sites of resistance in the text to the colonial appropriation of knowledge (B. Anderson 1990, 274).

Manuals are still common in Indonesia and throughout Southeast Asia, where we find treatises on war strategy, statecraft, healing therapies, law codes, and religious texts, as well as handbooks on sorcery, astrology, pharmacology, and invulnerability (C. Reynolds 1996; Quinn 1975; Turton 1991; Wolters 1999, 49, 116). This assemblage of knowledges, which was available to ordinary people as well as to the elite, is similar enough to the tradition of codifying knowledge in treatises and handbooks known as *śāstras* in India to warrant some discussion.

In his study on this topic, Pollock argues that *śāstras*, or shastras, represent "an attempt at an exhaustive classification of human cultural practices" (Pollock 1985, 502). What is distinctive about this knowledge is its sheer comprehensiveness, which embraces everything from cooking to sexual intercourse, elephant rearing, thievery, mathematics, logic, legends, ascetic renunciation, and spiritual liberation. We find this characteristic in the *Serat Centhini* and in the manual literature of Southeast Asia generally. Another shastric characteristic found in Southeast Asian manuals is the expression of the "centrality of rule-governance in human behaviour" (Pollock 1985, 500). Learning in early India, Pollock says, moved away from contact with direct experience toward a mastery of shastric codifications. But the question of the relationship between theory and practice was not a matter of trivial concern in the Indian intellectual tradition (Pollock 1985, 504). According to Pollock, "the relation of theoretical knowledge to actual practice" was given its "fullest and most pointed expression" in the *Kāmasūtra*, a manual on the art of love (Pollock 1985, 506). According to one ancient commentator on the *Kāmasūtra*:

> *Kāma* cannot be achieved without the application of a specific procedure. . . . *Kāma* is a function of the union of man and woman, and this requires some procedure, the knowledge of which comes only from the *kāmaśāstra*. . . . The procedure must therefore be enunciated, and the purpose of the *Kāmasūtra* is to do just this and so make it known. For how does one come to know anything except by means of a given *śāstra?* (Quoted in Pollock 1985, 506)

The subject of sexual knowledge and practice is also a major concern in the *Centhini* and its textual antecedents (B. Anderson 1990, 271–298; Kumar 1999). An early Javanese reference to the use of an Indic love manual as a theoretical guide to practice is contained in a passage from the twelfth-century *Bhāratayuddha* (a text that will be discussed in chapter 5), in which King Śalya and his wife Satyawatī "achieved the most sensuous enjoyment of sexual union in accordance with the *kāmatantra*" (Supomo 1993, 233). The oldest Javanese encyclopedic shastra in literary form is the Old Javanese *Rāmāyaṇa* from the tenth century (Hooykaas 1958b). The fact that this poem was based on an Indic version of the story of Rāma and Sītā that doubled as a manual of poetic technique—an Indic model that was at once theoretical and practical—underlines the importance of shastric knowledge in early Southeast Asia as a how-to guide to forming new kinds of states and civilizations.

Informed with Pollock's understanding of the Indian shastric concept of knowledge, we can read the first verse of the 1814 *Serat*

Centhini and take note of the way in which it alludes to the poem's character as a hybrid historical, narrative, localized, and vernacularized expression, late in the second millennium of the common era, of Pollock's Sanskrit cosmopolis:

> The excellent Crown Prince
> of Surakarta Adiningrat
> on the island of Java
> has ordered his servant, the scribe,
> Sutrasna, his close companion,
> to fashion a story taken from the past
> in such a way that all of Javanese knowledge [*kawruh Jawa*]
> is gathered together [*ingimpun*], arranged [*tinrap*] in metrical form
> so that all who hear it will be pleased, not bored. (translation, with
>   minor changes, from Behrend 1997, 41)

Several pertinent questions arise from this opening stanza. Why was the text compiled in 1814? Why was the compilation of *kawruh* given in the form of a historical "story" *(cariteng dangu)?* What is the significance of the seemingly shastric all-inclusiveness of its intent? What is the role of rules and rule making in its encyclopedic account? What is *kawruh Jawa*, Javanese knowledge, all about?

Peter Carey's work on the political and cultural history of Central Java during the first two decades of the nineteenth century is illuminating on the question of why the text was composed in 1814. The production of the text seems to have been caught up in and to have given expression to the politics of the court of the Surakarta ruler, Pakubuwana IV (r.1788–1820) (Carey 1977, 298–302). In 1811–1812, prior to the destruction of the Yogyakarta *kraton* by the British, Pakubuwana had been secretly plotting with the ruler of Yogyakarta to expel them, in the hope that Hamengkubuwana II's disloyalty would also be discovered, thus paving the way for Pakubuwana's possession of both thrones. The king of Surakarta was also at odds with the ruler of the Mangkunegaran principality, who sent forces to help the British assault on Yogyakarta. Pakubuwana's hatred of this prince, Pangeran Prangwedana, expressed itself when he refused to allow his daughter to marry the Mangkunagaran ruler, and it was further inflamed by the whisperings of another powerful prince at court, Mangkubumi. Mangkubumi also fomented intrigues against the crown prince, hoping to see him replaced as Pakubuwana's successor by his own son-in-law, Pangeran Purbaya. And it was Mangkubumi who made contact with a group of rebellious Sepoys in the British expeditionary force, introducing them to Pakubuwana, who became infatuated with their Hindu ritual. In Carey's words,

> This fascination on the part of the Sunan [i.e., Pakubuwana IV]
> for Hindu ceremonial was later stressed by Raffles as having
> been one of the main reasons why such close initial contacts were
> formed between the Surakarta court and the Sepoys. . . . Indeed,
> the Sepoy conspirators in Surakarta were at pains to emphasize
> to the Sunan that Java had a special Hindu heritage which in their
> opinion should be once again revitalized. . . . The fact that many
> of the Hindu temples and archaeological remains were in the pro-
> cess of being cleaned and surveyed by the British government at
> the time, may have also served to awaken an interest among the
> Central Javanese nobility in their Hindu past. . . . [Note: Raffles
> also used the Sepoys as informants during his visits to Hindu tem-
> ples in Central Java and commented on their admiration for these
> monuments, as well as their contempt for the Javanese of the
> day: "degenerate sons, with scarce a remnant of arts, science, or
> of any religion at all" (Raffles 1965 [1817], 2:27).] In Surakarta . . .
> the Sunan immediately responded to the Sepoys' overtures by
> lending them Hindu images from the Surakarta court collection
> and . . . also attended various Hindu ceremonies inside the fort.
> (Carey 1977, 301–302)

These contacts between Pakubuwana and the Sepoys continued during the later months of 1814 and early 1815, the conspiracy finally being discovered and the leaders of the Sepoy plot arrested in November 1815. The Surakarta court copy of the *Serat Centhini* is dated December 29, 1814 (Florida 1993, 252).

The political and religious tensions surrounding the Sepoy conspiracy help to explain the specific provenance and dating of the 1814 *Centhini*. The frame story of the poem, with its tale of the sacking of Giri, the flight and subsequent wanderings of the royal son and heir, and its representation of "religion" as depoliticized lists and conversations about various knowledges and practices, seems to comment on the situation in Surakarta in 1811–1814 from a point of view that reflected the experiences of the embattled crown prince and stated the fears of many courtiers about the volatile mix of politics and religion that was being prepared during the Sepoy conspiracy. The compendious exposition of Islamic knowledge in the text can certainly be read as a shastric exposition of all possible religious practices and theological positions, but there is also a polemical edge to the treatment of heterodoxy that reflects a critical rather than a tolerant assessment of Pakubuwana's neo-Hinduism (Soebardi 1971, 349). A political reading of the text is also supported by the realization that the 1814 *Centhini,* in its attention to rules and conduct, is similar to other shastric texts from the same period that repeatedly enunciated the injunction "Do not forget!" to courtiers and commoners who were ignoring the rules of proper conduct and dress as Europeans intruded more and more into Central Javanese politics and culture during the early nineteenth century, threatening the cultural and moral basis of hierarchy and social order (Kumar 1997, 367–429).

The *Serat Centhini,* therefore, can be read as a discourse about knowledge and power at a major turning point in the history of Central Java. Its hybrid form and content reflect its origins as shastric manual, political polemic, and Enlightenment-style, knowledge-gathering travelogue. Benedict Anderson has read the text from one point of view as the representation of a "phantasmagoric utopia" in which proto-Enlightenment Javanese intellectuals attack the ideology of Javanese kingship, a reading that emphasizes the struggle over knowledge and power evident in the poem (B. Anderson 1990, 271–298). But this interpretation underplays the way the poem emphasizes the views of the dominant male elite of the court (Florida 1996, 217) as well as its all-pervasive "rule-boundedness," which extends to characterizations of social and gender relationships that are anything but revolutionary. Notwithstanding occasional, carnivalesque but morally instructive upendings of the social order, the poem repeatedly illustrates the consequences of not following shastric rules even as it gives expression to subversive ideas and impulses (Pollock 1985, 509, 511; J. Scott 1990, 80, 166–182).

The *Centhini* is less an Enlightenment intellectual's antistate polemic or a Javanese subaltern's poetic "world-turned-upside-down," therefore, than a contested textual site, similar to the nineteenth-century Siamese poem *Nirat N'ongkhai,* analyzed by Craig

Reynolds, in which "a struggle over hierarchies and boundaries, a struggle for the terrain of some intermediary space between the court and the subaltern world" takes place (C. Reynolds 1991, 31). Anderson may be right that, in the scene he analyzes at length in which the wandering hero Cabolang sodomizes and is himself sodomized by a rural lord, an Enlightened note is being sounded about the triumph of intellectual expertise over political authority, thus setting the stage for the subsequent struggle of such heroes of the Enlightenment in Indonesia's history as the writer Pramoedya Ananta Toer against the forces of Javanese statism and cultural darkness (B. Anderson 1990, 279–282, 286). On the other hand, and this is my preferred reading, it can be argued that the authors of the text do not foresee the unintended, egalitarian consequences of their own cosmological, hierarchy-reinforcing Sufi doctrines about the interdependence of lord *(gusti)* and servant *(kawula)*, which are enunciated in response to the social and political disorder of the times (see Ortner 1984, 157). This topic of servant-master mysticism is examined several times in the *Centhini*, as it is in many Sufi manual texts from the early nineteenth century. The following passage from one such text contains a succinct statement of the *kawula-gusti* doctrine:

> If you devote yourself assiduously to religion (*literally*, if you carry out asceticism), ask about Lord and servant. Servant and Lord are the union of two: two unite and become one. That is the perfect knowledge and perfection of unity. Go and take instruction in this doctrine with another. This is the perfect worship. . . .
>
> One is man and at the same time woman; one venerates and at the same time is venerated; one gives orders and at the same time is ordered; one turns north yet goes south. For the [*dh*]*alang* [puppeteer] reveals himself in the puppets and the puppets reveal themselves in the [*dh*]*alang*. Think this through thoroughly! The Lord reveals himself in the servant and the servant reveals himself in the Lord. Do not be indifferent to this! (Zoetmulder 1995, 259)

Whatever the potential for subversive readings of the *Centhini*'s various presentations of this statist form of mysticism may be, the unity of master and servant in a stable political hierarchy is the desired alternative proposed in the poem to the political chaos of early nineteenth-century Central Java.

Anderson's Enlightenment interpretation of the text does, however, encourage us to think seriously about the fact that the *Centhini* pays abundant attention to practice as well as theory, to experience as well as rules. Is there an expression of Enlightened thinking here? Pollock notes a similar tension in Indian shastras, one that was resolved there in favor of theory and rules. One of the features that distinguishes the *Centhini* from contemporaneous European encyclopedic travel and historical accounts of Java is the vivid way in which it dwells on natural settings, social interaction, eating, music, performance, and sex before and after the "rules" of a particular kind of knowledge are expounded, a characteristic that is also found in the Thai *nirat* genre (C. Reynolds 1991; Wenk 1995).

Compare, for example, Mackenzie's account of his scientific expedition to the site of Prambanan (the Hindu temple ruin) near Yogyakarta, Central Java, with the poetic narrative of the visit by Mas Cabolang and his companions to the same place (Serat Centhini 1985–1990, 3:85 ff.). The Javanese travelers approach through a dawn landscape filled with bird song, sights of towering mountains, and the sound of people working in the rice fields. They arrive at the ruins and a spring whose refreshing qualities are sensuously evoked. A village woman fetching water tells them the name of the place and takes them to meet the village head Harsana, who is delighted to show them around the temples, over which it is his duty to watch. After a tour, during which the ruins and their features are minutely described (at one point the text makes use of verses from the *Serat Rama*, the modern Javanese poetic version of the *Rāmāyaṇa*, to describe a relief on one of the temples and evoke its emotional significance), the travelers retire to Harsana's home, where he offers them food and drink. The meal and their enjoyment of it are described at length. After eating, Mas Cabolang politely asks for the "story" about the temples, since he does not "know" *(weruh)* which of the two versions he has heard is correct. Harsana obliges with a tale that lasts several hundred verses and makes for a night of pleasurable listening.

There are certainly parallels between the details and stages of Mackenzie's visit to Prambanan and the one described in the *Centhini* that suggest either a Javanese awareness of European archaeological method or the agency of Javanese modes of making inquiries that have been incorporated into European practice through the use of native informants. But the differences between the two accounts are equally striking. Compared to the intensely serious and imperious Mackenzie and Raffles being borne aloft on the shoulders of coolies during their rigorous daily study routines, on the job by nine, home by six, the *Centhini's* scholars enjoy a relaxed, egalitarian, joyous, and sensuous learning experience in which "time" is noticed, if at all, at various moments of the day because people want to worship God, who has created all knowledge and existence. This mode of living and learning seems enlightened, but not in a European sense! For reasons that may have to do with the experiential rather than exclusively shastric orientation of the poem, the word used to designate most of the knowledges in the text is *"kawruh,"* from the root *"weruh,"* meaning to see or come to know by observing the exoteric, external appearance of things (Gericke and Roorda 1901, 2:14–15). The term *"ngelmu"* is reserved for the esoteric, mystical secrets of religion, such as those revealed by Amongraga to his bride-to-be Tambang Raras on their wedding night (see the *Centhini* passage translated and discussed in Zoetmulder 1995, 132–136). The important point is that without exception all forms of knowledge are explicated in the *Centhini* (B. Anderson 1990, 288). But the main protagonists Cabolang and Amongraga, who elicit or make these revelations, are hardly middle- or lower-class "professionals" in the modern, secular meaning of that term, as Anderson would like to imagine them in order to set up a parallel between early nineteenth-century Javanese and European Enlightenment intellectuals. Rather, the Javanese characters are men of spiritually superior ancestry *(trah utama)* who ultimately submit to the authority of fathers and kings, however *nakal* (naughty) they have been. At the end of the poem, the theologian Amongraga becomes a rattan worm so that he can be consumed by and so merge with the king. The perspective in the text on knowledge and social behavior is thoroughly elitist and mainly male, although mocking female opinions and transvestite acts that subvert hierarchy, religion, and male sexuality and dominance are also richly represented (Florida 1996; Kumar 1999, 484–486).

There is more to say about the shastric range of knowledges presented in the text. When they began appropriating bits and pieces of these knowledges, Western scholars took what interested them—theology, music, dance, and sex—which may have influenced the selection of the portion of the total text that was first transliterated and published in 1912–1915. Taken together, these selections constituted a certain construction of "the Javanese" that cast them in the role of a civilized yet erotic, impractical, and mystically inclined people fit to be the subjects of colonial rule, moral restraint, and philological study, a construction that dates from the writings of Thomas Stamford Raffles at the beginning of the nineteenth century. It is not hard to imagine that the intention of the authors of the *Centhini* in setting out a more cosmologically expansive range of knowledge about Java was a different one.

The basis for the universality of the text's scope is given in the first stanza of the poem quoted earlier, namely that the knowledges presented are Javanese, or *kawruh Jawa*. The earliest textual use of "Javanese" as a classifier for knowledge is possibly the sixteenth-century tract on Islamic ethics translated by G. W. J. Drewes (1978). In this text the question is asked, "Which is the better religion, Islam or the religion of the Javanese?" *(Ana ngucapa endi becik agama selam lawan gama jawa?)* (Drewes 1978, 36–37). The answer given: Islam. In early eighteenth-century Kartasura in Central Java, a didactic Sufi poem resolved the cultural clash between Islamic and Javanese identities by asserting that both must be cultivated in order to make the perfect courtier. "What is wrong with not knowing Arabic," the poem states, "is that you know not the order of life, the life of the All-Disposing" (quoted in Ricklefs 1998, 219). "What is wrong with not knowing Javanese is that your speech is confused and far from good. You know not the levels of language, for a king, warrior, a *bupati* [regional overlord], for a relative, for a holy *guru*, a lord and parents" (quoted in Ricklefs 1998, 219–220). Within the 1814 poetic Javanese landscape of dispersed knowledges, however, Islam and carnivalesque violations of normative language use and social hierarchy are both normal. But why must the "Javaneseness" of knowledges in the text be designated as such?

This question may appear to be the overriding one, particularly if, following Anderson, we take a historicizing view that the poem is an early enunciation of Indonesian nationalism. Such a reading would start with the historical context of early nineteenth-century Central Java, where decades of European regulation of court affairs and probings of their knowledges, followed by the pillage of manuscripts and heirlooms from the *kraton* of Yogyakarta, provided a powerful reason for self-reflexivity about the Javaneseness of knowledges and anxiety about their efficacy (Kumar 1997). Pemberton has given us an analysis of one aspect of this Javanese cultural self-reflexivity and response to European colonialism in his study of Central Javanese court ritual from the late eighteenth century onward by means of which there developed a "Javanese" concept of "order" *(tata)* and a self-consciously "Javanese style" *(cara Jawa)* of behaving that became the basis for "official" Javanese nationalism and culture in the late colonial and New Order periods (Pemberton 1994; B. Anderson 1991, 83–111; cf. Sutherland 1979 and Sartono et al. 1987).

A shastric reading of the 1814 *Centhini,* however, challenges this interpretation of early nineteenth-century Javanese culture by placing it in a much older historical framework, that of the Sanskrit cosmopolis. The shastric emphasis in the poem is on exposing, for all to know, the *sarat,* or effective means, for utilizing knowledge of many different kinds. The word *"cara"* (manner, style of doing something) as used in the text also possesses a plural rather than a monolithic meaning in the way in which it is used to describe a variety of Javanese ways of doing things—for example, *cara praja,* the way to do things in a *kraton* environment; *cara priyayi,* the way aristocrats do things; *cara basa Budha,* the way one would make a statement in pre-Islamic language. In the poem's encyclopedic approach to knowledge, "Java" consists of a multitude of orders and styles. The frequent occurrence of the phrase *"cara Jawa,"* or *"Javanese style,"* challenges Pemberton's understanding of the dominant role played by Dutch colonialism in the (further) codification and commodification of "Javanese" culture (cf. R. C. Morris 2000, 234, on northern Thailand) because the plurality of possible ways of being Javanese in the text is not limited by either place or time, thus allowing "Java" to escape totalizing colonial control. Space and time in the poem are cosmological, as well as here and now. This fact poses problems for a historicist reading of the text that would link it in a linear, teleological way to either the Indonesian nation or the New Order state.

In looking for another theoretical approach, we might consider the suggestion made by scholars of Javanese literature that the composition of texts served a ritual as well as literary purpose well into the nineteenth century (e.g., Zoetmulder 1974, 151–185; Ricklefs 1974, 176–226; Day 1982). The 1814 *Centhini* and the impulse behind its display of *kawruh Jawa* could thus be interpreted in a ritual framework.

The ideas of Victor Turner, an anthropologist of ritual and performance, offer one appealing way of understanding the broader cultural, historical, and ritual significance of the text's writing.

In Turner's terms, the "utopian" (as Anderson would put it) or
"subjunctive" (Turner's own term) mode of representation in the *Serat
Centhini* would not derive from the antifeudal ideology of an emerging professional class of Enlightened, nationalistic artists who produced the text, as Anderson argues in order to suggest a parallel between late eighteenth-century France and early nineteenth-century
Java. Rather, the *Centhini* and its hybrid characteristics would form a
"metacommunication" about Javanese culture in the early nineteenth
century, a self-reflexive ritual "framing" in literary form of cultural
practices and values in a period of rapid and violent change (Turner
1988, 102). Thus in a textual form (and we will see in a moment how
well the text's narrative content supports this view) the poem could
be viewed as analogous to the explicit framing of cultural values that
occurs during the middle, "liminal" phase of ritual as analyzed by the
anthropologist Van Gennep and by Turner himself (see Turner 1982,
24). "Liminality," writes Turner, in one of his eloquent definitions of
this concept,

> is often the scene and time for the emergence of a society's deepest
> values in the form of sacred dramas and objects—sometimes the
> re-enactment periodically of cosmogonic narratives or deeds of
> saintly, godly, or heroic establishers of morality, basic institutions,
> or ways of approaching transcendent beings or powers. But it
> may also be the venue and occasion for the most radical scepti-
> cism—always relative, of course, to the given culture's repertoire
> of sceptical concepts and images—about cherished values and
> rules. Ambiguity reigns; people and public policies may be judged
> sceptically in relation to deep values; the vices, follies, stupidities,
> and abuses of contemporary holders of high political, economic,
> or religious status may be satirized, ridiculed, or condemned in
> terms of axiomatic values, or these personages may be rebuked
> for gross failures in common sense. (Turner 1988, 102)

The *Serat Centhini*, it could be argued, displays all the hallmarks
of a metacommunication in Turner's "liminal" sense. The frame
story, involving the oldest son of the defeated ruler of Giri (one of the

most sacred sites of Islamic pilgrimage and once a powerful, theo-cratic maritime state on Java's northeast coast) and his quest for his brother and sister, who have become separated from him during the pillage of the city by the forces of Mataram, the Central Javanese inland state, has the basic ritual structure of separation, transition, and incorporation (Turner 1982, 24)—a structure that is recapitulated over and over again in narrative subplots and in the topics of Islamic debate and discussion throughout the text. The final "incorporation" sought by Amongraga, which is repeatedly parodied in the scenes of exuberantly raunchy sexual union (as well as disunion!), is with God, not with his two siblings, whose separation from him and from each other is symbolic of man's separation from God. Amongraga ("He who devotes himself to love") eventually achieves his own spiritual goal, but not before—by means of travels, discussions, per-formances, sexual unions, and displays of every kind of knowledge imaginable—the cultural values and paraphernalia of Central Java are put on display in the midst of a "liminal" realm of villages and places of pilgrimage situated outside Giri, outside Mataram, outside the normal, everyday world of Surakarta where the poem was com-posed. The world of the poem, which Anderson calls a "phantasma-goric utopia," could instead be defined as a concrete ritual space, situated in a real Javanese geography beyond the pale of "normal" courtly and increasingly colonized Surakarta society, where the char-acters of the poem, like participants in some Java-wide initiation ritual, are instructed in the *kawruh* of their culture. But this initiation reconfirms, rather than revolutionizes, the hierarchical social and political order. The dispersed and noncourtly location of knowledges in the text also reflects, in a directly referential way, the actual dis-persal of specific sites of experience and knowledge throughout the landscape of Java before the nineteenth century (see Prapañca 1995). This situation changed in the course of that century as the country-side was colonized and a Europe- and *kraton*-centric idea about the origin and location of knowledge and culture developed (Day and Derks 1999). A reading of the *Centhini* that treats it as ritual would insist that not just theology but every form of Javanese knowledge presented in the text is imbued with a ritualized sacredness and power to induce self-reflexivity about being "Javanese" at a time of cultural and political crisis. The shastric nature of the text, which has its origins in very old approaches to learning and literary production in India and Java (Noorduyn 1982, 418), conforms to and expresses this liminal, ritual function of the poem.

In a stimulating oral discussion of an earlier draft of this chapter presented at a seminar at the Australian National University in November 1996, in which I advanced a "liminal" reading of the poem based on Turner, Ranajit Guha argued that I had in fact fallen into the trap of reducing my treatment of knowledge to the "old story," that of the struggle between "tradition" and "modernity," the "East" and the "West," "freedom" and the "state," leading to the inevitable triumph of the latter term in each case. "The operation is a rationalist operation," he said. Guha proceeded to deconstruct my discussion of the *Serat Centhini* in the manner of his critique of Hegel's definition of "history" in which Hegel makes it identical to the "state" (Guha 1997, 75). I quote from my notes of Guha's remarks:

> The whole text is treated as "rational" by being called an "encyclopedia." Here's how it works: You call something which is non-unitary an "encyclopedia." Then you carry out three operations: historicize; explain; secularize. You give the text a genesis and link it to a political crisis, bringing a disorderly text to order. The "political crisis" is such because of the state, which has already been posited. The analysis searches for a nexus of "reason," while diversity is assigned to a "spiritual" category: "self-reflexivity." The "objectivity" of the text and all it contains is thereby destroyed, since its self-reflexivity is thought of as an allegory of separation-transition-incorporation, a classic mediation scheme in which abstract signifiers replace material ones. This mediation process takes place, not in the life of the community, but in relation to the "state" which has been secularized. Western, high modernity triumphs.
>
> But alternatively, is it not possible to embrace plurality and diversity in our representation of the past? Can we cope with the diversity of being human in past time and take care of that diversity? There is an obsession with unification, which makes it impossible to "take care of" the diversity found in the *Centhini*. The historiography of unification is linked to the rise of the nation-state. We have let the state thematize the past for us. The drift of "statism" governs our representation of the past. The problem with Foucault is that his notion of power is amenable to a statist

interpretation because there is nothing that is not an exercise in power.

Guha's criticism cogently illuminates the way in which an uncritical application of Turner's ritual framework to a reading of the *Serat Centhini* turns the text into a cultural manual that prepares the reader for national service under the Indonesian New Order state. This is in fact what happened historically to the text. In the second half of the nineteenth century the poem was extensively quoted in a European-style travelogue by R. M. A. A. Candranegara, an uncle of the nationalist Kartini, in ways that suggested an important role for the text in defining the cultural, if not also "national," identity of the colonial Javanese elite at that time (Bonneff 1986; Day and Derks 1999). A partial manuscript of the text also found its way into the Batavian Academy of the Arts and Sciences. There it was eventually edited by the future Mangkunegara VII, a descendant of Pakubuwana IV's rival and an aristocratic Javanese nationalist who identified himself with Amongraga, the chief seeker after mystical truth in the poem. This version of the poem was published in abbreviated form in 1912–1915 during the height of the Javanese nationalist awakening (Sears 1996a, 163–169; Muhlenfeld 1916/1917, 85). The *Serat Centhini* thus became, like the codified repertoire of Central Javanese shadow-puppet theatre or the Old Javanese *Deśawarṇana,* partially pacified "territory" in the colonial and postcolonial struggle over the truth about "Java."

In the case of the *Deśawarṇana,* this pacification was not uncontested. First published between 1905 and 1914 in the scholarly journal of the Royal Institute in Leiden, the only palm-leaf copy of the Old Javanese poem about the fourteenth-century reign of King Hayam Wuruk of Majapahit known to exist at that time had been seized during the Dutch conquest of the island of Lombok in 1894. But as S. Supomo observes,

It is, perhaps, more than a coincidence that it was during the period of the rebirth of Prapanca's Majapahit that Budi Utomo, the first embodiment of the Javanese national awakening, was founded in 1908—a decade after the publication of the *Pararaton* [i.e., another Old Javanese "historical" text about early Java], three years after the first installment of Kern's articles on the *Nagarak-*

rtagama [Deśawarṇana]. Initially this organization sought the stim-
ulation and advancement of the Javanese people only, but this
regionalism soon gave way to the idea of one Indonesia covering
the whole of the Netherlands East Indies, the idea which was
shared by other regional-based associations. And what better
model for this one Indonesia which was free and united than the
great Majapahit, the *real* Majapahit which had just been brought
back to life by the labour of great scholars like Brandes, Kern and
Krom, and the expanse of which coincided with, or was even
larger than, the Netherlands Indies? (Supomo 1979, 181)

The "discovery" of Majapahit and of the old Sumatran kingdom
of Srivijaya by Georges Coedès in 1918 thus allowed the truth about
the precolonial past to become available, in an Orientalized form, to
nationalist intellectuals (Reid 1979). The *Centhini,* meanwhile, with
its heterogeneous contents and conflicting radical and conservative
political messages, was turned into a Western-style "encyclopedia"
of normative Javanese culture, to be plundered for bits and pieces of
kawruh Jawa considered important for Western knowledge about
such topics as Islamic mysticism (Zoetmulder 1995), popular performance (Pigeaud 1938), and Central Javanese gamelan music (Kunst
1973). The *Centhini* subsequently became a state heirloom, a subject
of official Javanese cultural preservationism during the Suharto era
(Behrend 1997). The historical specificity and ambiguity of its relation
to colonial politics in Central Java in 1812–1814 and its "Enlightened" explicitness about knowledge of all sorts has been forgotten.
By 1862, when the Eurasian Javanologist C. F. Winter's "Javanese
Conversations" *(Javaansche Zamenspraken)* were published as a text-
book for Dutch Javanese-language learners, the *Serat Centhini* was
referred to, only briefly, as a "secret guide to mystical knowledge"
(perlambang ngelmi). The Orientalization and mystification of what is
presented in the text as empirical knowledge of all sorts, both mun-
dane and esoteric, about Java had thus been carried out by the principal Eurasian contributor to the invention of Dutch-style "Javanese"
culture in the first half of the nineteenth century (Winter 1862, 193).

If the *Serat Centhini* represents the first stage in the interaction
between Javanese and Westerners in the construction of Javanese
knowledge for the purposes of exercising (or resisting) domination
over Java, Winter's intervention in the construction of that knowl-

edge for the explicit purpose of training Dutch colonial officials constituted the second. The transformation of the text by Dutch Orien-
talists into an esoteric "encyclopedia" of Dutch knowledge about
"Java," along with its own message of political, sexual, and religious
submissiveness, is at least part of the reason why the poem never
became as seditious as the banned nineteenth-century Siamese *Nirat
N'ongkhai*, which vulgarized high culture and so challenged the hegemony of the Bangkok state—a challenge that continued to be powerful
long after its composition (C. Reynolds 1991, 27). Nor does the *Centhini* examine the conflict between family and state in a way that provokes seditious thoughts against the Javanese state in the manner of
the Siamese folk epic *Khun Chang Khun Phaen* (Sibunruang 1960; Pasuk
and Baker 1995, xv–xvii). Written in a language that did not become
the national language of Indonesia, and unconcerned with the question of political loyalty, it also never became a supreme literary expression of being "Javanese" in colonial and postcolonial situations,
as the early nineteenth-century Vietnamese *Tale of Kiều* did for Vietnamese of all classes and political persuasions (Nguyễn Du 1983; Tai
1992, 109–112). What the *Centhini* does share with these other encyclopedic texts from Siam and Vietnam is an interest in the role of
knowledge in relation to the exercise of power.

An Entropic Cosmological State

To eliminate power and the state altogether from the formation of
the text, as Guha and Anderson both argue, is to ignore its shastric,
normative message and what that might tell us about state formation
in Southeast Asia. What the shastric message calls attention to is not
a future state or national revolution, but the agency of Indic and Sufi
cosmological state formations still active within the thought world of
the poem. For the text is not just a compendium of shastras or a
European-style fact-finding travelogue; it can also be read as a colo-
nial-age, hybrid representation of several very old Southeast Asian
modes of cosmic journeying; as a royal progress (Prapañca 1995); as
the heroic, encyclopedic quest for potency outside the boundaries of
the state (Day and Derks 1999; Maier 1999); or as a search for the
reunion of separated siblings (Koolhof 1999; Robson 1971; also see
S. Errington 1989, 128, 237, 250–251, 264–265, 279, 289, 292). The setting for these simultaneous journeys is itself ambiguous: the "Java"

of the poem is a hybrid both cosmological and geographical, filled with pleasures that convey the "loose," "safe" feeling of territory fully under the control of a powerful king, yet also charged with the tension of a "dangerous," alien testing ground for heroes on a quest for new sources of potency or their missing siblings (S. Errington 1989, 251, 282). The prize of potency scattered throughout the landscape of the poem is *kawruh Jawa,* a veritable topographical archive of hybrid knowledges about Java. Until the early nineteenth century, before the codification and purification of "official" Javanese culture began, this hybridity was reflected in the cultural practices of the Javanese state itself, which were drawn from all over the island (Carey 1999). The cultural hybridity of the state was an assertion and representation of its cosmic universality and unity. In the *Serat Centhini,* however, the diversity and comprehensiveness of Javanese knowledges serve two other purposes: as a strategy of cultural self-defense and as a warning signal about the entropic disintegration of the Javanese cosmological state.

The strategy looks like a masterful transcultural appropriation and counterdeployment of the same British "strategy of heterogeneity" by which hegemony over Tibet, India, and early nineteenth-century Java and Malaya was sought through a "comprehensive knowledge of peoples" collected by nomadic scholar-officials like Colin Mackenzie wandering around the countryside "searching for reality" (Richards 1993, 27–29; Maier 1988, 13–50). Presented in a mode that appears random from a Western point of view (B. Anderson 1990, 274), information in the *Centhini* unravels not according to the logic of a colonial taxonomy, but along the meandering route of seekers after *kawruh.* Its acquisition is never demanded, but is subordinated to the willingness of village sages to divulge their knowledge and is governed by the etiquette of polite inquiry. A scientific collection and decipherment of written sources is replaced by the oral/aural pleasures of learning by listening and telling, followed by eating, music making, or sex. The fact-seeking expeditions of colonial officials are resisted in the form of wandering motivated by a religious quest that, once completed, leaves the living sources of knowledge alone and at peace. As an expression of textual resistance to colonialism in the early nineteenth century, the *Serat Centhini* deploys the heterogeneity of Javanese culture the way other Javanese poems use knowledge as a magical talisman to ward off evil and create well-being (Zoetmulder 1974; Ricklefs 1974).

Yet the poem's far-flung and heterogeneous cultural archive is also a sign of warning about the entropic decline of the Javanese cosmological state, which was disintegrating at the time the poem was written. Entropy is not solely a European scientific discovery (cf. Richards 1993, 73–109). Indic cosmological conceptions of the state posit the steady dissipation of its potency, which leads to the formation of new states by other "men of prowess" (B. Anderson 1990, 34). Sūryavarman built Angkor Wat to represent the entropy of his age in numerological and mythic terms and invited his followers to join him in reversing it. New leaders rose repeatedly in nineteenth- and twentieth-century Java in response to the entropic disorder of the state, of which the effects of colonialism were both symptom and cause (Sartono 1972). The quest for knowledge in the *Serat Centhini* is also an attempt to reverse this process. The poem's fictional party of nomadic exiles, who embody the civilizational norms of the Javanese state, journey from one location of cultural information to another, demonstrating their cultural prowess, eliciting information that is organized into shastric manuals of normalizing knowledge. As Ronald Inden writes of responses to entropy in early India,

> Unless people interacted repeatedly and correctly with the overlord of the cosmos with the purpose of acquiring new infusions of his *tejas* [luminous, goal-directed energy], the human world would quickly disintegrate, for people would be unable to complete themselves and eventually obtain the goal of union with the absolute godhead. There was, however, no firmly grounded knowledge on which people could automatically act. . . . It was only when knowledgeable action seemed to produce decisive manifestations, among which the most important was the "universal monarch", the king of kings who succeeded in conquering the quarters, that people would know and feel that they were on the right path. (Inden 1990, 236)

The *Serat Centhini* reads like a quest for a similar kind of redemptive, state-forming, all-inclusive cosmological power and knowledge, one that never, however, reaches its goal.

The exuberances and freedoms represented in the *Centhini*, indeed the very recognition by the text's courtly writers of the vast array of local knowledges to which they had access, can therefore be understood as a reaction to the colonial statist project that was underway in Central Java at the beginning of the nineteenth century. Anderson interprets knowledge in the text as a wholly subversive, barely veiled "hidden transcript" of subaltern rebelliousness against Javanese state authority. I read the role of knowledge in the text as ambiguous, cutting both ways at the same time in a struggle for power that did not have clear winners or losers (B. Anderson 1990, 271–298; J. Scott 1990; C. Reynolds 1991). The compilation of the text, I have argued, is at once a reflex of a colonial project and an act of resistance to it, both a shastric exercise in codifying rules of knowledge and a celebration of hybrid idiosyncrasies that cannot all be subjected to a single form of authority, the shastric mission of the main protagonists notwithstanding. The text is also a ritual act. To think of the text as also being what it records many instances of, as a ritual process, helps us to see that Javanese knowledge and relations of power are being interrogated in a special way that makes them "redemptive" in the colonial situation (Bell 1992, 196, 209). The articulation of hundreds of fragments of *kawruh Jawa* framed by a story of political and familial disintegration empowers the characters in the poem and the readers/hearers of the text to affirm their collective strength and cultural identity in the face of colonial conquest. If the normative teleology implicit in Turner's liminal model is removed, it can still be used to illuminate the ritual, celebratory nature of this nineteenth-century Javanese poem and its quest for redemptive knowledge.

The 1814 *Centhini,* together with the published and unpublished encyclopedic compendia produced by the Enlightenment in early nineteenth-century Java, also needs to be read in a way that reveals the strategic role of such texts in a transcultural network of power relationships spanning the cultural divide between "Java" and "Europe," the Sanskrit cosmopolis, Islam, and Western modernity. At the beginning of the nineteenth century, for reasons partly due to the appearance of the Enlightenment in Java, this divide was narrower than it had been or would again be for a long time (cf. Maier 1988, 43). More research is needed to uncover the nature and extent of contacts and conflicts between European and Javanese seekers after knowledge at the beginning of the nineteenth century. But on the basis of what we already know about this relationship, and on the strength of the many similarities between the encyclopedic interests pursued and facts gathered in both intellectual traditions, there are grounds for thinking that the early nineteenth century was a pivotal moment in Javanese history when, all other things being equal, a different and more convergently hybridizing historical turning point might have been achieved. As it turned out, of course, "Enlightened" Europeans and Javanese pursued divergent trajectories toward their own "legitimate," "authorized, " and "purified" futures, ignorant of the inevitability of the unintended, hybrid reconvergence of these paths (Bourdieu 1991; Latour 1993).

Purifying Regimes, Hybridizing Networks

As was the case elsewhere in Southeast Asia in the course of the nineteenth and early twentieth centuries, in Siam or the Malay world, for example (Gesick 1995; Maier 1988), local Javanese "intellectuals" and texts were transformed into "informants" and sources for knowledge about colonized peoples and their cultures. Although far less was recorded about them, the writers of the *Serat Centhini*, as well as the various Javanese princes who shared their learning and texts with Mackenzie and Raffles, were treated more nearly as intellectual equals by Europeans than was Ranggawarsita (1802–1873) of Surakarta, descendant of a long line of court writers. During his lifetime he labored anonymously and impecuniously as an assistant to Dutch lexicographers, only to be ridiculed for his ignorance of Old Javanese by one of the most prominent early Dutch philologists, A. B. Cohen Stuart (1825–1876) (Day 1982, 164 and passim; Tsuchiya 1990; Fasseur 1994). Ranggawarsita was seemingly crushed beneath a juggernaut of Dutch research on Central Javanese culture and relegated to the bottom of a new scientific and political pecking order that stretched from Leiden to Surakarta (Tsuchiya 1990; Day 1982; Florida 1987; J. Errington 1989). Yet by the 1930s, Ranggawarsita had been rehabilitated within the Javanese nationalist movement as a prophet of national independence. In an account of Ranggawarisita's life based on a biography compiled in the early twentieth century at the request of Dr. van Hinloopen Labberton, a theosophist and close friend of prominent members of Budi Utomo, the aristocratic nationalist organization, Ranggawarsita's education and mystical knowledge are presented as an alternative to Western rationalism and the educational methods that fostered it (Tsuchiya 1990, 96–106). As Kenji Tsuchiya shows, Ranggawarsita was thus "recuperated" in terms of the same hybrid kind of modernity that gave rise to the Taman Siswa educational system (Tsuchiya 1987).

Ranggawarsita's exposure to philological scrutiny in the mid-nineteenth century resulted from a shift in the focus of Western empirical research on Java. The shift can be seen in the pages of the *Transactions* (Dutch *Verhandelingen*) of the Batavian Academy of the Arts and Sciences after 1843. Interest turned from the natural sciences to language, literature, archaeology, and the collection of antiquities as the academy "approached several Dutch specialists in 'the heart of Java' [i.e., the principalities of Jogjakarta and Surakarta] with a request for assistance in selecting and translating important works from old Javanese" (The and van der Veur 1973, 8). The academy also promoted "the preservation of antiquities" and fought to protect its piece of the archaeological action when the State Ethnographical Museum of Leiden tried to arrange the transfer of its collection of ethnographic objects to the Netherlands. It also fostered the use of knowledge derived from the colonization of India to recover and colonize Java's "classical" Indic past:

> Another example of the Academy's activities . . . is the case of Rudolph H. Th. Friederich, a German student of Sanskrit who had enlisted as a regular soldier in the Colonial Army in order to obtain access to Hindu monuments and manuscripts. . . . Friederich's talents were soon put to more productive use. The Directors, alerted that the government intended to send a military expedition to Bali, petitioned the Governor-General to have "the interests of scholarship" represented by attaching Friederich to the expedition with the task of collecting manuscripts, statues, inscriptions, and information on the connection between Balinese and old Javanese. In the last decade of the century, similar efforts led to the "rescue" from the temple of the *radja* of Lombok of the *Nagarakretagama* [sic], the panegyric of the court poet Prapantja on King Hajam Wuruk. (The and van der Veur 1973, 11)

The pages of the academy's *Transactions* after 1843 recorded a deepening and totalizing appropriation of the Javanese past, involving a definition of that past as essentially "Hindu," "classically" Indic and non-Islamic, and thus "naturally" more akin to Europe rather than to the Middle East (Day 1983a; Sears 1996a). The content of its scholarly articles also began to prefigure, then parallel, the expansion of the Dutch imperium into the heartland of the Javanese countryside by means of the Cultivation System and out into the rest of the archipelago in the vanguard of military conquest (The and van der Veur 1973, 109–125). From 1853 onward, the academy also printed a journal, which, next to linguistic and philological matters, began publishing studies on subjects directly relevant to political, military, and economic concerns, such as Islamic and Chinese education, Muslim and Chinese sects and secret societies (information about the latter was passed on to French authorities in Cochinchina; see Tai 1983, 55), and, in the 1890s, Javanese village legends and beliefs. "Knowing" the Indies began to mean literally possessing it, and both the knowing and possessing were masculine in gender:

> Many colonial administrators, who were always male, imagined Asia as unfathomable . . . whereas they envisioned the physical terrain of colonial administration as a Pandora's box, the ultimate symbol of feminine inscrutability. . . . It was only the scientific scrutiny of Western men that could decipher the conundrum of colonial governance. Knowledgeable civil servants should strip away the layers of secrecy and ignorance that surround the *desa* [village], said the Dutch *adat* [village customary law] specialist Cornelis van Vollenhoven in 1909; only through a scholarly ethnographic analysis of the customs and cosmology of family life in the *desa* can the great divide between the formal colonial state and the informal village world be bridged. (Gouda 1993, 6)

Dutch philologists reenacted military conquest and administrative centralization on the dry pages of their journals. European scholars subjugated indigenous texts and redefined their universal truth-value as well as their multiple, potentially subversive meanings for indigenous readers by arranging variant versions into stemma leading to a single lost "original." In 1862 the Dutch government declared that "[t]he islands of the Indies Archipelago offer a wide field for scientific study" and concluded that the Netherlands should become the international center for studies of the region (quoted in Fasseur 1994, 196, 197). Elsbeth Locher-Scholten (1981, 176–208) links the liberalizing colonial "Ethical Movement" at the very end of the nineteenth century, which encouraged the development of Indonesian nationalism, to an upsurge of Dutch national self-confidence, military expansionism to the outer islands of the Indonesian archipelago, and an anxious concern for the "development" of the "natives." One of the decisive events in the reawakening of Dutch national self-confidence was the conquest of Lombok in 1894, where the Old Javanese *Deśawarṇana* was seized (Locher-Scholten 1981, 197). Textual editing of such colonial booty implied that only the Western philologist could guess at what such expressions of indigenous culture once "really" and originally meant. Philological editions also implicitly restated the view that contemporary Indonesian societies were, to use Raffles' words, mere vestiges "of humbled majesty and decay" (Raffles 1965 [1817], 15; Quilty 1998).

Margaret Wiener's examination of the clash between Dutch and Balinese ways of knowing implicit in the colonial conquest of territory and texts sheds further light on this kind of struggle over the possession of knowledge (Wiener 1995). Balinese still make use of historical texts, she says, "for aid in ritually 'remembering' their ancestors, persons transformed through death rituals into nonvisible agents. Such remembering is crucial to well-being, for 'forgetting' . . . is often diagnosed through healers as the cause of illness, dissension, and other misfortunes" (Wiener 1995, 78). For Europeans, on the other hand, vision, not memory, was "the primary trope for knowledge" (Wiener 1995, 76). Once the conquest of the island had been completed in 1908, the Dutch were routinely interested in only "statistics and regularities" (Wiener 1995, 90). But the texts that were looted from Klungkung and elsewhere reflected a world in which power was "inherently divided and dispersed" (Wiener 1995, 149) and in which competing individuals "acquired their power from differing sources." For the Balinese, the important question was, "There are many texts: which one is superior?" (Wiener 1995, 207). This attitude to knowledge is similar to the one that Peter Vandergeest thinks was held by peasants in prenational Buddhist states in Southeast Asia, where "notions of power were fragmented according to source and mode of access" (Vandergeest 1993, 851). For the authors of Javanese, Balinese, Malay, or Southern Thai *tamra* texts, it was the knowledge conveyed by, as well as the ritual uses and powerful attributes of, manuscripts that was important; for colonizing philologists and the regimes that employed them, it was the techniques of investigation and control acquired through such investigations that mattered most

(Foucault 1980, 102). It is not accidental that the detailed investigative reports on peasant uprisings and the early nationalist movement in the Netherlands Indies were written by trained Arabicists and Javanologists—men like Snouck Hurgronje, Hazeu, and Schrieke (T. Shiraishi 1990; Pramoedya 1992).

Hendrik Maier has argued in essays about the "creation" of official languages in the colonial and postcolonial periods in Indonesia that the general trend over the nineteenth and twentieth centuries was for what he calls "Authority" to transform the "hetero-glossia" of hybrid languages and knowledges, both native, white, and Eurasian, into a "polyglossia" of invented, purified, and discrete linguistic and cultural constructs called "Javanese," "Malay," and "Dutch" (Maier 1993, 1997b). Yet as Wiener has argued in an essay on the "politics of magic" in the Netherlands Indies, such tendencies were a response to the proliferation of hybridities that arose in the "contact zones" and "interstices" that were created by colonial rule (Wiener forthcoming; Bhabha 1994, 4, 38; Pratt 1992, 6–7). Purification gave rise to new hybridities in their turn.

> The various activities understood under the rubric "colonialism" —from the settling of territories to the extraction of wealth, from the administration of subject peoples to the deliberate reform of their ways of life—all involved interactions between Europeans and those they ruled. Minimally, these required some degree of mediation, of cultural and linguistic translation, however problematic the communications that resulted. Indeed such processes never occurred without friction, without the production of new forms of culture and the transformation of meanings and practices. Nor was the colonial work of mediation solely discursive. It included other forms of material relations, from the exchange of goods to sexual intercourse. The literature on colonialism makes increasingly obvious precisely how much hybridization occurred in colonial contact zones. . . . Yet at critical moments colonialism also entailed endless forms of purification, through which attempts were made to separate and distinguish subjects and phenomena. From living spaces and child-rearing to scientific racism, from sanitation works to the codification of customary laws, agents of colonialism tried to classify, discipline, and cleanse in the territories they administered. . . . [And yet] the work of purifi-

cation, the Cartesian work of analysis and critique, by constantly establishing new divisions, multiplies the sites where further hybridization is possible. (Wiener forthcoming, 16–18)

Thus the interaction between the state, languages, and knowledge in the colonial situation was not a linear one leading inevitably to the absolute dominance of "pure" and "official" forms, but a contested process in which hybrids were continually generated. The 1814 *Centhini* was itself a hybrid cosmological response to "the Cartesian work of analysis and critique" carried out by colonialists like Mackenzie and Raffles. As noted above, by the 1930s a century of philological and political "purification" led to new hybrids of "Javanese"/"Western" knowledge expressed in the mysterious life and prophecies of Ranggawarsita and the philosophy of the Taman Siswa movement. Maier offers another striking example of the process by which hybridity was generated by means of purification in his analysis of a 1940s Philips light bulb ad in Java in which the use of informal, spoken "Malay" in the text of the advertisement subverts the orderliness, stasis, and "whiteness" of the family scene depicted visually in the ad, as well as the "authorized," colonial "Indonesian" language used and promoted by the journal in which the ad appears (Maier 1997c, 191). Technological change in the Netherlands Indies spawned countless new forms of cultural hybridity, as it continues to do in Indonesia today (Mrázek 1997; Lindsay 1997; Sen and Hill 2000).

A "genealogical" history of knowledge and subject formation in the Indies colonial state, therefore, would pay attention to the day-to-day struggle over the absurd details of what it meant to be Javanese or Dutch, "modern" or "traditional," or a person who, like the nineteenth-century Javanese Christian Sadrach, was a new kind of hybrid located somewhere in-between (Guillot 1981; Day 1986). As Latour comments,

> Without the countless objects that ensured their durability as well as their solidity, the traditional objects of social theory—empire, classes, professions, organizations, States—become so many mysteries. . . . What, for example, is the size of IBM, or the Red Army, or the French Ministry of Education, or the world market? To be sure, these are all actors of great size, since they mobilize hundreds of thousands or even millions of agents. . . . However, if we

wander about inside IBM, if we follow the chains of command of the Red Army, if we inquire in the corridors of the Ministry of Education, if we study the process of selling and buying a bar of soap, we never leave the local level. . . . Could the macro-actors be made up of micro-actors. . . . The Red Army of an aggregate of conversations in the mess hall? The Ministry of Education of a mountain of pieces of paper? (Latour 1993, 121)

Peter Zinoman makes a similar remark with regard to the history of modern prisons in colonial Indochina. Contrary to what we might expect from Foucault's model of modern disciplinary punishment or Furnivall's depiction of the 1930s Southeast Asian state as a "Leviathan" (Furnivall 1991; cf. Rafael 1999, 10–12), the "technologies of power in Indochina—such as the prison system—were composed of diverse, countervailing elements which derived from the peculiarities of the colonial project and the enduring influence of pre-colonial traditions" (Zinoman 1999, 154).

Cornelis Fasseur's long study, "The Indologists: Bureaucrats for the East, 1825–1950" (1994), uncovers some of the miniscule and often ridiculous networks of bureaucratic activity and paperwork along which knowledge and power traveled to and from the Indies. Little did Ranggawarsita or other "natives" who were made to feel *minder*, that is, inferior, to arrogant Dutch taskmasters realize that from the time of Raffles until the end of the colonial period (if not beyond), Dutch officials and policymakers were themselves chronic sufferers of a cultural inferiority complex in relation to the English. The issue of "civilization" was the hegemonic cultural constraint that shaped both discourse and practice in colonial Java. It was Raffles who had "discovered" the natural gentlemanliness of the Javanese aristocracy and whose *History of Java* set the standard for Dutch scholarship on Indonesia in the nineteenth century (Forge 1994). As was the case for Dutch interest in Javanese and Balinese "antiquities," the inspiration and model for setting up institutes to provide future colonial bureaucrats with linguistic and other skills came from the British, who had established such institutions as the College at Fort William (1800) and Haileybury College (1809), both of which trained bureaucrats for service in India, as well as the Anglo-Chinese College in Malacca (1818) and the Malay College of Singapore (1823) (Fasseur 1994, 25–28, 60–61). In 1825–1826 the pros and cons of the English model were debated in the chambers of power in Batavia and The Hague. King William I, the minister for colonies, and the governor-general of the Indies all agreed that what was appealing about the selection and training of the British colonial official was that he was chosen from "the gentlemanly *(fatsoenlijken)* rank," his gentlemanliness further cultivated and enhanced through training in language and local knowledge. The result, according to Minister for Colonies J. C. Baud (1840–1848), was that the impression made on Asians by English bureaucrats was "none other than one of respect [*eerbied*] and admiration [*bewondering*], which explains the ease with which a people as populous as that of Hindustan is able to be kept in thrall by means which are small in comparison with their object" (Fasseur 1994, 47). On October 29, 1832, "Java received its Fort William" in the form of the Institute for the Javanese Language, Surakarta (Fasseur 1994, 62).

The decision to focus on Javanese and to found the first training school for colonial bureaucrats in the defunct capital of the old Central Javanese kingdom of Mataram was based on a mixture of practical needs, cultural prejudices, and Dutch national identity problems. The Javanese language was chosen partly because it had been selected by the Netherlands Bible Society, founded in 1814, again on a British model (that of the British and Foreign Bible Society [1804]), as the first Indonesian language to become a medium for the transmission of Holy Scriptures to the heathen; because the German Bible translator Johann Friederich Carl Gericke (1799–1857) had been sent to the Indies in 1827 and had settled in Surakarta, where the "best" Javanese was supposedly spoken; and because from there, with a view to using his pivotal role as a Javanese-language expert to advance the evangelical cause, Gericke was able to pressure the government in Batavia to found a training school in Surakarta (Fasseur 1994, 57–62). Also, colonial officials thought that Javanese was the language that those who would run the new Cultivation System needed to learn in order to make the system work (and the fewer the colonial administrators, the cheaper it would be to run). A deeper underlying reason for choosing Javanese was the one that echoed Minister Baud's admiration for the *fatsoenlijkheid,* or gentlemanliness, of the English and that contributed to the conceptualization of the ideal colonial bureaucrat as a man of "civilized habits and manners" (Fasseur 1994, 73). On April 14, 1841, the linguist Taco Roorda enunciated this reason when he delivered a speech before King William II in Amsterdam that helped pave the way for the establishment of a training course for colonial bureaucrats in Delft, where Roorda would be named Holland's first professor of Javanese. Roorda

> delivered a fiery address, in which, with argument after argument, he ridiculed the corrosive use of Malay in official dealings between the Dutch government and the [native] chiefs. Moreover, Malay for a Javanese was the language of the stranger, a language he despised. Not only did the use of Malay frequently lead to unfortunate misunderstandings, to speak to a Javanese in that language was, according to Roorda, "unstatesmanly," because it constantly reminded him of the foreign domination to which he was subjected. Most particularly, Malay was objectionable because it placed the person spoken to on the same footing as the speaker. It was "a language in which differences in rank and class were not expressed or considered," a feature so characteristic of Javanese. The Dutch bureaucrat who mastered Javanese would, in speaking to his Javanese interlocutor in Low Javanese, choose his words so as to make his superiority felt, while the Javanese, according to sanctified usage, should make use of High Javanese. (Fasseur 1994, 90 [my translation]; see also 1992b, 249)

The choice of Surakarta as the source of the purest Javanese, which was to be transmitted to colonial officials in a Western-style teaching institution to be located after 1842 in the Netherlands rather than in the colony, reenacted, on a pedagogical level, the same conquest of territory and knowledge that had taken place when Central Java was pacified in 1830 and Ranggawarsita was demoted from court poet to native informant. But who had ultimately conquered whom in Surakarta? As studies by John Pemberton (1994) and Laurie Sears (1996) have shown, the British and then Dutch colonial "invention" of Surakarta as the location of a vanquished yet still hegemonic, "high" aristocratic "civilization" had long-lasting, unintended consequences. "Surakarta" and its cosmological state legacies continued to influence state formation in extremely powerful ways after Indonesian independence. Surakarta was the place where Javanese radical nationalists were first impelled to contest the authority of the "Java" created by the authors of the *Serat Centhini* and by Ranggawarsita,

Taco Roorda, Mangkunegara VII, and others (T. Shiraishi 1990). Central Java was also selected by the Communist Party of Indonesia (PKI) in 1965 as the " 'model area' which would demonstrate the superiority of the PKI approach to development"; the heartland of colonial "Java" "was to be a sort of spiritual Yenan" for the PKI, as Ruth McVey puts it (1996, 113). Former president Suharto and his wife Ibu Tien completed the reconquest of this capital of a purely imaginary, authentic, all-powerful Javanese cultural homeland, assisted by several generations of philologists and anthropologists from the universities of Leiden and Cornell (Siegel 1986; Day 1982, 1983b; Pemberton 1994; Florida 1993, 1995; Brenner 1998). Suharto and his entourage of Western philologists and ethnologists were in reality "kissing the knee" of a phantasmatic but potent cosmological state of great antiquity.

Javanese was rejected as a language of state by the colonial regime for reasons that help explain the attraction of "purified" Javanese culture as a form of state power in New Order Indonesia. Almost from the beginning the Institute for the Javanese Language in Surakarta was criticized because it catered mainly to sons of Eurasians, who in large numbers were seeking positions in the lower ranks of the colonial bureaucracy during the expansive early years of the Cultivation System (Fasseur 1994, 65, 70–71, 118). These hybrid, "Indo" pupils were thought by "pure blood" officials, typically, to be congenitally unruly and "unscientifically" educated (by their largely Eurasian teachers) and were despised by their (pure-blood) classmates "born into a gentlemanly (*fatsoenlijk*) class" (Fasseur 1994, 65–67). In 1838, C. F. Winter, a Eurasian, was accused by a review committee of being unable to control his students, who lacked "moral guidance" (Fasseur 1994, 67). Fears also began to be voiced that a failure to learn perfect Javanese "with that tone, with that accent, that the gentlemanly Javanese wants to hear" would open the Dutch bureaucrat to ridicule and hence disrespect, an argument that resurfaced in 1872, when mandatory Javanese was dropped from the curriculum in "Indologie" at Leiden University (Fasseur 1994, 66, 267). From having regarded Surakarta Javanese as the linguistic medium sine qua non through which Dutch administrators could absorb a "pure" kind of Javanese cultural power for exercising political and economic dominance over Java (at low cost!), policymakers began to associate it with a dangerous hybridity that threatened to pollute another category that, as the century progressed, became even more essential for Dutch control: racial purity.

Not far beneath the surface of the debate about the Surakarta institute, which was closed in 1843, one year after the opening of the academy for colonial civil servants at Delft, was an old Dutch-male anxiety—which went back to the early days of the colony in the seventeenth century and became increasingly intense from the end of the nineteenth century onward, when pure-blood wives began to accompany their husbands to the Indies and establish "proper" European households—about loss of control to mixed-bloods, natives, and women (see J. Taylor 1983; Maier 1993; Stoler 1995b, especially 93–136). This anxiety was translated into the view that only the Europe-educated, proper Dutch-speaking, pure white (male) official could exercise authority and control, and only he could ever be a "gentleman." Minister Baud was particularly fearful of mixing the European and the "Indies-Polynesian" races, a miscegenation that would have "neither physically or morally happy results" (quoted in Fasseur 1994, 76). In 1851 Baud founded the Royal Institute for Linguistics, Geography, and Ethnography, dedicated, as he put it in his opening speech of June 4, 1851, not only to "pure research," but to guiding a "just, enlightened, and well disposed Government" (Baud 1853, 3). Racial and intellectual "purity" went hand in hand.

Stoler highlights the connection between the barring of racial and linguistic hybrids—that is, Eurasians with "native" language skills —from anything but the lowest levels of the colonial civil service and government concern with providing those very same linguistic skills to the "right" kind of candidate administrator: "At issue was obviously not whether civil servants knew local languages, but how those languages were learned and used and whether that knowledge was appropriately classified and controlled" (Stoler 1995b, 108). Anxiety about racial purity gave rise in turn to yet another kind of hybrid: a "shastra"-like colonial literature, "colonial guides to European survival 'at home' in the tropics" (Stoler 1995b, 109). Meanwhile, by the end of the nineteenth century, natives were exploring their own hybrid forms and concepts of "modern" domesticity, a subject left unexamined by Stoler (Pemberton 1994, 137–144; cf. Chakrabarty 1997).

The decision by the colonial state to maintain the purity of Javanese by relegating it to the hybrid world of Eurasians and natives was a form of cultural surrender to a submissive yet dangerous colonial subject, but it effectively excluded the language as a medium of transcultural exchange in Java during the colonial period. Javanese was also prevented from serving as a hybridizing language of cultural contact between Java and the West or as a language through which Javanese speakers could gain access to "modernity," even though at the level of popular usage in the late nineteenth and early twentieth centuries, there is every evidence that the boundaries between Javanese, Malay, and Dutch were fluid and permeable (Day 2001; Chambert-Loir 1984; Tickell 2002). The purifying effect of Dutch colonial policies on the development of Javanese is even reflected in the way in which the antistate, Javanese-peasant Samin movement in north Central Java, which has been active since the late nineteenth century, has attempted to purify Javanese words of their colonial, Islamic, "foreign" meanings (Widodo 1997). Colonial attitudes about Surakarta Javanese as the tongue of "high" civilization also carried over into postcolonial state doctrines about "correct" Indonesian. These dogmas, along with strikingly colonial-like policies that favored the preservation of what was "venerable" *(luhur)* and purely "traditional" *(asli)* over what was innovative, hybrid, and new, had a stultifying effect on the development of national culture during the thirty-two years of Suharto's rule.

But this is not to say that Javanese became totally subservient either to the New Order state or to the Indonesian language. In the 1980s and 1990s Javanese-Indonesian hybrids blossomed as a linguistic medium of opposition to the state (Foulcher 1987; Bodden 1996; Keeler 2002; Day 1999, 2001). In the Philippines, Singapore, and Thailand, where the purification of national languages was also carried out in the twentieth century, hybrid mixtures of Tagalog and English (i.e., Taglish), the reemergence of "counter-hegemonic" colloquial Tagalog in the Philippines as the language of intellectual discourse, the deliberate "slumming" use of Singapore English (Singlish), and non-Central Thai ways of speaking and printing Thai have all undermined the authority of "official" forms of linguistic expression (B. Anderson 1998, 235–262; Rafael 1995b; Hedman and Sidel 2000, 140–165; Lee Gek Ling 1994; Diller 1991). In Laos during the 1980s, people began resisting the purifying dress codes and normative speech demanded by the communist regime, opting for both sartorial and linguistic ways of asserting the diverse values of hierarchy

(G. Evans 1998, 86–87). Like knowledge, language has played both a purifying and hybridizing, a formative and deconstructive role in the history of the Southeast Asian state.

Knowledge: Talisman of "Primitive" Invulnerability or "Modern" Freedom?

> You are semen. White divinity. A clotted drop. Closed with a key. Fluid iron. Fluid semen. (Meratus Dayak spell for stopping bullets, told to Anna Tsing; Tsing 1993, 77)

Colonial regimes of truth, which assumed monolithic, bureaucratized form by way of thousands of petty strategems and conflicts, were no less universalizing than the state cosmologies in Southeast Asia that preceded and then overlapped with them. As we have seen in the case of colonial Java, Dutch truth and Javanese cosmology reinforced each other's hegemony in the minds of colonial agents in much the same way that science and Buddhism did in nineteenth-century Siam. The quality of shastric, totalizing authority and ethnographic completeness that we find in the *Serat Centhini* bears witness to the cosmological nature of that text in both a "traditional" and a colonial sense. But the *Serat Centhini* also contains a multitude of traces of another form of knowledge, what Foucault would call "subjugated knowledges" (Foucault 1980, 81–82), the array of competing and/or "inferior" concrete knowledges and skills possessed by experts of all kinds that form the historical content of the lists of rule-governed ways of knowing and acting that, in codified form, became more amenable to state and masculine control. Foucault calls these forms of knowledge popular, particular, local, and regional "differential" knowledges, "incapable of unanimity" (Foucault 1980, 82). We can also link the variegated knowledges presented in the *Serat Centhini* to the kind of "practical" knowledge or "cunning" that James Scott thinks has been progressively displaced by "scientific," standardized knowledge controlled by the modern state (J. Scott 1998).

But just how "subjugated" or "standaradized" are the knowledges surveyed in the *Serat Centhini?* On the one hand, the shastric regime that reduces all knowledge and experience to lists and precepts, together with the courtly ethos that pervades the text and explicitly ranks people, things, and experiences in a court-centric hierarchy, is clearly dominant. But it is not hegemonic (Guha 1997). As I have observed, there is plenty of sheer *jouissance* and irreverence, meandering, and exposition of kinds of knowledge that elude absolute categorization and control (Day and Derks 1999; B. Anderson 1990, 271–298; Kumar 1999). In his assessment of the struggle over the control of knowledge in rural New Order Java, Pemberton has recorded the survival of similar Javanese village "excesses," including belief in the efficacy of local spirits, in the face of New Order attempts to "modernize" and control the countryside (Pemberton 1994, 236–310). Although he clearly thinks that "the supernatural landscape of idiosyncracies" found in early nineteenth-century Java has been largely superceded by "a vast topography of monumental power" (Pemberton 1994, 276) under Suharto's rule, the evidence he presents is richly equivocal. As it has turned out, it is the New Order itself, rather than the plethora of local relations of power and identity that both constituted and resisted it, that has passed from the scene. As Latour remarks in his discussion of Hobbes' famous treatise, "The Leviathan is made up only of citizens, calculations, agreements or disputes. In short, it is made up of nothing but social relations" (Latour 1993, 28). Increased globalization and commercialization, moreover, appear to promise more rather than less "locality" of identity; we should not be surprised to find the same effects of globalization that have been noted elsewhere in Southeast Asia in Java as well (Appadurai 1996, 178–199; C. Reynolds 1998). Perhaps, as Guha argued, my own analysis of the *Serat Centhini* should have concentrated on the hybrid, state-resisting aspects of the text, on the effects of early nineteenth-century globalization, and on possibilities for developing a critical perspective on Foucault's notion of "subjugated knowledge," not to mention a thorough critique of the role of the state in Southeast Asian history.

Yet the sorts of knowledge found within the text have also been "subjugated" and rationalized according to shastric rules and in accordance with the ideology of the elite male authors who wrote the poem. The autonomy and subjugation of knowledge do not exist in antithetical states of total negation of one another, but in a process of struggle. It is not clear how complicit Javanese servants and masters have been in the formation of each other's places in the hierarchy of domination. By way of a few examples that follow, I want to conclude my discussion in this chapter by raising a more general question about the relationship between "subjugated" and cosmological forms of knowledge in Southeast Asia. Are they different or similar? How knowledge of both sorts relates to "modern" systems of knowledge in Southeast Asia is a further question I want to raise before bringing the chapter to a close.

Arguably the most important form of knowledge to be found throughout Southeast Asia at all levels of society and in any historical period is knowledge about "invulnerability." To borrow Anna Tsing's phrase, which echoes the argument and rhetoric of an essay by Charles Tilly (1985), Southeast Asian states themselves are "protection rackets" in worlds where violence, disease, and the sheer insecurity of being on one's own have exercised a powerfully determinant effect in bringing about and sustaining the formation of states (Tsing 1993, 96; McKenna 1998, 61–62; Aung-Thwin 1985, 82; R. C. Morris 2000, 66). The following quotation from Nicola Tannenbaum's study of tattoos, invulnerability, and power among the Shan in northern Thailand sketches the benign face of protection, one that conforms to a widely held assumption in Southeast Asia about the "proper" role of power and hence of the state:

> The proper behavior for beings with power is to be benevolent to their followers and to use their power to protect and aid their dependents, contingent on their dependents' proper behavior. . . . Beings with power provide their dependents with access to it. This power is primarily protective and passive. (Tannenbaum 1987, 703)

Tannenbaum shows specifically how knowledge about tattoos is used to create a "safe inner area surrounded by a barrier that keeps out dangers and evils" for the Shan wearer (Tannenbaum 1987, 703). Shan tattoos cause spirits and people to "treat the bearer with loving kindness," thus creating protective bonds and dependencies that bring people together in a way that transforms the "fear" of danger and insecurity into "respect" for the dominance of the powerful (Tannenbaum 1987, 696, 704). My sense is that, looking at Southeast Asian history as a whole, a culture of "security," conceived as a kind of "freedom," has been, and continues to be, the dominant constraint on the form and role of the state in Southeast Asian societies (Reid 1999, 143). As Wolters has remarked of "*maṇḍala* times," the effect of the "overlord's prowess would [be to] enlarge his *maṇḍala*'s sphere of influence and, ripple-like, persuade distant centers to seek his 'protection' " (Wolters 1999, 217). If this or similar statements could be made about the appeal of states during the whole course of Southeast Asian history, then we should look for state-forming tendencies in a wide variety of situations where "invulnerability" is at stake.

Examples of the connection between power, knowledge, invulnerability, and state-forming tendencies abound. The quotation at the beginning of this section, which suggests that male prowess and magical knowledge can transform an enemy's bullet into the amulet-possessor's potency and survival, is Tsing's translation of a spell spoken by a Meratus Dayak shaman to ward off bullets. It had protected him during conflicts of the late 1950s, its "secret words" also serving to create bonds of "masculine trust" with other Meratus as well as Banjar males (Tsing 1993, 77). In twelfth-century Sumatra, Buddhists studied the "Peacock" *sūtra* to learn "talismanic formulae . . . for protection against dangers" (Wolters 1983, 53). In contemporary northern Thailand, collections of verbal formulae *(katha)*, some of which are hundreds of years old and written in Burmese ("the language of a once conquering polity") make villagers invulnerable *(kham)* to the manifold dangers of subordination (Turton 1991; Tambiah 1984, 195–289). As Andrew Turton notes, erotic and martial magic is the chief form of knowledge described and repeatedly used by the characters of the Siamese folk epic *Khun Chang Khun Phaen,* a tale in which "the contrasting careers of the main characters highlight the importance of royal patronage for livelihood, protection, justice, and relief from the dangers of life" (Pasuk and Baker 1995, xv). The acquisition of *kham* stimulates "strong desires for individual enhancement, for acquiring special abilities and capacities" (Turton 1991, 163; Vandergeest 1993). But personal invulnerability also offers protection to those without it, thrusting the possessor of *kham* inevitably into the role of "teaching and sharing knowledge, and mobilizing others" (Turton 1991, 171). This process sounds very similar to the one Wolters describes in early Southeast Asia, when "men of prowess" who devoted themselves to Śiva attracted followers who "could come to realize that obedience to their leader was a gesture of homage that implied religious *rapport,* or *bhakti*" (Wolters 1999, 22). Wandering monks in Northeast Thailand helped the state and official Buddhism "develop" the region in the 1930s and 1940s by successfully persuading villagers to overcome their fear of local spirits and seek refuge in the teachings of Theravada Buddhism (Kamala 1997, 198–225). The knowledge deployed by adherents of the Buu Son Ky Huong religion in the "wild" southwest of Vietnam in the middle of the nineteenth century displayed similar characteristics that suggest the state-forming potential in the power of invulnerability:

> The apostles knew some magic and could perform healing, either with traditional medicine or through thaumaturgy. Some were geomancers who could be entrusted with the task of deciding where to locate new settlements. They knew ways of protecting the pioneers against wild beasts, had organizing abilities, and offered their own example of hard and selfless work. (Tai 1983, 16)

The Passion (Tagalog *Pasyon*) ideology of revolutionary movements in the Tagalog region of the Philippines at the end of the nineteenth century, derived from a native interpretation of Christ's suffering and death, also offered invulnerability and membership in a new "state," since it made a connection between the knowledge *(dunong)* attainable through participation in revolution and a state of "relief from pain, sickness or difficulties" *(kaginhawaan)*, "bodily pleasure" *(layao)*, and "freedom" *(laya)* (Ileto 1979, 102–122, 161–195). In his study of animist beliefs in the Visayan region of the Philippines between the sixteenth and early twentieth centuries, Alfred McCoy stresses the basis in fear of the loyalty shown to leaders who possessed powers of healing and invulnerability (McCoy 1982). In Bali and Malaysia the fear of "covert violence" through black magic is a major determinant in everyday life (Wikan 1990, 210–229; Peletz 1997, 263), which is why, during the 1960s, Indonesian soldiers posted to East Timor frequented Balinese masters in the magic of invulnerability *(balian kebal;* Connor 1995b). In seventeenth-century southern Thailand, a region prone to frequent attack by "pirates" from Johore, Aceh and Aru, *tamra* texts, written in Khmer script and containing passages of ornate language that gave voice to the authority of the distant king of Ayutthaya, protected the rights and freedoms of various Buddhist temples and the kin groups and lands associated with their upkeep (Gesick 1995). In contemporary Thailand and Singapore, popular stories from the third-century B.C.E. Chinese *The Romance of the Three Kingdoms* furnish the reader with "special powers" that promise survival and success in the raging wars of business and political life (C. Reynolds 1996, 145; Romance 2000).

Although the examples given above are a miscellaneous sampling of a very large and diverse range of sources from Southeast Asia, they share certain features in common. Notwithstanding the secrecy and procedures of ritual initiation that often govern access to particular fragments of knowledge in particular times and places, the knowledge of invulnerability is in fact accessible to all participating members of a Southeast Asian community. The Javanese homeowner can learn the secrets of the thief from the same printed *primbon* (Quinn 1975); the Siamese slave and king resorted to the same magic to ward off danger; the Tagalog *ilustrado* and the common peasant modeled their revolutionary aspirations on the same *Pasyon*. Anyone can learn the cunning survival skills of the heroes of *The Romance of the Three Kingdoms* (C. Reynolds 1996, 146). The knowledge of invulnerability in Southeast Asia is not the ideological preserve of a certain class, to be used exclusively as an instrument of class domination. It is directly concerned with relations of power, but its function is to assist the knowledgeable to exercise power, make it protective, or elude it. Such powerful knowledge also attracts adherents who form communities of the "protected." It is a state-forming kind of knowledge.

If we compare Angkor Wat or Suharto's mysticotechnological New Order to a Javanese thief's manual or an amulet from a Tagalog insurrectionary movement, what would the significant differences be? In all cases knowledge is transcultural and hybrid in the sense that it draws on knowledge about the natural and social worlds, both local and foreign. In all cases knowledge is cosmological and universalizing in its claim to control time, space, and power for both offensive and defensive purposes. In all cases knowledge acts as a talisman of invulnerability that transforms the bearer and those who seek the protection of the same talismanic sphere of influence into a "state" of well-being. What really differentiates one invulnerable "state" from the next is scale, rather than ideological and technological differences between, say, "Indic statecraft" and "German technology," animist religion and "science, " "modernity" and "tradition." For all of their massive size and dominance, neither Angkor Wat nor the New Order remained dominant and in control of their respective "protection rackets" forever, and many a wily peasant has remained invulnerable to, even thrived within, their seemingly timeless, authoritarian regimes of control (J. Scott 1990). The category of "subjugated knowledge" in Foucault's sense, therefore, disappears from view in Southeast Asia. Local knowledges continue to offer the lowly what Vandergeest calls a "creative power" that can never be entirely controlled or destroyed by a temporarily dominant state (Vandergeest 1993).

What happens to the issue of knowledge, invulnerability, and the state when we examine it in the context of the struggle for "modernity" in twentieth-century Southeast Asia? This is a very large question, but I want to raise it here briefly in order to suggest the outlines of an argument that has great relevance to the ideas I have been developing in this chapter.

Students of nationalism and modernization in Southeast Asia record attempts by intellectual elites to escape the subjugation of traditional beliefs and colonial rule through the acquisition of "true" and "modern" forms of knowledge. Vietnamese intellectuals during the 1920s and 1930s, for example, attacked familyism, determinism, and superstitition and embraced science, dialectical materialism, and information of all kinds about the world beyond Vietnam (Marr 1981, 327–367). David Marr comments that, as of 1977, the state's list of superstitions to be eliminated was still active and long. It included "fortune-telling, astrology, physiognomy, necromancy, going into trances, drawing lots before idols, making amulets, exorcism, worshipping ghosts, burning incense or sacrificial paper articles for spirits, and treating diseases with witchcraft" (Marr 1981, 366). The Malay intellectual and journalist Mohd. Eunos Abdullah received a Western-style education and formulated a modern political vocabulary in Malay during the 1920s so that his readers could think of themselves as "rational," "individual" "citizens" who "work" in a "nation-state" rather than as unthinking "subjects" of a "kingdom" (Milner 1995, 89–135). In the Gayo region of northern Sumatra, "much of the religious poetry written in the 1930s and 1940s argues that knowledge [of orthodox Islam and its practices] is required for acceptable worship, since only with knowledge can one formulate the correct intent for each act of worship" (Bowen 1997, 166). One Gayo poem criticizes the kind of praying carried out by those who seek an "invulnerability spell" ("from the *takbîr* all the way to the *salam*, his heart flies and shakes") as not "effective," according to the Prophet Muhammad

(Bowen 1997, 170). For Suharto and his New Order officials, "the source of true knowledge" lay "in the scientific knowledge and expertise of advanced capitalist societies" (McVey 1995a, 26). And for the Thai Marxist Jit Poumisak, true knowledge of the past was only accessible through the application of "scientific" Marxist historical analysis. As Jit wrote:

> In the saktina [feudal] age the struggle of the peasant class was manifest in the form of revolts or the flaring up of peasant disturbances. But time and time again the peasant struggle met with defeat: defeat at the hands of the law which was the instrument for safeguarding the profits of the Land-Lord class and defeat at the hands of the repressive powers of the Land-Lord class which was firmly and systematically entrenched. The causes of the defeats of the peasant class lay in its economic condition. The system of independent production kept individuals scattered here and there, each living off his own plot, and this prevented peasants from developing habits which would allow them to organize themselves systematically and unify their power. This was one factor. Another was the philosophy of life propounded by the saktina class to delude the peasants into believing that human beings could not thwart the destiny their merit decreed. Life was subject to merit, karma, and fate, and this aroused in the majority of peasants, who had no capital to fall back on, feelings of dejection, apathy, and despair. Thus the peasant struggles which erupted took the form of disturbances (MOB) which lacked tenacity, preparation, and organization, and which even lacked proper leadership. Such circumstances inevitably doomed these struggles to defeat. (C. Reynolds 1987, 54)

This is not the place to engage fully with Jit's analysis of Thai history. But one can observe that the "modern" categories in this passage, which define what is "true" about the past and lay the purifying ideological groundwork for the building of a revolutionary state, are presented in an argument that is as sweeping, as "universalizing," as that of the Three Worlds cosmology or the preachings of a messianic *phu mi bun* (man of merit; Murdoch 1974). Modern Thai elite notions and practices of *siwilai*, or being "civilized," are also a cosmological hybrid of ancient Tai and modern European concepts (Thongchai 2000). McVey has reminded us that in Indonesia,

Marxism was also "scientific" and so (given modern assumptions) superior to theories that could not make that claim. In addition, the Indonesian word for science, *ilmu,* is also the word for mystical knowledge, and had the resonance of recondite truth. The difficulty of Marxist philosophy, the need for study and for submission to a leadership adept in the thought, was something that could be accepted by people of strong mystical traditions. Hence, what seem on the surface to be among the most forbidding aspects of Marxism-Leninism actually made it more recognizable and powerful. (McVey 1996, 98)

Thus the more closely we examine forms of purely "modern" knowledge in Southeast Asia, the more hybrid and hybridizing many of them appear to be. In his discussion of the Gayo poem about prayer and invulnerability quoted above, John Bowen remarks that the poet makes no comment on the propriety or effectiveness of magic spells as such (Bowen 1997, 170). The development of Gayo "notions of religion as a scripture-based set of practices" has relied on and stimulated another "set of discourses that gives social and moral value to transactions with spirits" (Bowen 1993, 329–330). In modern Vietnam, "Ho Chi Minh," writes Marr,

was also intimately aware of a number of less orthodox teachings and stories which downgraded determinism almost entirely in favor of 'willpower' *(y, chi),* the capacity of certain individuals to overcome the worst historical odds, sometimes by magical means. Often Taost in origin, these ideas were deeply embedded in Vietnamese folklore and popular fiction. (Marr 1981, 355)

Hồ Chí Minh also made use of "the universalism of old concepts" to formulate his notion of "the great unity under heaven" in its new meaning of "the world revolution" (Lockhart 1989, 54–55). In the 1930s, Sumatran dime novels *(roman picisan)* fictionalized the adventures of Tan Malaka, the fervent Muslim-Marxist revolutionary from Minangkabau, casting him as the Scarlet Pimpernel (Pacar Merah) (Oshikawa 1990). This was the same Tan Malaka who wrote an autobiographical treatise while in jail during 1947–1948 in which he analyzed the "rise and fall of states" according the ideas of Engels and Marx (Malaka 1991, 45–55). In the Pacar Merah stories, packed with information about the world that "introduced a new dimension of space and time divorced from the controlled reality of colonial life" (Malaka 1991, 30), modernity works its magic to reproduce old concepts of male prowess and hierarchy (Siegel 1997, 172–173):

> The Scarlet Pimpernel always comes across enemies in his travels and is in constant danger. Yet there is an enviable quality of freedom in his adventures, a freedom he zealously maintains through the artifices of disguise and magical transformation. He possesses the supernatural ability to break out of the seemingly closed space of reality. His magical abilities are the Scarlet Pimpernel's most potent weapon and the source of his mystical aura. (Oshikawa 1990, 33)

In 1960s Indonesia, Communist leaders, while "striving for respectability and advancement" in modern Jakarta, were constrained by the realities of life in the countryside to reinterpret rather than replace "traditional" puppets and stories in their reform of the shadow-puppet theatre (McVey 1986, 37). The most refined puppets came to stand for the common man in an abstract, mythologized sense, which was "a hybrid, combining assumptions of socialist realism with the representational techniques of the *wayang purwa*" (McVey 1986, 37). McVey also quotes from Javanese Communist leader Sudisman's final statement, made when he was condemned to death in 1967, in which he compared himself and the four other members of the core party leadership to the five Pāndawa brothers, inseperable in the name of both "Communist solidarity" and ancient Javanese-Indic belief in the face of death (McVey 1986, 21). No less fervent and hybrid a declaration of modern truth came from the pen of the Javanese Muslim Communist H. Mohammad Misbach in 1926:

> Hai, brothers! Know this! I am a person who professes to be faithful to Religion and also enters the field of the communist movement. I also acknowledge that my thinking with regard to the truth of the commands of the Islamic Religion became more and more opened wide only after I studied the science [*ilmoe*] of communism. Therefore I now dare to say that the welfare of this world has been in chaos up to the present because of the devils of capitalism and imperialism with their cruel spirit. Because of them not merely our well-being and our freedom-of-life in this

world are being ruined but even our belief in Religion. (quoted in
T. Shiraishi 1990, 297)

These examples of "modern" knowledge in action in Southeast
Asia clearly suggest areas of intersection and overlap between state
cosmologies, spells of invulnerability, and ideas drawn from Western
modernity. In turning to new forms of knowledge in order to express
concepts of "freedom" from colonial domination, Southeast Asians
articulated hybrid concepts in which older notions of collective
safety mingled with newer ideas of risk-taking individual action and
freedom in search of states of well-being. They thus resemble the
cosmologies and the encyclopedic *Serat Centhini*, examined earlier in
the chapter, in which "freedom" is ultimately a "state" of invulnerability in a dangerous world.

Summary

Rather than understand state cosmologies in Southeast Asia as one
"pure" form of dominant knowledge, on the one hand, to be resisted
and opposed by quite different, but equally "pure," ideas about invulnerability or scientific "rationality" on the other, I have argued in
this chapter that we should think about the common features and
hybrid combinations of all three forms of knowledge in the context
of networks of agents, ideas, and power relations in Southeast Asia.
One of the most important of these hybrids is talismanic knowledge
that acts as a source of both cosmic dominance and daily survival, a
key to a kind of "freedom" that still makes sense in modern Southeast Asia today. The magic of the cosmological state in Southeast
Asia can still transform Americans into "ramifications of an indefi-
nitely extended 'famili' " in New Order Jakarta (B. Anderson 1990,
192) and create the illusion that the minority Khmu are vassal/citizens
in the contemporary Lao kingdom/nation-state (Trankell 1999, 210).
But can it also protect Singapore residents of subsidized housing
from the ghosts that continue to haunt these structures of domestication, challenging the state's "hegemony of pragmatism" (R. Lee 1989;
Chua 1997a, 20; 1997b)? In any case, why haven't the vestiges of
older cosmological orders in Southeast Asia been eradicated by the
"rational, modern, bureaucratic state"?

4
Bureaucracy, Reason, and Ritual

The answer to the question I asked at the end of the last chapter is embedded in another one: How do bureaucracies, "rationality," and ritual interact and inform state practices in Southeast Asia? "Ritual" and "rationality" have appeared as terms in chapters 2 and 3, but their significance for understanding the state in Southeast Asia has yet to be fully examined. My starting point here is the fact that it is difficult to map a linear, Weberian model of patrimonial patron-clientage leading to rational-legal bureaucracy on to actual historical processes in the region. Weber himself probably could not have imagined the typical Southeast Asian situation in which warrior-kings or military strongmen are at the same time rational and successful entrepreneurs who are able to sit still for hours at formal, ritualized events (cf. Weber 1951, 25). "Rationality" itself, I will argue, is in any case not a "pure" category, but a highly variable, context-specific mode of practice in Southeast Asia, as it is everywhere in the world (Adams 1999, 117). For the purposes of my discussion, "rationality" and "bureaucracy" in quotation marks will signify the Weberian variants of these inherently plural terms.

The Myth of the "Rational," "Bureaucratic" Southeast Asian State

Scholars of Southeast Asia, however, remain faithful to Weber's own typology of a succession of political formations through world-historical time in their desire to make "bureaucracy" and "rationalization" properties of the history of the modernization of Southeast Asia. Even before the advent of modernity, according to historians of

the sixteenth, seventeenth, and eighteenth centuries, the centralization of states went hand in hand with "administrative reform" (Lieberman 1984, 1993; Reid 1993, 261). Implicit in such accounts is the
assumption that we are looking at precursors to the more successfully "bureaucratized" states of the nineteenth and twentieth centuries, rather than altogether different types of state formation with an
alternative future. But can we be sure of finding Weberian concepts
and institutions in Southeast Asia even in the modern period?

The authors of the best-known history of Southeast Asia in the
nineteenth and twentieth centuries, *In Search of Southeast Asia* (Steinberg 1987), are certain they can. They explicitly link "bureaucratic
frameworks" and the modernization of the region. In their view of
the overall nature of bureaucratic change during this period, the
"bureaucratization" of Southeast Asia began at the end of the nineteenth century, with the arrival of colonial administrators (and the
modernizing Siamese king Chulalongkorn and his brothers) on the
scene. These men planted the "germ of change" (Steinberg 1987, 205).
The new bureaucratizers discouraged traditional elites from using
"ceremonial appurtenances" (Steinberg 1987, 205), and their efforts
were encouraged by "rapid economic change or large populations"
that called for "increasingly complex administrative methods" (Steinberg 1987, 206). In the early twentieth century, Southeast Asians
themselves were increasingly brought into the new bureaucratic
frameworks. The authors of *In Search of Southeast Asia* are struck by
"the plain courage of many Southeast Asians in the early twentieth
century who . . . accepted the premises of modern bureaucratic government—so alien to their own political culture" (Steinberg 1987, 209).

It is interesting, in light of such statements, to consider actual
examples of bureaucracy in modern Southeast Asia and to learn how
divergent these were from the model set forth in *In Search of Southeast
Asia*. The Southeast Asian administrations that developed in the
colonial nineteenth and twentieth centuries, contrary to what we are
led to expect, exhibited a hybrid mixture of characteristics, some of
them "cosmological" in the mode of early Southeast Asian states (see
Heine-Geldern 1956; Tambiah 1976, 132–158; Prapañca 1995; Mabbett
1977) or "familial," again in what historians usually associate with
"premodern" state forms (Vickery 1985; Sidel 1997), even though
there was undoubtedly growing pressure over the course of
this period to "rationalize" bureaucratic structures and practices in

response to the needs of an increasingly territorialized and exploitative state system (Butcher 1993; R. Taylor 1987, 66–147; Englehart 2001, 93–102; Vandergeest and Peluso 1995). In a bureaucratic state formation such as that of the Netherlands Indies in the 1920s and 1930s, for example, the white elite in the highest offices had been striving feverishly ever since the late nineteenth century ("living, eating and sleeping with pen in hand," to quote one critical colonial observer [Couperus 1985, 74, quoted in Rush 1990, 125]) to work by "rational-legal" norms. One of their signal successes was the preservation of older, family-oriented cultural beliefs and practices among the native elites who occupied bureaucratic positions lower down in the hierarchy, in the name of protecting "traditional" Indonesian "customs" (*adat*), but also white colonial rule itself in the face of nationalist agitation. Such a bureaucracy can hardly be said to exhibit a Weberian "pure rationality," although the rationality of a particular colonial "reason of state" was clearly at work (Sutherland 1979, 159; Foucault 1991b). Sociologist J. C. van Leur, writing to a friend from Tulungagung in East Java in 1935 during his tour of duty as a colonial civil servant, puzzled over the "rationality" of the Indies colonial bureaucracy of his day in a way that echoes Marx's critique of Hegel's concept of the state, in which Marx proclaimed that bureaucracy was an insidious "illusion of the state" (Tucker 1978, 23; Lefort 1986, 112; Day 1984):

> You must read Weber's characterization of bureaucracy some time. . . . The Indies bureaucracy is almost an ideal-type. . . . From institution to institution rolls every matter: everything ends up in the right place, through the laws peculiar to the system. For every action there is an instruction. . . . Always the slow pavane of the bureaucratic style, the magic of formulae and file numbers, the allegrettos of marginal annotations. As a gigantic mountain this bureaucracy waits for me, with its bureaucratic "thinking" (as such something completely different from scientifically based "knowledge" in general!). On Java, the BB [*Binnenlands Bestuur*, the white colonial civil service] has no more power. Diarchy is the rule [note: van Leur here refers to the unsuccessful liberal policy of "de-tutelization" of the native administrative corps adopted in 1918; see Sutherland 1979, 81 passim], even

though the status of the BB uniform is still high. I have been in regions where I rode like a knight on horseback along the road. . . . This situation is now in the process of breaking apart, but the power of this tradition can be measured by what still persists. (van Leur 1957, 277–278)

As H. Benda has argued (1966), in the highly bureaucratized, Orientalizing, and interventionist *beamtenstaat* of the 1930s Netherlands Indies, the apotheosis of the panoptic state depicted in Pramoedya Ananta Toer's novel *House of Glass* (1992), "sound administration" was dedicated to the fragmentation and retraditionalization of Indonesian society (see also Robinson 1995). This state was also responsible for the composition of endless pavanes and allegrettos of memoranda and reports, a ritualistic exchange of paperwork that suggests nothing more strikingly than the ceremonial handling of diplomatic letters, monastic records, and court documents in "traditional" Southeast Asia (Reid 1993, 235–236; Gesick 1995; Mannikka 1996, 125; Drakard 1999).

Indeed, models of modern Southeast Asian state formation such as Riggs' "bureaucratic polity" (1966) or Benda's *beamtenstaat* (1966) reveal the seemingly perverse irrationality and curious nonfunctionality of bureaucratic state organization in modern Southeast Asia. In these models, Weberian "rules" and "rationality" are bent to accommodate, in the case of Thailand, an older, "patrimonial" kind of patron-client politics, and in the case of Indonesia, the myth of a certain kind of modernity that can only be implemented by an entrenched, faction-ridden administrative elite. As reexamined by Ruth McVey (1982), the Indonesian colonial *beamtenstaat* and its postcolonial New Order avatar, state formations to which she also applies the label "bureaucratic polity," represent the institutionalization of a certain "myth" of "modernity" in which "society's peace and prosperity rested above all on organizational, technical, and economic expertise. Administration must therefore take command over politics" (McVey 1982, 87). Both the bureaucratic polity and the *beamtenstaat* are antidemocratic and nonmodernizing, since they serve the interests of elites and myths rather than "modernity"; they foster elite self-interest in the name of such shibboleths as "development" (see Heryanto 1988) rather than the modernization of society as a whole, carried out democratically with the help of genuine "experts." McVey's characterization of the "bureaucratic polity" is worth quoting at length:

> When an agrarian society evolves—either from its own traditions or a colonial experience—an elite which is almost wholly employed in or dependent on the bureaucracy, a business class that is weak (and most likely alien), and a passive peasantry, it is likely to assume this state. The bureaucracy modernizes enough to rout any traditional rivals and secure a firm grip on the state. It then, however, ceases to move in a modernizing direction. . . . Moreover, because it is the locus of power and of wealth (through its control of licenses and permissions, secured by a carefully nurtured statism), it becomes the arena for all meaningful political action. Real politics takes place not in parliament or whatever organs may exist outside the bureaucracy, but in the government apparatus itself. . . . Because the bureaucracy is the arena for politics, it cannot function effectively as an executive arm; it cannot be battlefield, commander, and soldier all at once. Because positions and criteria for advancement are not what they formally seem, an official's real status depends not on his formal title but on securing wealth, clients, and favor; and (quite aside from display requirements in a changing and increasingly materialistic society) this means utilizing the economic possibilities of one's position to the full. Hence the "commercialization of office" that is now a chronic Indonesian complaint. Because the bureaucracy cannot administer effectively, its social role becomes largely parasitic and its members, if ever they entered with the idea of achieving anything, soon slip into the prevailing inertia. The bureaucracy thus becomes alienated functionally from the population at large, in addition to the distance created by differences in wealth, power, and cultural westernization. (McVey 1982, 88)

The underlying assumption in the model of the bureaucratic polity is that the "reason" of state and of state bureaucracy in the modern era ought to be different from that which guided other bureaucratic formations throughout the region over many centuries. Somehow this "reason" has failed to take effect. As ineffective as modern Southeast Asian bureaucracies may have been or continue to be by ideal Weberian standards, however, the words "alienated" and "inertial" do not help us understand why the bureaucracy of Java increased five-hundredfold between the late nineteenth century and today (compared to a sixfold increase in population), or why that of Burma grew 89.6 percent for a population that increased only 32 percent between 1962 and 1974 (Emmerson 1978, 85; R. Taylor 1987, 310). Something significant in a cultural as well as a social and economic sense occurred in Java and Burma to produce these statistics, but it will not be clear what, unless we put the "bureaucratic polity" in historical context and try to understand the kinds of meaning people in Southeast Asia have attached to participation in bureaucracies over the centuries.

Such an investigation is called for especially since the definition of the "bureaucratic polity" has begun to blur. Fifteen years after first publishing her essay on the *beamtenstaat*, McVey shifted her perspective on the "bureaucratic polity" when she joined other commentators on Southeast and East Asian economic development in arguing that Southeast Asian bureaucracy has been in fact an engine, rather than an ox cart, of capitalist development (see the essays in McVey 1992b; on East Asia see Haggard 1990; Wade 1990; Weiss and Hobson 1995). As she restates the issue:

> From our present vantage-point the features of the bureaucratic polity—its inwardness, the indeterminacy of its institutions, its lack of direction—have less the aspect of a developmental bog than of a container for fundamental transformation, a chrysalis in whose apparently confused interior the change from one sort of socio-economic order to another was taking place. For it has now become clear that there is increasing intimacy and equality between business and political leadership, and that members of the indigenous power elite are playing serious business roles. (McVey 1992a, 22)

This quotation from McVey echoes passages from the work of Anthony Reid and others on Southeast Asian state entrepreneurialism in the sixteenth and seventeenth centuries. In the midst of capitalist, globalized contemporary Southeast Asia, we are still in a world of powerful kinship networks, their allies, and clients, who use a combination of brains, control over the bureaucratic institutions of the state, and physical violence to accumulate capital and power. McVey and her colleagues have challenged the supposed isolation of the Southeast Asian bureaucratic state from its surrounding social context (cf. B. Anderson 1990, 94–120), reembedding the state within a matrix of socioeconomic activity. But it is only by assuming that a certain kind of "rationality" and a need for bureaucratic forms of organization are necessary to or will automatically spring from the development of capitalism that one can make Weberian sense out of a situation in which advanced capitalism and old-fashioned "patrimonialism" continue to enjoy a predominantly happy symbiosis. And none of the studies in McVey's 1992 volume, her own essay included, provide historical depth to the analysis of the contemporary Southeast Asian bureaucratic state.

One of the difficulties in unraveling the bureaucratic riddle in Southeast Asia is the assumption that "modernity" entails a radical break with the past (Latour 1993). Scholarship on modern bureaucracy in other parts of the world is helpful here because it challenges this assumption (Herzfeld 1992; Lefort 1986). Claude Lefort is particularly suggestive about the Southeast Asian case as he attempts to answer the question that forms the title to his essay, "What is Bureaucracy?" Lefort speaks of the tendency for "clans" to form within modern bureaucracies. These family-like groupings engage "in a covert war between departments which is constantly nourished by their separation, each one rushing to blame the other for errors or delays in carrying out a programme" (Lefort 1986, 108; cf. Herzfeld 1992, 181). The result of such warfare is the constitution of bureaucracy "as a rich and differentiated milieu [that] acquires an existence for itself" (Lefort 1986,108). This picture of bureaucracies as battlegrounds of competing "families" preoccupied with their own power struggles rather than with the interests of society as a whole is similar to Marx's understanding and to McVey's definition of the "bureaucratic polity," but it also fits descriptions we have of bureaucratic processes ranging from eleventh-century Cambodia (Vickery 1985) to nineteenth-century Thailand (Wyatt 1994, 98–130) to twentieth-century Indonesia and the Philippines (B. Anderson 1990, 94–120; 1998, 192–226).

In another suggestive passage, one that is reminiscent of van Leur's depiction of Dutch Indies bureaucratic practice in the 1930s, Lefort suggests that "modern Western bureaucracies" are susceptible to ritualization. He writes:

The efficacy of bureaucratic work can thus be assessed in terms of the capacity of officials to preserve and extend the field of activity which they organize. But this assessment can be formulated in objective (shareable) terms only if one considers the formal aspect of the activity of the bureaucrat—the fetishism of the agenda at the regular assemblies of the party, the multiplicity of reunions, meetings, celebrations or commemorations, the existence of what could be called "activism": a feverish and vain agitation which has become routine. The number and diversity of ceremonies from which the institution draws its daily justification goes hand in hand with the proliferation of bureaucrats. (Lefort 1986, 112)

Does the suggestion that, even in the West, ritual is an important component of bureaucratic practices have any application to Southeast Asia? In studies of modern Southeast Asia, the characteristic approach to the question of ritual is to treat it as an expression of "unreason," as a form of mystification that masks the real workings of the state (e.g., Pemberton 1994). In their introduction to a collection of essays on religion and modern states in Southeast Asia, Charles Keyes, Laurel Kendall, and Helen Hardacre link "rational action" to "modernization," while "commitment of faith" and the reinvention of ritual is associated with the mystifying process of "nation-building" engaged in by the state (Keyes, Kendall, and Hardacre 1994). The editors assert that the "tension between these two stances as well as that between each of them and those religious practices that derive their authority from other than the state have contributed to the crisis of authority" in contemporary Southeast Asia (Keyes, Kendall, and Hardacre 1994, 5–6). States have engaged in the "ritual displacement" of authority from religious communities to the state, even though "ritual and magical symbols continue to hold great appeal even in highly rationalized social orders" outside the state sphere because they represent a "cosmic order" that transcends the imperfect "contingent ideals of particular political systems" (Keyes, Kendall, and Hardacre 1994, 6–10). As I have already suggested in chapter 3, "modern" nation-states in Southeast Asia are themselves "cosmic blueprints" in the manner Keyes, Kendall, and Hardacre reserve for religious movements in opposition to the state. Their argument also begs the question of the nature and role of rationality in religion and in other areas of social practice not reducible to "modernization" in a (Weberian) Western sense. But they do identify ritual as an important state activity in contemporary Southeast Asia in a way that invites attention.

Comparable doubts can also be raised about treatments of the seemingly "revolutionary" impact of conversions to certain world religions in an earlier period of Southeast Asian history. In a discussion titled "A Religious Revolution," from his two-volume work on the "age of commerce" (1450–1680), Reid argues that conversions to Islam and Christianity in Southeast Asia during the sixteenth and seventeenth centuries entailed "a major step towards what Weber characterized as rationalization of religion," a "new world-view" that "provided the necessary foundation" for engagement with "a wider world of international trade, of large-scale state operations" (Reid 1993, 159). Elsewhere, however, Reid links the development of "bureaucratic and legal institutions" most especially to centralized, "absolutist" government in the seventeenth century (Reid 1993, 260–262). By his own account, the "bureaucracies" of seventeenth-century Southeast Asia owed their rationality to factors other than religious ones. Nor has the participation of Southeast Asian societies in international trade, which was happening long before the sixteenth and seventeenth centuries, ever depended on religious conversion as distinct from long-standing local as well as global cultural and economic forces operating within the region (Wolters 1967; K. Hall 1985; Wicks 1992). Other scholars, together with Reid himself, argue as well that bureaucracies in this period were in fact (also) patronage networks "involving the nobility, officials, and other men of influence" (Kathirithamby-Wells 1993, 132; Nagtegaal 1996). Under pressure, particularly between 1620 and 1680, from the monopolistic practices of the English and the Dutch, Southeast Asian kings intervened directly in the market (Reid 1993, 248–249). Even though these were the same rulers who created "bureaucratic institutions," in practice ruler-entrepreneurs did business through loose networks of merchants, some of whom were "scarcely to be differentiated from the ... category ... of merchant-officials mediating explicitly between the court and the market-place" (Reid 1993, 120). From the ranks of such official-entrepreneurs sprang state-bureaucratic "dynasties" of entrepreneur-bureaucrats like that of the Bunnag of Siam or those of the Bendahara and Laksamana families of Melaka (Reid 1993, 121).

Thus for the period heralded as the "age of commerce" in a

Weberian mode in Southeast Asian history, the roles of "rationality" and "bureaucracy" in the historical process do not have a clear connection to one another and are difficult to define in a way that makes sense of them in Southeast Asia or that helps to demarcate the boundary between "state" and "society" (Mitchell 1999). What can be said about the role of "ritual" in this period of Southeast Asian history? As I have already noted, historians of Southeast Asia as well as other commentators on Southeast Asian culture and politics have been mostly hostile to Clifford Geertz's insistence that the ritual "theatre" of the Southeast Asian state from early to contemporary times has actually performed the work of constituting state power (C. Geertz 1980; Bell 1992, 194; B. Anderson 1990, 94–120; Pemberton 1994; Robinson 1995; Sidel 1997). Reid also assigns a minor role to state ritual, relegating the subject to a chapter on "festivals and amusements" in the first volume of his study. There he begins his treatment of the subject by quoting words from Geertz on the "theatre state," but he ignores Geertz's argument about the real political work performed by state ritual. Instead, Reid presents colorful examples that illustrate the purely "spectacular" nature of Southeast Asian state rituals where the majesty of kingship was put on "display" (Reid 1988, 174–182). Reid's view of Asian state ritual is no different from the one held by Lord Macartney, the late eighteenth-century British diplomat to the Qing court. As James Hevia shows, Macartney held the Enlightenment-British belief that "ceremony" was associated with the Asian love of external pomp, which placed the absolutism and despotism of the ruler on display before his easily duped and subdued subjects (Hevia 1995, 222). Macartney insisted on the same distinction between (Asian) "ritual" and (Western) "rationality" that Reid and other scholars make in their discussions of the Southeast Asian state.

　　Yet it can be shown with Reid's own data that identifying practices in which rationality and ritual were both in play provides the best understanding of commercial and political relationships during the "age of commerce." Reid observes that Southeast Asian states imitated the Chinese tribute system, which had long governed their trading relations with China, in their dealings with one another and with Europeans (Reid 1993, 234). At the beginning of the seventeenth century, Dutch trader Frederick de Houtman published the following fictional dialogue in Malay to illustrate the kinds of ritualized protocol that trade missions to the kingdom of Aceh at the northern tip of the island of Sumatra were required to observe:

> D[aud]: Who is coming on this great elephant, who has such a crowd of people behind him?
>
> I[brahim]: It is the Shahbandar [harbormaster] with the *Penghulu kerkun* [secretary].
>
> D: I also see some foreign traders sitting up there. Who are they?
>
> I: That is a Gujarati nakhoda [ship captain], who has just come with his ship, and whom they are going to take to salute the raja.
>
> D: What does it mean, that elephant caparisoned in red cloth, with those people in front of it playing on tambourines, trumpets, and flutes?
>
> I: The elephant you see and the man sitting on a palanquin upon it, means that a letter is being brought from their raja to our lord. . . .
>
> D: Who is seated there?
>
> I: It is one of the sultan's orangkaya [wealthy nobleman] that he has chosen for that.
>
> D: And what is all that for?
>
> I: To honour the raja whose letter it is.
>
> D: And what is that I see, so many men and slaves, each bringing a painted cloth in his hands?
>
> I: These are the presents which the nakhoda will offer to the king.
>
> D: Is that the tariff he must pay for his goods, or must he pay another tariff?
>
> I: No, the tariff is extra, 7 percent.
>
> D: What honour will the raja give him in return?
>
> I: Indeed, when they enter the raja's palace, they will be given great honour.
>
> D: What happens there?
>
> I: There they eat and drink, all sorts of food and fruits are brought, they play, dance, with all sorts of entertainments, they play on the trumpet, flute, clarinet, and *rebab* [bowed fiddle], and then the king asks for a garment of our local style to be brought, which he gives to the nakhoda. (quoted in Reid 1993, 237–238)

The seventeenth-century sultanate of Aceh was an Indic cosmological state in which there were four *syabandar,* who embodied the quarters of the universe and offered ritual tribute to the sultan on certain holy days of the Islamic calendar (Brakel 1979, 63–64). The dialogue from de Houtman alludes to such cosmological, ritual practices. It also gives a good example of what Catherine Bell calls the ritual constitution of power through "the lived body, which is both the body of society and the social body" (Bell 1992, 204). In de Houtman's dialogue we are introduced to the ritual procedures by which Acehnese and Europeans sought to create relations of dominance and subservience that were physically incorporated within the bodies of those who took part and were expressed through ritually appropriate clothes and gestures. The Acehnese raja, the foreign merchant, the foreign king who has sent a letter, the raja's *orang kaya,* as well as many other masters and servants in the Acehnese social hierarchy who were present in scenes similar to the one de Houtman described, engaged through this and similar rituals in an ongoing negotiation not just about economic relations, but about power itself—who wielded it, who submitted to it. In Bell's terms, rituals like this one enacted and embodied seventeenth-century economic and bureaucratic rationalities in Southeast Asia in a way that gave them efficacious meanings. These rationalities have less to do with "pure rationality" in a Weberian sense than they do with "participation" (Sanskrit *bhakti*) through ritual homage in the cosmological rationality of the state (Inden 1990, 235; Milner 1982, 25; 1995, 124–126). Southeast Asian rituals such as the one described above reenacted and reenforced the hierarchical separation of different ethnic groups in a way that allowed those who were lower down, a group that included the foreign traders in this case, to derive benefit from civilizing contacts with those who were above and at the same time to maintain their distance and maneuverability with respect to those who were unequal and higher (Jónsson 1996, 173–174). Rituals of ethnic inclusiveness could also assert the dominance of one group over another in a way that widened the distance between those above and those below (G. Evans 1998, 141–152). But even in situations in which subordinates openly resisted the authority of the state, such resistance could be ritually parlayed into a cosmologically rational strategy for acquiring potency from the dominant authority. J. H. Walker describes the case of the Bidayan Iban of nineteenth-century Sarawak who, in refusing to pay an unreasonable tax on their rice harvest, lured colonial officials to their villages so they could divest the officials of their potency *(semangat)* by ritual means (Walker 1998). Another major ritual context in which business and politics have been conducted throughout Southeast Asian history, one that we will consider at greater length shortly, was that of marriage (Andaya 1993; Pemberton 1994). "Negotiations between kings," Reid writes, "often began with a pragmatic need for trade or military cooperation but ended with a request for a royal daughter" (Reid 1993, 239). Again, this statement relegates "ritual" to a secondary role with respect to "rationality" in a way that begs the question of their intrinsic and constant interaction.

There are good reasons, therefore, for thinking that the question I asked at the start of this chapter is worth pursuing. We need to approach it free of assumptions about what terms such as "rationality" and "modernity" may actually mean in a historically deep, Southeast Asian sense. In the rest of this chapter I want to explore a variety of connections between rationality, ritual, and bureaucracy in examples taken from different periods of Southeast Asian history. My examples will provide substance to an observation from Weber himself, namely that the "concept of rationalism allows for widely different contents" (Gerth and Mills 1974, 240). They will also demonstrate that ritual activity is intrinsic to what bureaucracy means in Southeast Asia.

"Territorialization"

The "territorialization" of the modern Southeast Asian state is frequently mentioned as the cause and object of increased, "modern" bureaucratization, in contrast to a situation in "traditional" times where manpower, not territory, was the primary concern in land-rich, manpower-poor, premodern Southeast Asia (Vandergeest and Peluso 1995, 392; Steinberg 1987, 5). My definition of the state in chapter 1 and my discussion of cosmological spaces in chapter 3 have already indicated that "territory" needs to be considered as one among many kinds of state-controlled "space" and so relieved of its solemn duty as a signpost of "modernity." The question of territory, space, boundaries, and the state in Southeast Asian history is a very large and interesting one, but for the purposes of the discussion here

I want to focus on the role of territorialization and bureaucracy in early Southeast Asia.

From early times, kinship networks and entourages occupying hierarchical structures that were conceived of as cosmologies also carried out rational bureaucratic tasks and kept written records of these transactions (Mabbett and Chandler 1995, 166–168; Prapañca 1995). It is as mistaken to ignore the meanings of territory in early Southeast Asia or fail to think about the ways in which territory was administered bureaucratically as it is to ignore the ordering efficacy of ritual activity across the landscapes of Southeast Asia before the advent of "national" boundaries (Thongchai 1994, 23).

In early, supposedly pre-"territorial" Southeast Asia, states were able to expand their authority territorially because they successfully promoted wet-rice agriculture, but also because they were able to issue to individuals or temple communities land grants that were documented in writing and subject to legal proceedings if disputed (Ricklefs 1967; A. Jones 1984; Wicks 1992; Wyatt 1975; Aung-Thwin 1985, 123–128, 172–182; cf. Goody 1986). If "territorialization" is taken to mean "excluding or including people within particular geographic boundaries, and . . . controlling what people do and their access to natural resources within those boundaries" (Vandergeest and Peluso 1995, 388), then "territorialization" is precisely what is recorded in inscriptions like the one from Kubukubu in 905 c.e. (discussed in chapter 2) or in the chronicles about early southern Thailand. Like other *sīma* inscriptions, which in Java were written on copper plates for durability and portability, the Kubukubu document records details of land utilization and lists state and local officials who participated in the ritual inauguration of the *sīma* territory. The bounded, territorial character of the term *"sīma"* is indicated by its derivation from Sanskrit *sīman*, meaning "boundary, border." An even more important term in the political vocabulary of early Southeast Asia, *"maṇḍala,"* which O. W. Wolters prefers to the term "state" for describing political formations in the region, has a basic meaning of "a centred world . . . whose boundaries have been clearly defined . . . a sacred enclosure, a world or field from which demonic, which is to say disordered and distracting, influences have been expelled and within which rituals can be performed without hindrance or danger" (Snodgrass 1985, 105; Wolters 1999, 27–40, 126–154, 216–221). Whereas one set of Javanese officials was thus ritually "included" in territory made sacred under the protection of the state, another group of state officials and officially sanctioned merchants was ritually "excluded"—that is, the tax officers, inspectors, and taxable traders who were forbidden to enter or reside in the *sīma*. Tax exemption and enhanced status gained from endowing *sīma* were enticements to local lords and villagers to participate in the life of the state. In Java, such land grants were used strategically by the state to bring both manpower and territory under control, like the uncultivated grounds mentioned in the inscription of Kaladi (909 C.E.), which were "fearsome" and "endangered the traders and people from downstream by day and by night," until turned into settled, wet-rice farmland under the auspices of a *sīma* (A. Jones 1984, 80 and 181). The interplay of bureaucracy, written documents, and ritual in state practices in early Java is as fully described in the fourteenth-century *Deśawarṇana*, the "Description of the Country" of Majapahit, as it is anywhere in early Southeast Asia (Prapañca 1995). Although Geertz based his earliest formulation of the "theatre state" on this text because of its extensive descriptions of royal rituals (C. Geertz 1993 [1977], 121–146), the *Deśawarṇana* also documents in detail the processes by which the state was claimed, demarcated, and administered by the king using bureaucratic procedures that were carried out in a ritualistic way. Literacy as well as vernacular literature in early Java were closely associated with a concept of "landscape" that entailed the territorial expansion of the king's rule through repeated ritual processions across space that was conceived of in topographical, administrative, and cosmological terms. These ritual acts were later inscribed on metal charters and palm-leaf manuscripts (Day 1994; cf. Pollock 1998b, 2000). Landscape poetry in early northern Vietnam also plays with interrelationships between concrete territorial space and spiritual infinity, between bureaucratically controlled (or at least patrolled) territory and cosmologically organized space (Wolters 1982b; 1988, 54–153; 1999, 71–78).

Texts and inscriptions from early Java tend to conceal the struggle that took place between states as they attempted to demarcate and redefine localities as "their" space, and local as well as external powers that sought to maintain and extend their own forms of sovereignty in disregard of state boundaries. A good example of this kind of struggle from eighteenth-century Java can be found in a Kartasura text, the *Serat Cabolek,* which tells a story about the state's attempt to exclude heterodox Islam and its claim to domination over universal space from the bounded interior of the realm (Soebardi 1975; Day 1983a; Ricklefs 1998, 127–162). An analysis of a contemporary example, in which a territorializing, bureaucratic state is pitted against shamans who believe that the landscape of their domain has no boundaries whatsoever, can be found in Anna Tsing's study of the Meratus Dayak of Borneo (Tsing 1993). Tsing describes a woman shaman, Uma Adang, who counters the logic of the territorializing, Islamicizing New Order state with the logic of a timeless Majapahit empire, which came to Kalimantan, converting stone into iron and introducing religious pluralism and "custom" *(adat).* Yet of all the Meratus shamans she knew, notes Tsing, "it was Uma Adang who was most willing to dictate rules for social life, fines for every possible transgression, and models for the spectrum of ceremonial occasions," thus mimicking the bureaucratic rationality and procedures of the state whose authority she contested (Tsing 1993, 274).

A comparable case to this last one, told from the state's point of view, comes from the history of Lý Vietnam (1009–1224), where Buddhism and a cultic form of kingship were more important for state formation than Chinese-style dynastic and bureaucratic practices. The Lý state had only a rudimentary bureaucracy (K. Taylor 1986a). But there was already an important kind of territorialization underway in the form of the state's attempt to incorporate local spirit cults into a "Lý dynasty religion" (K. Taylor 1986a, 144; Lý 1999). From the fifteenth to the mid-nineteenth centuries, the territorialization of northern Vietnam continued to develop as the state endeavored to keep public and taxable lands out of the hands of local families and to Confucianize villagers in order to make them loyal to the state (Whitmore 1997). Under Lê Thánh-tông (r.1460–1497) in particular, there was a strong "desire to see the government become strongly involved in the affairs, moral and material, of the countryside," resulting in "a production of detailed reports and an accumulation of paperwork which created a 'documentary state' " (Whitmore 1997, 676). But the struggle between the state and local spirits for territorial control over the "realm of Việt" continued long into the modern period (Tai 1983).

Even the "cellular organization" of manpower in Pagan, where people were grouped by the state into villages according to their occupations—a mode of social organization alluded to in the *Serat Centhini*'s depiction of early nineteenth-century Java—is evidence of territorialization in premodern Southeast Asia, since leaders of such villages became hereditary leaders over territory as well as people (Aung-Thwin 1985, 87, 93). In early Burma, the state struggled to control the spiritual powers of conquered spaces (Aung-Thwin 1983). From the fourteenth to the early nineteenth centuries, Burmese rulers also carried out surveys to collect detailed information on cultivated lands and populations (Trager and Koenig 1979, 51). For example, in one *sit-tàn* (record of inquiry) from 1784, after learning the exact geographic location and service obligations of a particular population, we are given, inter alia, the following details of tax obligations in Kòn-baung Burma:

> Fifty jars of jams made from pumpkin, papaya, taro, coconuts, yams, several kinds of bananas, sweet potatoes, lily root and marian; twenty-seven jars of pickled mango, lime, marian, wood apple, ginger and caoutchouc; and three jars of sedge root and scented powder were levied from the inhabitants of the tract. When the officer in charge of jams and his men have prepared the produce, it is deposited in the crown storehouse at Taung-ngu *Myó* [district or town]. Once a year in time for the New Year Festival in Tagù, the officer in charge of jams and his men traditionally submit the produce to the king at the Western Court (women's quarters of the royal palace). As there are presently but a few men of the jams unit, the tax-payers are assessed for the expenses of transporting this produce. (Trager and Koenig 1979, 144)

This document territorializes Burmese space in detailed bureaucratic fashion. Although not as emphatically as in the description of people offering tribute to King Kyanzitthà (r.1084–1111) of Pagan, in which a "full-grown male elephant would pick up . . . flowers and come dancing and make their offerings to the king" (quoted and discussed in Wicks 1992, 122–123), the eighteenth-century *sit-tàn* also suggests a ritualized context for Burmese economic and bureaucratic activity. This is another example of how states in Southeast Asia have attempted to establish and expand their sovereignty by means of bureaucratic, territorial, as well as cosmological practices.

Rationality, Bureaucratic and Otherwise

Service to the state in Southeast Asia, from early times to the present, has demanded disciplined behavior based on rational rules that were articulated in concepts drawn from Indic shastras, Confucian treatises, or guides to modern, Western-style bureaucratic procedure. States have been staffed by "discerning" bureaucrats in fourteenth-century Vietnam (Wolters 1999, 200), "cunning" and "well-behaved" ones in fifteenth-century Melaka (Wolters 1999, 201–203), and "talented" and "educated" ones in twentieth-century Singapore (Lee Kuan Yew 2000, 664). Rational rules could both reinforce and oppose values of loyalty and "devotion," which were expressed in an idiom of familial relations and emotions. As is shown by examples from nineteenth- and twentieth-century Vietnam, early Java and nineteenth- and twentieth-century Philippines, loyal sentiments expressed in an idiom of kinship did not always bind individuals and families to the state (Woodside 1971; 1976, 95–102; Jamieson 1995; see chapter 5; Ileto 1979; Fegan 1994). Such emotions were essential for holding bureaucracies together, yet they also served to undermine bureaucratic cohesion when they acted in the interests of the family alone. As Alexander Woodside comments on the Nguyễn bureaucracy in relation to Chinese political ideology and practice in early nineteenth-century Vietnam:

> Characteristically Chinese dilemmas . . . came to be faithfully reflected in Vietnamese imperial politics. "Cliques inevitably issue primarily from the father-son and elder brother-young brother relationship and later spread to other men," Minh-mang noted in 1839. But if family ties united official cliques, which then conspired to diminish the influence of the emperor (whose peace of mind depended upon a politically atomistic bureaucracy), they were also the rudimentary sources of the bureaucracy's self-discipline. "Filial piety can be transferred to matters of state, so the prince who is searching for loyal ministers must visit households with filial sons," Gia-long remarked sententiously in 1814. (Woodside 1971, 38)

During the entire course of the twentieth century, bureaucracies as well as the thousands of new religious and political organizations, born of what Pangemanann (the panoptic, bureaucratic narrator of Pramoedya's *House of Glass*) calls "organization fever," were filled with people who struggled to uphold rules and standards of rationality (Pramoedya 1992, 151). The sources of the rationality that informed organizational practices in Southeast Asia during this period were partly secular. "In their education," write Pasuk Phongpaichit and Chris Baker of the situation in Thailand in the early part of the twentieth century,

> the new bureaucrats were taught the importance of principles, rules, and laws. In their jobs, they found that social power overrode legal principle. They expected to be rewarded for professional capability and efficiency. They found that appointments, promotions, and salaries depended more on birth, on connections, and on loyalty to the throne. They pressed for recruitment by competitive examinations, standardized salaries, and promotion by seniority and merit. They promoted the idea of *lak wicha*, the principle of administration based on law and rationality, in opposition to *lak ratchakan*, the principle of royal service. (Pasuk and Baker 1995, 248)

In 1930s Burma, the Marxist and nationalist student movement Do Bama Asiayon (Our Burma Association) called for organization "to purify, regulate, extend, and strengthen" the association (quoted in R. Taylor 1987, 212; Khin Yi 1988).

But rationality also emerged from religious beliefs and practices. In early twentieth-century West Sumatra, Minangkabau Muslim reformers stressed the use of "reasoning" *(akaliyah)* and the need for "organization," which one writer defined as

> [a]n institution for channeling the spirit of reform, . . . to encourage enterprising vigor and to enhance the nobility of knowledge *(kemuliaan ilmu)*. It is a place to cultivate (brotherhood) among mankind and nations. (quoted in Abdullah 1971, 17)

The secular, Dutch-educated Minangkabau rationalist Sjahrir, who criticized the bloated, inefficient Indonesian bureaucracy of the early 1960s (Emmerson 1978, 88), drew on Minangkabau Muslim ideas about rationality for his own ideas about "thinking" and "organization" (Mrázek 1994, 104). Although he opposed both Islam and other

"Eastern" religions as useless to men of "intellect," he wondered, in one of his letters written while in exile in 1935, "whether Islam, with regard to Hinduism, does not play the same role in history that Protestantism did against Catholicism in Europe, viz., articulating a bourgeois view of life against a feudal one" (quoted in Mrázek 1994, 149).

In a study of Buddhism in contemporary Thailand, Peter Jackson says of Chokechai Sutthawet, a Buddhist thinker of the 1990s, that he

> identifie[d] reason *(het phon)* as the key feature of the emerging global economic and political order, and locate[d] this reason in the core of Buddhist culture. According to Chokechai, it [wa]s therefore possible for Thailand to participate in the global culture of reason on an equal footing with the West. (Jackson 1997, 89)

The views of Chokechai and others challenged the authority of the "official" Buddhist *sangha*, fashioned by the Sangha Acts of 1902, 1941, and 1962 into a national organization serving the interests of a centralized state and the Chakri dynasty in the name of "a rationalization of social life, that is, the regularization of markets and the introduction of a meritocratic social order in which socio-economic advancement [is] determined more by individual skill and effort than by association with entrenched power" (Jackson 1997, 73 ,76; Ishii 1986, 67–170). This challenge, according to Jackson, posed less of a problem for the state in the 1990s than previously, because the Thai state no longer relied as heavily on "official" Buddhism for its legitimacy. Yet Buddhist ritual and calls for unity in the face of threats to "Thai" Buddhism still served the interests of those allied with the state, many of whom had close ties with monks who claimed supernatural powers. Rationalist Buddhism attacked such supernaturalism and the bureaucratic power holders and state-sponsored cults of Thai identity that it supported. Although this form of Buddhism was also divided within itself over issues of global capitalism and Western values, at the grass-roots level, "a common oppositional dynamic . . . facilitated the establishment of political alliances between karmic-animist villagers and rationalist monks and urban NGO advocates" (Jackson 1997, 92). This example is a good one for illustrating the hybrid nature of religious rationality in contemporary Southeast Asia, which draws on local as well as global resources in the struggle for control over the region's future.

Whereas Buddhism in Thailand flourished in the margins of

the state during the 1990s, in Indonesia Islam moved into the very center of it, with the election of Muslim intellectual and leader Abdurraham Wahid as the republic's fourth president. A part of this story that is relevant to my discussion here concerns the foundation of the Association of Indonesian Muslim Intellectuals (ICMI) in 1990 (Hefner 1993; 2000, 128–166). Robert Hefner argues that ICMI was the product of a renewed commitment to Islamic values during the 1970s and 1980s that took place inside the state bureaucracy as well as in civil society. Muslim intellectuals became openly critical of undemocratic "bureaucratic Javanism." At the same time, increasing numbers of Muslims motivated by clear, "precise ethical prescriptions" entered the bureaucracy in the 1980s "and quietly labored to promote Muslim interests" (Hefner 1993, 8, 14; Peacock 1978). During the same period the state promoted the building of mosques and Muslim educational institutions throughout Indonesia. In 1991, President Suharto made the pilgrimage to Mecca, not long after giving his approval for the establishment of an association of Muslim intellectuals under the chairmanship of the then minister for research and development, Dr. B. J. Habibie. Although criticized by some prominent Muslim intellectuals because of its close links to the bureaucracy, from which it drew most of its membership, ICMI attracted a wide range of Muslim intellectuals who endorsed such causes as the role of science and technology in Indonesian development, human rights, and the need to solve social problems caused by technological change. Although surrounded by controversy, its autonomy strictly circumscribed by the state, the formation of ICMI signaled the emergence within as well as outside the contemporary Indonesian state of groups committed to Islamic rationalism.

As in Thailand, however, the New Order Indonesian bureaucracy was also a breeding ground for a hybrid kind of rationality that mixed supernaturalism with Western rationality. Suharto and other top Javanese officials and generals, who were committed to "the scientific knowledge and expertise of advanced capitalist societies" (McVey 1995a, 26), also engaged in mystical practices, consulted with masters of supernatural knowledge *(dukun)*, and traveled to sites of magical potency on the island of Java (Pemberton 1994, 269–310; Bourchier 1984, 93–94). Javanese bureaucratic supernaturalism also served as a medium for rational criticism of the injustices of the New Order. In 1978, a mystic and minor former bureaucrat named Sawito

Kartowibowo was found guilty of subversion, having secured the signatures of Dr. Mohammad Hatta and several other prominent Indonesians for a document titled "Towards Salvation" in which Sawito asserted:

> If the current progress in national development is evaluated in the context of the way in which it has really benefitted the Indonesian people as a whole it is clear that apart from advances in the pioneering of physical means, it has brought about an obvious deterioration in the standard of human dignity. . . . The danger of this threat is already quite apparent in the throttling of the *sovereignty of law.* (quoted in Bourchier 1984, 23–24, emphasis in original)

In another document, Sawito directly blamed Suharto for the country's troubles and called upon him to resign. In the early 1970s Sawito and a small group of fellow mystics engaged in what he later called "metaphysical research expeditions" to caves, mosques, and Hindu-Buddhist temple ruins in Java (Bourchier 1984, 41). During these expeditions he received revelations of the dawning of a new age, in which the head of the Indonesian state would have to set an example of "Pancasila living," bureaucrats would have to "differentiate between the state's property and [their] own," and the unity of "moral, social, and cosmic dimensions of awareness, and between the spiritual, philosophical, and scientific foundations of knowledge" would be achieved (quoted in Bourchier 1984, 47–48).

In this section it has become clear that a variety of rationalities, some with their source in Western secular thought, others drawn from Southeast Asian religious thinking, still others formed from hybrids of the two, have helped shape the nature of bureaucratic practices in the region. In the next part of my argument I want to explore other sources of specifically hybrid kinds of bureaucratic formation in Southeast Asia.

Bureaucratic Tact and Other Assaults on "Rational" Bureaucracy

An interesting illustration of what economic historians Linda Weiss and John Hobson call the "synergy" between the bureaucratic state and commerce in Asia can be found in the colonial nineteenth century in an autobiographical text called the *Tarikh Datuk Bentara Luar Johor* (Weiss and Hobson 1995; Sweeney 1980a; 1980b). This is a collection of three autobiographical writings by Mohamed Salleh bin Perang (1841–1915), an important bureaucrat in Johor during the middle of the nineteenth century, which was a period of rapid modernization and economic and territorial expansion in this tiny Malay state (Trocki 1979). This is how the Datuk describes the beginning of his bureaucratic career in 1856 under Temenggong Daing Ibrahim (1810–1862), the founder of modern Johor:

> About two months after I had been forbidden to teach at the school in Kampung Gelam, . . . I was employed by Encik Long— on the orders of Marhum Ibrahim—and made a junior clerk. . . . The duties he assigned me entailed issuing identification papers for people involved in growing various kinds of plants and trees. He also gave me the task of copying letters into a register. I reaped enormous benefit from this, because Encik Long was a man of wisdom and generosity, and devoted much attention to me, teaching and advising me on all sorts of worthwhile matters, and state protocol, custom and ceremonial. He also taught me how to write letters to important rulers. In addition, my understanding was further increased by copying a number of letters which were of much use and benefit, in the offices of government [*kerajaan*] under his charge. Every day, moreover, I heard the beneficial and salutary words of wise men [*orang bijaksana*] endowed with incisive tongues, speaking in gatherings of rulers and ministers, and I noted their use of parables, their good breeding, cultured manners and refined behavior; for every other day or so, the dignitaries would all meet in conference and consider ways and means to improve the country, to induce more people to seek their livelihood in occupations which would increase the state revenues, and to improve the lot of the people of the country.
>
> I worked there for about two years and, by the grace of God, I was like a man doing business: my profits mounted day by day, and with my capital I was easily able to buy and obtain fine merchandise and property. (Sweeney 1980a, 83–84; 1980b, 39–40)

In this passage there is a mixture of rational-bureaucratic, entrepreneurial, and courtly-Malay activity and criteria for defining the
work of the mid-nineteenth-century Johor bureaucrat. Note the use
of the Sanskritic term *"bijaksana,"* "wise, insightful, tactically astute,"
to describe the exemplary Johor administrator, as well as references
to rhetorical skill, good manners, and "finesse" (Crouch 1996, 155),
as necessary attributes of the good Malay bureaucrat: these are the
same bureaucratic gifts possessed by the fourteenth-century Javanese prime minister Gajah Mada, according to the "Description of
the Country" (Prapañca 1995, 33). As Carl Trocki shows (1979), moreover, the "modernizing" nineteenth-century Johor state was embedded
in a system of Chinese revenue farms that were opening up new
land for commercial exploitation, and the "bureaucratic" structure of
the state was in reality an interlocking network of Malay and Chinese families who acquired wealth through their participation in the
state bureaucracy.

Next to familial "love," rules, and organization, therefore, networking skills and "cultural manners and refined behavior," what
Malays call *bahasa,* have long been a characteristic of bureaucratic
practices in Southeast Asia. In the following passage from an eighteenth-century Acehnese poem, a prince uses *bahasa* with ritual-like
efficacy to cause certain political alliances to take form, and others to
disintegrate:

> Now we tell of Pòtjoet Moehamat, a small man, always prepared
>   with a fitting reply.
> His words were all in verse, like doves descending through
>   the air.
> His commands and prohibitions were all sweet and captivating;
>   the leaders were thoroughly frightened of him.
> He forbade nothing in the wrong manner but prohibited all with
>   calmness;
> Hearing his delicious, savory voice, the hearts of the people soft-
>   ened. (Siegel 1979, 52–53)

This finesse is the same quality that a Malay text, the *Hikayat Pahang,*
bestows upon the nineteenth-century Pahang leader Bendahara Ali
(Milner 1982, 41), and which even the leftist, formerly bureaucratic

hero of an Indonesian Communist novel published in 1924 displays as he makes new friends during a tram ride:

> The sweet expression on Soedjanmo's face, his gentle manner of speaking together with his polite way of moving made everyone who made his acquaintance experience a delicious feeling [*rasa sedep*]. (Soemantri 1924, 48)

These examples remind us that "little scenarios of etiquette" (Ortner 1984, 154) are as formative of state or statelike authority as the machinations of "rational" bureaucracies.

Throughout the colonial era Southeast Asian states appropriated and exploited the familial deep structures and attractive, smooth-talking, and gently smiling ceremonial surfaces of bureaucratic practices in order to effectuate their dominance. But in so doing they often created a tension between older and newer meanings of bureaucracy for Southeast Asian bureaucrats. Still present and powerful was the appeal of bureaucratic office as a source of *nama* (Malay "reputation"; see Milner 1982, 105–111), status, and now "modernity." But to be a bureaucrat during the 1920s and 1930s in Southeast Asia was also to be directly subjected to the humiliations of racist colonial domination, as well as tainted by association with an illegitimate colonial or an antimodern, absolutist royal regime. In such circumstances working for family interests was no longer synonymous with loyalty to the emerging "nation," as it once had been to a state. *Bahasa* (appropriate language and behavior) became tainted, since smooth-talking European capitalists could also deploy it as a *"taktiek"* (tactic) to lure unsuspecting natives into dishonorable collaboration (Soemantri 1924, 51). Woodside describes the tension created in the countryside of Annam (central Vietnam) during the 1930s when "traditional" rituals in honor of state officials were staged, causing consternation among local populations whose acceptance of the old "hierarchical ethos" had already worn thin (Woodside 1976, 134–135).

In his powerful historical novels about the Indonesian nationalist movement, Pramoedya Ananta Toer recreates the nationalist abhorrence of the colonial bureaucracy, which can also be found in the novel *Rasa Merdika* (Meaning/Sensation of Freedom) (Soemantri 1924) and other Malay fiction of the 1920s. In the following depiction—which equals in savagery the assault that Douwes Dekker (or Multatuli, "He who has suffered much"), the disgruntled Dutch colonial former bureaucrat, launched against the mid-nineteenth-century Dutch colonial bureaucracy in his novel *Max Havelaar* (Multatuli 1982)—Pramoedya lambasts the character Sastrotomo, the father of the heroic Nyai Ontosoroh. Ontosoroh is speaking, explaining how her father handed her over to become the mistress of a Dutch factory foreman in exchange for a bureaucratic promotion:

> My father had many younger brothers and sisters as well as cousins. As a clerk he had great difficulty in getting them jobs at the factory. A higher post would have made it easier, and also it would have raised him up higher in the eyes of the world. . . .
>
> The post he dreamed of was paymaster: cashier, holder of the cash of the Tulangan sugar factory, in Sidoarjo. . . . As the factory paymaster he would become a big man in Tulangan. Merchants would bow down in respect. The Pure and Mixed-blood *Tuans* would greet him in Malay. The stroke of his pen meant money! He would be counted as among the powerful in the factory. People would listen to his words: *sit down on the bench there* in order to receive their money from his hands.
>
> Pathetic. It was not a rise in position, respect or esteem that he obtained from his dreams. On the contrary: people's hatred and disgust. (Pramoedya 1982, 65)

Pramoedya's example illustrates the nature of both the rational, nationalist rejection of bureaucratic status and its appeal in status-hungry, hierarchical Southeast Asia.

As in Java, writers who championed individualism and nationalism in Malaya or Vietnam found ways of detaching traditional definitions of "work" and "reputation" as "service" to a king or a bureaucracy from their older meanings in order to recast them in anticolonial, modern, and individualistic terms. The Malay journalist Mohd. Eunos Abdullah, in a newspaper editorial of 1907, declared that "every person who works hard for himself and looks after his dependents" is able to become "a person who has *nama* and is praised" (Milner 1995, 125). The Vietnamese nationalist intellectual and activist Phan Bội Châu (1867–1940) "was obsessed by the need to launch a war against the . . . upper-class appetite for the 'honors of office' *(cong danh)*, which he called 'empty names' *(hu danh)*" (Woodside 1976, 42). "Government officials, parents, and mothers-in-law," writes Neil Jamieson, became the villains of Vietnamese novels in the 1930s (Jamieson 1995, 105 and passim), but such views were not necessarily a good guide to the practices adopted by those who read them, and yet felt compelled to work to uphold and raise the family honor:

> In print and over bowls of soup at sidewalk cafes along the side streets of Hanoi and Saigon, young men and a few women grumbled about their families' old-fashioned ideas or lamented the narrow and self-serving conservatism of the colonial bureaucracy, but few of them put their ideas into action. At the office they were polite, respectful, and tried to please the boss. (Jamieson 1995, 134)

Southeast Asians could also draw on older forms of community organization and rational thinking in their responses to colonial bureaucracy or other forms of "foreign" organization (Woodside 1976, 31–36; Ileto 1979; Widodo 1997). Although reverence for Confucian bureaucratic norms has an old history in Vietnam (Wolters 1999, 198), the early nineteenth-century folk poem "Catfish and Toad," about a dispute between He-Toad and He-Catfish, pits Vietnamese common sense and the intractable realities of village family rivalries against the rationality and corruption of a Confucian-style bureaucracy that intervenes to settle the quarrel (Huỳnh 1996, 46–60; 1983). In the following passage from this allegorical satire, bureaucratic underlings officiously but mistakenly identify tadpoles as catfish in an attempt to verify whether He-Toad's children are his or He-Catfish's:

> The clerks obeyed their order, hit the road—
> All in a body hastened toward Clear Pond.
> Arriving there, they summoned village chiefs
> To show them round and help them learn the truth.
> They found those tadpoles in a frisk and romp
> Quite near the surface—little swarthy ones.
> "No shadow of a doubt!" the clerks agreed.
> "From head to tail they look like catfish, yes!"
> After recording what they observed,
> They hurried back, submitted their report. (Huỳnh 1996, 53)

Similarly, there are old precedents for Javanese nationalist resistance to bureaucracy and alien forms of rationality derived from foreign books, such as the long-standing argument, recorded in writing as early as the ninth century C.E., between priestly book learning and oral peasant wisdom vividly expressed in riddles and puns (Hooykaas 1958a). The following verses from the late nineteenth-century *Suluk Gatholoco* (B. Anderson 1981, 1982; 1990, 289–297) also draw on the resources of popular Javanese poetry and verbal wit to poke fun at pedantic book learning and priestly authority in rural Islamic schools of the period:

2. [...]
It was a famous place for education
Three hundred santri [orthodox Muslim students] studied there.
Now after Ngisa prayers,
Their salat [daily prayer] done, the guru three together sat
Within the *langgar* [prayer house] for instruction,
Teaching the Pekih and the Sitin,

3. As well as every other kitab [religious treatise]
According to each several santri's wish.
Now some were studying the texts
Explaining the Qur'ān,
Trick-questioning their comrades turn and turn about.
Those santri who were satiated
With learning the Sitin by heart

4. With jokes their recitation mixed,
In Purwakanthi meter supply phrased.
Those santri who had fully mastered
Texts and interpretation
Articulately argued with their teachers on
The meaning of Qur'anic texts,
Comparing illustrative cases

5. As they had come to know them, while
Still other students argued over texts
And what their essence truly was.
Tumultuous the war
Of words, as all approached the guru. (B. Anderson 1982, 31–32)

Both the *Suluk Gatholoco* and "Catfish and Toad" expose the gap between practical, everyday rationality and modes of knowledge deployed by dominant, organized groups in society. The Jakarta cartoonist Sudarta and his character Oom Pasikom, alternately a petty bureaucrat, peasant, peddler, or member of the rising middle class, explored a similar, glaringly obvious gap between common sense and official cant in New Order Indonesia during the 1970s and 1980s (Murai 1994).

The long history of ambivalent attitudes toward bureaucracy in Southeast Asia helps explain why indigenous bureaucracies, formed in response to colonial rule, sometimes assumed distinctly non-Western shapes. Throughout the region from the nineteenth century onward, to borrow what McVey has said of Indonesia, Southeast Asians "were confronted with the question of organization in two ways: first as a need for civilizational reordering, and second as the world's new secret of success" (McVey 1996, 97). In colonial Vietnam during the 1920s and 1930s, while civics texts explaining the intricacies of French colonial administration were being absorbed by primary students, experimentation with new kinds of organization involved practices undreamed of in French textbooks (Marr 1981, 94–96, 118–119). The Cao Đài sect, soon to be a mass organization, was founded in the south of Vietnam in 1926 by a former member of the Colonial Council. Most of its leadership was recruited from people who held positions in the colonial bureaucracy (Werner 1981, 20–24; Tai 1983, 84–88). But the "secret" of its success had little to do with the "rationality" of its Western antecedents. David Marr remarks that "Cao Dai apostles were more effective than anyone else in breathing new life into traditional hierarchical relations" (Marr 1981, 90).

Marr's comment about the retraditionalizing effect of Vietnamese bureaucratic reactions to colonialism in hierarchical Vietnamese society invites attention to the hybrid, hierarchy-reinforcing way in which bureaucratic practices developed elsewhere in Southeast Asia. In Java, intellectuals like Soetomo and Soewardi Soerjaningrat went to Western-style schools and learned how *not* to "imitate" Western forms of rationality (B. Anderson 1998, 96). The Yogyakarta aristocrat Soewardi (1889–1959) developed the Taman Siswa educational movement in the 1920s and 1930s in order to teach a new kind of rationality (Tsuchiya 1987). In his writings Soewardi attacked the *zakelijkheid,* or practical rationalism, of the Dutch colonial bureaucracy, while in his schools he instituted a form of benevolent authoritarianism based on neotraditional formulations of Javanese ideas about family and the authority of a fatherly leader. The most important qualification for fatherly leadership in Soewardi's familial state was that the leader must be *bijaksana,* like Gajah Mada or Mohamed Salleh bin Perang. In an article published in 1931, Soewardi (now Ki Hadjar Dewantara) explained the difference between rational-legal bureaucracy and his "family principle":

> Taman Siswa is both a physical body *(badan lahir)* and spiritual body *(badan batin).* . . .
>
> Who are the members of our great sacred family? Normal organizations are bound by "articles and regulations" *(statuten dan reglement),* and anyone may belong who has paid his "dues" *(contributie).* Providing he pays his dues and abides by the rules, he may do as he pleases. Solidarity among members of the organization can be found only in the fact that they attend "meetings" *(bervergadering)* where there are speeches and debates, motions are introduced, and after heckling, protest, and even bargaining, decisions are taken by majority vote.
>
> Our situation is very different from this.
>
> The members of Taman Siswa . . . should be called family members *(anggota keluarga).* They must not think they are tied by regulations; they must sense that they are united by feelings of *purity,* . . . that is, by the bonds of the family name. They should not behave well because of what is called in Javanese *mangèsti persatuan,* that is, because of regulations; they should behave well because they are aiming for an ideal. (quoted in Tsuchiya 1987, 141; see also S. Shiraishi 1997, 93)

An anticolonial, antibureaucratic idea during the Dutch period, Soewardi's "family principle" became one of the central features of bureaucratic ideology and practice under Sukarno and Suharto (see Reeve 1985; Bourchier 1997). Saya Shiraishi argues that the "family principle" became a fact of everyday social and bureaucratic life in New Order Indonesia, one that subverted the "rational"-legal potential of organizations because it catalyzed the conversion of official authority into personal power:

Historically, the concept of *kekeluargaan,* or family-ism, was born and developed in Taman Siswa. It then migrated to government offices as Taman Siswa teachers and graduates joined the government. Family-ism therefore manifests itself most clearly in modern, national, bureaucratic organizations. It resides most comfortably in government and corporate offices and school classrooms where Indonesian is used. Whatever their social or ethnic backgrounds are, once employed, people in government and corporate organizations . . . address their bosses "*Pak* So-and-So" or "*Bu* So-and-So" in Indonesian when they meet, and bring the relations of *bapak/ibu* [father/mother] and *anak* [child] into being. (S. Shiraishi 1997, 93, 108, and passim)

State-sponsored schools in contemporary Thailand, which began to replace monasteries from the end of the nineteenth century as the most important institutions of mass education, also inculcate certain kinds of state-inflected rationality and bureaucratic behavior, in addition to literacy and knowledge about the modern world. Keyes contrasts the pedagogical effect of the organization of space in the traditional monastery with that of the modern state school in the following way:

In entering the *wat* to go to school, a child was first oriented in space by the reliquary shrines that stood as a link between the present community of the living and the past community of the dead. Within the *wat* grounds, the child would recognize himself or herself as being within a ritual space that included both the structures where rituals were held and the critical ritual actors, the members of the Sangha. Within this ritual space, the school occupied a subordinate position. . . . Conspicuous in the Ban Nong Tun school, as in every village school, are the linked images of the Buddha, the king (sometimes the king and queen or the king and other members of the royal family), and the national flag or colors. These juxtaposed images point to the three pillars of national identity that have been promoted by the state since the time of King Vajiravudh. . . . The posters and charts that have been attached to the walls of village schools anticipate a bureaucratic domain of social action. (Keyes 1991a, 99–101)

In apparent contrast to the hybrid, familial modernity of the Taman Siswa and Cao Đài movements, both the Communist Party of Indonesia (PKI) during the 1950s and early 1960s (McVey 1996) and the bureaucratic opponents to the absolutist monarchy in Thailand in the late 1920s and early 1930s invoked what the Thai call *lak wicha,* "the principle of abiding by texts or rules," as opposed to *lak ratchakan,* "the principle of royal service" (Pasuk and Baker 1995, 238, 247–248). In the mass organizations promoted by the Communists in Indonesia during the 1950s,

> [w]orking one's way up as a cadre might eventually result in a full-time political career; more immediately, it provided a set of supportive relationships and activities with both economic and psychological value. Organizational work was seen to be modern, hence more respectable and efficacious than the *"bapakist"* patron-client ties which characterized postrevolutionary institutions generally and which were widely blamed for the Republic's corruption and drift. (McVey 1996, 99–100)

Yet even the ultramodern organizations of the PKI, comments McVey, "resembled a community" that "tapped energies that might not have been available to a more bureaucratic-rational structure" (McVey 1996, 105). "To modernize the villages," declared PKI official Nyoto in 1965, "means to bring about a democratic revolution in them. Therefore we must possess a modern organization, must organize [the villagers] in a modern manner, stressing efficiency and striving to overcome bureaucratism" (quoted in McVey 1996, 107). Nyoto suggests that, like the Cao Đài and Taman Siswa movements, the Indonesian Communist party had to reinvent the meanings of "modernity" and "rationality" as well as appeal to nonbureaucratic forms of cohesion in order to modernize Southeast Asia in a noncolonial way. But the question remains: Why have so many thousands of people been attracted to bureaucratic positions in Southeast Asian states?

Wealth, Bureaucracy, and Ritual

> The officials of the outer regions headed by Arya
> Singhadhikara and especially the Saiwas and Buddhists there
> Made gifts of food, immaculate and with due ceremony [*sopacara*],

> Which the King repaid with gold, clothing and titles, being
> pleased. . . .
> Duly at an auspicious time [the king] left Singhasari and went
> south to Kagenengan,
> To offer devotion to the lord of the sanctuary, with all his various
> groups of people following.
> Money, refreshments and food accompanied his flower-offerings
> with all the proper requisites [*sopacara*],
> As well as clothing carried on poles preceded by drums—the
> people who saw it were delighted. (Prapañca 1995, 48–49)

Participation in the bureaucracies of Majapahit or Angkor was supposed to be a religious experience. At the same time, it was an economic one, as the quotations from the fourteenth-century "Description of the Country" above and studies of state, religion, and economy in early Southeast Asia demonstrate (Aung-Thwin 1985; K. Hall 1985). Bureaucratic offices in premodern Southeast Asia were important because they conferred both high status and access to wealth in worlds where it was possible to acquire the former through individual religious devotionalism and the latter through commerce, but not both together except through participation in the organization and ethos of the state. Status acquired through service to the state was more than an end in itself, the gift of the ruler or lord, a mark of achievement in this life and the promise of advancement in the next. It provided access for extended families to wealth and "immortality," which was reckoned in material transgenerational as well as otherworldly religious terms. As Hong Lysa remarks of Siamese officials under King Rama III (r.1824–1851), "[O]fficial positions, ranks, and honours given by the king were the keys to the economic advancement of its holders. . . . They had the king's blessings to make what they could from their official positions" (Hong 1984, 12). William Koenig makes an almost identical comment about the relationship between bureaucratic office, status, and wealth in eighteenth- and early nineteenth-century Burma (Koenig 1990, 162–163). The ultimate punishment for transgressions against the socioeconomic order in Rama III's Siam, according to the king, was "rebirth as destitute without relatives or patrons to depend on" (Hong 1984, 28).

    In another part of Southeast Asia, Anthony Milner analyzes the interrelatedness of the terms *"belanja"* (outlay, expenditure), *"kaya"* (property, power), and *"karya"* (ritual work) in Malay court texts from the sixteenth through the nineteenth centuries. Milner shows that, according to the ideology of the ruling elite, "wealth" was meaningless outside a political context defined in terms of service to the king:

> The *Hikayat Hang Tuah* . . . tells how the rich Indian merchant, Parmadewan, hears that God has placed a Raja from Heaven in the Malay region. As his own land has no ruler, the merchant thinks: "It is best I expend *(berbelanjakan)* my property to bring a Raja to this land, because my property is very extensive, and the property of this world can have no use." The merchant's judgment . . . implies that, while a concept of property existed, property had no value in itself. In this case, it was valued only in so far as it could achieve what we might call a political end. (Milner 1982, 25 and passim)

Economic activity in the "Description of the Country"—referred to in descriptions of ritual exchanges of farm products offered as "homage" and royal tokens of honor, as well as gold, bestowed as "gifts" during kingly processions; in allusions to the presence of large numbers of foreign merchants in the territories of Majahapit; or in the mention of the dedication of productive land to the upkeep of rural communities in the countryside—is similarly embedded in the ritual routines established and staged by the state. It is through these routines that the connected meanings of "state," "work," and "wealth" were formed. Throughout premodern Southeast Asia the products of both agriculture and trade were gathered and exchanged following ritual procedures that allowed those who participated in them to embody and participate in the hierarchical social order of the state. What exactly was the role of wealth in this process?

In myths about the origins of states along the coasts of Java, Bali, Sumatra, and Kalimantan, wealth is the catalyst for state development (Manguin 1991). Origin stories also reflect the very old tension between traders and rulers, one that long predates the struggle between "absolutist" rulers and wealthy merchants in Reid's "age of commerce." Reid and his colleagues write as if the suppression of the *orang kaya* (men of wealth and power) during the "age of commerce" is a special characteristic of "absolutism" in this period, the principal cause of the failure of capitalism to emerge in Southeast Asia (Reid 1993, 114–123; Kathirithamby-Wells 1993). But state entrepreneurialism had long flourished throughout the region, with kings and merchants competing for control over trade and the wealth essential for entourage and state formation from very early times, as inscriptional evidence cited by Pierre-Yves Manguin attests:

> In the first ever written mention of a *puhawang* [shipmaster] in a late seventh century C.E. Sriwijayan inscription, the ship-master class appears among those who threaten the "treasure" of the ruler (and, interestingly enough, they are among the few that bear an Austronesian, non-imported, title). No doubt, if merchants stopped patronizing a harbor-city, the ruler's "treasure" would rapidly fade away. Similarly, in an inscription from Champa dated 797 C.E., merchants are mentioned, together with warriors, brahmins, and ministers, among those prone to steal the riches of the polity. (Manguin 1991, 51)

Manguin also notices the prevalence of boat symbolism in ritual objects and textiles used in "state or rank-related rituals" in island Southeast Asia (Manguin 1991, 52; 1986). An example of such ritual symbolism mentioned by Manguin is a scene in the Javanese "Description of the Country" in which floats in the form of ships were carried in the important ritual of 1362 commemorating the death of the king's grandmother Rajapatni, while money, food, and clothing were lavishly distributed to the crowds who took part (Prapañca 1995, 73).

Another ritual example could be added to Manguin's list, one that serves to expand the periodization of his topic. It comes from late nineteenth-century Siam and involves a reading of the *Vessantara Jataka,* the story of the last incarnation of the Buddha before he became Siddhatha Gotama, in which he demonstrated his nonattachment to worldly things by renouncing his family. Held in celebration of the crown prince's entry into the monkhood in December 1891, the ceremony included a "symbolical ship," built on the model of a Chinese trading junk,

> as also a numerous fleet of minor craft of all descriptions; of fishes both real and fantastic; and marine monsters, all made of or

filled with eatables and other offerings tastefully arranged. A new and very kindly feature also was introduced. The rich presents that decked the junk and its multifarious and picturesque *cortege,* though intended exclusively for the young Prince, were by him devoted partly to the relief of the sufferers from a recent cyclone in one of the Southern provinces of the realm, and partly to the hospitals and other charitable institutions of the capital. (Gerini 1976 [1892], 36)

In "shipshape" Southeast Asian trading societies, boats are metaphors for the dynamic interaction between wealth and "organized" society (Manguin 1986, 190). The examples taken from Java and Siam above have an additional significance: symbolic ships, laden with goods, were props in rituals that celebrated family unity and prosperity (C. Reynolds 1994, 81; Sombat 1981). The moral of the royal Vessantara ritual of 1891 was really an affirmation rather than a denial of the interconnections between the state, kinship networks, familial values, and wealth: the entire emergent Thai nation-state was defined as a Buddhist "family," with the future king as its fatherly head and chief business tycoon. The nineteenth-century Sino-Thai Bangkok kings were at once Indic rulers, Chinese merchants, and European governors-general, a hybrid identity that had its origins in the sixteenth century (C. Reynolds 1996, 125).

Along with wealth, merchants also brought bureaucratic skills to Southeast Asian states, as they did elsewhere in the premodern world (Subrahmanyam 1992). In Ayutthaya, Chinese, Arab, Persian, and European merchants "helped to run the royal trading monopolies, to manage the treasury, and to implement new techniques for trading, bookkeeping, and fiscal management" (Pasuk and Baker 1995, 92). This is the same pattern found in contemporary Southeast Asia, where entrepreneurs provide states with the business and technical skills needed for participation in the global economy. Rather than interpret the contemporary situation as a "neocolonial" one in which "bureaucratic polities" prey "parasitically" on "capitalists," we should recognize here an old Southeast Asian "king-merchant" symbiosis, one based on rivalry as well as cooperation (cf. McVey 1992a). In this symbiotic relationship, questions of economic development have long been inseparable from ones of state sovereignty (cf. Hawes 1992, 150–152). In the words of the seventeenth-century

Sejarah Melayu, "[W]here there is sovereignty there is gold" (quoted in Wolters 1999, 43)!

The tax-farming regimes of the nineteenth century represent another phase in the historical development of this relationship. In nineteenth-century Thailand and Java, Chinese tax-farmers were incorporated into the state bureaucracy and given official adminis- trative titles (Pasuk and Baker 1995, 95 and passim; Cushman 1991; Rush 1990, 83–107). In both places, the world of the tax-farm became a place within the bureaucratic system where colonial officials ac- quired the financial means with which to cultivate high status and "feudal" entourages. In late nineteenth-century Thailand Chinese tax-farmers who raised the most "splendid revenues" received titles, legal privileges, and the right to furnish wives to the royalty (Pasuk and Baker 1995, 96). In nineteenth-century Java wealthy Chinese tax- farmers regularly made "contributions" *(sumbangan)* to the aristo- cratic lifestyle of the Dutch colonial bureaucracy. According to James Rush,

> The quintessential sumbangan institution in colonial Java was the auction. It was customary for officials to auction off their pri- vate possessions and household furnishings—from flowerpots and teaspoons to carriages and cattle—at the end of each posting. Such auctions offered a final opportunity for an official's subor- dinates, associates, and other well-wishers to demonstrate their respect by purchasing items at highly inflated prices. On such occasions common teacups reportedly brought as much as f500, and native officials from regents to lowly mantris pledged a month's salary to buy the discarded bric-a-brac of the residency house. The higher the position of the departing official, the larger and more dignified the crowd and the more grandiose the bids. Because of this the auctions of departing residents were carnival affairs. (Rush 1990, 131–132)

The colonial auction in Java was a "ritual" comparable to others I have already mentioned, in which the relationship between power and wealth, and the hierarchical relationships between those who participated in the acquisition of both, were negotiated in strategi- cally significant ways. In nineteenth-century Java, it was crucial to the maintenance of that "reassuringly tranquil surface" so prized by

Dutch and Javanese officials alike as the proper mode for the exercise of power that the rigidities of the "statute book" be softened in "casual" environments in which "mutual obligations" could be "engendered" through ritualized activity (Rush 1990, 125, 133, and passim). Ritual events such as the colonial auction or the Javanese royal wedding (Pemberton 1994, 68–101) were themselves productive of state power; they were arenas in which relations of power were displayed, negotiated, and embodied (Pemberton 1994, 190; Bell 1992, 186 and passim). Like the colonial auction, marriage rituals in nineteenth-century Java generally allowed for negotiations about the relationship between hierarchy and wealth—a subject that was examined in Central Javanese writings from one end of the century to the other—to take place (Brenner 1991; Day 1983b; Padmosusastra 1980, 107–114, 290–293; cf. Pemberton 1994, 137–144).

Barbara Andaya gives another interesting example of the ritualization of commercial interaction in her study of the pepper trade in Palembang and Jambi in the seventeenth century, one that throws light on the objective historical reasons for the ideological construction of "wealth" as a "contribution" to be humbly offered to the king. Andaya shows that the rulers of Palembang and Jambi attempted to transform European "strangers" into "trusted merchants" through various ritual means (Andaya 1993, 57). First they tried to turn them into kin by offering them women in marriage, a method of securing kinship-like commercial ties that had worked well with Chinese and Portuguese traders. When Protestant English and Dutch merchants reacted to such proposals with "moral indignation," the rulers attempted to adopt them as "sons." "A formal ceremony was held," Andaya writes,

> and new names, clothing, and symbols of high office were bestowed. In 1640 the VOC factor in Jambi was given a pike and a gilded silk cloth woven by the wife of the pangeran anum and was told to address the ruler "no longer as king but as father." This was not simply a political gesture, for the status of "son" was accorded only selected Europeans and from the indigenous viewpoint established a unique bond. (Andaya 1993, 60)

Since this method of ritualized kinship also failed to create binding ties, other ritualized tactics for dealing with Europeans, such as the exchange of gifts and letters, acquired heightened, and over time an increasingly inflated, significance:

> When the Dutch and English first arrived, mirrors, spectacles, pictures of Amsterdam, muskets, and small amounts of cloth had been considered appropriate presents; a generation later Europeans anxious to attract court favor had to be prepared to offer cannon, precious stones, fine porcelain, jewelry, luxurious cloth, and exotic animals such as sheep. The necessity to obtain royal approval transformed every court ceremony—a royal birth, a marriage, even a death—into an opportunity to acquire commercial advantages. (Andaya 1993, 62)

As we know from the history of the pepper trade in South Sumatra and Southeast Borneo, ritual could not keep the desire of local rulers and European merchants for the accumulation of wealth in check. Unlimited pepper growing and headlong pursuit of wealth were a formula for "ruin," in the words of a seventeenth-century chronicle of the kingdom of Banjar in Southeast Borneo analyzed by Michael Dove (1997) and quoted by Andaya for their pertinence for southern Sumatra in the same period:

> And let not our country plant pepper as an export-crop, for the sake of making money, like Palembang and Jambi. Whenever a country cultivates pepper all food-stuffs will become expensive and anything planted will not grow well, because the vapours of pepper are hot. That will cause malice all over the country and even the government will fall into disorder. The rural people will become pretentious towards the townsfolk if pepper is grown for commercial purposes, for the sake of money. (quoted in Dove 1997, 342–343)

A similar note of alarm at the hierarchy- and hence state-destroying properties of wealth was sounded by the eighteenth-century northern Vietnamese scholar and bureaucrat Lê Quý Đôn (1726–1784) in his "Frontier Chronicles," an analytic survey of the government and economy of Central Vietnam (Woodside 1995). Lê Quý Đôn thought that the robust international trade of the region threatened the stability of the state's bureaucratic order. According to Woodside,

Ever the bureaucrat, one of Lê Quý Đôn's chief concerns about this international trade was the way in which it had created a rising tide of consumer expectations in central Việt Nam. This had dangerous consequences for the political maintenance of social hierarchy. The wealth had a levelling effect: horses and embroidered silk seemed accessible to all. (Woodside 1995, 166)

Both the author of the *Hikayat Banjar* and Lê Quý Đôn were concerned with what can be called the "moral economy" of the Southeast Asian state (cf. Dove 1997, 359, citing J. Scott 1976). For both authors, ritual and bureaucratic practices were rational strategies for converting wealth, with its potential for creating social and political disorder, into well-regulated states.

In the preceding sections of this chapter I have examined examples of the interaction between bureaucracy, ritual, and rationality in Southeast Asia. My interest has been to destabilize conventional meanings for these concepts in scholarly writing on Southeast Asia by looking closely at how they received their meanings in various contexts of Southeast Asian state formation. I have tried to do this in a comparative, nonchronological way so that I can also suggest the need for rethinking our linear notions of the history of the region. I have indicated ways of examining similarities and differences between historical eras that do not depend on either Weberian categories or on his teleology of historical change.

In the final section of this chapter I want to borrow a concept from the work of the social historian Charles Tilly, one that I have already used in formulating my definition of the state in chapter 1, in order to suggest an approach to writing histories of bureaucratic state practices that may avoid the pitfalls I have identified. How do we explain the fact that Benedict Anderson's New Order Indonesian state, for example, looks remarkably like a colonial one without resorting to his merely polemical, rhetorical flourish, namely that we are witnessing the "resurrection of the state and its triumph vis-à-vis society and nation" (B. Anderson 1990, 109 passim)? In historical terms, the question is not one of raising the alarm about the miraculous rebirth of a certain kind of malignant state formation, but of explaining how certain state practices, or what, following Tilly, could be better termed "repertoires" of state power, have come to assume certain enduring shapes over time (Tilly 1993).

Tilly proposes the concept of "repertoire" as a way of understanding the persistence and transformations of culturally specific forms of political "contention":

> The word repertoire identifies a limited set of routines that are learned, shared, and acted out through a relatively deliberate process of choice. Repertoires are learned cultural creations, but they do not descend from abstract philosophy or take shape as a result of political propaganda; they emerge from struggle. The limits of that learning, plus the fact that potential collaborators and antagonists likewise have learned a relatively limited set of means, constrain the choices available for collective action. The means, furthermore, articulate with and help shape a number of social arrangements that are not part of the collective action itself, but channel it to some degree. . . . Like their theatrical counterparts, repertoires of collective action designate not individual performances, but means of *inter*action among pairs or larger sets of actors. . . . Thus, repertoires of contention are the established ways in which pairs of actors make and receive claims bearing on each other's interests. (Tilly 1993, 264–266, emphasis in original)

Although Tilly proposes that the notion of "repertoire" be applied to the study of struggle between social classes in order to gain a better understanding of the "rules" and "constraints" that affect the nature of social change, I think that it can be as fruitfully applied to the question of bureaucracy as it has been to the study of peasant resistance to state power in Southeast Asia (Peluso 1994). To conceive of bureaucracies as cultural and transcultural repertoires rather than as "structures" or "institutions" encourages us to think of them as performative or ritual sets of contentious practices carried out by human agents. What appears to be a bureaucratic "structure" can be viewed as a temporary "arrangement" and "constraint" that binds agents to certain "rules of the game," which may either change or persist, constantly emerging out of the struggle between those who seek to construct or resist particular kinds of state formation. The concept of repertoire thus helps us to train our attention on the practices by which bureaucratic formations take or lose shape over time and to insist on the need for taking the full historical duration and contingency of this process into account. In the brief discussion that follows, I want to sketch what one particular Southeast Asian bureaucratic state repertoire might look like.

The Historical Development of a Bureaucratic Repertoire: The Javanese Case

More than one scholar writing on the history of bureaucracies and states in Indonesia (e.g., Benda 1966, 1982; Emmerson 1978; Sutherland 1979) has commented on the long-term interaction of Asian-traditional and Western-colonial and -postcolonial factors in the making of the modern state. But there is still need for greater precision about the particular aspects and effects of the interaction of cultural and transcultural forces that have gone into the making of bureaucratic-state repertoires over time. The usual coupling of "tradition" and "patrimonialism" with Asia and of "rationality" with the West in most analyses is, as I have been arguing, an assumption that is ripe for reexamination. The "rational"/"ritual," Western/Asian dichotomy is particularly noticeable in studies of modern Southeast Asian states, where there is a tendency toward polemical critique of cultural essentialism accompanied by renewed interest in colonialism and its influence on the present (e.g., B. Anderson 1990; Pemberton 1994; Robinson 1995; Sidel 1997). But to turn the abstract concept of "colonialism" into a hegemonic agent and hold it responsible for creating the modern Southeast Asian state not only deprives human beings of their historic role in a process that is neither linear nor one-sided, but it is just as reductive and essentializing as the concept of "culture" that is being critiqued! It has taken more historical agents, more transcultural interactions, and a far longer historical *durée* than these studies suggest to create the bureaucracies of Southeast Asia.

The representation of the state found in the fourteenth-century "Description of the Country" is a good starting point for an attempt to sketch an alternative history of the Javanese bureaucratic repertoire. In the text, the bureaucracy of Majapahit has the appearance, constantly recreated through ceremonial events and ritual progresses, of a Hindu-Buddhist cosmography. This "Indic" appearance creates the illusion that the hierarchy of state officials who form the dominant elite related to one another by marriage constitutes a "state." The bureaucracy, like the state itself, is also a fluid network of competing families and individuals with bases of power outside the state, but their practices as members of the state are constrained by repeatedly stated Indic rules of etiquette and morality. The function of state offices is both religiously symbolic and administratively functional: the bureaucracy administers the realm and enacts, through public rituals, a cosmological unity, which is embodied, through appropriate physical movements and modes of dress, in those who take part in ritual state activities. Bureaucratic service to the state is motivated by economic opportunism as well as the desire for religious merit and high social status; in fact, the three motives seem interdependent. What persuaded the "real" bureaucratic officials represented in the text to serve the state was probably a combination of possible motives, such as religious belief; a desire to participate in the "higher" and more "beautiful" Indic civilization of the king's court; a familial ethos of devotion and loyalty to the ruler; status envy; economic opportunism; and a fear of violence (see also Supomo 1977; Pollock 1996; chapter 5 below).

The Javanese "Majapahit" mode of Indic state formation outlived the demise assigned to it by historians and exerted long-lasting and far-reaching influence on state practices in many parts of the Indonesian archipelago outside Java. The Portuguese Tomé Pires described aspects of its hierarchical and ritual modus operandi when he visited the north coast of Java at the beginning of the sixteenth century (Cortesão 1967, 166–200). Variants of the formation were still active in Islamicized Central Java and in regions of the archipelago, such as Sumatra and Borneo, that came under the cultural and political influence of Majapahit-style Javanese states during the seventeenth and eighteenth centuries (Ricklefs 1998; Andaya 1993; Drakard 1999; Maier 1997b; Dove 1997; Ras 1968). In Bali during the nineteenth and twentieth centuries, a strong local variant of "Majapahit" developed, actively fostered by Dutch colonial officials and policies once the island had been pacified (C. Geertz 1980; Boon 1977; Robinson 1995). Another colonial variant of post-Majapahit bureaucratic practices was introduced into Sumatra in the nineteenth century (Dobbin 1983), and then in a New Order format throughout the Indonesian republic after 1965 (Pemberton 1994), where neo-Majapahit state practices were sometimes challenged by political forces shaped by alternative cultural memories of contact with Majapahit centuries earlier (Tsing 1993).

The civilizational authority of the Majapahit state formation, even if we allow for alterations and limitations brought about by Islamization, colonialism, and nationalism, has been remarkably far-reaching and long lasting (also see Gunn 1997). But a full examination of this assertion is impossible here. Instead, I want to move on to the question of how successive Dutch state formations interacted in transcultural ways with the state in Central Java over time. Other studies of such interactions in Java and Sumatra during the eighteenth century have stressed the absolute difference and nontransformative nature of cultural contact between the Dutch and indigenous peoples (Ricklefs 1974, 1998; Andaya 1993; Drakard 1999). I want to argue here that we consider cultural affinities and possible transcultural effects, at least in the case of those who participated in the successive formations of the Javanese state that came to dominate the archipelago until the end of the twentieth century.

As described in a series of articles by the sociologist Julia Adams (1994a, 1994b, 1996), the Dutch state that collided at the beginning of the seventeenth century with Mataram, the next large-scale Javanese state formation after Majapahit, was also a "familial state." In the Dutch case, "elite male family heads seized hold of local state offices, constituting themselves as a regent patriciate" that intermarried, formed lineages, fought among themselves, and used bureaucratic office to pursue economic gain, which was bequeathed to successive generations (Adams 1994a, 505 passim). Jean Taylor has shown that the Dutch East India Company (VOC), located in Batavia, was based on a network of family relationships. She also brings out the importance of ritual in the way the VOC conducted its business (J. Taylor 1983).

But there was less difference between the "Asian" and the "European" variants of the seventeenth-century Dutch state than Taylor argues (Day 1984). According to a Dutch pamphleteer writing of the situation at home in 1747, but in words that would apply perfectly to the situation in Java, "everyone knows that the quickest way to get rich is to get into the government and that is the reason that men pay to get in" (quoted in Adams 1994a, 507). Over time the effect of "the regents' embrace of politico-economic privilege and office" was that they became rentiers rather than active merchant capitalists (Adams 1994a, 518). In the course of the eighteenth century the Dutch political economy declined for this and other reasons. Adams stresses the role of familial practices and ideology, which facilitated the "accumulation and strengthening of patrimonial privilege" in the seventeenth century, as a major reason for the decline:

> To reform the state the regent family heads would have had to do away with its familial structure. Yet their money was secured in it. Their authority, status, and very identity were tied to the state, in part because it would also be their sons' and their sons' sons'. Instead, elite families embraced their piece of the polity more tightly, just as the legitimating political symbolism of heredity, birth, and blood began to conflict with the newer Enlightenment and popular attitudes of merit, utility, and reason pervading eighteenth-century Europe, including the Netherlands. (Adams 1994a, 522)

In a second essay (1994b), Adams argues against the assertion put forward in world-systems theory that only "strong states" are capable of achieving high levels of capital accumulation and hence dominance in the world economy. If the Dutch were, in Defoe's words, "the Carryers of the World, the middle persons in Trade, the Factors and Brokers of Europe" (quoted in Adams 1994b, 321), it was precisely because theirs was a nascent patrimonial state "marked by a segmentation or parcelization of sovereign power among the ruler (or rulers) and corporate elites" (Adams 1994b, 326). At the end of the sixteenth century, the mercantile elites of the states of Holland had successfully retained their control of maritime and trade policy, and under the Union of Utrecht the fifteen hundred regents were confirmed as the ruling elite (Adams 1994b, 329–330). When the VOC was established at the initiative of the Amsterdam regents in 1602, it was from the start "a patrimonial state creation and merged partnership of state and merchant class," and it pursued "an explicitly coercive politico-economic project" (Adams 1994b, 332–334). The most important factor that assisted Jan Pieterszoon Coen's aggressive colonial strategy in Asia was "the dispersed sovereignty inherent in patrimonial political structures," allowing him to operate "out of control" of the states-general and Heren XVII. In the words of the English ambassador to the Netherlands in 1612, the VOC was "a body by themselves, powerfull and mighty in this State, and will not acknowledge the authority of the States generally more than shall be for their private profits" (quoted in Adams 1994b, 336). As a char-

tered company operating in Java, the VOC, "like other powerful corporate bodies, joined towns, provinces . . . other corporations," and
the various power networks within the state of Mataram in "jockey-
ing for position and struggling to define themselves politically
within an emergent structured totality, the interstate system" (Adams
1994b, 337).

Fundamentally, seventeenth- and eighteenth-century post-Majapahit Mataram, which has been described by Luc Nagtegaal as a
"network state," more closely resembled the contemporaneous VOC
variant of the European Dutch state than it did the mythic, Javanese
"Oriental despotism" of VOC and later Dutch colonial thinking or
Moertono's idealized, purely indigenous "old" Javanese kingdom
(Nagtegaal 1996, 32 passim; Moertono 1981). Both state formations
were familial, ritualistic, and based, contrary to an "absolutist" model
of state power, on "dispersed" rather than "centralized" sovereignty
(cf. B. Anderson 1990, 17–77; Reid 1993, 202–266).

The similarities can be glimpsed if we compare two descriptions
of these states. The first passage below depicts the relationship
between the Susuhunan, king of Mataram, and the regents who governed in his name along the Pasisir (north coast of Java) during the
late seventeenth and early eighteenth centuries. The second describes power struggles in Holland from the same era.

> Relations between the Pasisir regents and the Susuhunan varied
> from one person to the next. Regents differed greatly in terms of
> their power and status. Some were almost the equals (in terms
> of military might and wealth, for instance) of the Mataram ruler
> himself, while other *bupati* were figures of little significance. A
> regent's standing was determined not by his position but by his
> successfulness [*sic*] in the power struggle. Some regents went so
> far as to adopt the stance of patron with respect to weaker *bupati*.
> (Nagtegaal 1996, 52)

> The regents also fought amongst themselves. Recruitment of rela-
> tives could lead to flagrant violations of traditional limits on
> town councils inscribed in civic charters, as regents sought to in-
> clude more of their male relatives. . . . Letters and legal cases decry
> alleged family take-overs of local East Indies Company boards.
> . . . Throughout the early modern era, power shifted back and

forth between patriciate families sympathetic to the Orangist cause and those intent on minimizing the stadholders' influence. (Adams 1994a, 515)

During the struggle between these two (in many ways) quite similar state formations, "political entrepreneurs" on both sides took advantage of the dispersed nature of sovereignty and control in their respective organizations to pursue ends that were simultaneously political and economic. Employees from the bottom to the top of the VOC hierarchy engaged in "practices like diluting the precious metals that arrived in Batavia, skimming off a percentage of goods bound for VOC warehouses, taking a brokerage percentage from indigenous suppliers, or defrauding the Company on its return cargo" (Adams 1996, 21). In the new economic and political conditions along the north coast brought about by VOC monopolistic policies and the treaty obligations imposed by the company on the king of Mataram to repay his war debts with cash money and rice, certain Javanese and Javanese-Chinese regents also became powerful and wealthy entrepreneurs, trading in political allegiances, bureaucratic offices, and economic prizes like any Dutch regent or VOC official worthy the name (J. Taylor 1983, 66 passim). According to Nagtegaal,

The most successful political entrepreneurs were members of a family of mixed Chinese-Javanese descent, of whom the best known was Jayadiningrat. He came from a commercially oriented background; his father farmed the tollgates along the road between Semarang and Kartasura. When he entered the service of Susuhunan Amangkurat III in 1703, Jayadiningrat's star soared, and he acquired the title of *tumenggung*. It was particularly at his insistence that the new Susuhunan adopted a cool attitude to the VOC. Jayadiningrat had himself appointed supreme commander of the army, and assured his sovereign that he would defeat the combined forces of Pakubuwana I and the Company. But before the first shot had been fired, Jayadiningrat had opened negotiations, and when the enemy promised him an important regency on the north coast, he went over to the other side. His reward proved to be Pekalongan, and in exchange for a payment of 3,000 *reales* he also acquired the [Javanese court] post of *wedana kilen*. (Nagtegaal 1996, 166)

Although the dispersal of authority and the destabilizing effects of political entrepreneurship, when combined with other factors, had similar effects within each state system (i.e., the collapse of both the VOC and the state of Mataram at the end of the eighteenth century), the Dutch state eventually triumphed over its Javanese rival by successfully transforming the latter into an agent of its own bureaucratic repertoire of economic exploitation, first of Java, then of the rest of what became the Netherlands Indies (Nagtegaal 1996, 84 passim). As that transformation occurred, "contentious struggles" took place within a hybrid state formation that continued to exhibit characteristics of both of its ancestors, as well as of Majapahit of old.

The administrative structure of Java after the final military pacification of Java in 1830 appeared to be and worked like a variation on the repertoire of VOC-Mataram relationships that had developed up to the end of the eighteenth century. The Cultivation System was in fact a conscious reversion to the policy of the VOC, whereby "native chiefs" would manage the agricultural production of the island and govern the native population, all on behalf of the penurious Dutch state (Fasseur 1992a, 50). From Batavia Java was ruled by the governor-general, who was given autocratic powers by the constitutional regulation of 1836 and assisted by a small, "revenue oriented" bureaucracy. In the provinces were found the faction-riven, tiny successor states to Mataram, Surakarta, and Yogyakarta, together with eighteen residencies and two assistant residencies (by 1860, nineteen and four, respectively), each headed by a Dutch resident and his European staff. In 1865 the total Indies BB (*binnenlands bestuur*, or internal administration) bureaucracy consisted of only 175 European officials (Fasseur 1992a, 21–22)! Cornelis Fasseur adds:

> Actual control over the population rested with a much larger administrative apparatus of "native" officials, who were at the same time the traditional leaders of the people. . . . The regents were the "trusted advisers" of the Residents and at the same time their "younger brothers" (one of those paternalistic touches that proliferated in every colonial society). The government did not see the regents solely as ordinary officials, who could be transferred or dismissed at the pleasure of the government, but as native chiefs (*volkshoofden*), who were entitled to special signs of respect. (Fasseur 1992a, 22)

In 1854 the "repeat performance" of first VOC, then Dutch colonial, respect for and political manipulation of notions of high birth and hierarchy was given clearer bureaucratic articulation through article 69 of the constitutional regulation, which made the office of native regent hereditary. Again, we might well ask, Who was kissing whom on the knee?

Historians have followed the paper trail of colonial regulations and policy decisions to sketch the growing "rationalization" of the Indies bureaucracy in the second half of the nineteenth century and the first two decades of the twentieth. But the paradox of an "irrational" ideal type of ritualized bureaucracy encountered by van Leur in 1935 calls for a better understanding of the way the "reason of state" in Indonesia developed within older repertoires of bureaucratic practice (Furnivall 1944; Sutherland 1979; Onghokham 1978). As the quote from van Leur's letter excerpted above suggests, two of the principal actors in the bureaucratic repertoire of Java at the end of the colonial period—the European BB and the Javanese native bureaucracy, the *pangreh praja*—exhibited many of the same characteristics possessed by those who had been playing similar roles for almost three centuries.

Throughout the colonial period, but also, indeed, since the days of Majapahit, bureaucracy and ritual were interlocking state practices. "Public ritual was an important part of the Dutch colonial style in Java," writes Rush of the nineteenth century. "In a fashion mimicking the old state pageantry of Mataram, the Dutch made a spectacle of important occasions" (Rush 1990, 43). Where once Hayam Wuruk had traveled to display and elicit participation in the cosmological universality of his dominance, Javanese kings (captive or exiled) (Kumar 1980; Day 1983b), *priyayi* bureaucrats (Bonneff 1986), visiting Southeast Asian monarchs (Chulalongkorn 1993), and Dutch officials now rode in stately procession (van Leur 1957). In his discussion of nineteenth-century Central Java, John Pemberton has argued that the meaning of *upacara* as "official ceremonial events" was a new colonial invention rather than an ancient Javanese one (Pemberton 1994, 189–196). But in the quotation taken from the fourteenth-century *Deśawarṇana* given at the beginning of "Wealth, Bureaucracy, and Ritual" above, the Old Javanese word *"upacāra"* is used in both an "old" sense, as "ritual appurtenances," and in its supposedly "new" one, as "rites, proper conduct" (for other instances of both meanings of the word in Old Javanese, see Zoetmulder 1982, 2128–

2129). Ritual had long been a part of both Dutch and Javanese state practices, and ritual practices in the nineteenth century, including the "royal progress," clearly had overlapping and conflicting cultural dimensions and political significances. Pemberton also invokes a variant of the familiar ritual-as-Oriental-mystification concept, asserting that colonial Javanese ritual was motivated by "nostalgia" for "tradition." A better explanation is that colonial Javanese rituals were variations on a long-standing repertoire of ritualized bureaucratic practices, and these cultural variations continued to shape Dutch-Javanese relations until the end of the colonial period. The following passage from Pemberton's study in fact suggests how colonial conditions allowed for a continuation of an ancient pas de deux between "administration" and "ritual" in the bureaucratic life of the Javanese state:

> Owing to the Javanese elite's nostalgia for its retreating, now "traditional," world and to the colonial government's desire to recover such a world as "Java" after the disturbing events in the Indies of the 1920s [caused by the rise of the nationalist movement], by the 1930s the term *ceremonie* gave way to the indigenous Javanese *upacârâra* and its Malay equivalent, *upacara*. These indigenous terms shifted to take over the role of *ceremonie* and, thus, acquired a second, more active meaning over and above regalia; *upacara* could now mean official ceremonial events. (Pemberton 1994, 192)

Ceremonialism is not the only element of an older bureaucratic repertoire that can be found, in reconfigured modes of interaction, in colonial Java. Fasseur's study of the Cultivation System (1992a) describes in detail how graft continued to be institutionalized in the colonial state, which was "sovereign" as well as "planter and merchant" until the liberal reforms of the 1860s and 1870s, through the payment of cultivation percentages to both native and European officials on low "official" salaries (Fasseur 1992a, 105 passim). Fabulous bonuses and nepotistic practices were particularly found in the sugar industry (Fasseur 1992a, 185–222). Fasseur comments:

> A notable example was I. D. Fransen van de Putte, later to become minister of colonies. In 1849, James Loudon and Cremer had appointed him as administrator of the sugar factory Pandji in

Besuki, then still to be built, at a salary of f350 per month. In 1851, he became the lessee; in 1854, owner of a quarter-share; and in 1857, owner of the remaining three-quarters. . . . In 1859, Fransen van de Putte, who also had fortunate interests in some "free" tobacco plantations, returned to the Netherlands as a millionaire. (Fasseur 1992a, 198)

Rush's study of the opium revenue farm in the second half of the nineteenth century (1990) is also revealing of how bureaucracy-as-ritualized-money-making-repertoire worked in colonial Java. The *cabang atas*, or "highest branch," of the Chinese community in Java attained wealth and high bureaucratic rank through control of the opium farms. Stories like the following read like variations on tales from the Pasisir of the early eighteenth century or the Netherlands in the seventeenth:

Nonya Be's great-grandfather, Tan Bing, had immigrated to Java in the late 1700s. As Liem [Thian Joe] tells his story, he arrived poor in Semarang and engaged in petty trade until he had acquired enough capital to open his own store. His business expanded, and he leased the teak-cutting concession and later still the lucrative salt monopoly. Then, like many successful Chinese entrepreneurs in Java, he invested in sugar milling. Tan Bing distributed his refined sugar to the towns and markets of central Java and gradually established shipping connections with Batavia, Ceribon, and Surabaya. His son, Tan Tiang Tjhing, later took over his various enterprises. . . . In recognition of his success, the Dutch appointed the younger Tan lieutenant of Semarang in 1809. Following this appointment, Tan became captain and ultimately in 1829 Semarang's first Chinese major. . . . His son, Tan Hong Yan, . . . became Chinese captain in 1828 and in the same year succeeded his father as opium farmer for all central Java. (Rush 1990, 92–93)

Such rags-to-bureaucratic-riches stories were made possible by the ways in which Chinese opium interests interacted with the Javanese *pangreh praja* bureaucracy and other institutions of the colonial state. The *pangreh praja* needed the cooperation of the Chinese opium networks in the villages to carry out their primary colonial and ancient cosmological function of preserving "order" and investigating crime, as well as to provide them with the necessary cash to maintain their status and ritual authority. The opium farmers needed the Javanese administrators to help control smuggling, which cut into their profit margin. Rush observes:

> Such collaboration was self-interested on both sides, for the pr[i]yayi [Javanese officials], too, had something to gain by protecting the local farm. Specifically, by means of gifts, bounties, loans, and salaries, the opium farm Chinese helped subsidize the regal manners and customs expected of pr[i]yayi by tradition—manners and customs that their own dwindling resources failed to support. (Rush 1990, 120)

As far as the Dutch were concerned, opium farms provided large amounts of official state revenue (16.8 percent of total revenue collected and 31.9 percent of daily administrative costs between 1848 and 1866), as well as lavish personal bonuses, since until the end of the nineteenth century Dutch officials also lived in regal Oriental style, beyond their official means (Rush 1990, 129–133). Dutch bureaucratic behavior was influenced by capitalistic "rationality," familial pride and status consciousness, and the civilizing, Orientalizing cosmological afterglow of the Majapahit sun.

Until the end of the nineteenth century, in other words, bureaucracy in Java operated according to a repertoire that can be traced back to Majapahit, via the seventeenth-century Netherlands. Although I have brought out the compatibility of Javanese and Dutch state formations in sketching this repertoire until the end of the nineteenth century, a more complete analysis would consider changes in the repertoire. By the end of the nineteenth century, for example, there were significant differences between Dutch and Javanese views of the hybrid practices of the Euro-Javanese state. From the Dutch side came mounting criticism of the "overall corrupting combination of opium, sinister profiteering Chinese, and greedy officials" and a push to "rationalize" the administration of the colony (Rush 1990, 202). There were certainly Western-style, modernizing "rationalists" on the Javanese side as well (Sutherland 1979). But as I have indicated in chapter 3 and in earlier portions of my discussion in this chapter, Javanese attempts were made throughout the colonial period to formulate non-Western, noncolonial modes of rationality in state practice, and these attempts eventually made important contributions to the formation of the Indonesian state in the independence period. A seemingly bizarre proposition of this kind during the late nineteenth century was made by the author of the *Suluk Gatholoco,* a Javanese text that I mentioned earlier in the context of Southeast Asian criticisms of bureaucratic forms of thinking and behavior. In this mystical Javanese poem, which celebrates the adventures and mishaps of an opium-smoking, ambulatory penis, a case is made for a kind of Javanese mode of reasoning that is diametrically opposed to that being advanced by the modernizers in either Westernized or Islamic Javanese circles at the time. The plot, theology, and physical form of the protagonist in the poem restate Javanese Sufi variants of Hindu-Buddhist cosmological thinking about state formation from even before the days of Majapahit.

In the course of the twentieth century, the expansion of the colonial state and its consolidation of territorial control over the entire archipelago took place; transportation and communications systems were expanded and modernized; and the inhabitants of the Indies were transformed into a "population" that needed general "welfare" as well as supervision (Furnivall 1944, 295; cf. Foucault 1991b, 99–100). These processes both stimulated and required the development of a less single-mindedly entrepreneurial, but no less ritualized, as well as vastly expanded, colonial state bureaucracy. But as I have already indicated, the bureaucratic repertoire was one in which the nature of rationalization, as one among many features of its already evolved and still developing formation, was conditioned by the nature of the repertoire. In ways that were less entrepreneurial than was the case in the seventeenth to nineteenth centuries, "bureaucracy" still meant "the intricate interplay of BB personalities, popular sentiment, and *priyayi* [Javanese state bureaucrat] intrigues," rather than a more impersonal process informed by Western ideas communicated by "newspapers, mass meetings, Marxism or nationalism" (Sutherland 1979, 80, 85). As a consequence of both Western and Javanese, new and old forces at work in the hybrid colonial context of Javanese state formation, a Western-educated Javanese aristocrat like Soewardi (Ki Hadjar Dewantara), who founded the Taman Siswa movement in 1922 and whose ideas helped lay the basis for Sukarno's Guided Democracy (Tsuchiya 1987,

213–215) as well Suharto's New Order (Reeve 1985; Bourchier 1997), was less likely to adopt the exploitative "rationality" of the Indies *beamtenstaat* as a feature of his own thinking about "wise" *(bijaksana)* leadership and bureaucratic rule. In an article that appeared in 1936 Soewardi wrote:

> When a "regulation" does not describe what it is meant to ac-
> complish, a leader can often do nothing at all. If you remember
> that no regulation whatsoever is completely perfect, you will see
> that Western "democracy" is often totally ineffective. It is for this
> very reason that I am proposing that leaders should inquire into
> ways and means to achieve *keselamatan* (tranquility) without being
> shackled. A leader can be regarded as a wise man by virtue of
> his being a leader, and he should also be regarded as more per-
> fect than any *reglement* (regulation). (quoted in Tsuchiya 1987, 4)

Soewardi understood and rejected the individualism, materialism, and domination concealed behind the reasonableness of
Dutch colonial *zakelijkheid*. But this understanding of "reason" as a
covert signifier of exploitation was not his insight alone: it already
informed Javanese understandings of the bureaucratic repertoire at
the end of the eighteenth century, when the author of the *Serat
Sakondhar*, a text written at the court of the first Sultan of Yogyakarta,
explained, in mythical terms, the dual structure of the Javanese-
Dutch bureaucratic state (Ricklefs 1974, 362–413; Sartono 1988, 209–
224). In the following passage the poem describes the "origin" of the
VOC, by command of the "Nakoda" (Merchant) to his twelve sons:

> Now it is my command:
> all worldly goods, I command,
> these I make to be king,
> adorning the *kraton;*
> my twelve sons, watch over them.
> Be not in discord, let your salaries be the same,
> take the salaries from profits.
>
> These worldly goods be regarded as king.
> Be set on your way (you) twelve.
> But be agreed in your consultations;

if one is not consulted
consider no further, think again,
do what is good.
Suffer no misfortune in what you desire,
even if it comes to thievery.
These worldly goods I name "The Company."
But to be consulted over by (you) twelve are

all of its affairs:
commerce, war, the destroying of cities.
These worldly goods be salaries then,
but omit not to calculate,
write up precisely
the profits and the losses,
remember these calculations. (quoted and translated in Ricklefs
      1974, 396–397)

These stanzas show a recognition, one that we have also met in the *Hikayat Banjar* and the "Frontier Chronicles" of Lê Quý Đôn, that "money" could usurp the sovereignty of the state, destroying the cosmological unity of Southeast Asian siblings bound together as one (Cannell 1999, 54; S. Errington 1989, 232–272). This threatened disintegration of the state is counteracted in genealogical terms in the text by the creation of a hybrid line of descent that links the rulers of the spirit world, Majapahit, Sunda (i.e., the location of Batavia), Islam, Holland, and Spain, to the governors-general of Batavia (Ricklefs 1974, 410). Also significant for our understanding of how the bureaucratic repertoire developed in Java from the seventeenth century onward is the implication in the text that rationality, in the meaning of disciplined unity and calculated control of the balance sheet of domination (cf. Andaya 1993, 74 and passim), was not located in the Javanese "interior" of the bureaucratic state. The poem asserts that this region was ruled by the sultan and his administration of local spirits, who are named along with their locations across the length and breadth of the island of Java. The Javanese "reason of state" as it developed during the seventeenth and eighteenth centuries came to require the participation of an agent external to the spiritual interior of the state, one that was crucial for access to wealth and violence—namely the VOC (Ricklefs 1998, 338). Thus a "duality" in the practices of the Javanese state developed in the course of seventeenth and eighteenth centuries as the VOC became the military and commercial arm of the Mataram ceremonial and "network" state, a relationship that was modified but not radically altered during the colonial period (Nagtegaal 1996, 69). By the 1930s the *beamtenstaat* still consisted of a dual, hybrid formation in which sovereignty was divided between the Dutch BB, presiding over wealth and violence, and the Javanese *pangreh praja,* who regulated ceremony, status, and patronage.

As Herbert Feith (1962), Donald Emmerson (1978), and especially Anderson (1990, 99–109) have suggested, the period from 1945, when Indonesia declared its independence, to 1965 could be seen as one in which a "weak" state failed to govern a "strong" and chaotic society. The failure of "administrators," the ascendancy of "solidarity makers," the tenfold increase in the size of the bureaucracy (from 250,000 in 1940 to 2.5 million in 1968) as political parties and patronage networks invaded state institutions and used them as a source of livelihood, social prestige, and power—these and other developments exerted new pressures on the bureaucratic repertoire that had developed up to the end of the colonial period. What Anderson has called the unique "porousness" of the state in the 1950s is certainly not unprecedented, however, nor were the uses to which the state bureaucracy was put, albeit by new forces and numbers. As Feith and McVey have pointed out, in the 1950s the bureaucracy was, more than ever before, a beacon of civilization, the destination of those who identified themselves with the modernity of "organization," education, and progress. If we entertain the possibility that the fourteenth century also had a concept of "modernity" based on the latest ideas received from India and elsewhere, then the same statement could probably be made about the courtiers, local gentry, and village heads who became bureaucrats in the days of the famous prime minister of Majapahit, Gajah Mada (Feith 1962, 103; McVey 1990, 20).

The ways in which the early independent state was "rescued" from democracy through the intervention of the army, which was dominated by Javanese officers and financed by the resources of seized Dutch economic interests, and the policies of Sukarno, particularly the banning of political parties and the introduction of Guided Democracy in 1958, are also in keeping with an older repertoire of contention within the Javanese state (B. Anderson 1990, 103–104). It was the VOC that rescued the Mataram state, the *beamtenstaat* that allowed its heirs to form a courtly bureaucracy that remained in power for a century. The repetition of these interventions in the workings of the state in the late 1950s, described in 1961 (see below) by a Cornell-trained Javanese bureaucrat from Yogyakarta, echoes the administrative ideals of Majapahit, Taman Siswa, and the *beamtenstaat*, even as it foreshadows the coming together of all three variations of the repertoire in Suharto's New Order (1966–1998):

> Within the organization of the administration itself, the personnel is no longer divided into overt factions which in the past were responsible for much of the administrative inefficiency because of intergroup conflicts, mutual suspicions, and political favoritism in the distribution of key positions and financially profitable jobs. . . . The focus of political life has shifted to the administration itself. Political parties no longer decide legislative and executive issues; the decisive powers are now entirely in the hands of the administrative officers, the President on the national level. . . . There is only one source of political norms: the President. (Selosoemardjan 1962, 128–129)

It would thus be reasonable to view the New Order bureaucratic state between 1966 and 1998 as not so much the "resurrection" of an older state form (B. Anderson 1990, 109) as the predictable outcome of a state repertoire that had been developing over centuries. In terms of this repertoire, Suharto was arguably more successful than Gajah Mada's master, King Hayam Wuruk, or three centuries of Dutch governors-general in creating a hybrid bureaucratic order of *priyayi* entrepreneurs and administrator-soldiers with armed violence, technocratic "rationality," cosmological mysticism, and ritual equally on tap (Emmerson 1978, 102 and passim; Jenkins 1984; Pemberton 1994). The New Order state also had a bureaucracy of spirits, consulted by the president, his administrators, and dissidents alike (Pemberton 1994, 236–268; Bourchier 1984).

As in the days of Majapahit, the VOC, or the opium farm, the New Order state was also a business (Winters 1996). In the words of Heri Akhmadi, a student leader tried and convicted for insulting the president in 1979:

The New Order regime has produced a prototype Indonesian human being frequently referred to as: government businessman-official. He's an official but also a businessman; he's a business-man but also an official. It is not hard to imagine how depraved a person is who holds two such titles simultaneously! . . . By their nature these people are not really cut out to be businessmen: they are not hard-working, persevering and thrifty, the way business-men should be. They act more like feudal lords who, because of their office, can put their feet up and wait for tribute or bribes from the cukong [Chinese financial backer]. (Akhmadi 1981, 103)

In this latter-day cosmological state, concealed, as in the days of the *beamtenstaat*, beneath a "tangle of rules and regulations" (Winters 1996, 165), were the operations of a bureaucratic repertoire that did not require an official to be "rational" in the Weberian sense de-manded by the International Monetary Fund, as long as international market conditions were right. In words that seem to pay obeisance to the admonitions of Ki Hadjar Dewantara, Ibnu Sutowo, erstwhile head of the state oil company PERTAMINA, remarked to Jeffrey Winters in 1989:

I paid no attention to bureaucratic rules and procedures. If there was a project being considered, I usually said I would have an answer in a month. If I said yes, they could start operations that afternoon. With the ministries, even after you got approval, you still had to wait. (Winters 1996, 85)

Sutowo, his king, their *cukong* (Chinese financiers), and the investors who allowed them to perform in a bureaucratic repertoire that dates back to the fourteenth century have now left the stage, at least for the moment. In light of the argument advanced in this chapter, it seems likely that the Indonesian state of the future will continue to be shaped within the constraints and practices of a bureau-cratic repertoire that has been assuming its present form over many centuries.

Summary

The similarities or differences between the model of a Javanese bureaucratic repertoire that I have just sketched and bureaucracies in other parts of Southeast Asia remain to be seen. But I have no doubt that the makings of a similar approach to Southeast Asian bureaucracies can already be extracted and synthesized from the scholarly works I have referred to in this study. Certain regional generalizations in advance of detailed local confirmation are worth drawing, even if they need qualification later on.

Notwithstanding the fact that specifically "Western" bureaucratic practices were introduced into Southeast Asia from the early seventeenth century onward, much of the history of the "impact" of Western bureaucratic practices and of modern "rationalization" on Southeast Asia misrepresents the nature of the transcultural processes involved and so distorts the history of the Southeast Asian state. The assumption that state practices from the West and those indigenous to Southeast Asia have at all times and in all respects been radically different from one another is wrong. If we think of the Southeast Asian state as having been situated in a network of individuals, economic relationships, and ideas extending across much of the globe since the beginning of the Christian era, then it is also misleading to privilege only the Western factors that have shaped the long progression of Southeast Asia toward some kind of (as yet poorly understood) alternative modernity (C. Taylor 1999). The interplay of similarities, as well as differences, between Southeast Asian and Western bureaucratic practices over time can much better be traced by means of Tilly's concept of repertoire. Like Latour's idea of the "network" or Foucault's " 'microrelations' of power, the local interactions and petty calculations of daily life" (Bell 1992, 200), the notion of repertoire keeps the analytic focus and explanatory center of gravity in the study of the Southeast Asian state at the level of actual social interactions between human agents, their paperwork, and ideas over the long duration of their entire history. These interactions have shaped bureaucratic practices in ways that cannot be neatly periodized in linear fashion along the standard chronology of Southeast Asian history. Nor do they lead from one pure and discrete historical stage to another, separated by "epistemic breaks" (Englehart 2001, 93, 102). In colonial Southeast Asia, older and newer modes of cultural, political, and economic production overlapped, and it is this overlapping that produced the distinctive trajectories of modern states in the region (McKenna 1998; Rush 1990; Day 1986; P. Anderson 1974). As J. M. Gullick has written of "the evolution of

Malay State governments towards a bureaucratic pattern" in a book that could serve as one of the important starting points for a "repertoire" approach to the history of the Malaysian state: "What happened in each case was the product of local circumstances, traditions, and personalities" (Gullick 1992, 162). I would add: "local" but also "global" circumstances, traditions, and personalities. There never was a time when global as well as local transcultural forces did not affect the power dynamic of bureaucracies and rituals in Southeast Asia. This assertion is borne out in many other studies that are richly suggestive of histories that could be written about bureaucratic repertoires in other parts of Southeast Asia (e.g., Pasuk and Baker 1995; Sidel 1999a).

Like the desire for status and hierarchy, as well as the "dynastic" familyism that these two cultural forces have continued to nourish and utilize, bureaucracies are crucial institutional repertoires that affect state formation in Southeast Asia. "Reasons of state" throughout the region are informed by cosmologies, the search for invulnerability, and various kinds of modern thinking, both secular and religious. They are also shaped by familyism and ritual modes of power that are practiced in bureaucratic contexts. Lefort suggests that ritualism is just as intrinsic to what is "modern" about bureaucracy as is "rationality." I have tried to show in this chapter that ritual is in any case not a new mode for creating relations of power in the context of bureaucracy in Southeast Asia (cf. Pemberton 1994, 190). Older concepts and approaches to ritual have shaped responses to the ritual resources of modern bureaucracies. Thus the importance of ritual in forming the Southeast Asian state has been constant and constantly renewed, especially by means of and in the context of bureaucratic practices, since the invention of the state idea in the region.

The sketch of a history of the bureaucratic repertoire in Java with which this chapter concludes has brought out similarities over time and across states and cultures at the expense of what may well have been even more important differences. The ritual negotiations of power as described over and over again in the *Serat Centhini* exhibit possibly significant differences from those that must have been embedded in the Independence Day rituals of a Central Javanese village in 1975 and 1978 described by Teruo Sekimoto (1990), for example. There is an obvious contrast between the free-flowing, almost anarchic feel of ritual celebrations described in the *Centhini* and the highly disciplined and bureaucratic nature of the New Order celebrations (Sekimoto 1990, 62). In both cases the village is the object of domination and the focal point for the formation of "official" identity. As we also learn from Pemberton (1994, 236–268), the balance of power between the village and the state has clearly shifted in the direction of the state since the late eighteenth century, although this may be about to change as Indonesians begin to decentralize and democratize their state. We cannot be sure what is going on exactly in Sekimoto's 1970s rituals because the agencies and negotiations at work beneath the surface of orderly, ritualized uniformity have not been brought to light. But when Sekimoto writes that "[i]n reality . . . the Independence Day celebration represents the ritualization of production and work themselves . . . assimilating village communal labor into a ritual form that is an end in itself and transforming this labor into ritual competition," we recognize the nature of ritual as it has been defined in this chapter and as it also appears in the *Serat Centhini*. To see state ritual in the New Order or other contemporary Southeast Asian contexts (e.g., Bowie 1997 for Thailand) not as a "despotic" method of control, but as a strategy for redefining relations of power in ways that make it possible for power to be exercised and accepted in circumstances where other methods of asserting dominance and giving assent might fail is an important insight produced by Sekimoto's study (see also Tsing 1993, 90, 172, and passim).

The pursuit of wealth is also still part of what goes on inside Southeast Asian bureaucratic repertoires. This fact does not make the predatory nature of contemporary Southeast Asian bureaucrats or entrepreneurial strongmen any less undemocratic or any more appealing; it simply reminds us that participation in the state, or a statelike entourage led by a "man of prowess," has implied the right to "eat" from it, as the old Burmese and Thai political metaphor for tax-farming practices puts it, for a very long time (cf. Pasuk and Sungsidh 1994; Sidel 1999a). Our attention to this aspect of Southeast Asian bureaucratic behavior should focus less on totalizing condemnation and more on nuanced, dehistoricized, comparative investigation (P. Evans 1989). Although Lefort (1986, 116–117) and commentators on Southeast Asian politics have also emphasized the totalitarian (or, in the terminology of the "age of commerce," absolutist) nature of modern bureaucracies generally, they ignore the workings of heterogeneous rationalities within bureaucratic formations. In the case of Southeast Asia, some of these rationalities have derived from religions like Islam and Buddhism; others have been drawn from "pragmatic" secular sources, both Asian and Western (Chua 1997a, 57–78); some of them are hybrids of several of the above. Some of these rationalities have also been entrepreneurial, while others have been critical of the corrupting influence of wealth. To think of the "reasons of state" in Southeast Asia as only serving the needs of totalitarian forms of domination is to remain within a reductive, purifying paradigm for understanding hybrid state practices in Southeast Asia that has dominated Western thinking about the region since the seventeenth century and that is still visible in the work of Reid, Benedict Anderson, and many others: the concept of "Oriental despotism." Such a paradigm helps to sustain and reproduce the very state form it is designed to combat (Sayer 1994, 372; Mitchell 1999, 76). Rituals and bureaucracies in Southeast Asia have constrained state practices and favored certain kinds of rationalities over others, but they have not achieved hegemonic dominance. Only through violence has the Southeast Asian state attempted, and occasionally managed, to establish a form of domination that transcends the heterogeneous workings of reason, the struggle for status and wealth, and the indeterminancies of power.

5
Violence and Beauty

The many horrific examples of state violence in Southeast Asia over the last half century, if nothing else, call for comment in a study of the state in the region. We should also recall the words from Max Weber's lecture "Politics as a Vocation": "If no social institutions existed which knew the use of violence, then the concept of 'state' would be eliminated, and a condition would emerge that could be designated as 'anarchy,' in the specific sense of this word" (Gerth and Mills 1974, 78). Clearly, for both theoretical and historical reasons, it is important to examine the ways in which violence and the state intersect in Southeast Asia.

In previous chapters I examined the kinds and contexts of relations of "power" in state practices and ideology. "Violence" is something else. As Catherine Bell observes, commenting on Michel Foucault's work on "modern" forms of power, "Foucault defines a relationship of power as a mode of action that does not intend to act directly on persons or things, which is what violence does, but indirectly on actions" (Bell 1992, 199). Bell's statement can be applied to Foucault's writing on torture and public executions in premodern France, where he speaks of "a power that not only did not hesitate to exert itself directly on bodies, but was exalted and strengthened by its visible manifestations" (Foucault 1991a, 57). As is clear from Foucault's analysis, the "power" of violence in this case was generated by the ceremonial, ritual, and spectacular mode in which it was carried out before large public audiences of "the people," whose subordinate relationship to the sovereign was reinforced by the powerful spectacle of violence. Whereas the exercise of power is shaped by and depends upon the freedom to resist it—it is that very resistance and the attempts made to overcome it that constitute the "relationship" of power—violence is nonnegotiable. Violence imposes a "final solution" on issues of dominance and subordination that are, by their very nature, contested and ongoing (Bell 1992, 200–201). But whence comes the "power" of violent acts to "exalt" it?

I begin this chapter by tracing the history of state violence in Southeast Asia, which develops over time in a different way from that in the West. The issue that interests me more, however, is the power of violence to enchant, to borrow and adapt Clifford Geertz's phrase. I will argue that, rather than think of the violence and aesthetics of Southeast Asian state practices as separate or antithetical modes of coercion (cf. Pollock 1998a, 32; 2000, 614), it is important to explore the ways in which violence is both the source and guarantor of the state's magical "beauty." Violent *Herrschaft,* not only familial *Gemeinschaft,* is beautiful in Southeast Asia and the object of state-engendering "political love" (B. Anderson 1991, 143).

Causes and Characteristics of State Violence in Southeast Asian History

An archaeologist has argued that "the prehistoric societies in the core areas of Southeast Asia had very little interest in developing *military might*" (quoted in Wolters 1999, 124). Although, as we shall see, stateless societies in Southeast Asia have given violence a function and form in their social practices, it is reasonable to think of violence and the state as developing in tandem in the history of the region (Wolters 1999, 164, n. 58). The transcultural models used for forming states, whether they came from India, China, or the West, all assigned violence a major role in the acquisition and maintenance of state control. Standard Western historical treatments of precolonial Southeast Asia (e.g., D. G. E. Hall 1981; Coedès 1968) document the role of violence in interstate rivalry and internecine struggle as a mere "fact of political life" (Mabbett and Chandler 1995, 157, quoted in Wolters 1999, 164). Noel Battye notes in passing that during the 417 years of Ayutthaya there were seventy wars (Battye 1974, 1). Barbara Andaya argues that the frequency and amount of state violence carried out against rival powers increased during the course of the sixteenth and seventeenth centuries; she suggests that this was due to the economic conditions of the period as well as the role of Europeans in the region

(Andaya 1999, 75–88). But everywhere in Southeast Asia before the colonial period, "men of prowess" resorted to violence when they sought vengeance, prestige, manpower, and wealth (Battye 1974, 2–5; Wolters 1999, 164). The imprint of male violence on the aesthetics of Southeast Asian theatrical forms as well as state practices can be traced from early times to the contemporary moment (Pauka 1998; Vail 1998).

But first it is worth asking the question, Did Southeast Asian states ever achieve the *"monopoly of the legitimate use of physical force* within a given territory" that, following this famous dictum of Weber, we are accustomed to associating with the modern nation-state in the West (Gerth and Mills 1974, 78, emphasis in original)? Anthony Giddens (1985) and Charles Tilly (1992), for example, treat Weber's formulation as axiomatic to their understandings of the history of the European state. Tilly defines the "state" in Europe as a product of the interaction between "the accumulation [of capital] and concentration of coercive means" (Tilly 1992, 19). Over time, states in Europe developed "distinct organizations that control[led] the chief concentrated means of coercion within well-defined territories" as well as standing armies for both offensive and defensive purposes (Tilly 1992, 19–20). In Europe since the seventeenth century, Tilly asserts,

> [t]he state's expansion of its own armed force began to overshadow the weaponry available to any of its domestic rivals. The distinction between "internal" and "external" politics, once quite unclear, became sharp and fateful. The link between warmaking and state structure strengthened. Max Weber's historically contestable definition of the state—"a state is a human community that (successfully) claims the *monopoly of the legitimate use of physical force* within a given territory"— . . . finally began to make sense for European states. . . .
>
> A ruler's creation of armed force generated durable state structure. It did so both because an army became a significant organization within the state and because its construction and maintenance brought complementary organizations—treasuries, supply services, mechanisms for conscription, tax bureaux, and much more—into life. . . . From A.D. 990 onward, major mobilizations for war provided the chief occasions on which states expanded, consolidated, and created new forms of political organization. (Tilly 1992, 69–70)

The history of the relationship between the state and armed force in Southeast Asia, however, follows a very different course from the one Tilly sketches for Europe. We can expect this for a number of reasons that are well known but worth briefly reviewing.

For one thing, until the twentieth century there was no obvious connection between a state's exercise of violence and the concept of "territoriality" in a Western sense. As has been frequently stated, boundaries in Southeast Asia until the last century were porous, its territories underpopulated. Wars were fought to capture manpower and bring it home rather than to maintain boundaries that kept people out. As I note in the previous chapter, this fact has led commentators to downplay the role of territoriality and space in the history of the premodern Southeast Asian state generally in ways that need to be reexamined. The fact that wars were waged to capture manpower also does not mean that they were not brutal and destructive (see Mayoury and Pheuiphanh 1998).

The "legitimate" monopolization of violence by the state has also been problematic rather than inevitable over the long course of Southeast Asian history. In premodern Southeast Asia, as the Siamese folktale from Ayutthayan times, *Khun Chang Khun Phaen,* and the Cambodian story of Tum Teav, set in the sixteenth century, both illustrate, Southeast Asian kings killed for glory, out of rage, or in revenge (Pasuk and Baker 1995, xv–xvii; Chigas 2000; Hinton 1998b, 353–355; Chandler 1996a, 94). This kind of violence neither sought nor required legitimation. In Burma, Siam, and Java in the seventeenth and eighteenth centuries—in contrast to European states during this same period that controlled violence inside their own territories, concentrating it in the form of standing armies and directing it outward toward their rivals in the emerging interstate system—dispersal and lack of control over, rather than concentration of military force within, the state was the characteristic feature of the state's relation to the means of violence. In chapter 2 I commented on the losing battle waged by the Restored Toungoo kings of Burma to maintain discipline and prevent defections from their groups of military *ahmú-dàn*s to the entourages of the powerful administrative elite (Lieberman 1984, 96–105, 152–181). In a reversal of Tilly's model, the role of capital in this struggle was to stimulate, rather than counteract, the dispersal of the state's military might (Lieberman 1984, 158). In Siam before the military reforms of the early twentieth century, which were motivated by an internal and "growing rural resistance to central control" rather than the needs of external conquest or defense (Pasuk and Baker 1995, 230), there was no standing army. Moreover, from the late seventeenth century until the period of modern reform, military power and authority in Siam were intentionally dispersed throughout the administrative system rather than concentrated in a single organization that might threaten the authority of the king (Battye 1974, 29–40; Wyatt 1984, 128). In Java, throughout the frequent conflicts between the kings of Mataram and their rivals in the late seventeenth and early eighteenth centuries, the structure of the army reflected "that of the state itself, with various leaders and their followers forming a fragmentary host of warriors" (Nagtegaal 1996, 58). Military force, says Luc Nagtegaal, was in any case the last rather than the first resort as a method of state control (Nagtegaal 1996, 58). In battles in which only a few aristocratic warriors took the lead, with the large mass of conscripted soldiers ready to flee when their leaders had been killed, small numbers of well-disciplined Dutch East Indies troops, like elephants in Siamese battles, made a decisive difference (Nagtegaal 1996, 63, 67; Vail 1998, 57–58). The difference was not based on technological superiority, since cannon and gunpowder were locally produced and rifles were widely available. Anthony Reid concludes that for all of Southeast Asia "by the late seventeenth century, muskets had become sufficiently light, manageable, and widespread as to neutralize the advantages initially brought to centralized rulers by the advent of firearms" (Reid 1993, 228). "The great advantage that the Europeans and, to a slightly lesser degree, the remaining Company troops, possessed in comparison to the Javanese," Nagtegaal writes, "was the fact that they operated in a relatively disciplined and orderly manner during battle" (Nagtegaal 1996, 68). For Mataram and other Southeast Asian states both early and late, lack of "discipline," however, should not be interpreted as an absence of concepts and practices of "order" that were actualized through ritual or other coercive means.

The dispersed nature of violence and of the means of violence in Southeast Asia before the end of the nineteenth century reflects the dispersal of sovereignty within the states of the region. When a degree of centralization occurred in the nineteenth and twentieth centuries, it was due to the threat or actualization of Western colonial conquest and the replacement of "traditional" states with Western-style, legalistic (but not therefore "legitimate") bureaucratic forms of rule that included standing armies and police forces. The Chakri kings of nineteenth- and early twentieth-century Siam, for example, began the process of transforming both the "sub-states" that had their centers in the large state ministries in Bangkok and the tributary kingdoms situated on the peripheries of the realm into a single, bureaucratically administered nation-state that attempted to monopolize both the accumulation of capital and the exercise of violence (Pasuk and Baker 1995, 215–243). Similar processes occurred in Burma and the Netherlands Indies (R. Taylor 1987; Furnivall 1956).

But in most of Southeast Asia, the introduction of centralized state institutions and practices modeled on those of the West did not lead to a "durable" state system in which a standing army, under civilian control, served its primary coercive role vis-à-vis external rather than internal enemies of the nation-state. In Thailand, Burma, Indonesia, and the Philippines, armies—and armies within armies— continued to struggle not only for control of the state, but also for a dominant position over other armed forces within their respective societies (Pasuk and Baker 1995, 244–366; R. Taylor 1987; Crouch 1988; McCoy 1999). Western-style "territoriality" and state control over "legitimate violence" did not map neatly onto Southeast Asia. On the island of Bali during the colonial period, levels of internal violence rose because, as Geoffrey Robinson observes,

> with the imposition of a territorially based system of political authority, control over people and control over land became enmeshed, and differences in landed wealth became an increasingly salient aspect of political and social power. Control of formal political office became similarly important. One consequence was that the focus of rivalry within and among noble houses expanded to encompass not simply claims to states and deference which Geertz argues were central in late-nineteenth-century Bali but also control over political office, land, and labor. (Robinson 1995, 29)

Overall, Robinson argues, colonial policies in Bali having to do with taxation, labor control, and the "Balinization" of structures of authority "reinforced and to some extent created a pattern of political affiliation and consciousness that divided Balinese over essentially internal issues" (Robinson 1995, 51). It is this entrenched pat-

tern of internal division that created enemies within rather than outside the Indonesian nation-state. Exacerbated and deepened by other
factors from 1942 to 1965, this pattern, in Robinson's view, explains
the violent massacres of 1965–1966 in Bali. In Indonesia as a whole in
1965–1966, when, with the active participation of the national army,
up to a million people lost their lives, the killings were the last battle
in a long campaign by which the army achieved (temporary) dominance over enemies and territory internal to the Indonesian nation-
state (Crouch 1988). With the exception of the military campaign to
"recover" West Irian in 1961–1962 and "confront" Malaysia in 1963–
1964 (a policy that the army actively opposed when it came to involve actual fighting), and the brutal invasion and occupation of East
Timor in 1975, during which two hundred thousand Timorese died,
all of the Indonesian army's fighting has been internal, against fellow
Indonesian citizens defined as "the enemy" (Siegel 1999, 214). And
none of the Indonesian army's "external" campaigns served the chief
purpose to which military aggression in Europe was put: the strengthening of the state.

In colonial Burma, to take another example, most of the army
and all of the military police were Indian, with the remainder of these
forces coming from non-Burmese minorities. The judicial system itself was "the apparatus of a foreign government" that had the effect
of stimulating rather than reducing litigation and crime (quoted in
R. Taylor 1987, 98–105). The Burma National Army, formed in 1942,
was nationalist in a narrowly Burmese sense, since, unlike the case of
the colonial army, members of both immigrant communities and hill
tribes were excluded from its ranks (R. Taylor 1987, 233). But the army
also "felt it necessary to involve itself in politics in order to compete
with other political groups and to achieve the officer corps' notions
of a correct social and political order" (R. Taylor 1987, 234). As was
the case in Indonesia during the 1950s and early 1960s, during the civil
war period in Burma from 1948 to 1952 the army had to deal with
Communist enemies, regional/ethnic separatists, and a weak civilian
government, an experience that taught it the "ability to function
independently of civilian control" (R. Taylor 1987, 237). The army implemented this lesson to the full when it took control of the country
in 1962. Mary Callahan argues that the violent, predatory behavior
of "state-authorized, often state-armed" local militias in Burma between 1948 and 1958 is entirely similar to that of precolonial "offi-

cials serving the kings, whose salary was based on taking a cut of whatever taxes or fees were collected on behalf of the central government" (Callahan 1998, 24–25).

There are a large number of economic, social, and geopolitical reasons that explain the dominant role of armies within most of the modern states of Southeast Asia today. I want to pay attention here, however, not to the causative factors involved in the creation of this situation, but to a property of the Southeast Asian state that can be identified in many times and places: the tendency for state violence to be enacted or conceptualized in terms of something "beautiful."

In Southeast Asia, female beauty and male prowess have been typically married or merged in representations of state authority (Supomo 1977; Van Esterik 2000, 155–158; McCoy 1999, 172–173). Studies of the military in contemporary Southeast Asia suggest other versions of the same aesthetic. Scholarly writing on the impact of Japanese military ethos and training on the nationalist youth of Southeast Asia in the early 1940s (B. Anderson 1972, 22–23) or of the history of the recovery and murderous excesses of "masculinity" in the postcolonial Philippines (Rafael 1995a; McCoy 1999; Sidel 1999b), for example, make it easier to see the important role of violent male prowess in creating an aura of male beauty around the postcolonial Southeast Asian state. Benedict Anderson, for example, offers the following evocation of the thrilling masculinity of the militarized, liberated, re-"masculinized" *pemuda* (revolutionary youth) of Java during October 1945:

> For the pemuda it was a time of improvization and exhilaration. Underneath the anarchic spontaneity of their movement, giving it power and conviction, were the fundamental impulses of every revolution. Liberty was merdeka, not a political concept of independence or freedom, but an experience of personal liberation. For many it was a release from the disciplined structures of the occupation period . . . as these disintegrated in the October days. For others it was liberation from the apparent fatality of their lives. . . . The pemuda rode free on buses, trains, and trams. They forced Japanese soldiers to kneel before them in the dirt. They scrawled their terse slogans on doors and walls. They emptied the tills of unguarded banks, and opened warehouses to the people of the kampung. They attacked tanks with sharpened bamboo

spears and homemade gasoline bombs. And they killed—Dutchmen, Englishmen, Japanese, Eurasians, Chinese, sometimes their
fellow-Indonesians. (B. Anderson 1972, 185)

Everywhere in modern Southeast Asia, posteffeminized/post-
colonial forms of violent masculinity have been represented in literature and film in ways that highlight its powerful aesthetic appeal,
even when the overall viewpoint represented is critical of male state
violence as such (B. Anderson 1989; 1998, 174–191; Sidel 1999b; C. Reynolds 1996; Hamilton 1991; Duong Thu Huong 1996; 2000; Nguyễn
Huy Thiệp 1994a, 1994b; Zinoman 1994). But how exactly have violence, beauty, and the state become synonymous with one another
over time in Southeast Asia? What is the deep history of their mu-
tuality? To address this question, I turn first to one of the earliest literary works from Southeast Asia to aestheticize political violence in
order to naturalize it within an ideology of loyal service to the state.

The Beauty of Death and Violence

3. Time passed and the *kali*-era dawned, bringing the destruction
of the whole world. The evidence was that in the delightful island
of Java, an island of incomparable beauty, people trembled in
fear under the rule of evil men and the country was in ruins because it lacked a strong protector. How sad that its beauty was
being destroyed, like the wood of the blossoming trees when the
king of beasts is absent.

4. Witnessing this, Lord Wiṣṇu was down-hearted and deeply
moved to compassion. He therefore descended to the world to
become the protector of the island and sedulously restored the
kingdom. In the past he was called Lord Kṛṣṇa and had succeeded in gaining victory in battle. Accordingly, he is called His
Majesty Lord Jayabhaya, famed throughout the world.

5. Without delay he destroyed every enemy who dared oppose
him and hunted down all the adversaries. Evil men were annihilated and scoundrels were completely swept away as in the past.
Throughout the entire land of Java, not one of those who escaped

death dares to disobey him, and indeed there is no (other) island
powerful enough to oppose him, for he is Wiṣṇu incarnate.

6. Moreover, he is one in essence with the Lord, the commander
of the army, the embodiment of the terrifying mountain torrent,
with seemingly inaccessible rugged ravines, forbidding and most
difficult to penetrate. If the trees of the forest are his protective
frame, then the branches, leaves and shoots are his poetic beauty
[*langö*]; the sweetness of his songs is so beautiful and pure, for he
is an eminent poet, to whom one most appropriately goes for
blessing.

7. So the world is now joyful and flourishing again and talk
about the poor and the needy has ceased; only the Law is discussed and no one makes mention of thieves if precious stones
were lost; disease has disappeared—the only sickness that has
increased is heartache of lovers in separation; many are stabbed
—but by seductive glances; and others are whipped by unbraided
hairknots. (Supomo 1993, 255)

A few lines later, the epic poem, written in East Java in 1157 at the
court of King Jayabhaya (r.1135–1157), continues, "In short, no one
opposes Lord Hari Jayabhaya who rules Daha." But how do we
account for Jayabhaya's dominance and for the role of violence in the
exercise of his rule? The verses from the end of the *Bhāratayuddha*,
which I quote above, speak first of Jayabhaya's own violent prowess,
but not of the means by which he forged his political alliances and
mustered his warriors and foot soldiers. And then there is the strange
and swift modulation in verse 6 from a metaphor of the king as savage
wilderness to his likeness to a gardenlike natural beauty, which he
can evoke through his own sweet poetry. And "so" the world flourished once again, a paradisiacal playground for lovers who only discuss the "Law" and engage in warlike sexual dalliance. But what
does this state of affairs have to do with violence, poetry, beauty, or
sex, and how is it maintained?

What interests me about the above verses, and indeed the whole
poem from which they are drawn, is that they raise the question not
of the existence of or justification for the exercise of state violence,

both of which are assumed, but of the intimate relationship between violence and other forms of domination, including "beauty." Most centrally, the poem examines the role of violence in transforming emotions associated with sex and the family into loyalty to the state. This transformation is effectuated and mediated by a notion of what makes the state "beautiful." As it unfolds, the poem also reveals tensions between foreign and indigenous concepts in early Southeast Asia that suggests that Sanskrit words, despite their "translation" and "localization" in vernacular Javanese texts, retained their foreignness and so assisted in the formation of a Javanese "state" that was distinct from a "kinship network" (cf. Christie 1995; Wolters 1999, 53, 131). I read the poem with the question in mind of how "domination," be it through violence or through other means, is defined and represented. One aspect of this question concerns the concept of "hegemony" and how foreign, Indic ideas about the ethics of war and service to the early Javanese state and indigenous notions of emotional attachment to family could have been reconciled and combined to form a single, hybrid, hegemonic state ideology that had the power to unify the armed and rivalrous members of the king's own network of family and subordinates.

Students of Indonesian history are familiar with the metaphors, ideas, and beliefs that make up a Javanese "world view" that is saturated with elements drawn from the stories of the Indic epic, *Mahābhārata*. The text that I will be discussing is the oldest written expression in a long history of Javanese representations of an elite, male, warrior ethos expressed in Indic terms, one that is widely held to have dominated Javanese cultural expression for centuries. "In Java, for historical reasons which are too complicated to enter into here, there is still an almost universally accepted religious mythology which commands deep emotional and intellectual adherence," Anderson wrote about the shadow-puppet repertoire, based on the *Mahābhārata*, in 1965 (B. Anderson 1969). "Imagery taken from wayang [shadow-puppet theatre]," comments Ward Keeler, "crops up frequently in Javanese speech, and the art form provides many a metaphor to Javanese comments on all sorts of events" (Keeler 1987, 15). These and many other statements about Javanese culture acknowledge the coherence and pervasiveness of a "world view," an "ethos," a "culture" that has been shaped by *wayang*, a form of shadow-puppet theatre that takes its repertoire from the *Mahābhārata*, although the issue of *wayang*'s hegemonic role in shaping Javanese culture is left unresolved (see also C. Geertz 1960, 262–278; McVey 1986; Sears 1996a).

And yet most of what has been written about *wayang* in Javanese society makes it sound very much like the source of a "lived system of meanings and values," which Raymond Williams defines as "hegemony" in his succinct and valuable discussion (Williams 1977, 108–114). By all accounts, the values inscribed in Javanese *wayang* stories about the heroes of the *Mahābhārata* have and do exercise some kind of sway over the hearts and minds of some Javanese "as in effect a saturation of the whole process of living," to quote Williams again (1977, 110). So are we dealing with hegemony here or not? In part, the disinterest displayed by scholars of Javanese *wayang* in the question of hegemony has to do with the presence in the scholarly tradition of Southeast Asian studies of two other concepts: that of "ideology," which is a formal system of meanings, and that of "culture," now postmodernistically termed "culture effect," which is broader than ideology, but has tended to be less concerned than hegemony with "relating the 'whole social process' to specific distributions of power and influence" (Williams 1977, 108–109). The best-known cultural analysis of early Java is Geertz's discussion of the fourteenth-century "Description of the Countryside" in which the representations of hierarchy, according to Geertz, "conveyed the structure of the cosmos—mirrored in the organization of the court—to the countryside" (C. Geertz 1993, 133). But neither the text nor Geertz's analysis of it explains how the ritual display of order or textual representations of the imitation of and subservience to kingly "magnificence" may have actually affected "the distributions of power and influence" in fourteenth-century Java. Missing from Geertz's account, and hidden in this particular Old Javanese poem, is an account of how the hegemony that the "Description of the Countryside" presents as an achieved, all-powerful reality was actively created and maintained. How did the dramaturgy of processions define and impose the state's dominance exactly? And when the processions had rumbled back to the capital, how were the relations of dominance and subservience that processions represented and helped create subsequently maintained in hierarchical orderliness in the countryside?

It is not accidental that Geertz's description of order-by-analogy in Majapahit is based on a text that gives the most static and least-contested account of power in early Java. "In most description and analysis," Williams comments, "culture and society are expressed in an habitual past tense" (Williams 1977, 128). Scholarly writers on Southeast Asia, too, have tended to treat ideology and culture as structures, "finished products," and static forms rather than as "forming and formative process[es]" in the sense stressed by Williams. The "hegemonic" or the "dominant," terms Williams prefers to "hegemony" and "domination" in order to bring out the processual and transient character of what he is talking about, by contrast, "has continually to be renewed, recreated, defended, and modified." "The most interesting and difficult part of any cultural analysis, in complex societies," Williams goes on, "is that which seeks to grasp the hegemonic in its active and formative but also its transformational processes." Williams particularly recommends works of art as sources for such an investigation (Williams 1977, 112–114, 128).

My interest in looking for the dominant in the Old Javanese *Bhāratayuddha* was stimulated by reading Williams, as well as by two studies of the representation of women in Old Javanese and Balinese literature (Creese 1993; Connor 1995a). Helen Creese makes a methodological decision to treat the "conventions" of Old Javanese literature as representations of social reality. In so doing she is able to draw attention to the distinctive characteristic of Javanese and Balinese versions of Indic prototypes: their interest in representations of women and femaleness. Linda Connor picks up particularly on the way in which women are represented in the *Bhāratayuddha,* where there are several long passages depicting female suicide. In her analysis of one such passage, which describes the suicide of Kṣitisundarī following the death in battle of her husband Abhimanyu, Connor is interested in establishing the woman's own agency in seeking death. She speaks of her "agony of separation" and of the centrality of the "idea of reunion" and of "images of following and joining" in the poem (Connor 1995a, 8). Connor also draws attention to the theme of the idealization of death in Old Javanese and Balinese literature generally.

Whereas Creese and Connor are particularly interested in representations of women and women's agency, my concern here is to analyze the way in which incidents and descriptions involving women or imagery connected to women are used to think about and influence political relationships more generally. Since I am attempting to read the *Bhāratayuddha* as a textual representation and enactment of the process by which relations of men and women dominating other men and women came into being in the court world of twelfth-century East Java (to paraphrase and slightly alter one of Weber's definitions of the "state" [Gerth and Mills 1974, 78]), the fact that the "introduction of women into the battle scenes in the Bhāratayuddha . . . constitutes the most significant departure from the Mahābhārata" becomes intriguing (Supomo 1993, 33; also Cohen Stuart 1860, 1:4).

Little is known about King Jayabhaya, at whose request the poem was written, except that, as one can gather from the opening and closing stanzas of the *Bhāratayuddha* and from those of a work written earlier in his reign, he was frequently at war (Supomo 1993; Zoetmulder 1974, 272). One thing that we can infer from our knowledge of Southeast Asian history generally is that politics in twelfth-century Java meant sexual politics, as bilateral relatives of the king and his predecessors intrigued and maneuvered to secure marriage partners and offspring who would one day take control of the state. The explicit source of political conflict in the *Bhāratayuddha* itself, the refusal of the Indic mythological Korawas to give half the kingdom of Hāstina to their relatives, the Pāṇḍawas, must have been a resonant political concern in Jayabhaya's time. His eleventh-century predecessor, Erlangga, divided his kingdom between his two sons when he abdicated some time after 1042. The political significance of this act was commemorated centuries later in the fourteenth-century "Description of the Countryside," and conflicts between brothers for political dominance were represented countless times in Old Javanese literary texts and on temple reliefs (Worsley 1991, 169–171).

The *Bhāratayuddha* suggests that the tension between a desire for unitary overlordship—as expressed, for example, in the god Wiṣṇu's exclamation to Jayabhaya in the fourth verse, "So be it, O King, you shall be the sovereign of the whole world"—and a more fluid and pluralistic contestation and sharing of power was ongoing and unresolved in early Java. The narrative of the *Bhāratayuddha* opens with Kṛṣṇa's mission to Hāstina to ask that half of the kingdom be given to the Pāṇḍawas. "If surrendered, there would be harmony; if not, a terrible war would ensue" (Supomo 1993, 165, v. 8). From the outset the dominant emotional and political state in the poem is one of separation and the desire for union in both a sexual and political sense. As Kṛṣṇa flies in his chariot to Hāstina he looks down upon banyan trees that "looked dejected, like a miserable woman covering herself with a blanket after her lover had left" because the Pāṇḍawas were not there (Supomo 1993, 165, v. 9). When he enters the city he is mobbed by sexually aroused female onlookers, some of whom climb trees and in their passionate haste expose "things which looked like the mouth (of a drunk) belching palmwine" (Supomo 1993, 167, v. 7–10). (Note: Mussolini was the object of a similar kind of adulatory "political love" [Berezin 1999, 369]!) Later that night, after Kṛṣṇa has retired from his first audience with the Korawa king Duryodhana and has met with Kuntī, mother of three of the Pāṇḍawas and of one of their bitterest enemies, Karna, a false peace settles over the palace, described in terms of an extended metaphor of marriage, deflowering, sexual union, and illicit elopement (Supomo 1993, 169, v. 9–14).

The descriptions of women and the allusions to sex evoke a particular atmosphere, one of aroused, desired, and irresolvable conflict, but they also function rhetorically to make the listener/reader participate in the textual examination of this issue. That this and other Old Javanese poems were meant to be read and their content heeded is indicated in numerous passages in many texts where allusions and comparisons refer to the writing of verse. These passages indicate that the purpose of writing was to elicit a passionate response from the reader. The readership was clearly both male and female, since both sexes are represented in Old Javanese poetry as writing, reading, and reacting to texts. Rhetorically, passages that refer to women and sex not only localize the Indic, epic subject matter of the poem in Java, they domesticate it, arousing both sexual desire and a longing for home in the reader.

Remembering that all such passages involving women were added to the story by the poets who recast the *Mahābhārata* as a Javanese narrative, it is striking how much "conviviality" and "familiarity" —to borrow two concepts that Achille Mbembe uses to explain how both the dominant and dominated become "inscribe[d] . . . in the same epistemological field" (Mbembe 1992, 14)—are conveyed by descriptions like the following one of the Hāstina court:

> 3. There the jewels among women were vying with each other in
> the moonlight admiring the beauty of the moon. Truly, the ladies
> of the inner court were as elegant as poems written on panels; so

sweet that their every movement and gesture arousing [*sic*] desire and love, as tantalizing as mangosteens collected during the spring, seasoned with pandanus petals covered with drawings.

4. At their ease, some played a whispering game, as they revelled in the moonlight. Suddenly a maiden was overcome by emotion that inflamed her passion. Then a maid-servant, acting as a medium of love, came forward furtively to speak words of affection. Under the pretext of whispering the message passed on in the game, she murmured the laments of an impassioned lover. (Supomo 1993, 170, v. 3–4)

This and many other passages that seem to depict early Javanese court life draw the Javanese reader into the foreign cultural world of the epic and make it as familiar as her or his own domestic surroundings. Domesticating moments recur repeatedly throughout the poem. Coupled with emotions of sexual arousal that allusions to courtship and sex create, such evocations of feelings of ease and familiarity must have helped seduce even plotting relatives and jilted lovers into participating in the civilizing formation of Jayabhaya's state. Yet the cultural flow of domesticating and civilizing "localization," to recall Wolters' keyword, is not one way. There is a tug and pull in the other direction, toward the "Indic," then back again in the direction of "Java," a debate about whether or how members of the court elite should call both India and Java their cultural "home."

This debate can be overheard in the impassioned dialogue that takes place between two value systems in the text. One of these value systems is expressed in terms of a Sanskrit vocabulary and is derived from Indic rules of conduct appropriate to what is referred to repeatedly as the warrior code *(kakṣatriyan)* (e.g., Supomo 1993, 68, v. 16; 175, v. 16). The other value system, conveyed in indigenous Javanese words, is concerned with sexual desire and family loyalty. The section of the poem I want to use in order to examine this debate is the longest of the passages that have been added by the Javanese poet to the main Indic narrative of the war: the story of the Korawa ally, King Śalya, and his wife Satyawatī (Supomo 1993, 226–238, cantos 34–42). Satyawatī is herself a Javanese interpolation, a character unknown in the Indian *Mahābhārata* (Supomo 1993, 33–34).

Of the many characters in the poem whose loyalties and affections are divided, Śalya's dilemma is made the most poignant and exemplary. After the death of Karna, the Korawas must find another commander to lead them into battle. Śakuni, who proposes Karna's charioteer, King Śalya of Madra, is explicit about what makes this choice problematic when he speaks to Duryodhana:

> 2. There is still king Śalya who is worthy to be your protector, for he is most reliable in battle. He is a valiant and mighty king, who is concerned with the welfare of others; he is famed for his meritorious deeds, and praised throughout the three worlds. Could any enemy survive if he dared to oppose him on the battlefield? However, the limits of his affection and his disaffection for you are difficult to ascertain.

> 3. His attachment is certainly unwavering. Here is some proof: Everyone knows that he is Nakula's [i.e., one of the Pāṇḍawas] uncle, and therefore he is an enemy to you. Yet he has not turned against you, nor does he wish to leave you. The only problem is that he has surrendered his life to the Pāṇḍawas. (Supomo 1993, 226)

The central problem in the practical politics of Old Java is expressed in concentrated form in verse 2, line 4: "However, the limits of his affection [*sih*] and his disaffection [*lalis*] for you are difficult to ascertain." The complementary opposites *sih* and *lalis* are both non-Sanskritic Javanese words. *Sih* is the key term for the emotion that holds lovers, masters and servants, and kings and subjects together; *lalis*, which means heartlessness or indifference, is "often used of somebody who has gone away or died without concern for the feelings of those left behind" (Zoetmulder 1982, 965). Arrayed in opposition to the value system of family and sexual emotion is a panoply of Sanskritic terms from the code of *kṣatriya* (warrior) conduct: almost all the words in the first three lines of verse 2 come from that lexicon. As if to make the tension between these two value systems even more emphatic and precarious, the Javanese in the last line of verse 3, which Supomo translates as "he has surrendered his life," is: *inanugrahākĕna nirâta hurip*, literally "he *may* bestow his life" (italics added). Śakuni thinks a danger exists that, despite his loyal service to the Korawas thus far, King Śalya *may yet* exercise his royal Sanskritic

attribute of benevolence *(anugraha)*, in effect fusing the two competing value systems, in a decisive act of commitment to the Pāṇḍawas.

Śalya says that he will agree to command the army provided
that Duryodhana agrees to sue for peace. In the ensuing debate
Duryodhana asks Śalya to feel a Sanskritic "misery" *(duhkha)* "for
those who have witnessed the slaughter of their relatives," while
Aśwatthāmā, another Korawa warrior, infuriates the king by accus-
ing him of "loving" *(sih)* the enemy. By having his *kṣatriya*hood called
into question, Śalya is maneuvered into declaring the "constancy"
(tulusa) of his "love" *(sih)* for the king of Hāstina, thus subordinating
his Javanese emotions to the code of conduct of an Indic state (Supomo
1993, 227, v. 4, 7, 9).

So Śalya is "consecrated without further obstruction" *(inabhi-
ṣekâpratihata)*, but as he returns to his camp he walks in a "daze":
"This affection for his near-kinsman [i.e., Nakula] was the source of
his distress," the poet writes, using the Javanese word *"lĕnglĕng"* to
describe Śalya's emotional state. *"Lĕnglĕng"* is one of the key terms in
the erotics and aesthetics of Old Javanese poetry, meaning a trance-
like feeling induced by beauty, and it can be an attribute both of
whatever causes the emotion and the emotion itself (Zoetmulder
1982, 1010). Its use here alerts us to the aesthetic dimension of the
representation of dominance in the poem, and I will return to this
aspect in a moment.

The intensity of Śalya's distress and of his dilemma of having to
choose between sexual desire and family love, on the one hand, and
adherence to a code of proper warrior conduct, on the other, is
increased when Nakula is brought before the king, offering to kill
himself rather than fight against a relative. Moreover, Nakula says,
using Sanskritic concepts from the code of proper behavior, "I would
be committing a most perfidious sin *(pāpā ning drohaka)* and be
branded as one who is disrespectful [literally "violates the bed of,"
ānalpaka] toward one's teacher." Śalya replies Sanskriticly by saying
that he would feel "mean and base" *(nīcâdhasta)* if he did not acknowledge the honors and gifts that the king of the Korawas has
bestowed upon him; he would prefer to die in battle rather than be
called an "evil man" (Sanskrit *kujana*). Then Śalya both foretells his
own death and clinches the argument at this stage of the debate in
favor of obedience to the code of *kṣatriya* conduct rather than to the
dictates of family love:

15. This is why I will give [*lĕpasakĕnê*, literally shoot, but in other inflected forms, to set a soul free from its earthly bonds] my power [*Śaktingkw*] to the king of Hāstina. However, as far as my life is concerned, I leave it in your hands. My only request is that my opponent shall be the son of Dharma [the "Law"], for by using the book as his weapon, he will be the cause of my death. (Supomo 1993, 230)

Śalya will be killed by Yudhiṣṭhira, the embodiment of the code, using his book-weapon, the Kalimahosadha. According to Supomo, the Javanese name Kalimahosadha, meaning "great medicine of Kali," is probably derived from the word for Yudhiṣṭhira's weapon in the Sanskrit text, which is *śakti,* meaning "spear, lance," but also "energy or active power of a deity personified as his wife" (Supomo 1993, 36 and 293). Within the thematics of the poem, it is clear why Yudhiṣṭhira, son and embodiment of Dharma, fights with a book containing Indic knowledge: it is the code of conduct transmitted to Java in Indic texts that is being aggressively used to transform sexual and family passions into loyalty to the state. When they are engaged in battle, Yudhiṣṭhira cannot be harmed by Śalya's arrows because they can only kill those who carry weapons and are subject to their passions. Yudhiṣṭhira is initially reluctant to kill Śalya because he "is truly like my own father. But now that he has gone too far in destroying the Law, it would be improper if I took no action."

7. Thus answered Yudhiṣṭhira. Then he rose and donned his battledress. His love [Sanskrit *karuna,* literally compassion] for Śalya vanished in his heart, and in its place was anger that raged like a mountain of fire. (Supomo 1993, 237)

Between Śalya's capitulation to Dharma and his death at the hands of the son of Dharma, however, comes one of the most significant Javanese interpolations in the Indic literature of early Java: Śalya's final lovemaking and farewell to Satywatī. The passage is intensely personal and emotional. Its force within the debate over hegemonic values in the poem is to contradict the incontrovertible dogma about proper conduct that is embedded in the Sanskritic original and that is invoked in the Javanese version as an ideological support for Jayabhaya's dominance. The passage challenges the dominance of the code of proper conduct, yet it also justifies it, since it is Śalya's "passion," described in familiarizing and sensuous Old Javanese poetry, that destines him to suffer extinction at the hands of the ascetic son of Dharma. Here are some excerpts of the scene from canto 38:

> 3. If it would make you happy, we can return to heaven together. But because we assume human body [*sic*], this can only be achieved through death. There we will both enjoy all the delights of Indra's heaven, and furthermore we will be young again and satisfy our love together.

> 4. There is no possibility that we could be separated, because we will be always one in nature. If you are the flower, my dearest one, I will be the bumble-bee, seeking your fragrance, and if you are a young spray blowing in the wind, I will be the tendrils of the *gaḍuṅ* creeper embracing you. We will be together for ever— if I live in poetic beauty [*langö*], then you will be the lyrics. . . .

> 9. Thus spoke the king, comforting her skillfully with loving words, interspersed with lyrics and songs, as well as jokes and passionate words of endearment, so that they achieved the most sensuous enjoyment of sexual union in accordance with the *kāma-tantra*. Then he continued to console her, to still her anxiety, and sang her soothingly to sleep. . . .

> 11. Then while she was asleep, using his arm as a pillow, the bell struck the seventh hour, as if to awaken him. The king awoke, but he was worried that the queen, sleeping on his arm, might be awakened too, and he could imagine how she would cling to him, lamenting and weeping.

> 12. This was why he moved aside and gently freed his arm from under her. But his outer garment was still beneath her, twisting around her awkwardly, so without regret he swiftly cut it with his kris, and rearranged the remainder of the garment that trailed on the bed, covering her with it. (Supomo 1993, 233–234)

The resolution of the argument between conduct and feeling, one that defers the fulfillment of familial love in favor of loyal service to the state, is death. Death is conceptualized as a continuation of life on earth. The poem represents the transformation of separation in life into reunion in death in a passage in which the conventions of descriptions of carefree kings and lovers wandering entranced through an enrapturing natural landscape are used to depict Satyawatī's royal "progress" across the battlefield, accompanied by a faithful servant, in search of her husband's body—an act of familial loyalty that has become a state-forming demonstration of the dominance of Dharma.

> 9. The flags that were left behind on their standards sheltering her from the sun, she took to be trees on the mountain slopes; she regarded the sound of crows cawing to each other as the singing of cuckoos comforting her; the stench of stinking corpses, she believed to be the fragrance of flowers; the breathing of the wounded warriors, with their blood still flowing, she considered a gentle breeze.

> 10. Even the lapping sea of blood she likened to an enchanting [*alangö*] ocean; the weapons to its islands and the fluttering flag-tussles to the blooming flowers on them; the metal-plated jackets to the gleaming fish, the armlets and necklaces to the *himi-himi* and *gĕtĕm* crabs; and the blades of the projectiles were likened to prawns in the crevices along the crag, crawling one after another along the coral of daggers.

> 11. There she was entranced [*lĕnglĕng*] by the sight of banners fluttering in the gentle wind like the sails of a ship—and this loyal wife looking for her beloved husband as master of the ship, shields as the ship, her life as its cargo, and reaching heaven, the reward for being a devoted wife, as the reason for crossing the ocean. But, alas! the ship suddenly sank as it crushed [*sic*] into an elephant, giving rise to despondency and regret. (Supomo 1993, 240–241)

Whereas earlier Śalya's dilemma is made to seem almost irresolvable and the necessity of taking leave of his wife almost unbearable, the poetics of "beauty" and "rapture" here effortlessly transmogrify carnage into a poetic premonition of heaven, where Śalya and Satyawatī are reunited. Before she stabs herself, Satyawatī asks her servant to report her death and "[i]mplore the prince of poets to write a lyrical poem about my suffering, so that the lovesick women will hear and know what I have done" (Supomo 1993, 242, v. 4). But her servant pledges to follow her in death, "even in the reincarnation of your reincarnation" (Supomo 1993, 242, v. 6). Thus are the deaths of master and servant inscribed and textually propagated as "worthy examples" to be emulated by Jayabhaya's courtiers and their retinues. Satyawatī and her servant both commit suicide.

> 10. Immediately thereafter their souls traveled quickly together. The king's soul was delighted—so one could say—for he had been waiting on an awe-inspiring cloud, bursting with impatience, accompanied by celestial nymphs, seers and hosts of gods.

> 11. He took the queen on his lap, and they returned to heaven in a splendid chariot. They came to an enchantingly beautiful heaven, with houses made of all kinds of jewels, shining and sparkling.

> 12. The queen was at a complete loss for words, enraptured by beauty [*mangö*, from *langö*] and overwhelmed with happiness and pleasure. Her only regret was that when they were born as mortals, why did not they immediately return to heaven while they were young? (Supomo 1993, 243)

What has taken place in the story of Śalya and Satyawatī, which comes late in the poem, after a series of passages that feature women and sexual imagery and in which the conflict between dogma and feeling is also examined, is the definition of a hegemonic set of values within the court world of Jayabhaya's state. As represented in the poem, this hegemony embraces powerfully contradictory sets of values, one associated with the concepts and institutions of Indic, male kingship, the other with women, sexual politics, "beauty," and family loyalty. The contradictions between these two value systems are resolved but not eliminated through the domestication of violence and death, so that engaging in the former and suffering the latter in fulfillment of the *kṣatriya* code of conduct is rewarded with sexual bliss in the embrace of the family in the afterlife.

The displacement of desire and love by self-control and duty to the Law does not of course eliminate either desire or love from the world of the poem. Sexual desire and family love are shown to be essential to, as well as dangerous for, the bonds of loyalty that bind courtiers to kings, servants to masters, wives to husbands. The Javanese interpolations in the work particularly evoke and illustrate the emotional makeup of such relationships. The attention paid in the Javanese version of the story to Śalya's sexual passion for Satyawatī, then to her passionate reunion with him in death, must be understood in part as a representation of the kind of emotional intensity that should inhere in every master-servant relationship. But in a bilateral society where women were not only political pawns, but also queens who exercised power in their own right over husbands, brothers, and sons, Satyawatī could also have chosen to be disloyal to the male code of *kṣatriya* conduct. Thus the story of Śalya and Satyawatī conceals possible contradictions that are internal to the definition of the hegemonic in the poem.

The aesthetic power of the poem works by awakening both sexual desire and a passion for right conduct in the reader; it evokes these emotions in order to tap them for the creation of assent to its own hegemonic message. The frequently repeated term for "beauty" and "rapture," *langö,* is thus central to the nature of the hegemonic as defined in the poem. Like the expressions of the *alus* (refined, "civilized") in nineteenth- and twentieth-century Javanese culture, *langö* is a powerfully political concept, not simply an aesthetic or religious one (cf. Zoetmulder 1974, 170–185; C. Geertz 1960, 232).

Perhaps the most important point to make, however, is that the hegemonic resolution of the struggle between desire and duty is inherently unstable. We can see this in the ambiguous lightness of the lines in verse 7, quoted at the beginning of this chapter, or in the following passage from the first canto of the poem:

> 5. The whole country is now tranquil; thieves are no more, they flee in fear of his [Jayabhaya's] power; only the stealers of beautiful women are not afraid of sneaking about in the moonlight. (Supomo 1993, 164)

Sex and sexual violence precipitate, but then outlive, the wars by which kings establish their dominance according to the *kṣatriya* code of conduct. Sexual desire generates new conflicts and more death, thus providing more opportunities for adherence to the Dharma in the service of kings in early Java, or, as we will see below, to the New Order state in the 1980s. The "hegemonic" code of *kakṣatriyan* (warrior-ness) is thus itself subject to the emotions that both bind lovers and families together and tear them apart. Ultimately, these emotions are the location and battleground of hegemony as represented in the Old Javanese *Bhāratayuddha*.

Violence and Social Order

The Old Javanese poem I have just examined is the earliest example of a discourse on family, violence, and the state that has been a key element in the "repertoire" of political struggle in Java from early times until the end of the New Order in 1998 (Robson 1971; T. Shiraishi 1981; McVey 1986; B. Anderson 1969; Yudhistira 1977; Scherer 1981; Sears 1996a). The text clearly documents the fact that "familyism" in Southeast Asia is a site of violent struggle within discourses about relations of power, not just a sociological cause of either political unity or disorder. Violence plays a state-forming role in the poem, the source of a certain kind of "beautiful" death that fuses familial love and loyalty to the state. I want now to examine some other examples from both early and modern Southeast Asia where violence is similarly shown to be a creative rather than a negative force, one that contributes to the formation of beautiful states.

King Jayabhaya's contemporary, Sūryavarman II of Angkor, for example, is represented on the southwest wall of the third gallery of Angkor Wat in the guise of the leader of the Pāṇḍawa army as he thrusts his spear into the neck of the commander of the Korawas (Mannikka 1996, 130–132, fig. 5.4). "At the axis of the battle," Eleanor Mannikka writes, "there is nothing but uninterrupted slaughter." Mannikka describes the representation of the battle of Kurukṣetra as one in which the "unperturbed line" and "neat geometry" of the victorious Pāṇḍawas leads into the "total entropy" of the vanquished Korawas in disarray (Mannikka 1996, 130). This image commemorates the battle Sūryavarman fought and won when he killed his great-uncle, united his family, and seized the throne (Mannikka 1996, 130, 133). But it also represents violence and death as an essential element of the king's victorious rule. The relief of the battle complements another image consisting of a stationary axis surrounded by whirling activity: the churning of the Sea of Milk, a process for generating immortality in which both gods and demons take part. This scene stands on the east wall of the same gallery of Angkor Wat, opposite the Kurukṣetra relief on the west. In both reliefs, the beauty of the scene is expressed through the representation of a creative tension between stillness and motion, death and life.

The juxtaposition of destructive and creative forms of violence can also be found within Southeast Asian representations of male violence itself. There are two kinds of violence being described, for example, in the following verses from the Old Javanese *Bhārata-yuddha* in which the slaying of the Pāṇḍawa hero Abhimanyu is described:

> Canto 13, 28. And so the Korawas were enraged. They fired their arrows to counter those of Abhimanyu, striking his horses and charioteer, not to mention his body, hands, legs, back, chest and his face. But, armed with a discus and a broken bow, the ever resplendent Abhimanyu continued to push forward. Striving after glory, he courageously pressed on with this furious attack, as he wished to die in close combat with Suyodhana [i.e., Duryodhana, king of the Korawas].

> 29. His assault could be compared to the performance of a youth deflowering a maiden, the quivering of his sharp arrows resembling her frowning eyebrows. When he saw the arrow wounds on his chest, he thought that they were scratches from the maiden's nails, and he mistook the clamour of the elephants, horses and chariots for her moaning.

> 35. He pressed his attack with great daring, like a humming bee desiring sweet honey, unperturbed by the buzzing arrows flying from the bowstrings that sounded like the drone of bees, nor by the eerie ravines of elephants, horses and chariots which were thick with arrows resembling sharp-pointed bamboos. Overwhelmed by the enemy, he was on the point of death, but truly his death was as beautiful as the search for sweetness (of honey).

Canto 14, 1. So Abhimanyu was slain in battle. His body, crushed as finely as moss in a golden bowl, lay motionless in the moonlight, cut to shreds as delicately as sliced cucumber.

2. The entire Pāṇḍawa army were in terrible anguish. . . .

3. Arjuna was deeply upset when he was informed of the death of his son, Abhimanyu. The brave son of Pāṇḍu then announced that he would launch an attack [*amuka*], with himself in the forefront of the troops so as to be slain.

4. Kṛṣṇa, however, immediately restrained him, saying: "It is against the Law. Do not do thus, O Prince, for all the Pāṇḍawas are in great distress." Thus spoke Kṛṣṇa to sooth him. (Supomo 1993, 188–189)

In this passage the same elisions between martial violence and sexual desire are made that we meet in the story of Śalya and Satyawatī. But there is also a tension present within the representation of male violence itself, between Abhimanyu's youthful energy and striving for glory on the one hand, and the grief and suicidal rage that make Arjuna want to run "amuck" (literally the Javanese word used in the text) on the other.

A similar range of male emotion, from focused, energetic, violent joy to aimless, destructive, violent grief is found in the Ilongot word for anger or passion (*liget*) and in the role of this emotion in head-hunting among the Ilongot mountain people of northern Luzon in the Philippines (M. Rosaldo 1980, 44–51). In the case of the Ilongot, such emotions and the violence to which they are connected do not underlie the formation of a state, but they are central to what, in early Java and elsewhere in Southeast Asia, is considered essential for state formation: a "beautiful," potentially violent energy that suffuses a healthy and orderly social life:

To say of someone, *Nantagal,* "What force!" is to give praise for *liget* manifested in hard work, fine ornaments, or forceful speeches; it is to recognize a passionate vibrato in a fellow's singing, a show of muscular grace and tension in a dance. Such

liget generates a "redness" in the self that wards off certain kinds
of illness; it makes for "energy" and is associated with a sense
of "focus" that encourages industry and success. (M. Rosaldo
1980, 46)

In other parts of island Southeast Asia, head-taking is explicitly linked to the foundation of the state (Hoskins 1996, 9–12, 90–
126, 127–166). In an oral epic that describes the founding of the
sultanate of Brunei, warrior-heroes serving the first ruler, Awang
Halak Batatar (later the first Muslim sultan of Brunei, Sultan Muhammad Shah), subdue the peoples of the interior through an orgy
of head-taking:

> The troops cut off, all the heads,
>> hither and thither, in a great tumult;
> the country of Sandungan, was struck by the force,
>> tens of thousands died, uncontrollably.
>
> The subjects died, not a few,
>> lying one on another, tight one against another;
> as far as the eye can see, corpses packed together,
>> the severed heads, like a hill. (Maxwell 1996, 115)

Allen Maxwell notes that this poem is performed at wedding rituals
in contemporary Brunei, which suggests a connection between violence, the foundation of the state, sexual conquest, and well-being
associated with marriage that is found in early Java (Maxwell 1996,
107; for more on Java, see Robson 1971). Maxwell is puzzled, however, by the fact that, as portrayed in the poem, the ruler Awang
Halak Batatar refuses to accept heads in tribute (Maxwell 1996, 104).
My own reading of this part of the text is that the sultan's refusal to
value heads as tribute marks the historical turning point between
"barbaric" and "civilized" Islamic times. The refusal helps define
him as a "sultan." But the continuation of head-taking in Islamic
Brunei, notwithstanding the formation of a civilized, Islamic state,
emphasizes the fact that violence still has an important role as a
means of maintaining hierarchy and demarcating a boundary around
the "state." As Maxwell puts it, "[I]n ancient Brunei, heads were
significant . . . for separating winners from losers, lords from sub-

jects, those who receive obeisance from those who gave it" (Maxwell 1996, 112).

A poetic description of a postcremation ritual *(ligya)* held in Klungkung, Bali, in 1842 presents another vivid illustration of the role of violence in what Bruce Kapferer, in his discussion of violence, ritual, and the state in Sri Lanka, calls "the formation or reformation of the wholeness and health of the state" (Kapferer 1988, 78). As presented in the poem, the ritual is marked by continuous outbreaks of disorder and violence (Vickers 1991). Peasants arrive in their disorderly hundreds to take part:

> The followers (of kings) came in scores,
> Flowing from the north, flowing from the east,
> Filling the streets to watch,
> Like a swarm of spreading wasps;
> There were probably more than 100,000
> People in Klungkung
> Crowding and jostling each other.
> Not knowing who was noble, who was not
> They jostled each other
> Uncertain of the way. (Vickers 1991, 92)

The crowds indulge in coarse speech, sexual improprieties, theft, and opium consumption—"excessive behaviour," Adrian Vickers writes, that "is a kind of surplus energy to be put to ritual use" (Vickers 1991, 93). The demon-offering *(buta yadnya)* stage of the *ligya* brings the potential violence to a head in the form of the destruction and seizure *(marebut)* of the ritual offerings by the crowd as part of the ritual process. The poem describes the anger and other negative emotions that accompany these actions. As Vickers summarizes the text:

> Those who attended upon the priests experienced some difficulty *(kocekan)* at the beginning of the destruction of the offering area. The priests themselves were troubled *(éweh)* to see the destruction of the pavilion from which they had carried out their worship. . . . The participants in the destruction themselves become angry *(krodha)* as they fight over the offerings, in particular they become angry because they are ashamed *(jengah)* when they cannot get what they want. (Vickers 1991, 99)

Vickers writes that the king who stages the ritual invites "the threat of chaos" by amassing a crowd of participants: "He provokes a crisis by testing whether he has the resources, in terms of subjects and support from the Brahmana and the other lords, to succeed with the ritual" (Vickers 1991, 103). His ritual function, Vickers concludes, is that of "The Respected Lord Who Spins Bali," a title that links the king's role in the *ligya* to the myth of the "Churning of the Sea of Milk" that produces the elixir of immortality (Forge 1978, figs. 7, 8; Mannikka 1996, 161–172). The poem describes a ritual regeneration of the state through violence that furnishes the social energy necessary for hierarchical order. The expression of violence here is central to the discursive formation of the Balinese state, not a carnivalesque, subaltern protest against it (J. Scott 1990, 172–182).

So far we have been examining conceptions of violence in Southeast Asia in which violence is generated, controlled, and beautified by the state. Violence can also assume a less controllable, more oppositional form, although here, too, the "beauty" of the state is highlighted through violence made manifest.

The problem of excessive violence is addressed in the most famous premodern Malay literary text, the *Hikayat Hang Tuah*, "a series of loosely connected tales" dating from the late seventeenth century about the adventures of Hang Tuah, a fighter and loyal servant of the Melaka sultans in the second half of the fifteenth century (S. Errington 1975; Braginsky 1990; Maier 1999). The ruler's favoritism toward Hang Tuah arouses the jealousy of the other members of the sultan's entourage. Hang Tuah is slandered and condemned to death, a sentence he avoids by escaping from Melaka with the help of a high official who knows the sentence is unjust. During his absence, Tuah's friend Hang Jebat takes outrageous liberties with the sultan's person and possessions, including his concubines, forcing the ruler out of his own palace. Jebat says he is taking revenge on the sultan for the murder of Tuah. Tuah returns and confronts his friend, who runs amuck, first slaughtering the sultan's concubines, then the inhabitants of Melaka, before being killed by his friend:

> Hang Jebat then went out and amucked in the marketplace. Thousands of Melakans died and were wounded, both men and women. Negeri Melaka was in turmoil. Hang Jebat entered and amucked in compound after compound, pathway after pathway,

palace after palace. Many died and were wounded. (translated
and quoted in S. Errington 1975, 111)

Shelly Errington argues that Jebat's violence arises from the
grievance he feels over the humiliation suffered by his friend Hang
Tuah. It represents the "chaotic" form of social energy that must
be contained and made "orderly," socially appropriate *(patut)*, by
the state (S. Errington 1975, 102–121). Commenting on another scene
in the *Hikayat Hang Tuah* in which Hang Tuah subdues amucks,
Errington writes:

> When amucks enter the scene, the negeri [state] becomes confus-
> ing, disorderly, in an uproar *(huru-hara)*. . . . The scene images a
> more extreme version of the human condition as it is before rajas
> come into the world and give it form. (S. Errington 1975, 63)

The passage quoted earlier about Arjuna's reaction to the death
of his son Abhimanyu records a similar kind of sorrow that threatens
to lead to indiscriminate killing that would destroy the order of the
state. According to Renato Rosaldo, "grief" would also be disruptive
of social order in the Ilongot world if it were not alleviated by the
taking of heads (R. Rosaldo 1989, 1–21). In the *Hikayat Hang Tuah*,
"amucking" and "appropriate" behavior, including the skillful display of martial violence in defense of the sultan, are frighteningly
interchangeable, separated from one another by nothing more than a
sudden shift of mood.

As Hendrik Maier's writing on the *Hikayat Hang Tuah* has
demonstrated, this volatility is never resolved in favor of a single,
dominant principle of order. The text deals with irresolvable contradictions in the practice of state affairs, and even the rules of proper
conduct as exemplified by Hang Tuah cannot save Melaka from conquest by the Portuguese (S. Errington 1975, 171). It is particularly the
episodes about Jebat's treachery, amucking, and slaying at the hands
of his dear friend Tuah that suggest a state-engendering and order-
threatening tension between sexuality, loyalty, rules of conduct, and
violence that is similar to the one represented in the twelfth-century
Old Javanese *Bhāratayuddha*. Both Errington and Maier quote from
the scene in the *Hikayat Hang Tuah* in which the sexual tensions that
undermine proper language and conduct *(bahasa)*, leading to chaotic

violence that must be contained (either through transformation into a "beautiful" death or courageously opposed as formless, "ugly" amucking), are examined. The passage comes after Hang Tuah has been "killed" on the order of the raja and Hang Jebat has insinuated himself into the ruler's household:

> And the ruler came out and sat down on the doorstep, pages paid homage to him. And also Hang Jebat came in and paid homage, and the ruler ordered him to read a tale because Jebat knew how to present a variety of voices, moreover those voices were very good. And Hang Jebat presented a tale, loud was his voice, and melodious too. And all the girl attendants and ladies in waiting and concubines of the ruler, they all sat down and peeped, and behind the screens they peeped at Hang Jebat reading the tale. And all the wives of the ruler lusted for Hang Jebat. . . . Everybody who heard [Hang Jebat's voice] felt love. And the ruler slumbered on the lap of Hang Jebat. (translated and quoted in Maier 1997a)

In his essay on the *Hikayat Hang Tuah* (1997a), Maier establishes the significance of this scene in relation to the text's multiplicity of voices and attitudes toward Malay politics and culture. Clearly both the ethical precepts associated with written texts and the raja's authority are flouted by Hang Jebat's orality and licentiousness. Following both Maier and Errington, and building on my analysis of the Old Javanese *Bhāratayuddha* earlier in this chapter, I read Jebat's seductive treason as the "formless" variant of the same male prowess and resourcefulness that save the sultanate repeatedly in their "appropriate" manifestation in the noble deeds of Hang Tuah. It is Hang Tuah's *bahasa*, or appropriate language and behavior based on written manuals of Islamic conduct, that translates slander *(fitnah)* and other forms of treasonous behavior, including the aimless violence of running amuck, into practices that serve the formation of the state. *Bahasa* channels sexuality, intelligence *(akal)*, and knowledge *(tahu)* away from the purposes of treachery *(derhaka)* to those that are "useful" *(berguna)* to the ruler (S. Errington 1975, 63–65, 71–72, 97–98, 121). In other words, as is the case of the Old Javanese *Bhāratayuddha*, the state is defined in the *Hikayat Hang Tuah* in terms of a violent tension between opposing tendencies that contest one another within state practices. The opposition in the *Hikayat Hang Tuah* turns on the difference between *bahasa*, a code of language and behavior derived from Indic and Islamic written texts (Maier 1997a, 14–15), and the powerful emotional appeal of male prowess—prowess that is sexual, oral, and martial. In the scene where Jebat seduces the raja and all his wives and concubines with his recitation, his appeal is irresistibly beautiful. In the *Hikayat Hang Tuah* "beauty" is thus also linked to violent forces that can destroy the state, rather than to violent deeds and deaths that confirm the order of the state alone, as in the Old Javanese *Bhāratayuddha*. The palace women, who pelt Jebat with packets of betel and containers of perfume and ointments in their infatuation with him as he recites his tale while the raja sleeps in his lap, are the first to be slaughtered when Jebat runs amuck (S. Errington 1975, 107–109). Even though Jebat is killed, Hang Tuah and his *bahasa* only partially recuperate for the state the power that makes Jebat sexually attractive and politically dominant when he is alive.

While the *Hikayat Hang Tuah* imagines the contradictions inherent in male prowess and its role within the state in terms of two different characters, and the *Bhāratayuddha* poem imagines them in terms of several, the "tales from stone and paper" that portray Đỗ Anh Vũ (1114–1159), a high official from Lý Vietnam and contemporary of the East Javanese King Jayabhaya, does so in terms of one and the same person (K. Taylor 1995). According to the classical Chinese text of the inscription from his tomb, Anh Vũ was a paragon of Confucian virtue, as well as a man whose beauty and martial skills enabled him to penetrate the affairs of the court in the most intimate ways:

> From his youth, the Duke . . . was slender and graceful with a snowy pure complexion and a radiant countenance. . . . The Duke was eminent in dancing upon embroidered cushions with shield and battleaxe and in singing "The Return of the Phoenix" while dancing with supple elegance. Merchants arriving from afar and those traveling for pleasure never failed to attend his performances.
>
> In the year of Đinh Mùi (1127), Thần Tông's court chose him to serve in the pavilion; he was ranked in a capped position . . . over the six lords-in-waiting to administer the women's apartments of the inner court. He governed every kind of affair; the

Emperor entrusted everything to him. When it came to writing, numerical calculation, archery, chariot driving, medicine, acupuncture, and diagnosing illness by taking the pulse, there was nothing in which he was not proficient. (translated and quoted in K. Taylor 1995, 64)

In later passages from the tomb inscription, Anh Vũ's military prowess and reforms are lauded. When he died in 1159 at the age of forty-six, the inscription says, "the Emperor and Empress Dowager wept bitterly for seven days, lamenting [the collapse of] the ridgepole and roof tiles of the kingdom" (quoted in K. Taylor 1995, 69). Yet could a man endowed with so much male beauty, intelligence, and military prowess, notwithstanding his Confucian virtuousness, have been entirely chaste in his comings and goings among the women of the inner court?

Keith Taylor reads Anh Vũ's career as a penetration of successive barriers into the inner chambers of state power, a penetration that was treasonously sexual. According to thirteenth- and fifteenth-century chronicles, Anh Vũ had "secret illicit intercourse" with the mother of the Emperor (quoted in K. Taylor 1995, 72). Like some Vietnamese Hang Jebat, "his arrogance grew; sitting as emperor in the hall of audience, he belligerently dared anyone to oppose him and gained a reputation for cruelty" (quoted in K. Taylor 1995, 72). A plot was formed to seize Anh Vũ, but he defeated his enemies with bribes and guile. At a crucial turning point, when one of the plotters was about to kill Anh Vũ but was restrained from doing so, the annalist makes a scatological pun in Vietnamese, the only moment in the account when, as Taylor puts it, "the Vietnamese language penetrates the barrier of the Chinese language, in which educated Vietnamese had learned to textualize their experience and their memories" (K. Taylor 1995, 73).

Read together, Anh Vũ's funerary inscription and the later chronicle accounts about him display a tension and debate at the heart of the early Vietnamese state between "male prowess" and "rules of conduct" that is similar to the one we have observed in the *Hikayat Hang Tuah* and the *Bhāratayuddha*. The inscription's representation of Anh Vũ 's manly beauty and skill suggests that such qualities were "virtues" no less essential for the well-being of the state than Confucian rules of proper conduct. This at least is the point of

view of the "strongmen," of Anh Vũ and two of his male relatives, who were the de facto rulers of Vietnam from 1137 until 1188
(K. Taylor 1995, 75). The thirteenth- and fifteenth-century annalists,
on the other hand, read the tale of Anh Vũ's affair with the "rules"
foremost in mind, albeit in different ways. According to Taylor, the
fifteenth-century annalist's "real criticism . . . is not at the level of
proper procedure but at the level of political calculation" (K. Taylor
1995, 77). In this account, the "categorical condemnation of Đỗ Anh
Vũ at the beginning of his comment is almost lost amidst his [the
annalist's] passionate critique of Vũ Đái's stupidity" at not listening
to the advice that Anh Vũ should be immediately seized and killed
(K. Taylor 1995, 78). The name of the feckless leader of the conspiracy, Vũ Đái, served as the basis for the scatological pun in Vietnamese that linked the lust for wealth and status in the Lý court to
"shit" and "piss" and to the violent end that greeted the indecisive
plotters (K. Taylor 1995, 72). What the plotters lack, as does Abhimanyu (who is criticized in the *Bhāratayuddha* for rushing heroically
into battle even though he has not yet mastered "the withdrawal
tactic" [Supomo 1993, 187, v. 23]), is the wily, masculine intelligence
of usurpers like Hang Jebat and Anh Vũ (or Suharto!). This faculty is
also expressed in the earthy wit of the Vietnamese pun and displayed
by Hang Tuah's *akal* (wit, intelligence, strategem; Wilkinson 1959, 13)
when he outsmarts and eliminates violent amucks (see S. Errington
1975, 87; Maier 1997a, 15). Taylor suggests that from the perspective
of the late fifteenth-century Vietnamese literati who "could look
back and contemplate the vicissitudes by which they had recently
emerged as custodians of the state," it was "knowing how to survive
and to eliminate enemies" that needed to be stressed (K. Taylor 1995,
78). In other words, neither physical male prowess as such nor the
discipline instilled by proper rules of conduct set forth in Indic,
Islamic, or Sinic texts ensured the survival of the individual or of the
state in the violent worlds depicted in the *Bhāratayuddha*, the *Hikayat
Hang Tuah*, and the tales about Đỗ Anh Vũ. Rather, it was the wit of
the wily mousedeer (the hero of the animal fables known throughout
South and Southeast Asia who defeats the lion, the elephant, and the
crocodile), the wiliness of the peasant trickster, and the cunning of
the ancient Chinese war strategist that was being invoked and
praised (Winstedt 1969, 6–16; C. Reynolds 1996, 146; cf. J. Scott 1990,
162–166). This is the quality that is also being alluded to by Singa-

pore's Lee Kuan Yew in the opening passage of his autobiography and that he utilized as the basis for an official ideology of state "pragmatism":

> There are books to teach you to build a house, how to repair engines, how to write a book. But I have not seen a book on how to build a nation out of a disparate collection of immigrants from China, British India, and the Dutch East Indies, or how to make a living for its people when its former economic role as the entre-pôt of the region is becoming defunct. (Lee Kuan Yew 2000, 3; cf. Chua 1997a, 57–78)

This kind of intelligence, what a modern Indonesian writer I will discuss later in the chapter might call *nyali* (guts, daring), is directly linked to both the exercise and avoidance of violence within the state. Cunning is as much a characteristic of those who seek to dominate affairs of state from within as it is of those who pit their "practical knowledge" against state power from without (Wolters 1999, 201; J. Scott 1998, 309–341). It both predates and underlies tamer, more "civilized," and formal Islamic, Indic, or Confucian forms of "reason," behavior, and speech that were incorporated into state ideologies in Southeast Asia over the course of time (cf. J. Scott 1998, 310).

Other examples come to mind of violent eruptions in both speech and behavior that challenge, but at the same time highlight, the "beauty" of state control in Southeast Asia. The compulsive, often obscene, verbal and physical outbursts of women and servants afflicted with a mental disorder known as *latah* in Java and Malaysia, for example, are a kind of "running amuck" against state-sanctioned norms of speech and behavior (Winzeler 1984; Siegel 1986, 28–33). As in the case of Hang Jebat's feeling of *sakit hati* (brooding resentment) about the misuse of the sultan's authority against his friend Hang Tuah, or the scatological pun on Vũ Đái's name at the moment in the story when Chinese proprieties should have been restored to the affairs of the Vietnamese state, the violence of *latah* is a startled reaction to, but also a defiant, theatricalized elaboration upon, a fortuitous breach of propriety that threatens the dominance and beauty of the state (Siegel 1986, 31–32, 87–116). In colonial situations such reactions could occur when Europeans violated the rules of *bahasa*, as seems to have been the case in the following incident from 1849, when the visit of a European official, J. R. Logan, put a Malay "villager" into an impossible social situation. As Logan recalled the encounter:

> At first his manner was embarrassed and apparently dry, and his efforts to break through the restraint under which he laboured were abrupt and highly grotesque. When we ascended into the veranda he blurted out his welcome again, jerked his head about and bent his body forward, and shifted his position every second. He was most delighted, he said, highly honoured, but oppressed with shame. His house was a miserable hut, and he was such a poor, ignorant, vile person, mere dung in fact! *Saya orang meskin tuan,—orang bodo—tai"* [I'm just a poor man, sir, a stupid man, shit], and so he continued vilifying himself, and accompanying each new expression of humility by a sudden and antic alteration of his attitude and position. (quoted in Winzeler 1984, 78–79)

Here, I imagine, the startling nature of the Malay's encounter with the European and the impropriety felt by one so humble of having to offer hospitality to someone both strange and powerful triggered the *latah* reaction, in which the Malay's speech and body "ran amuck" against the very social norms of *bahasa* that he was constrained, unexpectedly and inappropriately, to observe.

Some of the best representations from the colonial period of the confrontation between the "beauty" of the state and the "ugly" violence that serves to create and sustain it are found in José Rizal's famous anticolonial novel, *Noli Me Tangere*, published in 1887. In one scene during a November fiesta, the awesome grandeur of the colonial state can barely contain the potential for mass violence as a crowd of natives arrives at church for Mass. The following passage is reminiscent of the description of the riotous crowds assembled for the postcremation ritual held in Klungkung, Bali, in 1842 or of the sexually aroused women who mob Kṛṣṇa when he enters Hāstina:

> The structure known to man as the dwelling of the Creator of all that exists was full of people from end to end. They pushed each other, pressed upon each other, trod on each other: the few who were going out and the many who were entering exhaling *Ayes!*

From afar an arm would stretch out to dip a finger in holy water,
but for the most part the crush would come and separate hand
from font; then a growl would be heard, a woman whose feet
had been stepped on would curse, but it did not stop the shov-
ing that went on. (Rizal 1997, 201; cf. Rafael 1984, 114)

When it is time for the sermon, Father Damaso begins speaking
in Latin and Spanish, the *bahasa-* or Sanskrit-like languages of the
colonial Philippines that enunciated the beauty and authority of
the Catholic-colonial regime:

Radiant and resplendent is the altar, and spacious the portals of
this church; but between them is the air that will transport the
holy and divine message that will spring forth from my lips.
Listen then, with the ears of the soul and the heart. . . . Ye great
sinners, captives of those Moro [Islamic] pirates of the spirit who
prowl the seas of eternal life in powerful vessels of the flesh and
the world, . . . behold with reverent remorse one who rescues souls
from the devil's thrall, an intrepid Gideon, a valiant David, . . . the
Constable of Heaven, braver than all the constabulary [*guardia
civil*] put together. (translated and quoted in Rafael 1988, 1)

What the "unlettered natives" hear in these metaphoric words
in languages they cannot literally understand, however, is a familiar
account of state practices in which supernatural forces, rather than
either the Catholic Church or the Spanish civil guard, protect them
from the violence of the state:

The illiterate *Indios* mentioned by the correspondent were not able
to catch anything except for the words civil guard, bandits, San
Diego and Saint Francis; they observed the scowl that the *Alferez*
[lieutenant] put on and the preacher's contentious gesture, and
concluded that he was scolding the *Alferez* for not going after the
bandits. San Diego and Saint Francis would take care of the matter
on hand, and very well too, as proven by an existing painting in
the Order's Manila convent in which Saint Francis, using only
his cincture as weapon, repelled the Chinese invasion during the
first years of the Spanish discovery of the Philippines. They re-
joiced and thanked God for this help, never doubting that once

the bandits were done away with, Saint Francis would also destroy the Civil Guards. (Rizal 1997, 206–207)

The first part of the sermon, delivered in the fluent, incomprehensible, yet "beautiful" languages of state, allows the congregation to imagine the restoration of a precolonial social order within the disorder of the existing colonial state. When Father Damaso switches to Tagalog, in which he "improvises" and "blunders," however, the result is uncontrollable, rebellious boredom and "random violence" (Rafael 1988, 214). Vicente Rafael reads this passage as a representation of the failure of translation in colonial situations. We could also characterize it as an outbreak of *latah*-like disrespect for male colonial authority, as an incidence of people running amuck because the ruler himself has violated the rules of state. As the disorderly reaction to the Tagalog portion of the sermon intensifies, Father Damaso himself loses control. Rafael explains:

> Assailed on all sides by Damaso's anger, people . . . are confronted by language out of control. Unable to appropriate anything from the priest, the people grow bored. Boredom leads to random explosions of violence, followed by automatic responses. A man slumps in sleep against his neighbor, crushing her dress; she explodes in words that seem to repeat those of the priest. Blows follow: she hits the man with her slipper; the priest pounds the pulpit with his fist; the woman responds by repeatedly kneeling. These events register in a series of exclamations: "Aaah! Aaah!" (Rafael 1988, 216)

Father Damaso's improvised, error-ridden, and rhetorically "ugly" Tagalog is itself a kind of violation of the state order evoked in the first part of the sermon. This transgression stimulates more violence and rebellion among the congregation, until near anarchy reigns.

One character in the novel is the embodiment of such anarchy: the Tagalog wife of the Spanish *alferez*, Doña Consolacion. Ugly, violent, and cruel, she defies easy gender categorization. Neither the physical brutality of her Spanish husband nor the satiric violence of Rizal's male-bourgeois discourse can subdue her (Rafael 1984, 129). She refuses to internalize any kind of *bahasa*. Pretending to have forgotten Tagalog, she is no better in Spanish, which her husband has attempted in vain to beat into her. When Consolacion "remembers" Tagalog and even speaks it perfectly, in a scene in which a mad-woman's Tagalog singing evokes memories of feeling and identity long repressed by Consolacion, she suffers a *latah*-like sequence of manic and repetitive outbursts that disrupt the alignment of the colonial state, which is momentarily sheltering the madwoman, Sisa, with the beauty of the "traditional" Tagalog song:

> "No, don't sing!" exclaimed the *alferez*'s wife in perfect Tagalog, standing up all agitated, "don't sing! Those verses hurt me!"
>
> The mad woman kept quiet. The assistant exclaimed: "Aba, she knows Tagalog *pala*!" and stared at the lady in admiration.
>
> The latter understood that she had betrayed herself, and felt ashamed. Since her nature was not that of a woman, her feeling of shame converted into anger and hate. . . . She took a few turns in the room, twisting the whip in her calloused hands and, stop-ping all of a sudden in front of Sisa, told her in Spanish: "Dance!"
>
> Sisa did not move.
>
> "Dance! Dance!" she repeated in a threatening voice.
>
> The mad woman regarded her with vague eyes, without ex-pression. The *alferez*'s wife raised one arm, then another, and started to shake her. It was useless: Sisa did not understand.
>
> She began to jump and agitate herself, prodding Sisa to imitate her. Music was heard from afar, the band of the procession play-ing a grave and stately march, but the lady was jumping furi-ously following a different tempo, a different music, that which resounded inside her. (Rizal 1997, 264–265)

Rizal's representation of the Tagalog washerwoman Doña Con-solacion, as dysfunctionally married as she is out of sync with the music of the "grave and stately march," portrays the same kind of failure to subsume various kinds of social energies within a beauti-fully ordered state that is found in the tales of Hang Jebat and Đỗ Anh Vũ. In each of the three stories there are different kinds of con-tingent and objective historical circumstances that explain why this failure occurs, but the results are similar: eruptions of violence that shatter aesthetic norms of beauty and the political standards of stately order that are synonymous with them. The ideal state of affairs is imagined in the Old Javanese story of Satyawatī and Śalya, where sexual passion, female initiative and beauty, male violence, marital harmony, loyalty to the state, martial carnage, and the aesthetics of poetic rapture are brought into perfect alignment with one another.

Modern echoes of similar themes and attempted alignments can be found in Rafael's study of Ferdinand and Imelda Marcos (Rafael 1993). Idealized in paintings and epic poems as reincarnations of "the first Filipino man and woman," Malakas (Strong) and Maganda (Beautiful), the Marcoses fused familyism and nationalism, beauty and violence, in terms of a discourse in which modern "Western" and "traditional" Filipino idioms competed for dominance. As Rafael writes,

> Philippine politics in the 1960s was caught up in the profound contradiction between the ideology of patronage and the material and social conditions set forth by capitalism, between an apparently generalized wish for social hierarchy, stabilized by traditional idioms of reciprocity, and a national state whose links with various localities were mediated by money. It was precisely at this historical juncture that the Marcoses emerged into the national scene. Their success was a function of their ability to seize upon —rather than resolve—the central contradictions of postwar Philippine politics. Ferdinand and Imelda played on them, seeking to utilize money and what it could buy in order to simulate patronage and the imaging of benevolent power (inexhaustible "strength" and eternal "beauty") at the top of the national hierarchy. Herein lay one source of their popularity: they seemed to be able to furnish a way of conceiving the "new" and the alienating changes it implied in the familiar and familial terms of patronage. (Rafael 1993, 65–66)

In the case of Java, since the days when the aesthetic concept of *langö* mediated between sexual passion, family loyalty, and subservience to the state at the court of Jayabhaya, a Javanese statist concept of "beauty" consistent with its ancient political meaning has developed. During the 1980s under the New Order, policies were violently enacted to promote settled wet-rice agriculture instead of the "disorderly farming" carried out by shifting cultivators (quoted in Tsing 1993, 156; cf. Dove 1985). Environmentally destructive approaches to logging were motivated not just by greed but also by a Javanese fear of the forest as a place inhabited by "troublesome plants," wild animals, and savages (quoted in Tsing 1993, 166–171). Both of these approaches to non-Javanese populations and environments owe something directly traceable to an aesthetic that pervades the following landscape description of the settled East Javanese countryside in the fifteenth century:

> 5. Now there was a village which he also viewed from above, lying below in a valley between the ridges.
> Its buildings were fine to behold, while the *lalang* roofs of the pavilions were veiled in the drizzling rain.
> Wisps of dark smoke stretched far, trailing away in the sky,
> And in the shelter of a banyan tree stood the hall, roofed with rushes, always the scene of many deliberations.
>
> 6. To the west of this were mountain ridges covered with ricefields [*pasawahan*], their dikes running sharp and clear.
> The gardens were close together and laid out in rows, and the many coconut palms were all shaded by mist.
> A heron's wing glistened as it flew along, faintly visible in the distance in the midst of the clouds;
> Then it disappeared, apparently merging with the mist, for it was finally lost from view. (Teeuw et al. 1969, 71; Day 1994, 186 passim)

This ancient landscape is not only "ordered" *(teratur)*, but the violence that has been required to make it so has been obscured from view by the misty "beauty" effect with which it is described, an effect that also acts to create a longing for sexual/political subservience, as well as wealth. As P. J. Zoetmulder observes in his discussion of *langö*,

> Objectively *langö* is the quality by which an object appeals to the aesthetic sense. It does so not by the clarity and immediacy of its beauty, but, on the contrary, because it seems distant, half hidden and apparently inaccessible; because it is suggestive, but does not reveal itself fully; because it allures, hinting at as yet unrevealed riches, so that the seeker after beauty is consumed by longing and the desire to reach it. (Zoetmulder 1974, 173)

In the case of the Philippines, I think that a similar aesthetic, one that mystifies violence and the enticements of greed, is at work in the ideological constructions of the Marcos era. An oil painting of Imelda Marcos was described in a 1969 newspaper article in the following terms:

> [T]he figure moves in a line that never was on sea or land. The details are precise: that parasol tugs at the hand and is tugged by the wind blowing a skirt into rich folds. Yet the landscape is not so much seen as felt: a seaside, early in the morning, on a cool day. And the figure seems not to walk but to float on the stirred air. The expression on the face is remote; this is a woman beyond politics and palaces, a figure from dream or myth. It's the pale ivory color that makes the scene unearthly, as though this were a frieze from some classic ruin. Just beyond the frame will be sirens choiring, the swell of a striped sail and, across the perfumed seas, Troy's burning roof and tower. (quoted in Rafael 1993, 73)

I am persuaded by Rafael that the effect of the painting's "hallucinatory quality" is "the imaging of patronage as something to which one may lay claim," but I think that it also conflates violent "strength" with winsome "beauty" so that the agency of the former merges with that of the latter. In this way, the portrait of Imelda Marcos could be likened to a passage of Old Javanese poetry in which the enticements of patronage and mystifications of violence lie hidden within the misty veils of an already conquered and wet-rice-growing landscape, in which subservience is like the dalliance of lovers or the raptures of poetic *langö* (Day 1997).

Elsewhere in Southeast Asia, poetry yields evidence of the violent processes of state formation in a way that beautifies the spoils of conquest and war. Court poetry in troubled fourteenth-century Vietnam contains images of military expeditions, natural barriers against invasion, subservient local spirits, and evocations of a Vietnamese golden age when "over ten thousand miles there were writing and chariots," a Chinese poetic metaphor for "a well-regulated State" (quoted in Wolters 1988, 27; 1999, 72–78). Classical Chinese poetic conventions enabled Trần officials to imagine a unified Vietnam ruled by "simple and pure customs" and a fatherly king. "By good customs," Wolters comments, "[the officials] meant obedience to the ruler's regulations" (Wolters 1988, 31). A variation on this secular poetic "landscaping" of conquered territory occurs in the Buddhist *dhyāna* poetry of King Minh-tôn (r.1320–1357). In his landscape poetry the king represented his troubled state as a *dharmadhātu*, a realm in which "[the] harmonious interplay between particularities and also between each particularity and universality creates a luminous universe . . . free from spacial and temporal limitations" (quoted in Wolters 1988, 114). This political vision is similar to the cosmological statement made by the builders of Angkor Wat and to the Sanskrit poetic assertions made at the end of the ninth century about Yaśovarman I (Wolters 1999, 78–85). In verses that allude to a lake built to the east of Angkor, the king's commands are compared to ambrosia, the elixir of immortality that "purified the hearts" and brought prosperity to his subjects. "To read of the king," writes Wolters, "is to read of Śiva, and vice versa" and to imagine his ambrosia spreading everywhere, ceaselessly, gloriously (Wolters 1999, 83).

States of Anarchy

Thus far in my discussion I have examined representations of violence and its role in state practices. There is an aesthetic quality to this role that acts in powerful collaboration with violence itself to effectuate state dominance. I have also suggested by way of comparative examples both temporal and regional that there are analogies between very old and contemporary instances of the way state violence is subsumed within a state aesthetic of the "beautiful" in Southeast Asia.

But what about horrors like the Indonesian killings of 1965–1966 or the Cambodian genocide of 1975–1978? How do we fit these and other mass killings on behalf of modern Southeast Asian states, unprecedented in their scale if not savagery, into older aesthetic frames? What kinds of new state aesthetic may be emerging because such killings have occurred? What aesthetic norms govern the perpetration and reception of killings in contemporary Southeast Asia that many citizens of Southeast Asia as well as Western observers label "criminal" but that contemporary Southeast Asian states, and many who serve them, appear to condone?

To begin with the last question first, a number of studies that examine what James Siegel calls the "conflation of criminal menace and state power" in contemporary Southeast Asia suggest continuities between a contemporary and an older aesthetics of violence (Siegel 1998, 99). In the Philippines, according to John Sidel, "[p]olitical office has served as an instrument for predation (e.g. in the protection of criminal activities and the acquisition of landholdings)" (Sidel 1998, 77). Sidel shows how a 1972 film about the Cavite criminal Nardong Putik, who was active in the 1950s and 1960s, emphasizes "the Cavite bandit's good looks, possession of *anting-anting* [amulets], and supposed Robin Hood–like popularity [which] served to identify him as a latter-day 'man of prowess' " (Sidel 1999b, 89). A similar kind of "insurgent masculinity" is evoked in the Clint Eastwood– and Rambo-based persona of "Gringo" Honasan, the leader of the Reform the Armed Forces Movement, which carried out killings, abductions, and torture against students and leftists during the later Marcos years and staged nine unsuccessful coups after Marcos' fall (McCoy 1999, 218, 263, 308–312, 346). Just as Imelda Marcos' "beauty" acted to naturalize the violent politics of her husband's rule in a seemingly ancient form of benevolent familyism, so the filmic

> legend of Nardong Putik and other Philippine gangsters work[s] to claim that power is not simply reducible to money and state office. The *anting-anting* of Nardong Putik, the weddings and town *fiestas* sponsored by Governor Remulla, the movie-star good looks and cockfighting victories of Senator Revilla—all locate the source of power in the intrinsic personal qualities of these aspiring powerbrokers. These various mechanisms thus represent claims that power—unlike money and electoral office—does not circulate and that the "big man" is essentially irreplaceable and indispensable. (Sidel 1999b, 93)

Another way of putting Sidel's point would be to say that films and stories about Nardong Putik and other Filipino strongmen turn their lives and deeds into exemplary representations of beautiful "states" in the Southeast Asian sense I have been discussing. Rather like the representation of Angkorean kingship in the relief depicting the battle of Kurukṣetra at Angkor Wat, the statelike spheres of influence surrounding Filipino bosses and rebel military officers have as their churning axis the "big man," "irreplaceable and indispensable" in the midst of violent upheavals that generate wealth, fear, and kinship solidarity.

In Thailand "the words 'godfather' (*jaopho*, a literal translation) and 'mafia' (adapted from Italian via English) are commonly used . . . to describe powerful figures from police to military leaders to cabinet ministers and business leaders—and not always in a derogatory fashion" (Ockey 1998, 39). James Ockey connects long-standing Thai traditions of "big men" *(phuyai)* and village toughs *(nakleng)*, via the history of tax farming in the nineteenth century and of "development" under Prime Minister Sarit (1958–1963), to the prominent role of criminal bosses in local and national politics in Thailand of the 1990s (Ockey 1998; Pasuk and Sungsidh 1994, 57–107; McVey 2000). During the same period Thai entrepreneurship was both guided and aestheticized by popularized versions of the Chinese *Romance of the Three Kingdoms* that celebrate the wiliness and derring-do of ancient Chinese warriors (C. Reynolds 1996). As the use of the terms "godfather" and "mafia" suggests, Hollywood idols such as Marlon Brando also served as models for Thai gangsters and the rising middle class whose glamour, wealth, and violence rivaled that of the Thai military and the state (B. Anderson 1998, 174–191). Both cultural models acted to create an aesthetic of masculine prowess and guile that has appealed to "tycoons" and "warlords" in contemporary Thailand (C. Reynolds 1996, 147). But possession of a female "radiant beauty" has also continued to be associated with powerful men (Van Esterik 2000, 156). The gendering of bossism itself has shifted as control over access to wealth and a desire for social respectability, rather than the macho display of sheer physical force, have (once more) become dominant in Thai political life (Ockey 1999; 1996; Pasuk and Sungsidh 1994, 102). Middle-age women (cf. Andaya 2000a) have also become prominent bosses *(jaomae)*, and some of "the less savory type" exploit the ambiguities of their hybrid identity as tough *jaopho* and merciful, bodhisattva-like "mothers" modeled on the middle-class cult deity Kuan Yin (Ockey 1999, 1055).

Studies that examine the killing that occurred in Indonesia during 1965–1966 and Cambodia between 1975–1978 also assign an important role to spectacular (i.e., public) displays of male "courage" and "honor" that fulfill aesthetic requirements of state-engendering and -preserving violence similar to those we have encountered in sources from early Southeast Asia. Writing of the massacres of PKI (Communist Party of Indonesia) members and other enemies carried out by youthful gangs in Bali, Robinson comments:

> Like their predecessors in the Revolution and the 1950s, the vigilantes of 1965–66 were primarily young men eager to demonstrate their "courage" and their sense of "revolutionary" commitment. Many, too, were martial arts adepts, something that gave them special status and added to their aura of power. (Robinson 1995, 300)

Such displays of prowess were also contextualized within discourses of "holy war" and religious "purification" by military and party leaders who directed the killings. Robinson sees this as a conscious manipulation and perversion of older cultural and religious symbols, which Hildred Geertz thinks were still powerfully alive during the Revolution (1991):

> The manipulation of cultural and religious symbols was crucial to the dynamic of the massacre. For while the PKI was in some respects iconoclastic, it was not self-evidently atheistic, nor was it obviously responsible for the island's economic and social problems or for the apparent cosmic imbalance. These ideas about the PKI's nature and culpability had to be, and were, nourished as the foundation for collective action. Likewise, the idea that the problem of cosmic imbalance or impurity would best be resolved by mass murder did not emerge naturally from precepts of Balinese Hinduism but originated rather with the Indonesian military leadership. (Robinson 1995, 301–302)

Writing on the Cambodian killings, Alexander Hinton sees less outside manipulation of and more compelling continuities between pre-Democratic Kampuchea (DK) notions of revenge, bravery, honor, and competition for praise and the role such notions played in the genocidal killings of the DK regime (Hinton 1998a, 1998b). Transposed into the new organizational and ideological context of the Khmer Rouge, which "glorified violence done in the name of the revolution" (Hinton 1998a, 115), "honor" and murder enacted before an audience of one's superiors and peers became synonymous:

> It is . . . crucial to note that executions usually took place in front of a perpetrator's peers and/or superiors. Within this structured setting, the killers attempted to gain honor through the positive evaluations of others in a manner analogous to student exam competition. . . . Earlier I noted that during indoctrination sessions and political meetings, Khmer Rouge were repeatedly asked if they would "dare" *(hean)* to kill an enemy, even if the person was a parent, sibling, spouse, or relative. Such propaganda played upon a traditional cultural model of bravery *(klahan)* that is an important part of "Cambodian machismo"—the brave who dare gain face, cowards who do not dare are shamed. (Hinton 1998a, 115–116)

Hinton thinks that the "frequent attempts to seize power and authority" during the DK period could also be construed as "offensive honor competitions" (Hinton 1998a, 116).

The Cambodian state that arose out of a churning sea of blood and that was built upon a mountain of corpses during the DK period was dependent, therefore, upon the energy and violence generated by competition between Cambodian males. It is hard not to recall once again the relief of the battle of Kurukṣetra at Angkor Wat and to wonder about continuities between the states of Angkor and the DK. The Khmer Rouge leadership, in fact, consciously invoked the memory of Angkor in its grandiose projects and pronouncements (Chandler 1996b, 316; Ponchaud 1989, 161; Marston 1994). Guards at the infamous interrogation and torture facility "S-21" referred to prisoners as "damned souls," recalling scenes of Buddhist hells painted on the walls of Buddhist temples as well as those carved on the south side, east half, of the third gallery of Angkor Wat, which they may have seen during at least one outing to the temple, recorded in a published photograph (Chandler 1999, 118, 121; Kiernan 1996, photo 21). In the following description from the fourteenth-century Three Worlds cosmology, a text that was republished by the Thai state in 1974 and that helped legitimize the violent repression of the left-wing insurgency there (Pasuk and Baker 1995, 316), we find a description of a hell that seems specifically designed for the class enemies of the peasant Khmer Rouge:

> The first of [the] auxiliary hells is called Vetaranī. The beings who live in this land are those who used to be well-to-do, having

property and men and slaves. But they harmed others and took their property by force, since they were stronger; and thus when they died they were born in this hell which is called Vetaranī. The guardians in the Vetaranī hell have clubs, large knives, lances, swords, spears, and all kinds of weapons for killing, stabbing, shooting and beating, all of which are made of fiery red iron, have flames that shoot upward like a fire in the sky, and blaze without ceasing. The *yama* guardians hold these throwing and stabbing weapons; they chase the hell beings, throw at them, stab them, and beat them with these weapons. These beings suffer great pain and anguish that is too much for them to bear. (Reynolds and Reynolds 1982, 71–72)

In the Angkor Wat relief, Yama, the god of death and king of the ancestors, and Citragupta, the scribe who records the good and bad karma of those being sent to hell, preside over two scenes: that of the damned, "unceremoniously thrown headfirst to their fate," and another where, "oblivious to the horror and uproar . . . virtuous men and women . . . sit in quiet splendor in the royal palaces of the heavens, attended by a multitude of servants" (Mannikka 1996, 155). Apart from the parallel nature of Citragupta's scribal function and the archive of forced confessions found at S-21, one could also point to similarly stark, heaven-versus-hell juxtapositions between opposing verbal registers in what one Cambodian commentator has described as the way "gentleness entwines with cruelty to the point where they become confused" in Khmer Rouge language use (quoted in Marston 1994, 110). The following lines from the song "Children of the New Kampuchea" also evoke the blissfulness mixed with obliviousness to contiguous slaughter that characterizes the heavenly elect as depicted on the third gallery of Angkor Wat:

> We the children have the good fortune
> to live the rest of our time in precious harmony
> under the affectionate care
> of the Kampuchean revolution, immense, most clear and shining.
> (quoted in Marston 1994, 111)

In the manner of the juxtaposed reliefs of heaven and hell on the walls of Angkor Wat, the aesthetic of the state in DK was created out of a deadly synergy between forces that became "diabolically" and "sweetly" intertwined (Chandler 1991, 110).

Throughout this chapter I have pointed out some of the ways in which violence has connected with beauty in the creation and maintenance of Southeast Asian states. In the examples we have just examined from the Philippines, Thailand, Bali, and Cambodia a link is made between male violence that exceeds the bounds of either law or morality and the order and majesty of the state. In his study of violence and criminality in Indonesia's New Order, Siegel argues that the kind of continuity between bandits, bosses, and gangsters and legitimate rulers that existed in Indonesia until the end of the nineteenth century was broken at the end of the Indonesian revolution (Rush 1990; Onghokham 1978; Schulte Nordholt and van Till 1999). "Jago [village toughs] and criminals furnished much of the push for revolution," Siegel writes, "[b]ut they [have] never been part of the national celebration of revolutionary heroes on any scale" (Siegel 1998, 49).

Under Sukarno, the first president of the Republic, the word "*rakyat*," once used to describe the entourages of powerful men in Indonesia that also included "criminals," was turned into the term for the "people" of the nation (Siegel 1999, 212–213). During Sukarno's presidency the "people" were denied the social reforms promised by the revolution; under Suharto this disenfranchisement was completed. "It was just at this point, when 'the people' had been suppressed, that a notion of criminality developed in Indonesia," Siegel writes (1999, 213). Whereas the killings that took place during the revolution or the anti-Communist massacres of 1965–1966 have the character of "an intermittent civil war in which, by definition, members of the same nation kill each other," violence in the New Order was typically carried out by and against "criminals," in which neither vengeance nor ideological differences (both of which played an important role in the Cambodian revolution of 1975–1978) were centrally important (Siegel 1999, 214).

Siegel describes the New Order state of the 1980s as being haunted by a fear of "organizations without form" *(organisasi tanpa bentuk)*, a term for an insurgency without name or shape that served to justify political repression and outbursts of state-sponsored violence. One such outburst was known as the "mysterious killings," or Petrus, which left the mutilated bodies of thousands of petty criminals on grotesque display in public places during 1983–1984. Since the New Order turned its own repressed and alienated "people" into "criminals," Siegel reasons, then carrying out "criminal" violence of its own was a way of making a connection with them, so as to constitute the "nation" (Siegel 1998, 90–119). By showing Indonesians that "terror rests in the control of the government," the New Order sought to "rebind the state to the nation" not in terms of social reform, but through spectacular displays of violence (Siegel 1998, 115).

Siegel's study focuses on the failure of national revolution in Indonesia and on the steps taken by an authoritarian military regime to detach the nation from its revolutionary past, rebinding it to the New Order state. But it is also possible to read state violence under Suharto in three other ways that contribute to our understanding of state formation in Southeast Asia more generally.

The first is to think of the Petrus killings as a kind of premodern public execution, carried out by Rambo-like, hooded killers trained in U.S. Army counterinsurgency techniques that had their own kind of aesthetic appeal and power. With even less of a context of legality to worry about than the monarchs of the French old regime, Suharto's aim was the restoration of "power" in the sense described by Foucault in the following passage:

> The public execution, however hasty and everyday, belongs to a whole series of great rituals in which power is eclipsed and restored . . . ; over and above the crime that has placed the sovereign in contempt, it deploys before all eyes an invincible force. Its aim is not so much to re-establish a balance as to bring into play . . . the dissymmetry between the subject who has dared to violate the law and the all-powerful sovereign who displays his strength. . . . [It was] a policy of terror: to make everyone aware, through the body of the criminal, of the unrestrained presence of the sovereign. The public execution did not re-establish justice; it reactivated power. (Foucault 1991a, 48–49)

As David Chandler observes, commenting on the testimony of a former S-21 interrogator, violence is "a dead end and its own reward" (Chandler 1999, 129). Carried to extremes, final solutions eliminate the very possibility of power and dominance, which depend on defiance and struggle for their own existence. But read in Foucauldian terms, Petrus was a judicious use of spectacular violence designed to regenerate power and hierarchy at a time when Indonesian society was undergoing economic and social deregulation (Mackie and McIntyre 1994). Petrus reminded the newly emerging popular forces in Indonesia "of the unrestrained presence of the sovereign," violently destroying assertions of private identity and invulnerability (expressed by the wearing of tattoos), so that these could be relocated and re-identified "within the hierarchy of the state" (Barker 2001, 41; Siegel 2001, 43). Joshua Barker argues that, by the mid-1990s, the prevalence of "magically powerful letters" *(surat sakti)* on behalf of business ventures, "invulnerability to the law" *(kebal hukum),* and all manner of club stickers and name cards received from officials served the function of authorized tattoos that (re)inscribed the identities of ordinary people and their localities within the space of the state (Barker 2001, 51). We could even say that, by means of Petrus, the New Order state reinvented the kind of manpower control, based on the tattooing and registration of all males eligible for labor service, that was once deployed by the state of Ayutthaya and by the early Chakri kings of Siam (Englehart 2001, 64–65; Mayoury and Pheuiphanh 1998, 145–148).

This last thought suggests a second way of reading Petrus, one that would put the killings in an older context of political violence in Java, like the one described in the long passage from the end of the *Bhāratayuddha.* Such a reading would imply a disagreement with John Pemberton's argument about New Order ritual and politics, in which he stresses the reinvented inauthenticity of state versions of Javanese "tradition" since the nineteenth century. Pemberton reads expressions of disorder and *"ekses"* in both the colonial and New Order periods as signs of popular rebellion against a repressive state obsessed with "order" (Pemberton 1994). Rather than think of "disorder" as a property of "society" outside the "state," however, I have been suggesting throughout this chapter that disorder is the very ground and source of statist definitions of beauty and order and hence of the boundary that separates the "state" from "society." It is impossible to imagine the Orde Baru, the "New Order," without contiguous mayhem to give that order its raison d'être. For all the continuities between the policies of the New Order and the *"rust en orde"* (tranquility and order) ideology of the Dutch colonial state, it is the absence of *rust* from both state formations that links them to a long and continuous history of turbulent politics at the heart of the Java-nese state (see Rush 1990; Schulte Nordholt and van Till 1999).

Compare the swiftness and savagery with which King Jaya-bhaya restored order to his realm in the Kali time—"Without delay he destroyed every enemy who dared oppose him and hunted down all the adversaries. Evil men were annihilated and scoundrels were completely swept away as in the past"—with Suharto's description of Petrus in his autobiography:

> The real problem is that these events (Petrus) were preceded by fear and nervousness among the people (rakyat). Threats from the criminals (jahat), robberies, murder and so on all happened. Stability was shaken. It was as though the country no longer had any stability. There was only fear. Criminals (jahat) went beyond human limits. They not only broke the law, but they stepped beyond the limits of humanity. . . . Doesn't that demand action? (translated and quoted in Siegel 1998, 107)

In *Bhāratayuddha* terms, Suharto was a modern Jayabhaya, restoring order through violence to his realm, so that "thieves . . . flee in fear of his power" (Supomo 1993, 104). As I argued in my reading of the twelfth-century text, violence receives its ultimate sanction and meaning within the familial political economy of a "beautiful" state that guarantees a loyal participant fulfillment of his or her desires in death. In attempting to make his state the dominant source of both death and invulnerability, Suharto established his genealogical resemblance to Jayabhaya (cf. Siegel 2001, 67).

It is also worth remembering that during the 1980s the New Order carried out beautification campaigns in Indonesian cities and villages, "cleaning" out unsightly rubbish of all kinds, including the tattooed and theatrically mutilated corpses of the Petrus victims left, overnight, on public display. Teruo Sekimoto observes that the Indo-nesian word for "clean" *(bersih)* had a political as well as an environ-mental meaning during this period:

> The word *bersih* first came into favour with the government in the sense of being free of communist influence. This sense of ·*bersih* still prevails today. . . . Then, in the 1970s and 1980s, *bersih* prevailed in the more literal sense of the physical cleanliness of

villages and towns. *Bersih* is often coupled with similar slogans such as *sehat* (healthy), *nyaman* (refreshing), *aman* (safe), and *tertib* (orderly), as many local governments organize large campaigns to clean and decorate the environment. Such campaigns gained momentum in the 1980s and many cities and regencies competed with each other and mobilized people for it. (Sekimoto 1997, 334)

Like New Order logging and transmigration practices that rid forests in the outer islands of the archipelago of "troublesome plants" and replaced them with transplanted and orderly people, Petrus and other campaigns to make Indonesia *bersih* recapitulated a sequence of steps (first rid the countryside of "evil men," then "develop" it into a flourishing garden) as old as the state in Java.

We can even observe a struggle between unrestrained sexuality and loyalty to the Javanese state in the early 1980s, although the terms of the debate changed in an interesting way compared to their first recorded occurrence in the twelfth century. Saraswati Sunindyo discusses the trial and conviction of two police intelligence officers in 1981 for the attempted murder of Mrs. Supadmi, the mistress of one of the men, Lieutenant Colonel Suyono (Saraswati 1996, 125–131). The Indonesian press compared the scandal to the British Profumo-Keeler affair, portraying Supadmi as an "immoral woman" bent on wrecking not only the lawful marriage of her assailant and former lover, but also "both the police corps and the country" (Saraswati 1996, 127). In their coverage of the trial, the newspapers also highlighted the sex appeal of the victim:

> Mrs. Supadmi showed up in a dazzling outfit and looked sexy. She was wearing a light brown *kebaya* [blouse], brown high heels, and a bun hairdo. An officer in charge commented, "Mrs. Ludewijk is definitely an extraordinary beauty, better than a movie star." (*Sinar Harapan*, March 15, 1981, translated and quoted in Saraswati 1996, 129)

As would have been the case in the twelfth century, Supadmi's beauty and sexual energy were forces threatening the order of the state. But accounts of the trial show that the New Order suppressed these forces rather than utilize them in order to create new bonds of loyalty and subservience. In the New Order's ideological representation of the incident, Supadmi herself became an enemy of the state, narrowly escaping death at the hands of two of its loyal defenders. Supadmi more closely resembles Hang Jebat or Malaysian Deputy Prime Minister Anwar Ibrahim, who was deposed, then tried and convicted of sodomy in 1998, because she was made an example of a dangerously attractive and treasonous sexuality that threatened to usurp the power of the state (Maier 1999; Andaya and Andaya 2001, 329; The Anwar Ibrahim Judgment 1999).

A third reading of Petrus and other instances of New Order violence, one that provides an optic for viewing high-tech violence of every sort throughout contemporary Southeast Asia, is offered by the novel *Nyali* (Guts), written by the Indonesian writer and theatre director Putu Wijaya in 1981 (Wijaya 1988; Widodo 1985). This is how Amrih Widodo characterizes, in incisive fashion, the blood-soaked world of the story and its main character, Kropos, whose name means "easily destroyed, weak, useless" (Widodo 1985, 87):

> The tale of Kropos has its setting in a state which is originally a Kingdom but becomes a Republic. In contrast with the atmosphere of "master planning" carefully built up by the author, the state has no clear, hierarchical governmental structure. Instead, one finds merely offices and ranks which do not at all imply the existence of a structure that limits and defines the activities and powers of people within it. Higher ranks simply indicate that some people have higher positions than others; they say nothing about their real importance or the authority they are seen to exercise. . . . Relations between commanders and subordinates . . . are not based on personal loyalty but on ideology and plan. Under such conditions rapid changes in these relations become quite understandable. . . . Since Zabaza is [an insurgent] band created by the state in the person of General Leonel, there is no clearcut dividing line between the state and Zabaza. Kropos, too, belongs to both. Each "side" continually infiltrates its spies into the other in order to ferret out its secrets; often it is unclear who is spying for whom. Everything is confused and confusing, a person may be on one side or the other, or both, and known to be such. . . . The "obscurity" of the social structure and political structure of the country, compounded by the obscurity of the dividing line

between opposing sides, and the general atmosphere of chaos
and brutality, enables the author . . . [to] create a feeling of sus-
pense, mystery, perplexity, and sometimes of deception. . . . We
are thus given a picture of a state in which the population experiences an atmosphere of control and terror, while the rulers feel
the need for something to terrorize the populations, but no need
to actually control it, since terror by itself will do the job. In fact,
it is precisely the terror that creates the atmosphere of "order"
and "organization." (Widodo 1985, 83–84)

While the two earlier readings of Petrus stress the similarities
between state violence in Southeast Asia today and state violence in
the past, this reading seems entirely concerned with what is different
about the two cases. In the world of *Nyali*, "order" and "organization"—devoid of logic, deprived of bonds of sex, love, or loyalty, and
based on uncontrolled violence and terror—are properties of a state
that is itself "an organization without form," a state that has run
amuck. Wijaya's state is an anarchy, which is an oxymoron in Weber's
terms. But the anarchy imagined by Wijaya in fact recalls accounts of
earlier Southeast Asian states that we have examined in this book, in
which fluid structures and chaotic "order," betrayals, and mass killings also held sway. There are many states in the course of Southeast
Asia's long history that could be called "organizations without form"
in which the boundaries that separate the "state" from family and
society are constantly breaking down. According to Widodo, the
character who exhibits the *nyali* (guts) of the novel's title is the killer
Kropos, a weak person who nonetheless has the courage and guile to
survive. Kropos has, therefore, genealogical links to other cunning
and invulnerable state-forming protagonists we have encountered in
this book. In Widodo's view Wijaya also has "guts" because he resists
the temptation to give his story a cyclical rather than an aimlessly
repetitive structure, a refusal that also denies the possibility of ex-
tracting a sense of "justice" or "morality" from the tale (Widodo 1985,
82). Wijaya's language and descriptions of violence are also intentionally "ugly," causing the reader to be "disgusted, nauseated,
puzzled, and annoyed" (Widodo 1985, 87)—emotions of fear and
nyali rather than of hope and submission. As a textual representation
of the Southeast Asian state, *Nyali* makes, therefore, a real break with

the past, since there is no incipient Golden Age, Viṣṇu ex machina, or "beautiful" state that will rescue Kropos' world from its interminable, post-Kali time.

Summary

In this chapter I have built my argument on two key concepts in Southeast Asian studies—Wolters' notion of the "man of prowess" and Geertz's idea of the "theatre state"—in order to suggest the long-term significance of the interaction of violence and aesthetics in the ideologies and practices of Southeast Asian states. Read against Weber's lecture, "Politics as a Vocation," or Giddens' *The Nation-State and Violence* (1985), the material I have examined here makes clear why the history of state violence in Southeast Asia differs from that in the West. "Bourgeois rights" and democracy (or as Giddens prefers to call it, polyarchy, the rule of the many through persuasion and debate) do not hold sway. The state does not control either violence or the definitions of what makes its use "right" or "legitimate." Internal pacification is uneven, the nature of punishment still violent and spectacular, rather than disciplinary and monotonous, even when hidden from public view (think here of the "spectacular" effect of the much-publicized physical injuries inflicted on Malaysia's Anwar Ibrahim while in custody!). "Crime" is still considered a form of "rebellion" rather than one of social "deviance." Violence still characterizes the labor contract, a subject that has not been examined in my discussion here but one that is symptomatic of the lack of separation of the economic from the political sphere in Southeast Asia, a topic I consider in chapter 4. Finally, for all the expansion of bureaucracies in nineteenth- and twentieth-century Southeast Asia, "administrative power" has failed to replace physical violence as the primary "sanctioning capacity" of the modern Southeast Asian nation-state (Giddens 1985, 188 and passim). Even in its most authoritarian and totalitarian forms, the Southeast Asian state is closer to anarchy than to statehood in a Weberian sense.

I have avoided entering into a major discussion of the manifold differences between the causes and uses of state violence in Southeast Asia and the West. Instead, I have tried to bring the particular aesthetic quality of state violence in the region into view in ways that will support my contention throughout this book that there are strong similarities in the conceptualization and practice of state formation across the region and over time. The "beautiful" attractions of state violence in Southeast Asia also point to the presence of what Michael Taussig would call "state fetishism" (Taussig 1992, 11–40). Taussig proposes that the *"fantasies of the people prohibited"* from initiation into the sacred knowledge and rites of state practices play a central role in the creation of the state as a magical object of worship (Taussig 1992, 130, italics in original). In other words, even those who are marginal to or victimized by the state help imagine and sustain its power, which in all the cases examined in this chapter was magically and irresistibly attractive to many, for long periods of time (cf. Siegel 2001, 46). I don't want to hazard a guess about how widely held or hegemonic ideas about the magical synergy between violence, beauty, and the state in Southeast Asia may have been or may continue to be. But the evidence I have discussed demonstrates that such a synergy is long-standing and significant. The question remains to be answered how many subjects and citizens of Southeast Asian states both past and present have helped erect the "cruel and brutal" beauty of the Southeast Asian state as an object of worship, as "awe-inspiring as royal glory" (Taussig 1992, 135, quoting from Jean Genêt's *The Thief's Journal*). Even when hierarchy collapses, Siegel reminds us in his discussion of witch killings in the post-Suharto Indonesia of 1998, "the impulse toward hierarchy does not end" (Siegel 2001, 68).

Conclusion
Alternative States, Incongruous Region

In his painting of the sorcerer Begawan Mercukunda (see page 286), the Balinese artist Ida Bagus Madé Togog represents the same kind of dynamic transformations of benevolent and violent identity and agency that characterize state formations in Southeast Asia over the centuries (H. Geertz 1994, 84, 83–95). Togog's sorcerer explodes with potency, which he has obtained from a book of magical knowledge given to him by a god. As Togog explained to anthropologists Gregory Bateson and Margaret Mead in the 1930s, the ability to change heads enables Begawan Mercukunda strategically to redeploy his power so that he can prevent anyone from defeating him (H. Geertz 1994, 85). In Southeast Asian worlds of "fluctuating, flowing, shifting forces," to borrow words from some of Hildred Geertz's eloquent reflections on magical power in Bali, states have always competed with rival sources of wealth and power to create, however "momentarily and precariously," safe havens for the kinship networks and entourages of those who seek to participate in their spheres of invulnerability and well-being.

In other ways as well, Togog's painting is emblematic of the "fluid iron" of coercive state repertoires that have been examined in this study. Togog barely spoke Malay and was apparently uninterested in "Western matters," unlike some of the other Batuan painters of his day (H. Geertz 1994, 19). He was immersed in seemingly "traditional" concerns about "religious and mythical subjects" and "magical events." Togog's interest in Begawan Mercukunda, however, was surely not a product of either a residual or a reinvented "traditionalism," but rather an expression of an emerging Balinese "alternative modernity" (C. Taylor 1999) in which changing patterns

The Making of a Mythic Sorcerer by Ida Bagus Madé Togog (from Hildred Geertz, *Images of Power*, 1994).

of magic, witchcraft, and other Balinese cultural practices would continue to play a part. This alternative modernity had already been long in the making (Vickers 1996). Like the "coexistent and conflicting modes of production" that constituted the Western Enlightenment (P. Anderson 1974, 421), overlapping stages and kinds of transcultural localization have shaped the formation of Southeast Asian states in ways that cannot be reduced to a single trajectory that converges with dominant Western modes of "civilization" and "development" (cf. Huntington 1997; Harrison and Huntington 2000). The interplay of autochthonous, Indic, and Western pictorial styles in Togog's painting recalls similar hybridities in the forms and practices of Southeast Asian states, some of which have been described in these pages, from early to contemporary times.

I began this book by surveying the principal ways in which the state has been studied and represented in the scholarship on Southeast Asia and by proposing my own definition of the "state" in order to help focus attention on the processes of state formation in the region rather than on a typology or teleology of "traditional" and "modern" states. In an effort to break down the traditional/modern dichotomization of states and historical periods, I argued that (at least) four state-forming processes have been at work in many Southeast Asian eras and localities.

The first is the agency of kinship networks in responding to state-forming possibilities. I showed that bilateral kinship groups, whether in response to Indic or Confucian models of a cosmological state or to (post)colonial ones of a rational-bureaucratic state order, seized opportunities to participate in building states in order to increase their status and solidarity. In the course of this process emotions of family love have been transformed into political love and loyalty, while gender identities have been contested and manipulated by states, but also by those who have opposed them. If the Southeast Asian state over time might best be characterized in gender terms as "masculine," that same masculinity has been challenged by the constantly resurgent power of women and by both men and women who have used "transvestite" strategies for appropriating state power for purposes of their own. The "beauty" of Southeast Asian states has both male and female attributes that offer a better understanding of the cultural meaning of state order and state violence in Southeast Asian societies than the Weberian concept of "legitimacy."

The second process I studied was the role of knowledge in forming cosmological states. Although conventionally relegated to "traditional" Southeast Asia and most especially to the formation of Indic and Confucian states by elites who acquired special knowledge from foreign sources to do so, I argued that cosmological state forms and the concepts that underlie them can also be found in colonial and modern, Western and Southeast Asian, elite and peasant variants. State-forming knowledge at all levels and in all eras, I proposed, can best be characterized as talismanic, serving to provide access to both universal truth and invulnerability. But cosmologies and truth regimes are not monolithic. They are constructed out of arguments, conflicts, and hybridizing networks of practices, texts, and ideas that offer more than one mode of participation and escape. Although Southeast Asian cosmological states look like examples of Hobbes' Leviathan—witness the monuments of Angkor Wat or the August 17 military parades during the New Order—this is an illusion of their state form. In fact, they are nothing more than networks of human relationships, practices, and concepts, repertoires that are very old and well rehearsed, but nonetheless susceptible to change. I stressed the fact that all state/knowledge formations are universalizing, which helps explain how colonial regimes of truth, as well as modern, anticolonial, and antistate ideologies, formed hybrids that have accommodated and preserved older Southeast Asian cosmological forms, so that cosmological states and modes of thinking continue to exist to this very day, even in Marxist writings. Yet the contested, hybridizing internal workings of these formations need to be brought to light, for in deconstructing them, new possibilities for thought and action are revealed.

Bureaucracy is the third state-forming practice I considered. If the cosmological state has long been associated with "traditions" that have been relegated to the past, bureaucracy has been the "modern" state form par excellence, a sure sign of the Southeast Asian state's success or failure to "develop." I argued that modern Southeast Asian bureaucracies, in their "pure" Weberian form—witness the prevalence of "bureaucratic polities"—are manifestly not out there, but this left a more interesting, if obvious, question unanswered: so what *is* out there that looks like a bureaucracy, in early as well as contemporary times, but is not one, according to a Weberian definition? My answer was that Southeast Asian bureaucracies have always exhibited Weberian characteristics of "rationality" and "territorialization," but the practices that have taken place inside them have also derived from a variety of other, "impure" kinds of rational practices as well as rituals and what Sherry Ortner calls "little scenarios of etiquette" that are reproducible in everyday life (Ortner 1984, 154). By thinking of bureaucracies as "repertoires" rather than "structures," it is possible to perform the same kind of deconstructive operation on their Southeast Asian historical forms that I attempted on cosmologies and truth regimes. Turned into practices, Southeast Asian bureaucracies reveal kinship-like networks, alternative rationalities, and rituals at work, as well as the exercise of Western-style "rational-choice" (Adams 1999) in the pursuit of wealth and status. The case of the formation of a dominant bureaucratic repertoire in Java suggests that, notwithstanding variations and changes over time that I was not able to bring out fully, bureaucratic practices and habits die hard, particularly since they involve ritual activity and the acquisition of wealth. And like the cosmological form of the Southeast Asian state, the bureaucratic form has taken shape by means of a repeated, overlapping series of transcultural encounters in which cultural similarities as well as differences between the interacting parties have played a role. Yet when all is said and done, bureaucracies are only repertoires and only illusions of the "state." They can be changed.

The final state form that concerned me was violence. Next to the apparent failure of modern Southeast Asian states to be really "bureaucratic," perhaps no other aspect of state practice in Southeast Asia has attracted more attention in the West than the question of state violence, either by way of silencing the issue, as in the writings of O. W. Wolters and Clifford Geertz, or by way of emphasizing its brutality and malevolence, as in most of the scholarly literature on the criminality and murderousness of the state in the modern era. Once again, I have tried to shift the focus of attention away from a dichotomous impasse in our understanding to one based on historical and regional comparison combined with a synthesis of seemingly incompatible models of state formation, in order to understand state violence, rather than either condemn or avoid it. After saying something about the failure of Southeast Asian states to make use of or monopolize violence in service of their rise to dominance, as in the West, I turned to the more interesting (for me) cultural question of the role of violence in expressing and maintaining an aesthetic of state "beauty." This synergy seems to have been operative in Southeast Asia for a very long time, although it is impossible to determine how hegemonic it has been except in terms of its various representations in works of art. Here, as throughout my study, I used works of art to illuminate the conceptual work involved in building states in the region. I concluded that, as Putu Wijaya shows, violence will lose its formative role in reinforcing the powerful aesthetic effect of the Southeast Asian state only if it is disarmed of its fetishistic, magical appeal, which also involves finding a way to modify and control the competitive, hierarchical nature of Southeast Asian societies themselves. In general, throughout my book I showed that transcultural interaction in Southeast Asia has stimulated the growth of newer, hybrid forms of hierarchy, which have in turn contributed to the elaboration of state forms. The fact that the West has historically been a source of more hierarchy and statism in Southeast Asia should give pause to those who only think of the West as the bearer of gifts such as modernity, nationalism, and democracy.

I have read and reread scholarly as well as artistic texts in order to bring out the practical ways in which Southeast Asian states have been formed. This has involved putting culture back into the study of states, which also means making more use of current ethnographies to understand state forms in early Southeast Asia that have already been studied with culture in mind. Cultural understandings, even if they come to us in essentialized formulations, raise doubts about the nature, extent, direction, and rapidity of "change," that great fetish-concept of the historian. If putting culture into studies of history helps to dehistoricize our understandings of the past, it helps as well to de-essentialize our understanding of culture, which also consists of heterogeneous human practices ever on the move and always shaped by economic and political forces.

State formation, as I have tried to show, is not an impersonal process that creates structures of authority in a vacuum or imposes dominance at will. It is a question of people dominating and submitting to each other. Since my focus has been on the making of states, I have not treated resistance as a "hidden transcript" or overt subaltern rebellion in opposition to the state, but rather as a crucial determinant in its formation. I have also indicated, without pursuing the matter in these pages, that expressions of resistance to the state are themselves power plays that, were they to succeed, would often lead to alternative kinds of state formation, rather than to some utopian alternative to the state as such (cf. Pasuk and Baker 2000, 193–216; Chatthip 1991; Hedman and Sidel 2000, 140–165).

In terms of their response to transcultural interactions over the centuries, Southeast Asian states have already, always been "alternative states"—alternative because of their specific cultural identities within historical frameworks that are, despite the dominant teleology of Western "development," uniquely their own and unlike others around the world that have been shaped by different concatenations and overlappings of forces. This does not mean that globalizing, generalizing labels like comprador, familial, absolutist, cosmological, bureaucratic, predatory, network, patrimonial, traditional, Indic, Confucian, colonial, and so on, should not be applied to Southeast Asian states. The use of these labels does suggest similarities with other state formations to which they can also be applied, and so they usefully serve to place state formations in Southeast Asia in still sharper relief as being, "comparatively speaking" and at a deeper level of characterization, historical formations like no other on earth. I also do not mean to suggest that one should never propose ways of constructing a " 'real' bureaucratic apparatus," say, in Southeast Asia as opposed to the hybrid, predatory, illusory bureaucratic repertoires now in place (P. Evans 1989, 582; Harrison and Huntington 2000). The consultant for "developmental," "civilizing" enterprises should be forewarned, however, that such attempts have already been made before in Southeast Asia many times, with mixed results.

I will say nothing here about where I think the "Southeast Asian state" is or should be heading. The task I set myself was to provide "partial, situated" understandings of state formation in Southeast Asia based on my reading of the scholarship and primary sources on the subject. But what of my use of "Southeast Asia" as a heuristic, comparative framework for analysis? Have I been trying to re-legitimize, by assembling, quoting, and implicitly assigning value to scholarly writings on "the region," the viability of Southeast Asia as an "area" of academic study at a time when it is being questioned, even dismissed, as such? Martin Lewis and Kären Wigen, for example, have strong doubts about Southeast Asia as a regional concept because of its "incoherence," "derivativeness," "arbitrariness," "artificiality," and "inauthenticity" (Lewis and Wigen 1997, 170–176). Mary Steedley writes: "Southeast Asia is arguably the most insubstantial of world areas, being at once territorially porous, internally diverse, and inherently hybrid" (Weighing 1999, 13). What kind of meaning do the words "Southeast Asia" have in front of the word "state" in the context of such remarks, or even of those that celebrate the "distinctiveness" of Southeast Asia's "diversity" (Acharya 2000, 4)?

My own understanding of the derivativeness and hybridity of Southeast Asian states is that these qualities define them. I cannot think of a single example of a Southeast Asian state form that is essentially, purely authentic. Foreignness haunts the formation of Southeast Asian states, as it does the formation of its many cultures generally. Southeast Asian pasts, like their modernities and states, are "alternative." But having said that, the incoherence, arbitrariness, and artificiality that we have observed in Southeast Asian state formations are not criteria that define their historical uniqueness. These characteristics make them like any other state formation, once we start thinking of all states as culturally constructed repertoires of practices reticulating out into the world at large, saved only from total dissolution into the multiplicity of power networks that constitute them by the magical and illusory boundaries that define their "statehood." As for Southeast Asia's much discussed "diversity," I understand this to be a relative term. Compare the contemporary Indonesian state to that of Thailand alone, and their differences are readily apparent. Compare them both to the states of Europe, or put them in a comparative, historical framework of state formation throughout all of Southeast Asia, and their similarities begin to come into view.

I do not endorse, in any case, the concept of Southeast Asia as a substantial, essentialized "region" in the normative way that informs the assumptions about world regions in the discussions of Lewis, Wigen, and Steedley. Instead, I think of the "region" of Southeast Asia as a space created by a vast number of cultural interactions, to borrow and adapt a definition of the word "region" proposed by Michel de Certeau (1988, 126). Southeast Asian states, complex agents acting through transcultural repertoires since their inception centuries ago, have never ceased to interact with the space of Southeast Asia in order "to orient it, situate it, temporalize it, and make it function in a polyvalent unity of conflictual programs or contractual proximities," again to borrow words and ideas from de Certeau. The authors of the *Hikayat Hang Tuah* or the *Serat Centhini*, modern scholarship on Southeast Asia, no less than the Association of Southeast Asian Nations (ASEAN), founded in 1967 (Acharya 2000, 83 and passim)—all of these have been constrained to work with a definition of "Southeast Asia" that is more like "a polyvalent unity of con-flictual programs or contractual proximities" than one based on the idea of a shared, coherent, pure "civilization." Neither scholars nor politicians should imagine that the latter should be the object of their investigations or policies.

Porosity is not a term that defines "Southeast Asia" as distinct from any other region around the globe either, since this term has become a master trope for a world without borders, consisting of "significant areas of human organization as precipitates of various kinds of action, interaction, and motion" (Appadurai 2000, 7). My own provisional, working label for Southeast Asia is "incongruous." What makes Southeast Asia "incongruous," both within itself and compared to other regions of the world, is its long history as a trans-cultural crossroads (Lombard 1990) in which—to borrow felicitous phrasing from Rudolf Mrázek's characterization of the "fluid" thought, politics, and career of Sjahrir, the Indonesian nationalist from West Sumatra—there has always been a need for "incongruous things" ulti-mately "to be placed safely side by side" (Mrázek 1994, 430). South-east Asia has not always been a safe or tolerant place, and its states still tend, as Wolters writes of early Southeast Asian *maṇḍala*s, to be-have as "self-styled 'unique' centers [in a way that] reduces the pos-sibility that [such] centers would accept each other on equal terms and gradually develop closer relations with each other" (Wolters 1999, 39). But much of my discussion has touched on the continuous pro-liferation of incongruities in the region, in the shape of ways of both forming and evading states, of crisscrossing identities, and of creating alternative havens of well-being inside state borders. Southeast Asian history is full of transformations that have allowed incongruities to coexist, but also to merge. As the Indonesian state proceeds to imple-ment decentralization (Kahin 1999, 277 and passim), as Thais walk "backwards into a *khlong*" in search of an alternative modernity (Pasuk and Baker 2000, 193), and as the ASEAN nation-states search for regional identity, international security, and economic well-being, it is important to recall and rethink the history of state formation in the region as the product of human aspirations and collective en-deavor. Southeast Asians need to exploit their knowledge of this past as they experiment with new ways of building states and of "playing at being relatives" (Maier 1997b). In doing both in the full light of history, they can transform who they are as they approach the cross-roads of the future.

References

Abdullah, Taufik. 1971. *Schools and Politics: The Kaum Muda Movement in West Sumatra (1927–1933)*. Modern Indonesia Project Monograph Series. Ithaca, N.Y.: Cornell University Modern Indonesia Project.

Abrams, Philip. 1988. Notes on the Difficulty of Studying the State. *Journal of Historical Sociology* 1:58–89.

Abu-Lughod, Janet L. 1989. *Before European Hegemony: The World System A.D. 1250–1350*. New York and Oxford: Oxford University Press (OUP).

Acharya, Amitav. 2000. *The Quest for Identity: International Relations of Southeast Asia*. Oxford: OUP.

Adams, Julia. 1994a. The Familial State: Elite Family Practices and State-Making in the Early Modern Netherlands. *Theory and Society* 23: 503–539.

———. 1994b. Trading States, Trading Places: The Role of Patrimonialism in Early Modern Dutch Development. *CSSH* 36(2):319–355.

———. 1996. Principals and Agents, Colonialists and Company Men: The Decay of Colonial Control in the Dutch East Indies. *American Sociological Review* 61(1):12–28.

———. 1999. Culture in Rational-Choice Theories of State-Formation. In *State/Culture: State-Formation after the Cultural Turn*, ed. George Steinmetz. Ithaca and London: Cornell University Press.

Akhmadi, Heri. 1981. *Breaking the Chains of Oppression of the Indonesian People: Defense Statement at His Trial on Charges of Insulting the Head of State*. Translation Series. Ithaca, N.Y.: Cornell University Modern Indonesia Project.

D'Alembert, Jean Le Rond. 1995 [1751]. *Preliminary Discourse to the Encyclopedia of Diderot*, trans. Richard N. Schwab. Chicago and London: The University of Chicago Press.

Andaya, Barbara Watson. 1979. The Nature of the State in Eighteenth Century Perak. In *Pre-Colonial State Systems in Southeast Asia*, ed. Anthony Reid and Lance Castles. Monographs of the Malaysian Branch of the Royal Asiatic Society no. 6. Kuala Lumpur: Council of the Malaysian Branch of the Royal Asiatic Society.

———. 1993. *To Live as Brothers: Southeast Sumatra in the Seventeenth and Eighteenth Centuries.* Honolulu: University of Hawai'i Press.

———. 1994. The Changing Religious Role of Women in Premodern South East Asia. *South East Asia Research* 2(2):99–116.

———. 1999. Political Development Between the Sixteenth and Eighteenth Centuries. In *The Cambridge History of Southeast Asia. Vol. 2: From c.1500 to c.1800,* ed. Nicholas Tarling. Cambridge: Cambridge University Press (CUP).

———. 2000a. Delineating Female Space: Seclusion and the State in Pre-Modern Island Southeast Asia. In *Other Pasts: Women, Gender and History in Early Modern Southeast Asia,* ed. Barbara Watson Andaya. Honolulu: University of Hawai'i at Mānoa, Center for Southeast Asian Studies.

———., ed. 2000b. *Other Pasts: Women, Gender and History in Early Modern Southeast Asia.* Honolulu: University of Hawai'i at Mānoa, Center for Southeast Asian Studies.

Andaya, Barbara Watson, and Leonard Y. Andaya. 2001. *A History of Malaysia.* 2d. ed. Basingstoke, Hampshire: Palgrave.

Anderson, Benedict R. O'G. 1969. *Mythology and the Tolerance of the Javanese.* Cornell Indonesia Project Monograph no. 37. Ithaca, N.Y.: Cornell University Modern Indonesia Project.

———. 1972. *Java in a Time of Revolution: Occupation and Resistance, 1944–1946.* Ithaca and London: Cornell University Press.

———. 1981 and 1982. The *Suluk Gatoloco. Indonesia* 32, 33:105–150 and 31–88.

———. 1989. Reading "Revenge" by Pramoedya Ananta Toer (1978–1982). In *Writing on the Tongue,* ed. A. L. Becker. Michigan Papers on South and Southeast Asia no. 33. Ann Arbor: University of Michigan Center for South and Southeast Asian Studies.

———. 1990. *Language and Power: Exploring Political Cultures in Indonesia.* Ithaca and London: Cornell University Press.

———. 1991. *Imagined Communities. Reflections on the Origin and Spread of Nationalism.* Rev. ed. London and New York: Verso.

———. 1992. The Changing Ecology of Southeast Asian Studies in the United States, 1950–1990. In *Southeast Asian Studies in the Balance: Reflections from America,* ed. Charles Hirschman et al. Ann Arbor, Mich.: The Association for Asian Studies.

———. 1996. "Bullshit!" S/he Said: The Happy, Modern, Sexy, Indonesian Married Woman as Transsexual. In *Fantasizing the Feminine in Indonesia,* ed. Laurie J. Sears. Durham and London: Duke University Press.

————. 1998. *The Spectre of Comparisons: Nationalism, Southeast Asia, and the World*. London and New York: Verso.

Anderson, Benedict, and Audrey Kahin, eds. 1982. *Interpreting Indonesian Politics: Thirteen Contributions to the Debate, 1964–1981*. Interim Reports Series no. 62. Ithaca, N.Y.: Cornell University Modern Indonesia Project.

Anderson, Perry. 1974. *Lineages of the Absolutist State*. London: Verso Editions.

The Anwar Ibrahim Judgment. 1999. *The Anwar Ibrahim Judgment*. Kuala Lumpur: Malayan Law Journal Sdn. Bhd.

Appadurai, Arjun. 1996. *Modernity at Large: Cultural Dimensions of Globalization*. Minneapolis and London: University of Minnesota Press.

————. 2000. Grassroots Globalization and the Research Imagination. *Public Culture* 12(1):1–19.

Aung-Thwin, Michael. 1979. The Role of *Sasana* Reform in Burmese History: Economic Dimensions of a Religious Purification. *JAS* 38(4):671–688.

————. 1983. Divinity, Spirit, and Human: Conceptions of Classical Burmese Kingship. In *Centers, Symbols, and Hierarchies: Essays on the Classical States of Southeast Asia*, ed. Lorraine Gesick. Monograph Series no. 26. New Haven, Conn.: Yale University Southeast Asia Studies.

————. 1985. *Pagan: The Origins of Modern Burma*. Honolulu: University of Hawai'i Press.

————. 1998. *Myth and History in the Historiography of Early Burma: Paradigms, Primary Sources, and Prejudices*. Monographs in International Studies, Southeast Asia Series no. 102. Athens: Ohio University Center for International Studies.

Barker, Joshua. 2001. State of Fear: Controlling the Criminal Contagion in Suharto's New Order. In *Violence and the State in Suharto's Indonesia*, ed. Benedict R. O'G. Anderson. Southeast Asia Program Publications. Ithaca, N.Y.: Cornell University Southeast Asia Program.

Barmé, Scot. 1993. *Luang Wichit Wathakan and the Creation of a Thai Identity*. Singapore: Institute of Southeast Asian Studies.

Battye, Noel Alfred. 1974. The Military, Government and Society in Siam, 1868–1910: Politics and Military Reform during the Reign of King Chulalongkorn. Ph.D. dissertation, Cornell University.

Baud, J. C. 1853. Aanspraak tot Opening van de Eerste Algemeene Vergadering van het Koninklijk Instituut voor de Taal-, Land- en Volkenkunde van Neêrlandsch-Indië. Gehouden op den 4den Junij 1851. *BKI* 1:1–6.

Bayly, C. A. 1996. *Empire and Information: Intelligence Gathering and Social Communication in India, 1780–1870*. Cambridge: CUP.

Beckett, Jeremy. 1994. Political Families and Family Politics among the Muslim Maguindanaon of Cotabato. In *An Anarchy of Families: State and*

Family in the Philippines, ed. Alfred W. McCoy. Quezon City and Madison: Ateneo de Manila University Press and University of Wisconsin-Madison, Center for Southeast Asian Studies.

Behrend, Tim. 1987. The *Serat Jatiswara:* Structure and Change in a Javanese Poem, 1600–1930. Ph.D. dissertation, the Australian National University.

———. 1997. Technical Prolegomena to Any Future *Centhini*-Critique: Manuscript Survey of the Textual Corpus and Outline of Recensions. Paper presented at the workshop "Encompassing Knowledge: Indigenous Encyclopedias in Indonesia in the 17th–20th Centuries." Leiden University, 8–10 December.

Bell, Catherine. 1992. *Ritual Theory, Ritual Practice.* New York and Oxford: OUP.

Benda, H. 1966. The Pattern of Administrative Reform in the Closing Years of Dutch Rule in Indonesia. *JAS* 25:589–605.

———. 1982. Democracy in Indonesia. In *Interpreting Indonesian Politics: Thirteen Contributions to the Debate, 1964–1981,* ed. Benedict Anderson and Audrey Kahin. Interim Reports Series no. 62. Ithaca, N.Y.: Cornell University Modern Indonesia Project.

Bendix, Reinhard. 1960. *Max Weber: An Intellectual Portrait.* Garden City, N.J.: Doubleday and Company, Inc.

Bentley, G. Carter. 1986. Indigenous States of Southeast Asia. *Annual Review of Anthropology* 15:275–305.

Berezin, Mabel. 1999. Political Belonging: Emotion, Nation, and Identity in Fascist Italy. In *State/Culture: State-Formation after the Cultural Turn,* ed. George Steinmetz. Ithaca and London: Cornell University Press.

Bhabha, Homi K. 1994. *The Location of Culture.* London and New York: Routledge.

Blagden, C. O. 1916. *Catalogue of Manuscripts in European Languages Belonging to the Library of the India Office. Vol. 1: The Mackenzie Collections. Part 1: The 1822 Collection and the Private Collection.* London, Edinburgh, Glasgow, New York, Toronto, Melbourne, and Bombay: OUP.

Blum, J. 1978. *The End of the Old Order in Rural Europe.* Princeton, N.J.: Princeton University Press.

Bodden, Michael H. 1996. Woman as Nation in Mangunwijaya's *Durga Umayi. Indonesia* 62:53–82.

Bonneff, Marcel. 1986. *Pérégrinations Javanaises. Les* Voyages de R.M.A. Purwa Lelana: *Une vision de Java au XIXe siècle (c.1860–1875).* Études insulindiennes, Archipel 7. Paris: Éditions de la Maison des Sciences de l'Homme.

Boomgaard, Peter. 1989. *Children of the Colonial State: Population Growth and Economic Development in Java, 1795–1880.* Amsterdam: Free University Press.

Boon, James A. 1977. *The Anthropological Romance of Bali 1597–1972: Dynamic Perspectives in Marriage and Caste, Politics and Religion.* Cambridge: CUP.

———. 1990. *Affinities and Extremes: Crisscrossing the Bittersweet Ethnology of East Indies History, Hindu-Balinese Culture, and Indo-European Allure.* Chicago and London: The University of Chicago Press.

Bourchier, David. 1984. *Dynamics of Dissent in Indonesia: Sawito and the Phantom Coup.* Interim Reports Series no. 63. Ithaca, N.Y.: Cornell University Modern Indonesia Project.

———. 1997. Totalitarianism and the "National Personality": Recent Controversy about the Philosophical Basis of the Indonesian State. In *Imagining Indonesia: Cultural Politics and Political Culture,* ed. Jim Schiller and Barbara Martin-Schiller. Monographs in International Studies, Southeast Asia Series no. 97. Athens: Ohio University Center for International Studies.

Bourdieu, Pierre. 1991. *Language and Symbolic Power.* Cambridge, Mass.: Harvard University Press.

———. 1999. Rethinking the State: Genesis and Structure of the Bureaucratic Field. In *State/Culture: State-Formation after the Cultural Turn,* ed. George Steinmetz. Ithaca and London: Cornell University Press.

Bowen, John. R. 1993. *Muslims through Discourse: Religion and Ritual in Gayo Society.* Princeton, N.J.: Princeton University Press.

———. 1995. The Forms Culture Takes: A State-of-the-Field Essay on the Anthropology of Southeast Asia. *JAS* 54(4):1047–1078.

———. 1997. Modern Intentions: Reshaping Subjectivities in an Indonesian Muslim Society. In *Politics and Religious Renewal in Muslim Southeast Asia,* ed. Robert W. Hefner and Patricia Horvatich. Honolulu: University of Hawai'i Press.

Bowie, Katherine A. 1996. Slavery in Nineteenth-Century Northern Thailand: Archival Anecdotes and Village Voices. In *State Power and Culture in Thailand,* ed. E. Paul Durrenberger. Monograph 44. New Haven, Conn.: Yale University Southeast Asia Studies.

———. 1997. *Rituals of National Loyalty: An Anthropology of the State and the Village Scout Movement in Thailand.* New York: Columbia University Press.

Braginsky, V. I. 1990. *Hikayat Hang Tuah:* Malay Epic and Muslim Mirror. Some Considerations on Its Date, Meaning and Structure. *BKI* 146(4): 399–412.

Brakel, L. F. 1979. State and Statecraft in 17th Century Aceh. In *Pre-Colonial State Systems in Southeast Asia,* ed. Anthony Reid and Lance Castles. Monographs of the Malaysian Branch of the Royal Asiatic Society no. 6. Kuala Lumpur: Council of the Malaysian Branch of the Royal Asiatic Society.

Breckenridge, Carol A., and Peter van der Veer, eds. 1993. *Orientalism and the Postcolonial Predicament: Perspectives on South Asia*. Philadelphia: University of Pennsylvania Press.

Brenner, Suzanne A. 1991. Competing Hierarchies: Javanese Merchants and the *Priyayi* Elite in Solo, Central Java. *Indonesia* 52:55–83.

———. 1995. Why Women Rule the Roost: Rethinking Javanese Ideologies of Gender and Self-Control. In *Bewitching Women, Pious Men: Gender and Body Politics in Southeast Asia*, ed. Aihwa Ong and Michael G. Peletz. Berkeley, Los Angeles, and London: University of California Press.

———. 1998. *The Domestication of Desire: Women, Wealth, and Modernity in Java*. Princeton, N.J.: Princeton University Press.

Burchell, Graham, Colin Gordon, and Peter Miller, eds. 1991. *The Foucault Effect: Studies in Governmentality*. Chicago: University of Chicago Press.

Butcher, John. 1993. Revenue Farming and the Changing State in Southeast Asia. In *The Rise and Fall of Revenue Farming: Business Elites and the Emergence of the Modern State in Southeast Asia*, ed. John Butcher and Howard Dick. Basingstoke and London: St. Martin's Press.

Callahan, Mary P. 1998. The Sinking Schooner: Murder and the State in Independent Burma, 1948–1958. In *Gangsters, Democracy, and the State in Southeast Asia*, ed. Carl A. Trocki. Southeast Asia Publications. Ithaca, N.Y.: Cornell University Southeast Asia Program.

Cannell, Fenella. 1999. *Power and Intimacy in the Christian Philippines*. Cambridge: CUP.

Carey, P. B. R. 1977. The Sepoy Conspiracy of 1815 in Java. *BKI* 133(2–3):294–322.

———. 1999. Civilization on Loan: The Making of an Upstart Polity. Mataram and its Successors, 1600–1800. In *Beyond Binary Histories: Re-Imagining Eurasia to c.1830*, ed. Victor Lieberman. Ann Arbor: University of Michigan Press.

Carey, Peter, and Vincent Houben. 1987. Spirited Srikandhis and sly Sumbadras: The Social, Political and Economic Role of Women at the Central Javanese Courts in the 18th and 19th Centuries. In *Indonesian Women in Focus: Past and Present Notions*, ed. Elsbeth Locher-Scholten and Anke Niehof. Dordrecht and Providence, R.I.: Foris Publications.

Cary, Caverlee. 2000. In the Image of the King: Two Photographs from Nineteenth-Century Siam. In *Studies in Southeast Asian Art: Essays in Honor of Stanley J. O'Connor*, ed. Nora A. Taylor. Southeast Asia Program Publications. Ithaca, N.Y.: Cornell University Southeast Asia Program.

de Casparis, J. G. 1981. Pour une histoire sociale de l'ancienne Java principalement au Xème s. *Archipel* 21:125–151.

de Certeau, Michel. 1988. *The Practice of Everyday Life*. Berkeley, Los Angeles, and London: University of California Press.

Chakrabarty, Dipesh. 1997. The Difference—Deferral of a Colonial Modernity: Public Debates on Domesticity in British Bengal. In *Tensions of Empire: Colonial Cultures in a Bourgeois World*, ed. Frederick Cooper and Ann Laura Stoler. Berkeley, Los Angles, and London: University of California Press.

————. 2000. *Provincializing Europe: Postcolonial Thought and Historical Difference*. Princeton, N.J., and Oxford: Princeton University Press.

Chambert-Loir, Henri. 1984. Muhammad Bakir: A Batavian Scribe and Author in the Nineteenth Century. *RIMA* 18:44–71.

Chandler, David P. 1991. *The Tragedy of Cambodian History: Politics, War, and Revolution since 1945*. New Haven and London: Yale University Press.

————. 1996a. *A History of Cambodia*. 2d. ed., updated. Boulder, Colo.: Westview Press.

————. 1996b. *Facing the Cambodian Past: Selected Essays 1971–1994*. St. Leonards, NSW: Allen and Unwin.

————. 1999. *Voices from S-21: Terror and History in Pol Pot's Secret Prison*. Berkeley: University of California Press.

Chatthip Nartsupha. 1991. The Community Culture School of Thought. In *Thai Constructions of Knowledge*, ed. Manas Chitakasem and Andrew Turton. London: University of London School of Oriental and African Studies.

Chigas, George. 2000. A Draft Translation of the Story of *Tum Teav* by Preah Botumthera Som. Master's thesis, Cornell University.

Christie, Jan Wisseman. 1983. Rāja and Rāma: The Classical State in Early Java. In *Centers, Symbols, and Hierarchies: Essays on the Classical States of Southeast Asia*, ed. Lorraine Gesick. Monograph Series No. 26. New Haven, Conn.: Yale University Southeast Asia Studies.

————. 1986. Negara, Mandala, and Despotic State: Images of Early Java. In *Southeast Asia in the 9th to 14th Centuries*, ed. David G. Marr and A. C. Milner. Singapore and Canberra: Australian National University, Institute of Southeast Asian Studies, and Research School of Pacific Studies.

————. 1991. States without Cities: Demographic Trends in Early Java. *Indonesia* 52:23–40.

————. 1995. State Formation in Early Maritime Southeast Asia: A Consideration of the Theories and the Data. *BKI* 151(2):235–288.

Chua, Beng-Huat. 1997a. *Communitarian Ideology and Democracy in Singapore*.

London and New York: Routledge and Asia Research Centre, Murdoch University.

———. 1997b. *Political Legitimacy and Housing: Stakeholding in Singapore.* London and New York: Routledge.

Chulalongkorn. 1993. *Itinéraire d'un Voyage à Java en 1896.* Trans. and ed. Chanatip Kesavadhana. Cahier d'Archipel 20. Paris: Association Archipel.

Coedès, George. 1951 (1937–1966). *Inscriptions du Cambodge.* Vol. 3. Paris: École Française d'Extrême-Orient.

———. 1963. *Angkor: An Introduction.* Hong Kong: OUP.

———. 1968. *The Indianized States of Southeast Asia.* Honolulu: East-West Center Press.

Cohen Stuart, A. B. 1860. *Brata-Joeda, Indisch-Javaansch Heldendicht.* 2 vols. *VBG* 27 and 28. Batavia: Lange en Co.

Cohn, Bernard S. 1996. *Colonialism and Its Forms of Knowledge: The British in India.* Princeton, N.J.: Princeton University Press.

Connor, Linda. 1995a. Dying by Fire and Kris: Speaking to Women in the Realm of Death. Paper presented to the Third International Bali Studies Workshop, University of Sydney, 3–7 July.

———. 1995b. Acquiring Invisible Strength: A Balinese Discourse of Harm and Well-Being. *Indonesia Circle* 66:124–153.

Corrigan, Philip, and Derek Sayer. 1985. *The Great Arch: English State Formation as Cultural Revolution.* Oxford: Basil Blackwell.

Cortesão, Amando, ed. 1967. *The Suma Oriental of Tomé Pires.* Vol. 1. Nendeln/Liechtenstein: Kraus Reprint Limited.

Couperus, Louis. 1985. *The Hidden Force.* London: Quartet Books.

Creese, Helen. 1993. Love, Lust and Loyalty: Representations of Women in Traditional Javanese and Balinese Literature. Paper presented to the Fourth Women in Asia Conference, University of Melbourne, 1–3 October.

Crouch, Harold. 1988. *The Army and Politics in Indonesia.* Rev. ed. Ithaca and London: Cornell University Press.

———. 1996. *Government and Society in Malaysia.* Ithaca and London: Cornell University Press.

Cushman, Jennifer W. 1991. *Family and State: The Formation of a Sino-Thai Tin-Mining Dynasty 1797–1932,* ed. Craig J. Reynolds. Singapore: OUP.

Day, Tony. 1982. Ranggawarsita's Prophecy of Mystery. In *Moral Order and the Question of Change: Essays on Southeast Asian Thought,* ed. D. K. Wyatt and A. Woodside. New Haven, Conn.: Yale University Southeast Asia Studies.

———. 1983a. Islam and Literature in Southeast Asia: Some Pre-Modern,

Mainly Javanese Perspectives. In *Islam in Southeast Asia*, ed. M. B. Hooker. Leiden: E. J. Brill.

———. 1983b. The Drama of Bangun Tapa's Exile in Ambon, the Poetry of Kingship in Surakarta, 1830–1858. In *Centers, Symbols, and Hierarchies: Essays on the Classical States of Southeast Asia*, ed. Lorraine Gesick. Monograph Series no. 26. New Haven, Conn.: Yale University Southeast Asia Studies.

———. 1984. Second Thoughts about a History of Batavia. *Indonesia* 38: 147–161.

———. 1986. How Modern Was Modernity, How Traditional Tradition, in Nineteenth-Century Java? *RIMA* 20(1):1–36.

———. 1994. "Landscape" in Early Java. In *Recovering the Orient: Artists, Scholars, Appropriations*, ed. A. Gerstle and A. C. Milner. Chur, Switzerland: Harwood Academic Publishers.

———. 1996a. Review of Vincent J. H. Houben, *Kraton and Kumpeni: Surakarta and Yogyakarta, 1830–1870*. *JAS* 55(3):782–784.

———. 1996b. Ties That (Un)Bind: Families and States in Premodern Southeast Asia. *JAS* 55(2):384–409.

———. 1997. What Lies Behind the Veils of *Semu*? *Indonesia* 64:139–148.

———. 1999. Language and Roles, Culture and Violence: Teater Gapit's *Rol* (1983) and the Question of "Interculturalism" in Contemporary Indonesia. In *Dis/Orientations: Cultural Praxis in Theatre. Asia, Pacific, Australia*, ed. Rachel Fensham and Peter Eckersall. Clayton, Vic.: Monash University, Centre for Drama and Theatre Studies.

———. 2001. Wayang Kulit and Internal "Otherness" in East Java. In *Puppet Theatre in Contemporary Indonesia: New Approaches to Performance-Events*, ed. Jan Mrázek. Michigan Papers on South and Southeast Asia no. 50. Ann Arbor: University of Michigan Center for South and Southeast Asian Studies.

Day, Tony et al. 1996. Perceiving Citizenship. In *Australia in Asia: Comparing Cultures*, ed. A. Milner and M. Quilty. Melbourne: OUP.

Day, Tony, and Will Derks. 1999. Narrating Knowledge: Reflections on the Encyclopedic Impulse in Literary Texts from Indonesian and Malay Worlds. *BKI* 155(3):309–341.

Day, Tony, and Craig J. Reynolds. 2000. Cosmologies, Truth Regimes, and the State in Southeast Asia. *MAS* 43(1):1–55.

Diller, Anthony. 1991. What Makes Central Thai a National Language? In *National Identity and Its Defenders: Thailand, 1939–1989*, ed. Craig J. Reynolds. Monash Papers on Southeast Asia no. 25. Clayton, Vic.: Monash University Centre of Southeast Asian Studies.

Dirks, Nicholas B. 1993. Colonial Histories and Native Informants: Biography of an Archive. In *Orientalism and the Postcolonial Predicament: Perspectives on South Asia,* ed. Carol A. Breckenridge and Peter van der Veer. Philadelphia: University of Pennsylvania Press.

———. 1994. Guiltless Spoliations: Picturesque Beauty, Colonial Knowledge, and Colin Mackenzie's Survey of India. In *Perceptions of South Asia's Visual Past,* ed. Catherine B. Asher and Thomas R. Metcalf. New Delhi, Bombay, and Calcutta: OUP and IBH Publishing Co. Pvt. Ltd.

Dirks, Nicholas B., Geoff Eley, and Sherry B. Ortner, eds. 1994. *Culture/Power/History: A Reader in Contemporary Social Theory.* Princeton, N.J.: Princeton University Press.

Dobbin, Christine. 1983. *Islamic Revivalism in a Changing Economy: Central Sumatra, 1784–1847.* Scandinavian Institute of Asian Studies Monograph Series no. 47. London and Malmö: Curzon Press.

Dove, Michael. 1985. The Agroecological Mythology of the Javanese and the Political Economy of Indonesia. *Indonesia* 39:1–36.

———. 1997. The Political Ecology of Pepper in the *Hikayat Banjar:* The Historiography of Commodity Production in a Bornean Kingdom. In *Paper Landscapes: Explorations in the Environmental History of Indonesia,* ed. P. Boomgaard, F. Colombijn, and D. Henley. Leiden: KITLV Press.

Drakard, Jane. 1999. *The Kingdom of Words.* Oxford: OUP.

Drewes, G. W. J. 1966. The Struggle between Javanism and Islam as Illustrated by the *Serat Dermagaṇḍul. BKI* 122(3):309–365.

———. 1978. *An Early Javanese Code of Muslim Ethics.* Bibliotheca Indonesica 18. The Hague: Martinus Nijhoff.

Drewes, G. W. J., and L. F. Brakel, eds. and trans. 1986. *The Poems of Hamzah Fansuri.* Bibliotheca Indonesica 26. Dordrecht and Cinnaminson: Foris Publications.

Dreyfus, Hubert L., and Paul Rabinow. 1983. *Michel Foucault: Beyond Structuralism and Hermeneutics.* Chicago: The University of Chicago Press.

Duong Thu Huong. 1994. *Paradise of the Blind.* New York: Penguin Books USA.

———. 1996. *Novel without a Name.* New York: Penguin Books USA.

———. 2000. *Memories of a Pure Spring.* New York: Hyperion East.

Elson, R. E. 1994. *Village Java under the Cultivation System, 1830–1870.* Sydney: Asian Studies Association of Australia in association with Allen and Unwin.

Emmerson, Donald K. 1978. The Bureaucracy in Political Context: Weakness in Strength. In *Political Power and Communications in Indonesia,* ed. Karl D. Jackson and Lucian W. Pye. Los Angeles and London: University of California Press.

Englehart, Neil A. 2001. *Culture and Power in Traditional Siamese Government.* Southeast Asia Program Publications. Ithaca, N.Y.: Cornell University Southeast Asia Program.

Enloe, Cynthia. 1990. *Bananas, Beaches, and Bases: Making Feminist Sense of International Politics*. Berkeley, Los Angeles, and London: University of California Press.

Errington, J. Joseph. 1989. To Know Oneself the Troubled Times: Ronggawarsita's *Serat Kala Tidha*. In *Writing on the Tongue*, ed. A. L. Becker. Michigan Papers on South and Southeast Asia no. 33. Ann Arbor: University of Michigan Center for South and Southeast Asian Studies.

Errington, Shelly. 1975. A Study of Genre: Meaning and Form in the Malay *Hikayat Hang Tuah*. Ph.D. dissertation, Cornell University.

———. 1989. *Meaning and Power in a Southeast Asian Realm*. Princeton, N.J.: Princeton University Press.

———. 1990. Recasting Sex, Gender, and Power: A Theoretical and Regional Overview. In *Power and Difference: Gender in Island Southeast Asia*, ed. Jane Monnig Atkinson and Shelly Errington. Stanford: Stanford University Press.

———. 1998. *The Death of the Authentic: Primitive Art and Other Tales of Progress*. Berkeley, Los Angeles, and London: University of California Press.

Evans, Grant. 1998. *The Politics of Ritual and Remembrance: Laos since 1975*. Honolulu: University of Hawai'i Press.

Evans, Peter B. 1989. Predatory, Developmental, and Other Apparatuses: A Comparative Political Economy Perspective on the Third World State. *Sociological Forum* 4(4):561–587.

Explore 2001. Explore the Mysterious Angkor Wat with StarHub. *The Straits Times*, 19 May: H3.

Fasseur, Cornelis. 1992a. *The Politics of Colonial Exploitation: Java, the Dutch, and the Cultivation System*. Studies on Southeast Asia. Ithaca, N.Y.: Cornell University Southeast Asia Program.

———. 1992b. The French Scare: Taco Roorda and the Origins of Javanese Studies in the Netherlands. In *Looking in Odd Mirrors: The Java Sea*, ed. V. J. H. Houben, H. M. J. Maier, and W. van der Molen. Semaian 5. Leiden: Vakgroep Talen en Culturen van Zuidoost-Azië en Oceanië, Rijksuniversiteit te Leiden.

———. 1994. *De Indologen. Ambtenaren voor de Oost 1825–1950*. Amsterdam: Bert Bakker.

Fegan, Brian. 1994. Entrepreneurs in Votes and Violence: Three Generations of a Peasant Political Family. In *An Anarchy of Families: State and Family in the Philippines*, ed. Alfred W. McCoy. Quezon City and Madison: Ateneo de Manila University Press and University of Wisconsin-Madison Center for Southeast Asian Studies.

Feith, Herbert. 1962. *The Decline of Constitutional Democracy in Indonesia*. Ithaca, N.Y.: Cornell University Press.

Fishel, Thamora V. 1999. Romances in the Sixth Reign: Gender, Sexuality, and Siamese Nationalism. In *Genders and Sexualities in Modern Thailand*, ed. Peter A. Jackson and Nerida M. Cook. Chiang Mai, Thailand: Silkworm Books.

Florida, Nancy K. 1987. Reading the Unread in Traditional Javanese Literature. *Indonesia* 44:1–15.

———. 1993. *Javanese Literature in Surakarta Manuscripts*. Vol. 1. Ithaca, N.Y.: Cornell University Southeast Asia Program.

———. 1995. *Writing the Past, Inscribing the Future: History as Prophecy in Colonial Java*. Durham and London: Duke University Press.

———. 1996. Sex Wars: Writing Gender Relations in Nineteenth-Century Java. In *Fantasizing the Feminine in Indonesia*, ed. Laurie J. Sears. Durham and London: Duke University Press.

Forge, Anthony. 1978. *Balinese Traditional Paintings: A Selection from the Forge Collection of the Australian Museum, Sydney*. Sydney: The Australian Museum.

———. 1994. Raffles and Daniell: Making the Image Fit. In *Recovering the Orient: Artists, Scholars, Appropriations*, ed. A. Gerstle and A. C. Milner. Chur, Switzerland: Harwood Academic Publishers.

Forster, Robert, and Orest Ranum, eds. 1976. *Family and Society: Selections from the Annales*. Baltimore and London: The Johns Hopkins University Press.

Foucault, Michel. 1973. *The Order of Things: An Archaeology of the Human Sciences*. New York: Vintage Books.

———. 1980. *Power/Knowledge. Selected Interviews and Other Writings 1972–1977*, ed. Colin Gordon. New York: Pantheon Books.

———. 1991a. *Discipline and Punish: The Birth of the Prison*. New York: Penguin Books.

———. 1991b. Govermentality. In *The Foucault Effect: Studies in Governmentality*, ed. Graham Burchell, Colin Gordon, and Peter Miller. Chicago: University of Chicago Press.

Foulcher, Keith. 1987. *Sastra Kontekstual:* Recent Developments in Indonesian Literary Politics. *RIMA* 21(1):6–28.

Freeman, Michael, and Claude Jacques. 1999. *Ancient Angkor*. London: Thames and Hudson Ltd.

Friedman, Thomas L. 2000. What a Mess! *The New York Times*, 3 October.

Furnivall, J. S. 1944. *Netherlands India: A Study of Plural Economy*. Cambridge: CUP.

———. 1956. *Colonial Policy and Practice: A Comparative Study of Burma and Netherlands India*. New York: New York University Press.

———. 1991. *The Fashioning of Leviathan: The Beginnings of British Rule in Burma*, ed. Gehan Wijeyewardene. Economic History of Southeast

Asia Project and Thai Yunnan Project. Canberra: Australian National University.

Geertz, Clifford. 1960. *The Religion of Java*. New York: The Free Press.

———. 1980. *Negara: The Theatre State in Nineteenth-Century Bali*. Princeton, N.J.: Princeton University Press.

———. 1993. *Local Knowledge: Further Essays in Interpretive Anthropology*. London: Fontana Press.

Geertz, Hildred. 1991. A Theatre of Cruelty: The Contexts of a Topéng Performance. In *State and Society in Bali: Historical, Textual and Anthropological Approaches*, ed. Hildred Geertz. Leiden: KITLV Press.

———. 1994. *Images of Power: Balinese Paintings Made for Gregory Bateson and Margaret Mead*. Honolulu: University of Hawai'i Press.

Gericke, J. F. C., and T. Roorda. 1901. *Javaansch-Nederlandsch Handwoordenboek*. 2 vols. Amsterdam/Leiden: Johannes Müller/E. J. Brill.

Gerini, G. E. 1976 [1892]. *A Retrospective View and Account of the Origin of the* Thet Maha Ch'at *Ceremony* (Maha Jati Desana) *or Exposition of the Tale of the Great Birth as Performed in Siam*. Bangkok: Sathirakoses-Nagapradipa Foundation.

Gerth, H. H., and G. Wright Mills, eds. 1974. *From Max Weber: Essays in Sociology*. London and Boston: Routledge and Kegan Paul Ltd.

Gesick, Lorraine M. 1995. *In the Land of Lady White Blood: Southern Thailand and the Meaning of History*. Studies on Southeast Asia. Ithaca, N.Y.: Cornell University Southeast Asia Program.

Giddens, Anthony. 1984. *The Constitution of Society*. Cambridge: Polity Press.

———. 1985. *The Nation-State and Violence*. Cambridge: Polity Press.

Girling, John L. S. 1981. *Thailand: Society and Politics*. Ithaca and London: Cornell University Press.

Gomez, Edmund Terence, and Jomo K. S. 1997. *Malaysia's Political Economy: Politics, Patronage and Profits*. Cambridge: CUP.

Goody, Jack. 1986. *The Logic of Writing and the Organization of Society*. Cambridge: CUP.

Gordon, Colin. 1980. Afterword. In *Power/Knowledge. Selected Interviews and Other Writings 1972–1977*, ed. Colin Gordon. New York: Pantheon Books.

Gouda, Frances. 1993. The Gendered Rhetoric of Colonialism and Anti-Colonialism in Twentieth-Century Indonesia. *Indonesia* 55:1–22.

Guha, Ranajit. 1997. *Dominance without Hegemony: History and Power in Colonial India*. Cambridge, Mass., and London: Harvard University Press.

Guillot, C. 1981. *L'Affaire Sadrach: Un Essai de Christianisation a Java au XIXe Siècle*. Paris: Éditions de la Maison des Sciences de l'Homme.

Gullick, J. M. 1992. *Rulers and Residents: Influence and Power in the Malay States 1870–1920*. Singapore: OUP.

Gunn, Geoffrey C. 1997. *Language, Power and Ideology in Brunei Darussalam.* Monographs in International Studies, Southeast Asia Series no. 99. Athens: Ohio University Center for International Studies.

de Haan, F. 1935. Personalia der Periode van het Engelsch Bestuur over Java 1811–1816. *BKI* 92(4):477–681.

Hagesteijn, Renee. 1987. The Angkor State: Rise, Fall and In Between. In *Early State Dynamics,* ed. Henri J. M. Claessen and Pieter van de Velde. Leiden and New York: E. J. Brill.

Haggard, Stephan. 1990. *Pathways from the Periphery: The Politics of Growth in the Newly Industrializing Countries.* Ithaca, N.Y.: Cornell University Press.

Hall, D. G. E. 1981. *A History of South-East Asia.* 4th ed. London and Basingstoke: The Macmillan Press Ltd.

Hall, Kenneth R. 1985. *Maritime Trade and State Development in Early Southeast Asia.* Sydney and Wellington: George Allen and Unwin.

Hamilton, Annette. 1991. Rumours, Foul Calumnies and the Safety of the State: Mass Media and National Identity in Thailand. In *National Identity and Its Defenders: Thailand, 1939–1989,* ed. Craig J. Reynolds. Monash Papers on Southeast Asia no. 25. Clayton, Vic.: Monash University Centre of Southeast Asian Studies.

———. 1992. Family Dramas: Film and Modernity in Thailand. *Screen* 33 (3):259–273.

Harrison, Lawrence E., and Samuel P. Huntington, eds. 2000. *Culture Matters: How Values Shape Human Progress.* New York: Basic Books.

Hawes, Gary. 1992. Marcos, His Cronies, and the Philippines' Failure to Develop. In *Southeast Asian Capitalists,* ed. Ruth McVey. Ithaca, N.Y.: Cornell University Southeast Asia Program.

Hedman, Eva-Lotta E., and John T. Sidel. 2000. *Philippine Politics and Society in the Twentieth Century: Colonial Legacies, Post-Colonial Trajectories.* London and New York: Routledge.

Hefner, Robert W. 1985. *Hindu Javanese: Tengger Tradition and Islam.* Princeton, N.J.: Princeton University Press.

———. 1987. Islamizing Java? Religion and Politics in Rural East Java. *JAS* 46(3):533–554.

———. 1993. Islam, State, and Civil Society: ICMI and the Struggle for the Indonesian Middle Class. *Indonesia* 56:1–35.

———. 2000. *Civil Islam: Muslims and Democratization in Indonesia.* Princeton, N.J., and Oxford: Princeton University Press.

Heine-Geldern, Robert. 1956. *Conceptions of State and Kingship in Southeast Asia.* Data Paper no. 18. Ithaca, N.Y.: Cornell University Southeast Asia Program.

Held, David, ed. 1985. *States and Societies*. Oxford: Basil Blackwell and the Open University.

Heng, Geraldine, and Janadas Devan. 1995. State Fatherhood: The Politics of Nationalism, Sexuality, and Race in Singapore. In *Bewitching Women, Pious Men: Gender and Body Politics in Southeast Asia*, ed. Aihwa Ong and Michael G. Peletz. Berkeley, Los Angeles, and London: University of California Press.

Heryanto, Ariel. 1988. The "Development" of Development. *Indonesia* 46:1–24.

Herzfeld, Michael.1992. *The Social Production of Indifference: Exploring the Symbolic Roots of Western Bureaucracy*. Chicago and London: The University of Chicago Press.

Hevia, James L. 1995. *Cherishing Men from Afar: Qing Guest Ritual and the Macartney Embassy of 1793*. Durham and London: Duke University Press.

Hewison, Kevin. 1989. *Bankers and Bureaucrats: Capital and the Role of the State in Thailand*. Monograph Series no. 34. Yale University Southeast Asia Studies. New Haven, Conn.: Yale University Center for International and Area Studies.

Higham, Charles. 1989. *The Archaeology of Mainland Southeast Asia from 10,000 B.C. to the Fall of Angkor*. Cambridge: CUP.

Hinton, Alexander Laban. 1998a. Why Did You Kill?: The Cambodian Genocide and the Dark Side of Face and Honor. *JAS* 57(1):93–122.

———. 1998b. A Head for an Eye: Revenge in the Cambodian Genocide. *American Ethnologist* 25(3):352–377.

Hobart, Mark. 1987. Summer's Days and Salad Days: The Coming of Age of Anthropology? In *Comparative Anthropology*, ed. Ladislav Holy. Oxford: Basil Blackwell.

———. 1990a. The Patience of Plants: A Note on Agency in Bali. *RIMA* 24(2):90–135.

———. 1990b. Who Do You Think You Are? The Authorized Balinese. In *Localizing Strategies: Regional Traditions of Ethnographic Writing*, ed. Richard Fardon. Edinburgh and Washington, D.C.: Scottish Academic Press and Smithsonian Institution Press.

Hobsbawm, Eric, and Terence Ranger, eds. 1983. *The Invention of Tradition*. Cambridge: CUP.

Hong Lysa. 1984. *Thailand in the Nineteenth Century: Evolution of the Economy and Society*. Singapore: Institute of Southeast Asian Studies.

———. 1998. Of Consorts and Harlots in Thai Popular History. *JAS* 57(2): 333–353.

Hooker, M. B. 1978. *A Concise Legal History of South-East Asia*. Oxford: Clarendon Press.

Hooykaas, C. 1958a. The Paradise on Earth in Lĕṅkā. *BKI* 114:265–291.

———. 1958b. The Old-Javanese *Rāmāyaṇa:* An Exemplary Kakawin as to Form and Content. *Verhandelingen der Koninklijke Nederlandse Akademie van Wetenschappen, Afd. Letterkunde.* Nieuwe Reeks, Deel LXV, no. 1. Amsterdam: N.V. Noord-Hollandsche Uitgevers Maatschappij.

Horsfield, Thomas. 1814. Over de Rivier van Solo en een Reis naar de Oosterstreken van Java. *VBG* 7.

Hoskins, Janet, ed. 1996. *Headhunting and the Social Imagination in Southeast Asia.* Stanford: Stanford University Press.

Hunt, Lynn. 1993. *The Family Romance of the French Revolution.* Berkeley and Los Angeles: University of California Press.

Huntington, Samuel P. 1997. *The Clash of Civilizations and the Remaking of World Order.* New York: Touchstone.

Hüsken, Frans. 1989. Cycles of Commercialization and Accumulation in a Central Javanese Village. In *Agrarian Transformations: Local Processes and the State in Southeast Asia,* ed. Gillian Hart, Andrew Turton, and Benjamin White. Berkeley, Los Angeles, and Oxford: University of California Press.

Hüsken, Frans, and Jeremy Kemp, eds. 1991. *Cognation and Social Organization in Southeast Asia.* Leiden: KITLV Press.

Huỳnh Sanh Thông. 1983. Toads and Frogs as Vietnamese Peasants. *The Vietnam Forum* 1:70–84.

Huỳnh Sanh Thông, ed. and trans. 1996. *An Anthology of Vietnamese Poems from the Eleventh through the Twentieth Centuries.* New Haven and London: Yale University Press.

Ileto, Reynaldo Clemeña. 1979. *Pasyon and Revolution: Popular Movements in the Philippines, 1840–1910.* Quezon City: Ateneo de Manila University Press.

———. 1982. Rizal and the Underside of Philippine History. In *Moral Order and the Question of Change: Essays on Southeast Asian Thought,* ed. D. K. Wyatt and A. Woodside. New Haven, Conn.: Yale University Southeast Asia Studies.

———. 1998. *Filipinos and their Revolution: Event, Discourse, and Historiography.* Manila: Ateneo de Manila University Press.

Inden, Ronald. 1990. *Imagining India.* Oxford and Cambridge, Mass.: Blackwell.

Ishii, Yoneo. 1986. *Sangha, State, and Society: Thai Buddhism in History.* Monograph of the Center for Southeast Asian Studies, Kyoto University. Honolulu: University of Hawai'i Press.

Jackson, Peter A. 1997. Withering Centre, Flourishing Margins: Buddhism's Changing Political Roles. In *Political Change in Thailand: Democracy and Participation,* ed. Kevin Hewison. London and New York: Routledge.

Jacob, Judith M. 1996. *The Traditional Literature of Cambodia: A Preliminary Guide*. London Oriental Series vol. 40. Oxford: OUP.

Jamieson, Neil. L. 1995. *Understanding Vietnam*. Berkeley, Los Angeles, and London: University of California Press.

Jay, Robert. 1969. *Javanese Villagers: Social Relations in Rural Modjokerto*. Cambridge, Mass.: MIT Press.

Jenkins, David. 1984. *Suharto and His Generals: Indonesian Military Politics, 1975–1983*. Monograph Series no. 64. Ithaca, N.Y.: Cornell University Modern Indonesia Project.

Johnson, Mark. 1997. *Beauty and Power: Transgendering and Cultural Transformation in the Southern Philippines*. Oxford and New York: Berg.

Jomo Kwame Sundarum. 1986. *A Question of Class: Capital, the State, and Uneven Development in Malaya*. Singapore: OUP.

Jones, Antoinette M. Barrett. 1984. *Early Tenth Century Java from the Inscriptions: A Study of Economic, Social and Administrative Conditions in the First Quarter of the Century*. Dordrecht and Cinnaminson: Foris Publications.

Jones, Russell. 1979. Ten Conversion Myths from Indonesia. In *Conversion to Islam*, ed. Nehemia Levtzion. New York and London: Holmes and Meier Publishers.

Jónsson, Hjörleifur R. 1996. Rhetorics and Relations: Tai States, Forests, and Upland Groups. In *State Power and Culture in Thailand*, ed. E. Paul Durrenberger. Monograph no. 44. New Haven, Conn.: Yale University Southeast Asia Studies.

Joseph, Gilbert M., and Daniel Nugent, eds. 1994. *Everyday Forms of State Formation: Revolution and the Negotiations of Rule in Modern Mexico*. Durham and London: Duke University Press.

Kahin, Audrey. 1999. *Rebellion to Integration: West Sumatra and the Indonesian Polity 1926–1998*. Amsterdam: Amsterdam University Press.

Kahn, Joel S., and Francis Loh Kok Wah, eds. 1992. *Fragmented Vision: Culture and Politics in Contemporary Malaysia*. North Sydney, Aus.: Asian Studies Association of Australia and Allen and Unwin Pty Ltd.

Kamala Tiyavanich. 1997. *Forest Recollections: Wandering Monks in Twentieth-Century Thailand*. Honolulu: University of Hawai'i Press.

Kapferer, Bruce. 1988. *Legends of People, Myths of State: Violence, Intolerance, and Political Culture in Sri Lanka and Australia*. Washington, D.C., and London: Smithsonian Institution Press.

Kathirithamby-Wells, Jeyamalar. 1993. Restraints on the Development of Merchant Capitalism in Southeast Asia before c.1800. In *Southeast Asia in the Early Modern Era*, ed. Anthony Reid. Ithaca and London: Cornell University Press.

Keeler, Ward. 1987. *Javanese Shadow Plays, Javanese Selves*. Princeton, N.J.: Princeton University Press.

———. 2002. *Durga/Umayi* and the Postcolonialist Dilemma. In *Clearing a Space: Postcolonial Readings of Modern Indonesian Literature*, ed. Keith Foulcher and Tony Day. Leiden: KITLV Press.

Kerkvliet, Benedict J. Tria. 1995. Village-State Relations in Vietnam: The Effect of Everyday Politics on Decollectivization. *JAS* 54(2):396–418.

Kessler, Clive S. 1977. Conflict and Sovereignty in Kelantanese Malay Spirit Seances. In *Case Studies in Spirit Possession*, ed. Vincent Crapanzano and Vivian Garrison. New York: John Wiley and Sons.

Keyes, Charles. 1977. *The Golden Peninsula: Culture and Adaptation in Mainland Southeast Asia*. New York: Macmillan.

———. 1991a. The Proposed World of the School: Thai Villagers' Entry into a Bureaucratic State System. In *Reshaping Local Worlds: Formal Education and Cultural Change in Rural Southeast Asia*, ed. Charles F. Keyes. Yale Southeast Asia Studies Monograph no. 36. New Haven, Conn.: Yale University Center for International and Area Studies.

———. 1991b. The Case of the Purloined Lintel: The Politics of a Khmer Shrine as a Thai National Treasure. In *National Thai Identity and Its Defenders: Thailand, 1939–1989*, ed. Craig J. Reynolds. Monash Papers on Southeast Asia no. 25. Clayton, Vic.: Monash University Centre for Southeast Asian Studies.

Keyes, Charles F., Laurel Kendall, and Helen Hardacre, eds. 1994. *Asian Visions of Authority: Religion and the Modern States of East and Southeast Asia*. Honolulu: University of Hawai'i Press.

Khin Yi. 1988. *The Dobama Movement in Burma (1930–1938)*. Southeast Asia Program Monographs no. 2. Ithaca, N.Y.: Cornell University Southeast Asia Program.

Kiernan, Ben. 1996. *The Pol Pot Regime: Race, Power, and Genocide in Cambodia under the Khmer Rouge, 1975–79*. New Haven and London: Yale University Press.

Kipp, Rita Smith. 1996. *Dissociated Identities: Ethnicity, Religion, and Class in an Indonesian Society*. Ann Arbor: The University of Michigan Press.

Kirsch, A. T. 1976. Kinship, Genealogical Claims and Social Integration in Ancient Khmer Society: An Interpretation. In *Southeast Asian History and Historiography: Essays Presented to D. G. E. Hall*, ed. C. D. Cowan and O. W. Wolters. Ithaca and London: Cornell University Press.

———. 1984. Cosmology and Ecology as Factors in Interpreting Early Thai Social Organization. *JSEAS* 10(2):253–265.

Koenig, William J. 1990. *The Burmese Polity, 1752–1819: Politics, Administration, and Social Organization in the Early Kòn-baung Period*. Michigan Papers on South and Southeast Asia no. 34. Ann Arbor: The University of Michigan Center for South and Southeast Asian Studies.

Koolhof, Sirtjo. 1999. The "la Galigo": A Bugis Encyclopedia and its Growth. *BKI* 155(3):362–387.

Kulke, Hermann. 1991. Epigraphical References to the "City" and the "State" in Early Indonesia. *Indonesia* 52:3–22.

Kumar, Ann. 1980. Javanese Court Society and Politics in the Late Eighteenth Century: The Record of a Lady Soldier. Two parts. *Indonesia* 29:1–46 and 30:67–111.

———. 1997. *Java and Modern Europe: Ambiguous Encounters*. Richmond, Surrey: Curzon.

———. 1999. Encyclopedia-izing and the Organization of Knowledge: A Cross-Cultural Perspective. *BKI* 155(3):472–488.

Kunst, J. 1973. *Music in Java: Its History, Its Theory and Its Techniques*. 2 vols. The Hague: Martinus Nijhoff.

Latour, Bruno. 1993. *We Have Never Been Modern*. Cambridge, Mass.: Harvard University Press.

Leach, E. R. 1965. *Political Systems of Highland Burma*. Boston: Beacon Press.

Lee Gek Ling. 1994. Is Singlish Becoming a Language of Prestige? In *Debating Singapore: Reflective Essays*, ed. Derek da Cunha. Singapore: Institute of Southeast Asian Studies.

Lee Kuan Yew. 2000. *From Third World to First. The Singapore Story: 1965–2000*. New York: Harper Collins Publishers.

Lee, Russell. 1989. *True Singapore Ghost Stories. Book 1*. Singapore: Angsanna Books.

Lefort, Claude. 1986. *The Political Forms of Modern Society*. Cambridge, Mass.: MIT Press.

van Leur, J. C. 1957. Java, Vreemd en Vertrouwd. Fragmenten uit Brieven van J. C. van Leur. *De Nieuwe Stem* XII: 276–293.

Lewis, Martin W., and Kären E. Wigen. 1997. *The Myth of Continents: A Critique of Metageography*. Berkeley, Los Angles, and London: University of California Press.

Li Tana. 1998. *Nguyễn Cochinchina: Southern Vietnam in the Seventeenth and Eighteenth Centuries*. Southeast Asia Publications. Ithaca, N.Y.: Cornell University Southeast Asia Program.

Lieberman, Victor. 1984. *Burmese Administrative Cycles: Anarchy and Conquest, c.1580–1760*. Princeton, N.J.: Princeton University Press.

———. 1993. Local Integration and Eurasian Analogies: Structuring Southeast Asian History, c.1350–c.1830. *MAS* 27(3):475–572.

———. 1995. An Age of Commerce in Southeast Asia? Problems of Regional Coherence—A Review Article. *JAS* 54(3):796–807.

———. 1999. Transcending East-West Dichotomies: State and Culture Formation in Six Ostensibly Disparate Areas. In *Beyond Binary Histories: Re-Imagining Eurasia to c.1830*, ed. Victor Lieberman. Ann Arbor: University of Michigan Press.

Lindsay, Jennifer. 1997. Making Waves: Private Radio and Local Identities in Indonesia. *Indonesia* 64:105–123.

Locher-Scholten, Elsbeth. 1981. *Ethiek in Fragmenten. Vijf Studies over Koloniaal Denken en Doen van Nederlanders in de Indonesische Archipel, 1877–1941.* Utrecht: HES Publishers.

————. 1994. Orientalism and the Rhetoric of the Family: Javanese Servants in European Household Manuals and Children's Fiction. *Indonesia* 58:19–39.

Lockhart, Greg. 1989. *Nation in Arms: The Origins of the People's Army of Vietnam.* Asian Studies Association of Australia Southeast Asia Publications Series no. 17. Wellington, London, and Boston: Allen and Unwin.

Lombard, Denys. 1990. *Le Carrefour Javanais: Essai d'histoire globale.* III. *L'héritage des royaumes concentriques.* Paris: Éditions de l'École des Hautes Études en Sciences Sociales.

Ludden, David. 1993. Orientalist Empiricism: Transformations of Colonial Knowledge. In *Orientalism and the Postcolonial Predicament. Perspectives on South Asia,* ed. Carol A. Breckenridge and Peter van der Veer. Philadelphia: University of Pennsylvania Press.

Lý Tế Xuyên. 1999. *Departed Spirits of the Việt Realm.* Ithaca, N.Y.: Cornell University Southeast Asia Program.

Mabbett, I. W. 1969. *Devarāja. JSEAS* 10(2):202–223.

————. 1977. *Varṇas* in Angkor and the Indian Caste System. *JAS* 36(3):429–442.

————. 1983. The Symbolism of Mount Meru. *History of Religions* 23(1):64–83.

Mabbett, Ian, and David Chandler. 1995. *The Khmers.* Oxford and Cambridge, Mass.: Blackwell.

MacIntyre, Andrew. 1990. *Business and Politics in Indonesia.* Sydney: Allen and Unwin Pty Ltd.

Mackenzie, Colonel. 1814. Narrative of a Journey to Examine the Remains of an Ancient City and Temples at Brambana in Java. *VBG* 7.

Mackie, Jamie, and Andrew MacIntyre. 1994. Politics. In *Indonesia's New Order: The Dynamics of Socio-economic Transformation,* ed. Hal Hill. St. Leonards, NSW: Allen and Unwin.

Mahathir Mohamad. 1998. *Excerpts from the Speeches of Mahathir Mohamad on the Multimedia Super Corridor.* Selangor Darul Ehsan, Malaysia: Pelanduk Publications.

Maier, Hendrik M. J. 1988. *In the Center of Authority: The Malay Hikayat Merong Mahawangsa.* Studies on Southeast Asia. Ithaca, N.Y.: Cornell University Southeast Asia Program.

————. 1993. From Heteroglossia to Polyglossia: The Creation of Malay and Dutch in the Indies. *Indonesia* 56:37–65.

————. 1997a. A Vademecum of Malay Writing: The Fragrant Flowers of the

Tale of Hang Tuah. Paper presented at the workshop "Encompassing Knowledge: Indigenous Encyclopedias in Indonesia in the 17th–20th Centuries," Leiden University, 8–10 December.

———. 1997b. "We Are Playing Relatives": Riau, the Cradle of Reality and Hybridity. *BKI* 153(4):672–698.

———. 1997c. Maelstrom and Electricity: Modernity in the Indies. In *Outward Appearances: Dressing State and Society in Indonesia,* ed. Henk Schulte Nordholt. Leiden: KITLV Press.

———. 1999. Tales of Hang Tuah: In Search of Wisdom and Good Behavior. *BKI* 155(3):342–361.

Malaka, Tan. 1991. *From Jail to Jail.* Trans., ed., and intro. Helen Jarvis. Vol. 3. Monographs in International Studies, Southeast Asia Series no. 83. Athens: Ohio University Center for International Studies.

Malarney, Shaun Kingsley. 1996. The Limits of "State Functionalism" and the Reconstruction of Funerary Ritual in Contemporary Northern Vietnam. *American Ethnologist* 23(3):540–560.

———. 1997. Culture, Virtue, and Political Transformation in Contemporary Northern Viet Nam. *JAS* 56(4):899–920.

Manas Chitakasem and Andrew Turton, eds. 1991. *Thai Constructions of Knowledge.* London: University of London School of Oriental and African Studies.

Manguin, Pierre-Yves. 1986. Shipshape Societies: Boat Symbolism and Political Systems in Insular Southeast Asia. In *Southeast Asia in the 9th to 14th Centuries,* ed. David G. Marr and A. C. Milner. Singapore and Canberra: Institute of Southeast Asian Studies and Australian National University Research School of Pacific Studies.

———. 1991. The Merchant and the King: Political Myths of Southeast Asian Coastal Polities. *Indonesia* 52:41–54.

Mannikka, Eleanor. 1996. *Angkor Wat: Time, Space, and Kingship.* Honolulu: University of Hawai'i Press.

Marr, David G. 1981. *Vietnamese Tradition on Trial, 1920–1945.* Berkeley, Los Angeles, and London: University of California Press.

Marston, John. 1994. Metaphors of the Khmer Rouge. In *Cambodian Culture since 1975: Homeland and Exile,* ed. May M. Ebihara, Carol A. Mortland, and Judy Ledgerwood. Ithaca and London: Cornell University Press.

Maxwell, Allen R. Headtaking and the Consolidation of Political Power in the Early Brunei State. In *Headhunting and the Social Imagination in Southeast Asia,* ed. Janet Hoskins. Stanford: Stanford University Press.

Mayoury Ngaosyvathn and Pheuiphanh Ngaosyvathn. 1998. *Paths to Conflagration: Fifty Years of Diplomacy and Warfare in Laos, Thailand, and*

Vietnam, 1778–1828. Southeast Asia Program Publications. Ithaca, N.Y.: Cornell University Southeast Asia Program.

Mbembe, Achille. 1992. The Banality of Power and the Aesthetics of Vulgarity in the Postcolony. *Public Culture* 4(2):1–30.

McCoy, Alfred W. 1982. *Baylan*: Animist Religion and Philippine Peasant Ideology. In *Moral Order and the Question of Change: Essays on Southeast Asian Thought*, ed. D. K. Wyatt and A. Woodside. New Haven, Conn.: Yale University Southeast Asian Studies.

———, ed. 1994. *An Anarchy of Families: State and Family in the Philippines.* Quezon City and Madison: Ateneo de Manila University Press and University of Wisconsin-Madison Center for Southeast Asia Studies.

———. 1999. *Closer Than Brothers: Manhood in the Philippine Military Academy.* New Haven and London: Yale University Press.

McKenna, Thomas M. 1998. *Muslim Rulers and Rebels: Everyday Politics and Armed Separatism in the Southern Philippines.* Berkeley, Los Angeles, and London: University of California Press.

McVey, Ruth T. 1982. The Beamtenstaat in Indonesia. In *Interpreting Indonesian Politics: Thirteen Contributions to the Debate, 1964–1981,* ed. Benedict Anderson and Audrey Kahin. Interim Reports Series no. 62. Ithaca, N.Y.: Cornell University Modern Indonesia Project.

———. 1986. The *Wayang* Controversy in Indonesian Communism. In *Context, Meaning, and Power in Southeast Asia,* ed. Mark Hobart and Robert H. Taylor. Studies on Southeast Asia. Ithaca, N.Y.: Cornell University Southeast Asia Program.

———. 1990. Teaching Modernity: The PKI as an Educational Institution. *Indonesia* 50:5–27.

———. 1992a. The Materialization of the Southeast Asian Entrepreneur. In *Southeast Asian Capitalists,* ed. Ruth McVey. Ithaca, N.Y.: Cornell University Southeast Asia Program.

———, ed. 1992b. *Southeast Asian Capitalists.* Ithaca, N.Y.: Cornell University Southeast Asia Program.

———. 1995a. *Redesigning the Cosmos: Belief Systems and State Power in Indonesia.* NIAS Reports no. 14. Copenhagen: Nordic Institute of Asian Studies.

———. 1995b. Change and Continuity in Southeast Asian Studies. *JSEAS* 26(1):1–9.

———. 1996. Nationalism, Revolution, and Organization in Indonesian Communism. In *Making Indonesia,* ed. Daniel S. Lev and Ruth McVey. Studies on Southeast Asia. Ithaca, N.Y.: Cornell University Southeast Asia Program.

———. 1998. Globalization, Marginalization, and the Study of Southeast Asia. In *Southeast Asian Studies: Reorientations.* The Frank H. Golay

Memorial Lectures 2 and 3. Southeast Asia Program Publications. Ithaca, N.Y.: Cornell University Southeast Asia Program.

————, ed. 2000. *Money and Power in Provincial Thailand*. Honolulu: University of Hawai'i Press.

Migdal, Joel S. 1988. *Strong Societies and Weak States: State-Society Relations and State Capabilities in the Third World*. Princeton, N.J.: Princeton University Press.

Mills, Mary Beth. 1995. Attack of the Widow Ghosts: Gender, Death, and Modernity in Northeast Thailand. In *Bewitching Women, Pious Men: Gender and Body Politics in Southeast Asia*, ed. Aihwa Ong and Michael G. Peletz. Berkeley, Los Angeles, and London: University of California Press.

Milner, Anthony. 1982. *Kerajaan: Malay Political Culture on the Eve of Colonial Rule*. The Association for Asian Studies Monograph no. 40. Tucson: The University of Arizona Press.

————. 1983. Islam and the Muslim State. In *Islam in Southeast Asia*, ed. M. B. Hooker. Leiden: E. J. Brill.

————. 1995. *The Invention of Politics in Colonial Malaya: Contesting Nationalism and the Expansion of the Public Sphere*. Cambridge: CUP.

Mitchell, Timothy. 1999. Society, Economy, and the State Effect. In *State/Culture: State-Formation after the Cultural Turn*, ed. George Steinmetz. Ithaca and London: Cornell University Press.

Moertono, Soemarsaid. 1981. *State and Statecraft in Old Java: A Study of the Later Mataram Period, 16th to 19th Century*. Monograph Series, Modern Indonesia Project. Ithaca, N.Y.: Cornell University Southeast Asia Program.

Morón, Eleanor. 1977. Configurations of Time and Space at Angkor Wat. *Studies in Indo-Asian Art and Culture* 5:217–261.

Morris, Regan. 2001. Chips' Fall Weighs on Asian Jobs. *International Herald Tribune*, 24 May: 13.

Morris, Rosalind C. 2000. *In the Place of Origins: Modernity and Mediums in Northern Thailand*. Durham and London: Duke University Press.

Mrázek, Rudolf. 1994. *Sjahrir: Politics and Exile in Indonesia*. Studies on Southeast Asia. Ithaca, N.Y.: Cornell University Southeast Asia Program.

————. 1997a. Indonesian Dandy: The Politics of Clothes in the Late Colonial Period, 1893–1942. In *Outward Appearances: Dressing State and Society in Indonesia*, ed. Henk Schulte Nordholt. Leiden: KITLV Press.

————. 1997b. "Let Us Become Radio Mechanics": Technology and National Identity in Late-Colonial Netherlands Indies. *CSSH* 39(1):3–33.

Muhlenfeld, A. 1916/1917. Een Troonswisseling in de Vorstenlanden. *Nederlandsh-Indië Oud en Nieuw* 1:79–88.

Multatuli. 1982. *Max Havelaar, Or the Coffee Auctions of the Dutch Trading Company*. Amherst: The University of Massachusetts Press.

Murai, Yoshinori. 1994. The Authoritarian Bureaucratic Politics of Development: Indonesia under Suharto's New Order. In *Approaching Suharto's Indonesia from the Margins*, ed. Takashi Shiraishi. Translation Series. Ithaca, N.Y.: Cornell University Southeast Asia Program.

Murdoch, John B. 1974. The 1901–1902 "Holy Man's" Rebellion. *JSS* 62(1): 47–66.

Mus, Paul. 1975 [1933]. *India Seen from the East: Indian and Indigenous Cults in Champa*, trans. David P. Chandler and I. W. Mabbett. Monash Papers on Southeast Asia no. 3. Clayton, Vic.: Monash University Centre of Southeast Asian Studies.

Nagazumi, Akira. 1972. *The Dawn of Indonesian Nationalism. The Early Years of the Budi Utomo, 1908–1918*. Institute of Developing Economies Occasional Papers Series no. 10. Tokyo: Institute of Developing Economies.

Nagtegaal, Luc. 1996. *Riding the Dutch Tiger: The Dutch East Indies Company and the Northeast Coast of Java 1680–1743*. Leiden: KITLV Press.

Nandy, Ashis. 1983. *The Intimate Enemy: Loss and Recovery of Self under Colonialism*. Delhi: OUP.

Nguyễn Du. 1983. *The Tale of Kiều*. New Haven and London: Yale University Press.

Nguyễn Huy Thiệp. 1994a. Kiếm Sác (A Sharp Sword), trans. Peter Zinoman. *Việt Nam Forum* 14:7–17.

———. 1994b. Vàng Lửa (Fired Gold), trans. Peter Zinoman. *Việt Nam Forum* 14:18–25.

Noorduyn, J. 1982. Bujangga Manik's Journeys through Java: Topographical Data from an Old Sundanese Source. *BKI* 138(4):413–442.

Noorduyn, J., and A. Teeuw. 1999. A Panorama of the World from Sundanese Perspective. *Archipel* 57:209–221.

Norindr, Panivong. 1996. *Phantasmatic Indochina: French Colonial Ideology in Architecture, Film, and Literature*. Durham and London: Duke University Press.

O'Brien, K. 1988. Candi Jago as Mandala: Symbolism of its Narratives. Part 1. *RIMA* 22(2):1–61.

———. 1990. Candi Jago: A Javanese Interpretation of the Wheel of Existence? Part 2. *RIMA* 24(1):23–85.

Ockey, James. 1996. Thai Society and Patterns of Political Leadership. *Asian Survey* 36(4):345–360.

———. 1998. Crime, Society, and Politics in Thailand. In *Gangsters, Democracy, and the State in Southeast Asia*, ed. Carl A. Trocki. Southeast Asia Publications. Ithaca, N.Y.: Cornell University Southeast Asia Program.

————. 1999. God Mothers, Good Mothers, Good Lovers, Godmothers: Gender Images in Thailand. *JAS* 58(4):1033–1058.

O'Connor, Richard A. 1991. Sukhothai: Rule, Religion, and Elite Rivalry. In *The Ram Khamhaeng Controversy*, ed. James R. Chamberlain. Bangkok: The Siam Society.

Ong, Aiwha. 1990. State versus Islam: Malay Families, Women's Bodies, and the Body Politic in Malaysia. *American Ethnologist* 17(2):258–276.

————. 1995. State versus Islam: Malay Families, Women's Bodies, and the Body Politic in Malaysia. In *Bewitching Women, Pious Men: Gender and Body Politics in Southeast Asia*, ed. Aihwa Ong and Michael G. Peletz. Berkeley, Los Angeles, and London: University of California Press.

————. 1999. *Flexible Citizenship: The Cultural Logics of Transnationality.* Durham and London: Duke University Press.

Ong, Aihwa, and Michael G. Peletz, eds. 1995. *Bewitching Women, Pious Men: Gender and Body Politics in Southeast Asia.* Berkeley, Los Angeles, and London: University of California Press.

Onghokham. 1978. The Inscrutable and the Paranoid: An Investigation into the Sources of the Brotodiningrat Affair. In *Southeast Asian Transitions: Approaches through Social History*, ed. Ruth T. McVey. New Haven and London: Yale University Press.

Ortner, Sherry B. 1984. Theory in Anthropology since the Sixties. *CSSH* 26 (1):126–166.

————. 1995. Resistance and the Problem of Ethnographic Refusal. *CSSH* 37 (1):173–193.

————. 1996. *Making Gender: The Politics and Erotics of Culture.* Boston: Beacon Press.

————, ed. 1999. *The Fate of "Culture": Geertz and Beyond.* Berkeley, Los Angeles, and London: University of California Press.

Oshikawa, Noriaki. 1990. *Patjar Merah Indonesia* and Tan Malaka: A Popular Novel and a Revolutionary Legend. In *Reading Southeast Asia*, ed. Takashi Shiraishi. Translation Series. Ithaca, N.Y.: Cornell University Southeast Asia Program.

Padmosusastra. 1980. *Tatacara* (Etiquette and customs). Jakarta: Departemen Pendidikan dan Kebudayaan.

Pasuk Pongpaichit and Sungsidh Piriyarangsan. 1994. *Corruption and Democracy in Thailand.* Chiang Mai: Silkworm Books.

Pasuk Phongpaichit and Chris Baker. 1995. *Thailand: Economy and Politics.* Kuala Lumpur: OUP.

————. 1998. *Thailand's Boom and Bust.* Chiang Mai: Silkworm Books.

————. 2000. *Thailand's Crisis.* Chiang Mai: Silkworm Books.

Pauka, Kirstin. 1998. *Theater and Martial Arts in West Sumatra: Randai and*

Silek of the Minangkabau. Monographs in International Studies, Southeast Asia Series no. 103. Athens: Ohio University Center for International Studies.

Peacock, James L. 1968. *Rites of Modernization: Symbolic and Social Aspects of Indonesian Proletarian Drama.* Chicago and London: The University of Chicago Press.

———. 1978. *Muslim Puritans: Reformist Psychology in Southeast Asian Islam.* Berkeley, Los Angeles, and London: University of California Press.

Peletz, Michael G. 1993. Sacred Texts and Dangerous Words: The Politics of Law and Cultural Rationalization in Malaysia. *CSSH* 35(1):66–109.

———. 1995. Neither Reasonable nor Responsible: Contrasting Representations of Masculinity in a Malay Society. In *Bewitching Women, Pious Men: Gender and Body Politics in Southeast Asia,* ed. Aihwa Ong and Michael G. Peletz. Berkeley, Los Angeles, and London: University of California Press.

———. 1996. *Reason and Passion: Representations of Gender in a Malay Society.* Berkeley, Los Angeles, and London: University of California Press.

———. 1997. "Ordinary Muslims" and Muslim Resurgents in Contemporary Malaysia. In *Islam in an Era of Nation-States,* ed. Robert W. Hefner and Patricia Horvatich. Honolulu: University of Hawai'i Press.

Peluso, Nancy Lee. 1994. *Rich Forests, Poor People: Resource Control and Resistance in Java.* Berkeley, Los Angeles, and London: University of California Press.

Pemberton, John. 1994. *On the Subject of "Java."* London and Ithaca: Cornell University Press.

Phelan, John Leddy. 1959. *The Hispanization of the Philippines: Spanish Aims and Filipino Responses, 1565–1700.* Madison: University of Wisconsin Press.

Pigeaud, Theodore G. Th. 1933. De Serat Tjabolang en de Serat Tjentini: Inhoudsopgaven. *VBG* 72(2). Bandung: A. C. Nix.

———. 1938. *Javaanse Volksvertoningen: Bijdrage tot de Beschrijving van Land en Volk.* Batavia: Uitgave Volkslectuur.

———. 1960–63. *Java in the 14th Century: A Study in Cultural History.* 5 vols. The Hague: Martinus Nijhoff.

Pollock, Sheldon. 1985. The Theory of Practice and the Practice of Theory in Indian Intellectual History. *Journal of the American Oriental Society* 105(3):499–519.

———. 1996. The Sanskrit Cosmopolis, 300–1300: Transculturation, Vernacularization, and the Question of Ideology. In *Ideology and Status of Sanskrit: Contributions to the History of the Sanskrit Language,* ed. Jan E. M. Houben. Leiden, New York, and Köln: E. J. Brill.

———. 1998a. The Cosmopolitan Vernacular. *JAS* 57(1):6–37.

————. 1998b. India in the Vernacular Millennium: Literary Culture and Polity, 1000–1500. *Daedalus* 127(3):41–74.

————. 2000. Cosmopolitan and Vernacular in History. *Public Culture* 12(3): 591–625.

Ponchaud, François. 1989. Social Change in the Vortex of Revolution. In *Cambodia 1975–1978: Rendezvous with Death*, ed. Karl D. Jackson. Princeton, N.J.: Princeton University Press.

Pramoedya Ananta Toer. 1982. *This Earth of Mankind*. Ringwood, Vic.: Penguin Books.

————. 1992. *House of Glass*. Ringwood, Vic.: Penguin Books.

Prapañca, Mpu. 1995. *Deśawarṇana (Nāgarakṛtāgama)*, trans. Stuart Robson. Leiden: KITLV Press.

Prasert Nagara and A. B. Griswold. 1992. *Epigraphic and Historical Studies*. Bangkok: The Historical Society.

Pratt, Mary Louise. 1992. *Travel Writing and Transculturation*. London and New York: Routledge.

Quilty, Mary Catherine. 1998. *Textual Empires: A Reading of Early British Histories of Southeast Asia*. Clayton, Vic.: Monash University Asia Institute.

Quinn, George. 1975. The Javanese Science of Burglary. *RIMA* 9(1):33–54.

Rafael, Vicente L. 1984. Language, Identity, and Gender in Rizal's *Noli*. *RIMA* 18:110–140.

————. 1988. *Contracting Colonialism: Translation and Christian Conversion in Tagalog Society under Spanish Rule*. Ithaca and London: Cornell University Press.

————. 1993. Patronage and Pornography: Ideology and Spectatorship during the Early Marcos Years. In *Text/Politics in Island Southeast Asia*, ed. D. M. Roskies. Monographs in International Studies, Southeast Asia Series no. 91. Athens: Ohio University Center for International Studies.

————. 1995a. Nationalism, Imagery, and the Filipino Intelligentsia in the Nineteenth Century. In *Discrepant Histories: Translocal Essays on Filipino Cultures*, ed. Vicente L. Rafael. Philadelphia: Temple University Press.

————. 1995b. Taglish, or the Phantom Power of the Lingua Franca. *Public Culture* 8(1):101–126.

————, ed. 1995c. *Discrepant Histories: Translocal Essays on Filipino Cultures*. Philadelphia: Temple University Press.

————. 1997. "Your Grief is Our Gossip": Overseas Filipinos and Other Spectral Presences. *Public Culture* 9(2):267–291.

————. 1999. Introduction: Criminality and Its Others. In *Figures of Criminality in Indonesia, the Philippines, and Colonial Vietnam*, ed. Vicente L. Rafael.

Southeast Asia Program Publications. Ithaca, N.Y.: Cornell University Southeast Asia Program.

———. 2000. *White Love and Other Events in Filipino History*. Durham and London: Duke University Press.

Raffles, Thomas Stamford. 1965 [1817]. *The History of Java*. Vol. 2. Kuala Lumpur: OUP.

Ras, J. J. 1968. *Hikajat Bandjar: A Study in Malay Historiography*. The Hague: Nijhoff.

Reeve, David. 1985. *Golkar of Indonesia: An Alternative to the Party System*. Singapore: OUP.

Reid, Anthony. 1979. The Nationalist Quest for an Indonesian Past. In *Perceptions of the Past in Southeast Asia*, ed. Anthony Reid and David Marr. Singapore: Heinemann Educational Books (Asia) Ltd.

———, ed. 1983. *Slavery, Bondage and Dependency in Southeast Asia*. St. Lucia, London, and New York: University of Queensland Press.

———. 1988. *Southeast Asia in the Age of Commerce. Vol. 1: The Lands below the Winds, 1450–1680*. New Haven and London: Yale University Press.

———. 1993. *Southeast Asia in the Age of Commerce 1450–1680. Vol. 2: Expansion and Crisis*. New Haven and London: Yale University Press.

———. 1998. Merdeka: The Concept of Freedom in Indonesia. In *Asian Freedoms: The Idea of Freedom in East and Southeast Asia*, ed. David Kelly and Anthony Reid. Cambridge: CUP.

———. 1999. Economic and Social Change, c.1400–1800. In *The Cambridge History of Southeast Asia. Vol. 2: From c.1500 to c.1800*, ed. Nicholas Tarling. Cambridge: CUP.

Rendra. 1979. *The Struggle of the Naga Tribe*. Brisbane: Queensland University Press.

Reynolds, Craig. 1976. Buddhist Cosmography in Thai History, with Special Reference to Nineteenth-Century Culture Change. *JAS* 35(2):203–220.

———. 1987. *Thai Radical Discourse: The Real Face of Thai Feudalism Today*. Studies on Southeast Asia. Ithaca, N.Y.: Cornell University Southeast Asia Program.

———. 1990. Models of State Formation in Southeast Asian History. Paper presented to the Biennial Conference of the Asian Studies Association of Australia. Griffith University, Brisbane, July 2–5.

———. 1991. Sedition in Thai History: A Nineteenth-Century Poem and its Critics. In *Thai Constructions of Knowledge*, ed. Manas Chitakasem and Andrew Turton. London: University of London School of Oriental and African Studies.

———. 1994. Predicaments of Modern Thai History. *South East Asia Research* 2(1):64–90.

———. 1995. A New Look at Old Southeast Asia. *JAS* 54(2):419–446.

———. 1996. Tycoons and Warlords: Modern Thai Social Formations and Chinese Historical Romance. In *Sojourners and Settlers: Histories of Southeast Asia and the Chinese,* ed. Anthony Reid. St. Leonards, NSW: Asian Studies Association of Australia in association with Allen and Unwin.

———. 1998. Globalization and Cultural Nationalism in Modern Thailand. In *Southeast Asian Identities: Culture and the Politics of Representation in Indonesia, Malaysia, Singapore, and Thailand,* ed. Joel S. Kahn. New York: St. Martin's Press.

———. n.d. Cultural Production and Militarism in the Narrative of the Thai Nation. Unpublished paper.

Reynolds, Frank E., and Mani B. Reynolds, trans. 1982. *Three Worlds According to King Ruang: A Thai Buddhist Cosmology.* Berkeley Buddhist Studies Series no. 4. Berkeley: University of California Center for South and Southeast Asian Studies.

Richards, Thomas. 1993. *The Imperial Archive: Knowledge and the Fantasy of Empire.* London and New York: Verso.

Ricklefs, Merle C. 1967. Land and Law in the Epigraphy of Tenth-Century Cambodia. *JAS* 26(3):411–420.

———. 1972. A Consideration of Three Versions of the *Babad Tanah Djawi,* with excerpts on the Fall of Majapahit. *BSOAS* 35(2):285–315.

———. 1974. *Jogjakarta under Sultan Mangkubumi 1749–1792: A History of the Division of Java.* London Oriental Series vol. 30. London: OUP.

———. 1993. *War, Culture and Economy in Java, 1677–1726.* Sydney: Allen and Unwin.

———. 1998. *The Seen and Unseen Worlds in Java, 1726–1749: History, Literature, and Islam in the Court of Pakubuwana II.* St. Leonards, NSW: Allen and Unwin.

Riggs, Fred. W. 1966. *Thailand: The Modernization of a Bureaucratic Polity.* Honolulu: East-West Center Press.

Rizal, José. 1997. *Noli Me Tangere,* trans. Ma. Soledad Lacson-Locsin. SHAPS Library of Translations. Honolulu: University of Hawai'i Press.

Robinson, Geoffrey. 1995. *The Dark Side of Paradise: Political Violence in Bali.* Ithaca and London: Cornell University Press.

Robison, Richard. 1986. *Indonesia: The Rise of Capital.* Sydney: Allen and Unwin Pty Ltd.

Robson, Stuart O. 1971. *Wangbang Wideya: A Javanese Panji Romance.* Bibliotheca Indonesica no. 6. The Hague: Martinus Nijhoff.

Romance. 2000. *Romance of the Three Kingdoms.* Pictorial Series in English and Chinese, ed. and trans. C. C. Low and Associates. 3d. ed. 4 vols. Singapore: Canfonian Pte Ltd.

Rosaldo, Michelle Z. 1980. *Knowledge and Passion: Ilongot Notions of Self and Social Life.* Cambridge: CUP.

Rosaldo, Renato. 1989. *Culture and Truth: The Remaking of Social Analysis.* Boston: Beacon Press.

Rush, James R. 1990. *Opium to Java: Revenue Farming and Chinese Enterprise in Colonial Indonesia, 1860–1910.* Ithaca and London: Cornell University Press.

Saraswati Sunindyo. 1996. Murder, Gender, and the Media: Sexualizing Politics and Violence. In *Fantasizing the Feminine in Indonesia,* ed. Laurie J. Sears. Durham and London: Duke University Press.

Sartono Kartodirdjo. 1972. Agrarian Radicalism in Java: Its Setting and Development. In *Culture and Politics in Indonesia,* ed. Benedict R. O'G. Anderson and James Siegel. Ithaca and London: Cornell University Press.

———. 1988. *Modern Indonesia: Tradition and Transformation, A Socio-Historical Perspective.* Yogyakarta: Gadjah Mada University Press.

Sartono Kartodirdjo, A. Sudewo, and Suhardjo Hatmosuprobo. 1987. *Perkembangan Perabadan Priyayi* (The flowering of *priyayi* civilization). Yogyakarta: Gadjah Mada University Press.

Sayer, Derek. 1994. Everyday Forms of State Formation: Some Dissident Remarks on "Hegemony." In *Everyday Forms of State Formation: Revolution and the Negotiations of Rule in Modern Mexico,* ed. Gilbert M. Joseph and Daniel Nugent. Durham and London: Duke University Press.

Scherer, Savitri. 1981. Yudhistira Ardi Noegraha: Social Attitudes in the Works of a Popular Writer. *Indonesia* 31:31–52.

Schulte Nordholt, Henk. 1991. Temple and Authority in South Bali, 1900–1980. In *State and Society in Bali: Historical, Textual and Anthropological Approaches,* ed. Hildred Geertz. Leiden: KITLV Press.

———. 1996. *The Spell of Power: A History of Balinese Politics 1650–1940.* Leiden: KITLV Press.

Schulte Nordholt, Henk, and Margreet van Till. 1999. Colonial Criminals in Java, 1870–1910. In *Figures of Criminality in Indonesia, the Philippines, and Colonial Vietnam,* ed. Vicente L. Rafael. Southeast Asia Program Publications. Ithaca, N.Y.: Cornell University Southeast Asia Program.

Scott, James C. 1976. *The Moral Economy of the Peasant: Rebellion and Subsistence in Southeast Asia.* New Haven and London: Yale University Press.

———. 1985. *Weapons of the Weak: Everyday Forms of Peasant Resistance.* New Haven and London: Yale University Press.

———. 1990. *Domination and the Arts of Resistance: Hidden Transcripts.* New Haven and London: Yale University Press.

———. 1998. *Seeing Like a State: How Certain Schemes to Improve the Human Condition Have Failed.* New Haven and London: Yale University Press.

Scott, William Henry. 1982. *Cracks in the Parchment Curtain*. Quezon City: New Day.

———. 1994. *Barangay: Sixteenth-Century Philippine Culture and Society*. Manila: Ateneo de Manila University Press.

Searle, Peter. 1999. *The Riddle of Malaysian Capitalism: Rent-Seekers or Real Capitalists?* Singapore: Allen and Unwin and University of Hawai'i Press.

Sears, Laurie J. 1993. The Contingency of Autonomous History. In *Autonomous Histories, Particular Truths: Essays in Honor of John R. W. Smail*, ed. Laurie J. Sears. Center for Southeast Asian Studies Monograph no. 11. Madison: University of Wisconsin Center for Southeast Asian Studies.

———. 1996a. *Shadows of Empire. Colonial Discourse and Javanese Tales*. Durham and London: Duke University Press.

———, ed. 1996b. *Fantasizing the Feminine in Indonesia*. Durham and London: Duke University Press.

Sedov, Leonid A. 1978. Angkor: State and Society. In *The Early State*, ed. Henri J. M. Claessen and Peter Skalnik. The Hague, Paris, and New York: Mouton.

Sekimoto, Teruo. 1990. State Ritual and the Village: An Indonesian Case Study. In *Reading Southeast Asia*, ed. Takashi Shiraishi. Translation Series. Ithaca, N.Y.: Cornell University Southeast Asia Program.

———. 1997. Uniforms and Concrete Walls: Dressing the Village under the New Order in the 1970s and 1980s. In *Outward Appearances: Dressing State and Society in Indonesia*, ed. Henk Schulte Nordholt. Leiden: KITLV Press.

Selosoemardjan. 1962. *Social Changes in Jogjakarta*. Ithaca, N.Y.: Cornell University Press.

Sen, Krishna. 1998. Indonesian Women at Work: Reframing the Subject. In *Gender and Power in Affluent Asia*, ed. Krishna Sen and Maila Stivens. London and New York: Routledge.

Sen, Krishna, and David T. Hill. 2000. *Media, Culture, and Politics in Indonesia*. Oxford: OUP.

Sen, Krishna, and Maila Stivens, eds. 1998. *Gender and Power in Affluent Asia*. London and New York: Routledge.

Serat Centhini. 1985–1990. *Serat Centhini Latin*. 12 vols. Yogyakarta: Yayasan Centhini.

Shiraishi, Saya S. 1997. *Young Heroes: The Indonesian Family in Politics*. Ithaca, N.Y.: Cornell University Southeast Asia Program.

Shiraishi, Takashi. 1981. The Disputes between Tjipto Mangoenkoesoemo and Soetatmo Soeriokoesoemo: Satria vs. Pandita. *Indonesia* 32: 93–108.

———. 1990. *An Age in Motion: Popular Radicalism in Java, 1912–1926*. Ithaca and London: Cornell University Press.

———. 1996. Rewiring the Indonesian State. In *Making Indonesia*, ed. Daniel S. Lev and Ruth McVey. Studies on Southeast Asia. Ithaca, N.Y.: Cornell University Southeast Asia Program.

Sibunruang, J. Kasem. 1960. *La Femme, le Héros et le Vilain: Poème Populaire Thaï*. Annales du Musée Guimet Tome LXV. Paris: Presses Universitaires de France.

Sidel, John T. 1995. The Philippines: The Languages of Legitimation. In *Political Legitimacy in Southeast Asia: The Quest for Moral Authority*, ed. Muthiah Alagappa. Stanford: Stanford University Press.

———. 1997. Philippine Politics in Town, District, and Province: Bossism in Cavite and Cebu. *JAS* 56(4):947–966.

———. 1998. Murder, Inc., Cavite: Capitalist Development and Political Gangsterism in a Philippine Province. In *Gangsters, Democracy, and the State in Southeast Asia*, ed. Carl A. Trocki. Southeast Asia Publications. Ithaca, N.Y.: Cornell University Southeast Asia Program.

———. 1999a. *Capital, Coercion, and Crime: Bossism in the Philippines*. Stanford: Stanford University Press.

———. 1999b. The Usual Suspects: Nardong Putik, Don Pepe Oyson, and Robin Hood. In *Figures of Criminality in Indonesia, the Philippines, and Colonial Vietnam*, ed. Vicente L. Rafael. Southeast Asia Program Publications. Ithaca, N.Y.: Cornell University Southeast Asia Program.

Siegel, James. 1979. *Shadow and Sound: The Historical Thought of a Sumatran People*. Chicago and London: The University of Chicago Press.

———. 1986. *Solo in the New Order: Language and Hierarchy in an Indonesian City*. Princeton, N.J.: Princeton University Press.

———. 1997. *Fetish, Recognition, Revolution*. Princeton, N.J.: Princeton University Press.

———. 1998. *A New Criminal Type in Jakarta: Counter-Revolution Today*. Durham and London: Duke University Press.

———. 1999. A New Criminal Type in Jakarta: The Nationalization of "Death." In *Figures of Criminality in Indonesia, the Philippines, and Colonial Vietnam*, ed. Vicente L. Rafael. Southeast Asia Program Publications. Ithaca, N.Y.: Cornell University Southeast Asia Program.

———. 2001. Suharto, Witches. *Indonesia* 71:27–78.

Skocpol, Theda. 1979. *States and Social Revolutions: A Comparative Analysis of France, Russia, and China*. Cambridge: CUP.

Smail, John R. W. 1993. On the Possibility of an Autonomous History of Modern Southeast Asia. In *Autonomous Histories, Particular Truths: Essays in Honor of John R. W. Smail*, ed. Laurie J. Sears. Center for Southeast Asian Studies Monograph no. 11. Madison: University of Wisconsin Center for Southeast Asian Studies.

Snodgrass, Adrian. 1985. *The Symbolism of the Stupa*. Ithaca, N.Y.: Cornell University Southeast Asia Program.

Soebardi. 1971. Santri-Religious Elements as Reflected in the Book of Tjentini. *BKI* 127:331–349.

———. 1975. *The Book of Cabolek*. Bibliotheca Indonesica 10. The Hague: Martinus Nijhoff.

Soemantri. 1924. *Rasa Merdeka. Hikajat Soedjanmo* (The feeling of freedom: The story of Soedjanmo). Semarang: Drukkerij V.S.P.P.

Sombat Chantornvong. 1981. Religious Literature in Thai Political Perspective: The Case of the *Maha Chat Kamluang*. In *Essays on Literature and Society in Southeast Asia: Political and Sociological Perspectives*, ed. Tham Seong Chee. Singapore: Singapore University Press.

Steedley, Mary Margaret. 1993. *Hanging without a Rope: Narrative Experience in Colonial and Postcolonial Karoland*. Princeton, N.J.: Princeton University Press.

———. 1999. The State of Culture Theory in the Anthropology of Southeast Asia. *Annual Review of Anthropology* 28:431–454.

Steinberg, David Joel, ed. 1987. *In Search of Southeast Asia: A Modern History*. Rev. ed. Sydney and Wellington: Allen and Unwin.

Steinmetz, George, ed. 1999. *State/Culture: State-Formation after the Cultural Turn*. Ithaca and London: Cornell University Press.

Stivens, Maila. 1998. Sex, Gender and the Making of the New Malay Middle Classes. In *Gender and Power in Affluent Asia*, ed. Krishna Sen and Maila Stivens. London and New York: Routledge.

Stoler, Ann Laura. 1995a. *Capitalism and Confrontation in Sumatra's Plantation Belt, 1870–1979*. 2d. ed. Ann Arbor: The University of Michigan Press.

———. 1995b. *Race and the Education of Desire: Foucault's* History of Sexuality *and the Colonial Order of Things*. Durham and London: Duke University Press.

———. 1996. A Sentimental Education: Native Servants and the Cultivation of European Children in the Netherlands Indies. In *Fantasizing the Feminine in Indonesia*, ed. Laurie J. Sears. Durham and London: Duke University Press.

———. 1997. Sexual Affronts and Racial Frontiers: European Identities and the Cultural Politics of Exclusion in Colonial Southeast Asia. In *Tensions of Empire: Colonial Cultures in a Bourgeois World*, ed. Frederick Cooper and Ann Laura Stoler. Berkeley, Los Angeles, and London: University of California Press.

Stone, Lawrence. 1979. *The Family, Sex and Marriage in England 1500–1800*. London: Pelican Books.

Subrahmanyam, Sanjay. 1992. Iranians Abroad: Intra-Asian Elite Migration and Early Modern State Formation. *JAS* 51(2):340–363.

Suharto. 1989. *Soeharto: Pikiran, Ucapan, dan Tindakan Saya. Otobiografi, seperti dipaparkan kepada G. Dwipayana dan Ramadhan K. H.* (My thoughts, sayings, and deeds: Autobiography, as related to G. Dwipayana and Ramadhan K. H.). Jakarta: PT. Citra Lamtoro Gung Persada.

Sullivan, Patrick. 1982. *Social Relations of Dependence in a Malay State: Nineteenth Century Perak.* The Malaysian Branch of the Royal Asiatic Society Monograph no. 10. Kuala Lumpur: Art Printing Works Sdn. Bhd.

Supomo, S. 1977. *Arjunawijaya: A Kakawin of Mpu Tantular.* Bibliotheca Indonesica 14. The Hague: Martinus Nijhoff.

———. 1979. The Image of Majapahit in Later Javanese and Indonesian Writing. In *Perceptions of the Past in Southeast Asia,* ed. Anthony Reid and David Marr. Singapore: Heinemann Educational Books (Asia) Ltd.

———. 1993. *Bhāratayuddha: An Old Javanese Poem and its Indian Sources.* New Delhi: International Academy of Indian Culture and Aditya Prakashan.

Suryakusuma, Julia I. 1996. The State and Sexuality in New Order Indonesia. In *Fantasizing the Feminine in Indonesia,* ed. Laurie J. Sears. Durham and London: Duke University Press.

Sutherland, Heather. 1979. *The Making of a Bureaucratic Elite: The Colonial Transformation of the Javanese Priyayi.* Singapore: Heinemann Educational Books (Asia) Ltd.

Sweeney, Amin. 1980a. *Reputations Live On: An Early Malay Autobiography.* Berkeley: University of California Press.

———, ed. 1980b. *The Tarikh Datu' Bentara Luar.* Berkeley: University of California Center for South and Southeast Asian Studies.

Tai, Hue-Tam Ho. 1983. *Millenarianism and Peasant Politics in Vietnam.* Cambridge, Mass., and London: Harvard University Press.

———. 1992. *Radicalism and the Origins of the Vietnamese Revolution.* Cambridge, Mass., and London: Harvard University Press.

Tambiah, S. J. 1976. *World Conqueror and World Renouncer: A Study of Buddhism and Polity in Thailand against a Historical Background.* Cambridge: CUP.

———. 1984. *The Buddhist Saints of the Forest and the Cult of Amulets.* Cambridge: CUP.

Tannenbaum, Nicola. 1987. Tattoos: Invulnerability and Power in Shan Cosmology. *American Ethnologist* 14(4):693–711.

Taussig, Michael. 1992. *The Nervous System.* New York and London: Routledge.

———. 1997. *The Magic of the State.* New York and London: Routledge.

Taylor, Charles. 1999. Two Theories of Modernity. *Public Culture* 11(1): 153–174.

Taylor, Jean Gelman. 1983. *The Social World of Batavia: European and Eurasian in Dutch Asia*. Madison and London: The University of Wisconsin Press.

Taylor, Keith Weller. 1983. *The Birth of Vietnam*. Berkeley, Los Angeles, and London: University of California Press.

———. 1986a. Authority and Legitimacy in 11th Century Vietnam. In *Southeast Asia in the 9th to 14th Centuries*, ed. David G. Marr and A. C. Milner. Singapore and Canberra: Institute of Southeast Asian Studies and Australian National University Research School of Pacific Studies.

———. 1986b. Phùng Hưng: Mencian King or Austric Paramount? *The Việtnam Forum* 8:10–25.

———. 1995. Voices Within and Without: Tales from Stone and Paper about Đỗ Anh Vũ (1114–1159). In *Essays into Vietnamese Pasts*, ed. K. W. Taylor and John K. Whitmore. Studies on Southeast Asia. Ithaca, N.Y.: Cornell University Southeast Asia Program.

———. 1998. Surface Orientations in Vietnam: Beyond Histories of Nation and Region. *JAS* 57(4):949–978.

Taylor, Robert. H. 1987. *The State in Burma*. Honolulu: University of Hawai'i Press.

Teeuw, A. et al. 1969. *Śiwarātrikalpa of Mpu Tanakuṅ: An Old Javanese Poem, Its Indian Source and Balinese Illustrations*. Bibliotheca Indonesica 3. The Hague: Martinus Nijhoff.

Than Tun, ed. 1985. *The Royal Orders of Burma, A.D. 1598–1888*. Part 2: A.D. 1649–1750. Kyoto: Kyoto University Centre for Southeast Asian Studies.

Thanet Aphornsuvan. 1998. Slavery and Modernity: Freedom in the Making of Modern Siam. In *Asian Freedoms: The Idea of Freedom in East and Southeast Asia*, ed. David Kelly and Anthony Reid. Cambridge: CUP.

The, Lian, and Paul W. van der Veur. 1973. *The Verhandelingen van het Bataviaasch Genootschap: An Annotated Content Analysis*. Papers in International Studies, Southeast Asia Series no. 26. Athens: Ohio University Center for International Studies.

Thongchai Winichakul. 1994. *Siam Mapped: A History of the Geo-Body of a Nation*. Honolulu: University of Hawai'i Press.

———. 2000. The Quest for *"Siwilai"*: A Geographical Discourse of Civilizational Thinking in the Late Nineteenth and Early Twentieth-Century Siam. *JAS* 59(3):528–549.

Tickell, Paul. 2002. Love in a Time of Colonialism: Race and Romance in an Early Indonesian Novel. In *Clearing a Space: Postcolonial Readings of Modern Indonesian Literature*, ed. Keith Foulcher and Tony Day. Leiden: KITLV Press.

Tilly, Charles. 1985. War Making and State Making as Organized Crime. In *Bringing the State Back In*, ed. Peter B. Evans, Dietrich Rueschemeyer, and Theda Skocpol. Cambridge: CUP.

———. 1992. *Coercion, Capital, and European States, A.D. 990–1992*. Cambridge, Mass., and Oxford: Blackwell.

———. 1993. Contentious Repertoires in Great Britain, 1758–1834. *Social Science History* 17(2):253–280.

Trager, Frank N., and William J. Koenig. 1979. *Burmese Sit-tàns, 1764–1826: Records of Rural Life and Administration*. Association for Asian Studies Monograph no. 36. Tucson: The University of Arizona Press.

Trankell, Ing-Britt. 1999. Royal Relics: Ritual and Social Memory in Louang Prabang. In *Laos: Culture and Society*, ed. Grant Evans. Chiang Mai, Thailand: Silkworm Books.

Trocki, Carl A. 1979. *Prince of Pirates: The Temenggongs and the Development of Johor and Singapore, 1784–1885*. Singapore: Singapore University Press.

Tsing, Anna Lowenhaupt. 1993. *In the Realm of the Diamond Queen: Marginality in an Out-of-the Way Place*. Princeton, N.J.: Princeton University Press.

Tsuchiya, Kenji. 1987. *Democracy and Leadership: The Rise of the Taman Siswa Movement in Indonesia*. Monographs of the Center for Southeast Asian Studies, Kyoto University. Honolulu: University of Hawai'i Press.

———. 1990. Javanology and the Age of Ranggawarsita: An Introduction to Nineteenth-Century Javanese Culture. In *Reading Southeast Asia*, ed. Takashi Shiraishi. Translation Series. Ithaca, N.Y.: Cornell University Southeast Asia Program.

Tucker, Robert C. 1978. *The Marx-Engels Reader*. New York and London: W. W. Norton and Company.

Turner, Victor. 1982. *From Ritual to Theatre: The Human Seriousness of Play*. New York: Performing Arts Journal Publications.

———. 1988. *The Anthropology of Performance*. New York: Performing Arts Journal Publications.

Turton, Andrew. 1991. Invulnerability and Local Knowledge. In *Thai Constructions of Knowledge*, ed. Manas Chitakasem and Andrew Turton. London: University of London School of Oriental and African Studies.

Vail, Peter Thomas. 1998. Violence and Control: Social and Cultural Dimensions of Violence in Thailand. Ph.D. dissertation, Cornell University.

Vandergeest, Peter. 1993. Hierarchy and Power in Pre-National Buddhist States. *MAS* 27(4):843–870.

Vandergeest, Peter, and Nancy Lee Peluso. 1995. Territorialization and State Power in Thailand. *Theory and Society* 24:385–426.

Van Esterik, Penny. 2000. *Materializing Thailand*. Oxford and New York: Berg.

Vickers, Adrian. 1991. Ritual Written: The Song of the Ligya, or the Killing of the Rhinoceros. In *State and Society in Bali: Historical, Textual and Anthropological Approaches*, ed. Hildred Geertz. Leiden: KITLV Press.

———. 1996. Modernity and Being *Moderen*: An Introduction. In *Being Modern in Bali: Image and Change*, ed. Adrian Vickers. Monograph no. 43. New Haven, Conn.: Yale University Southeast Asia Studies.

Vickery, Michael. 1985. The Rise of Sūryavarman I and Royal Factionalism at Angkor. *JSEAS* 16(2):226–244.

Wade, Robert. 1990. *Governing the Market: Economic Theory and the Role of Government in East Asian Industrialization*. Princeton, N.J.: Princeton University Press.

Walker, J. H. 1998. James Brooke and the Bidayuh: Some Ritual Dimensions of Dependency and Resistance in Nineteenth-Century Sarawak. *MAS* 32(1):91–115.

Warren, James Francis. 1981. *The Sulu Zone 1768–1898: The Dynamics of External Trade, Slavery, and Ethnicity in the Transformation of a Southeast Asian Maritime State*. Singapore: Singapore University Press.

Weatherbee, Donald E. 1978. Raffles' Sources for Traditional Javanese Historiography and the Mackenzie Collection. *Indonesia* 26:63–93.

Weber, Max. 1951. *The Religion of China: Confucianism and Taoism*. Glencoe, Ill.: The Free Press.

Weighing. 1999. *Weighing the Balance: Southeast Asian Studies Ten Years After*. New York: Southeast Asia Program, Social Science Research Council.

Weiss, Linda, and John M. Hobson. 1995. *States and Economic Development: A Comparative Historical Analysis*. Cambridge: Polity Press.

Wenk, Klaus. 1995. *Thai Literature: An Introduction*. Bangkok: White Lotus Co., Ltd.

Werner, Jane Susan. 1981. *Peasant Politics and Religious Sectarianism: Peasant and Priest in the Cao Dai in Viet Nam*. Monograph Series no. 23. New Haven, Conn.: Yale University Southeast Asia Studies.

Whitmore, John K. 1997. Literati Culture and Integration in Dai Viet, c.1430–c.1840. *MAS* 31(3):665–687.

Wicks, Robert S. 1992. *Money, Markets, and Trade in Early Southeast Asia: The Development of Indigenous Monetary Systems to A.D. 1400*. Studies on Southeast Asia. Ithaca, N.Y.: Cornell University Southeast Asia Program.

Widodo, Amrih. 1985. The *"Roh"* of the System: On the Unification of Meaning and Expression in a Contemporary Indonesian Novel. *Indonesia* 40:75–88.

———. 1997. Samin in the New Order: The Politics of Encounter and Isolation. In *Imagining Indonesia: Cultural Politics and Political Culture*, ed. Jim Schiller and Barbara Martin-Schiller. Monographs in International Studies, Southeast Asia Series no. 97. Athens: Ohio University Center for International Studies.

Wiener, Margaret J. 1995. *Visible and Invisible Realms: Power, Magic, and Colonial Conquest in Bali*. Chicago and London: The University of Chicago Press.

————. forthcoming. Hidden Force: Colonialism and the Politics of Magic in the Netherlands Indies. In *Magic and Modernity: Interfaces of Revelation and Concealment*, ed. Birgit Meyer and Peter Pels. Stanford: Stanford University Press.

Wijaya, Putu. 1988. *Nyali* (Guts). Jakarta: Balai Pustaka.

Wikan, Unni. 1990. *Managing Turbulent Hearts: A Balinese Formula for Living.* Chicago and London: The University of Chicago Press.

Wilkinson, R. J. 1959. *A Malay-English Dictionary (Romanised).* Part 1 (A–K). London: Macmillan and Co. Ltd.

Williams, Raymond. 1977. *Marxism and Literature.* Oxford: OUP.

Winstedt, Sir Richard. 1969. *A History of Classical Malay Literature.* Kuala Lumpur and Singapore: OUP.

Winter, C. F., Sr. 1862. *Javaansche Zamnenspraken.* Eerste deel. Amsterdam: Johannes Müller.

Winters, Jeffrey A. 1996. *Power in Motion: Capital Mobility and the Indonesian State.* Ithaca and London: Cornell University Press.

Winzeler, Robert L. 1984. The Study of Malayan Latah. *Indonesia* 37:77–104.

Wolters, O. W. 1967. *Early Indonesian Commerce: A Study of the Origins of Srivijaya.* Ithaca, N.Y.: Cornell University Press.

————. 1976. Lê Văn Hưu's Treatment of Lý Thần Tôn's Reign (1127–1137). In *Southeast Asian History and Historiography: Essays Presented to D. G. E. Hall,* ed. C. D. Cowan and O. W. Wolters. Ithaca and London: Cornell University Press.

————. 1979. Assertions of Cultural Well-Being in Fourteenth-Century Vietnam: Part 1. *JSEAS* 10(2):435–450.

————. 1982a. *History, Culture, and Region in Southeast Asian Perspectives.* Singapore: Institute of Southeast Asian Studies.

————. 1982b. Phạm Sư Mạnh's Poems Written While Patrolling the Vietnamese Northern Border in the Middle of the Fourteenth Century. *JSEAS* 13(1):107–119.

————. 1983. A Few and Miscellaneous *Pi-chi* Jottings on Early Indonesia. *Indonesia* 36:49–65.

————. 1988. *Two Essays on Đại-Việt in the Fourteenth Century.* The Lạc-Việt Series no. 9. New Haven, Conn.: Yale University Southeast Asian Studies.

————. 1994. Southeast Asia as a Southeast Asian Field of Study. *Indonesia* 58:1–17.

————. 1999. *History, Culture, and Region in Southeast Asian Perspectives.* Rev. ed. Ithaca and Singapore: Cornell University Southeast Asia Program Publications, and Institute of Southeast Asian Studies.

Woodside, Alexander Barton. 1971. *Vietnam and the Chinese Model: A Comparative Study of Nguyễn and Ch'ing Civil Government in the First Half of the Nineteenth Century.* Cambridge, Mass.: Harvard University Press.

———. 1976. *Community and Revolution in Modern Vietnam.* Boston: Houghton Mifflin Company.

———. 1995. Central Việt Nam's Trading World in the Eighteenth Century as Seen in Lê Quý Đôn's "Frontier Chronicles." In *Essays into Vietnamese Pasts,* ed. K. W. Taylor and John K. Whitmore. Studies on Southeast Asia. Ithaca, N.Y.: Cornell University Southeast Asia Program.

Worsley, P. J. 1972. *Babad Buleleng: A Balinese Dynastic Genealogy.* The Hague: Martinus Nijhoff.

———. 1991. Mpu Tantular's Kakawin Arjunawijaya and Conceptions of Kingship in Fourteenth Century Java. In *Variation, Transformation and Meaning: Studies on Indonesian Literatures in Honour of A. Teeuw,* ed. J. J. Ras and S. O. Robson. Leiden: KITLV Press.

Wyatt, David K. 1975. *The Crystal Sands: The Chronicles of Nagara Śrī Dharrmarāja.* Trans., ed., and intro. David K. Wyatt. Data Paper no. 98. Ithaca, N.Y.: Cornell University Southeast Asia Program.

———. 1982. The "Subtle Revolution" of King Rama I of Siam. In *Moral Order and the Question of Change: Essays on Southeast Asian Thought,* ed. D. K. Wyatt and A. Woodside. New Haven, Conn.: Yale University Southeast Asian Studies.

———. 1984. *Thailand: A Short History.* New Haven, Conn.: Yale University Press.

———. 1994. *Studies in Thai History: Collected Articles.* Chiang Mai, Thailand: Silkworm Books.

Young, Robert J. C. 1995. *Colonial Desire: Hybridity in Theory, Culture and Race.* London and New York: Routledge.

Yudhistira Ardi Noegraha. 1977. *Arjuna Mencari Cinta* (Arjuna searches for romance). Jakarta: Cypress.

Zinoman, Peter. 1994. Nguyễn Huy Thiệp's "Vàng Lửa" and the Nature of Intellectual Dissent in Contemporary Việt Nam. *Việt Nam Forum* 14: 36–44.

———. 1999. The History of the Modern Prison and the Case of Indochina. In *Figures of Criminality in Indonesia, the Philippines, and Colonial Vietnam,* ed. Vicente L. Rafael. Southeast Asia Program Publications. Ithaca, N.Y.: Cornell University Southeast Asia Program.

Zoetmulder, P. J. 1974. *Kalangwan: A Survey of Old Javanese Literature.* The Hague: Martinus Nijhoff.

———. 1982. *Old Javanese-English Dictionary.* 's-Gravenhage: Martinus Nijhoff.

———. 1995. *Pantheism and Monism in Javanese Suluk Literature: Islamic and Indian Mysticism in an Indonesian Setting,* trans. and ed. M. C. Ricklefs. Leiden: KITLV Press.

Index

Absolutism, 22–23, 24
Aceh, 78, 176–177
Ancestors, worship of, 50, 53–54, 56, 108–109; consciousness of, 57, 76
Anderson, Benedict, 7, 10–12, 27–28, 106–107, 205, 235–236, 238; and *Serat Centhini*, 124, 128, 129, 131, 132, 134, 135, 139, 142
Angkor, 9; Buddhism in, 48, 51, 71; bureaucracy in, 198; and cosmography, 103, 104; and geography, 104; Hinduism in, 49, 50, 51, 94–95, 97, 98–99; kings in, 48–49; kinship networks in, 42, 44–46, 48, 50–52; paternalism in, 70–71; role of mothers in, 50, 51–52; temples in, 1, 50–51, 54–55, 95–98, 99; violence in, 251–252. *See also* Cambodia
Angkor Wat, 1, 95–98, 103, 107, 108, 111, 141, 160, 251–252, 274–275
Anh Vũ, Đỗ, 259–261
Asiatic Mode of Production (AMP), 4–5, 22–23, 25
Aung-Thwin, Michael, 12, 13
Ayutthaya, 229, 231

Bali, 7–8; bureaucracy in, 208, 233–234; and Dutch, 29–30; hybridization in, 287; knowledge in, 146; political violence in, 29–30, 233–234, 255–256, 273
Batavia, 16, 18, 150, 209

Batavian Academy of the Arts and Sciences, 118, 144–145
Bhāratayuddha, 237–238, 240, 241–251, 252–253
British: and Java, 118–121; scholarship of, 149–150 (*see also* Mackenzie, Colin; Raffles, Thomas Stamford)
Brunei, 254
Buddhism, 15, 17, 74; in Angkor, 48, 51, 71; and Chinese, 82–83; and rationality, 185; in Siam, 99, 101, 200–201; in Thailand, 88, 158–159, 185, 196; Theraveda, 56–57, 159; in Vietnam, 20, 60–61, 62, 77–78
Burma, 12, 13; armed force in, 234–235; and Hinduization, 9; and territory, 182; Toungoo, 65–67

Cambodia: Hinduization of, 9, 42–44; violence in, 273–276. *See also* Angkor
Capitalism, 23–25, 199–200
Ceremony. *See* Theatre: of state
Charisma, 3, 7–8, 9, 10–11, 16
China, 4; and Buddhism, 82–83; and Java, 216–217; and masculinity, 82; and tax-farming, 202; and Vietnamese, 19–20
Christianity, 18, 19, 20–21, 74–75, 76–77, 78–79, 84–85, 159
Colonialism, 24–25, 26, 31–34; and

About the Author

Tony Day grew up in Washington, D.C. He received a B.A. in history and literature from Harvard University in 1967 and his Ph.D. in Southeast Asian history from Cornell University in 1981. He has worked as a Peace Corps volunteer in the Philippines, for the Bureau Indonesische Studien at the University of Leiden, and, for twenty years, at the University of Sydney where he taught Indonesian and performance studies. He is currently an independent scholar and visiting lecturer in history and comparative literature at the University of North Carolina, Chapel Hill. His present project is a book on postcoloniality and modern Indonesian literature with Keith Foulcher.

9470011